God Still Comes

From the Manger to the Heart

The publication of this book would not have been possible without the substantial financial contribution of M. Roger Glass, owner of Marion's Piazza, and friend of the International Marian Research Institute at the University of Dayton.

Author Fr. Johann G. Roten, S.M.

Design Ann E. Zlotnik

Photography Kenneth Breakall, Robert Breen, Jane Dunwoodie, Dawson Powell, Nichole Rustad, Anne Sventy, Sara Vrabel

Special Contributors Clare Jones, Sr. Jean Frisk, S.S.M., Michele Devitt, Richard Lenar

Printer Meyers Printing & Design, Inc. Dayton, Ohio

ISBN 978-0-692-26661-8

Contents

In loving and grateful memory of
Connie Breen
Ginny and Herb Whalen
Marion and Irene Glass
and their respective Families,
as well as that of
Danuta Romanowska

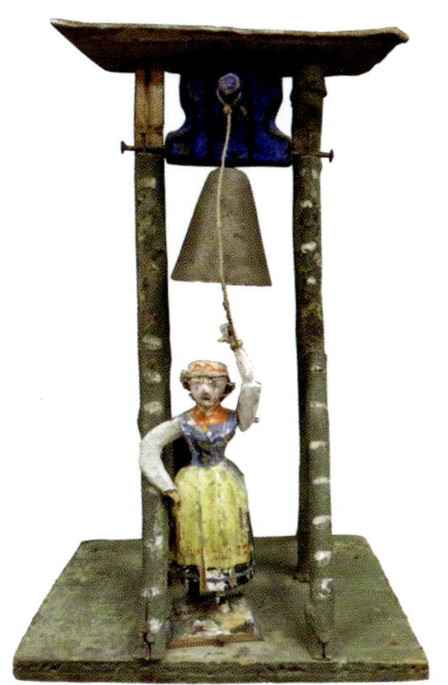
Grulich Tradition

An Invitation

These pages are an invitation to enter the magic world of Christmas, its joyful celebration and deeper meaning. The world of Christmas as presented reflects the tradition of the manger, of nativity sets, cribs, or crèches as we colloquially call them. Entering the world of the crèche the reader will discover some of its traditions and manifold expressions.

If the one and only Incarnation was a gesture of gratuitious love on the part of God, the re-enacting and reconstructing of the Nativity scene has always been a challenge and a labor of love. Thus, these pages are a travelogue of sorts, sharing with the reader the story of a beautiful experience of dedicated people, lovers of beauty, and skillful artisans. For almost twenty years now, the Marian Library/International Marian Research Institute has proudly shared its many nativity sets, and the unique way of displaying them, with local and national communities. Some of the more characteristic manger scenes of our collection are shown in this book.

Mainly a picture book, we wanted to avoid producing still another coffee table book on nativities. Aside from reaching back into the religious roots of the Nativity tradition, we would like to expose the reader to some historical and symbolic aspects of this age-old and rich custom. The sets featured are from many countries, showing a wide variety of local customs and traditions. These manger scenes tell us that a nativity set is not just a nativity set, but is part of the story how Christianity has shaped the culture of the people whose faith was captured by the good news of Christ's birth. Likewise, our nativity sets are signs of the many ways in which culture has helped the message of the Bible to be better understood and more gratefully cherished.

Our invitation includes a joyful walk down memory lane. We are grateful for what has been accomplished. But, a more pressing invitation is addressed to all of us. The Incarnation of Christ reaches its practical meaning in the heart of the believer. Incarnation is ever new, and never ending as long as there is Christianity. Nativity sets are only a humble reminder of what is called ongoing Incarnation. They are the little white pebbles helping us to find our way home.

Collecting and displaying nativity sets is never an end in itself

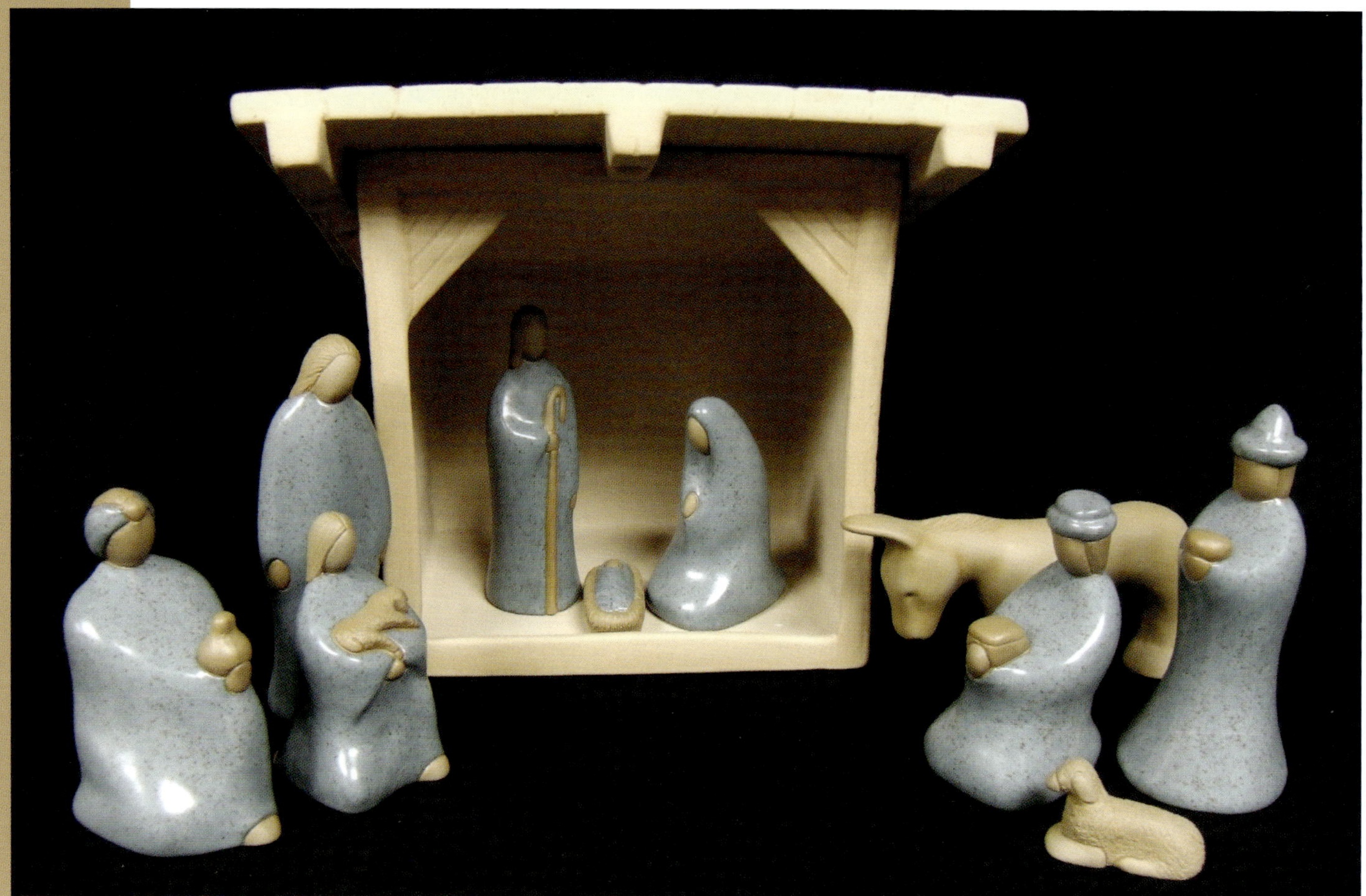

Jack Black, United States

Why Nativity Sets?

Recreating the scene of Christ's birth is one of the most tender and enduring Christmas traditions. It has its origin in the middle ages, and came to bloom as popular culture during the 17th and 18th centuries. Rooted originally in three geographical centers – Naples, Southern France (Provence), and Southern Germany as well as Austria – nativity sets spread all over the world thanks, not least, to missionary efforts. Contemporary culture with its noted penchant for the visual and tactile seems to have rediscovered this popular religious tradition and art.

In late summer of 1994, the Marian Library/International Marian Research Institute at the University of Dayton made a first and tentative effort to collect some contemporary cultural expressions of the Nativity scene. Today the collection holds several thousand artifacts from many regions of the world. Some of these artifacts are on permanent display in the Marian Library's Crèche Museum. Collecting and displaying of nativity sets was never an end in itself.

The Marian Library uses its manger scenes to promote the study of culture and religion. It has set the following goals for this endeavor:

1. To make the Christmas event, its meaning and celebration better known.

2. To highlight the aesthetic dimension of religious culture.

3. To show how strongly and permanently culture and religion influence and enrich each other.

4. To explore the sociological and psychological implications of the Christmas culture.

A Short History

A complete history of the Marian Library's Crèche Collection would involve the gathering of countless little episodes and names in order to weave together what turned out to be an ongoing adventure and constant labor of love. A labor of love! The expression comes easily, and has an almost conventional ring. In fact, without a deep love for the good news of the Christian message, the solidarity of like-minded people, the generosity of believers, and the sense of adventure of the few, the building of the collection and, more important, the related crèche activities would not have seen the light of day.

This short history highlights a few major episodes in the development of a beautiful and ongoing endeavor. It represents a humble and grateful testimonial to the many friends, volunteers, and donors whose hearts, hands, and minds are forever part of the joys the Marian Library Nativity Collection is and will be able to share and dispense.

A Humble Beginning

The Nativity tradition of the University of Dayton begins with the year 1995 when the Marian Library put little crèches on top of book cases and in between rows of books. Some of these nativity sets were gifts that came from Europe; others were purchased in antique malls and shops of Dayton, Springfield, and Waynesville. As Connie Breen observed: "I saw those darling nativity sets hidden between books and thought, they have to come down and need to be properly exhibited."

This is what happened. Over the next three years the number of crèches of the Marian Library Crèche Collection increased, and so did the number of *aficionados* and helpers of what soon came to be known as Crèches International. The group was spearheaded by the dynamic co-chairs, Connie Breen and Ginny Whalen, and helped for various tasks from maintenance to fund-raising by a group of dedicated volunteers.

The Inspiration

In an attempt to gather information about the nativity culture and tradition, several visits to the Oratory of St. Joseph in Montreal were organized. It is there that Michel Forest, designer and artist, was discovered. For ten years, he would be the builder of our nativity settings.

A Vision and Style

With the help of his artistic inspiration and practical know-how we developed our own nativity tradition based on museum-worthy displays highlighting (1) the message of the Incarnation of Jesus Christ, (2) the cultural and historical background of the nativity artifacts, (3) the socio-political context, and, of course (4) the aesthetic quality of the displays.

From then on, to reach these goals, the nativity sets were presented in glass-topped and moveable cases containing the nativity figures placed in a special setting. Usually, the setting represents an artistic and symbolic/realistic landscape expressive of the culture from where the figures originated. Each case is accompanied with a description based on the above listed criteria (1-4). It is our custom to limit displays to 30-40 cases.

The Growth of the Collection

An important event during this initial period was the encounter between George Drake from Bellingham, Washington and Fr. Johann Roten, S.M. For years, George Drake had been instrumental in encouraging artisanal activities in Latin America and other regions of the world concentrating on the crafting of nativity sets. Nativity sets of outstanding quality were exhibited and awarded annually in Bellingham. Thus, over the years Mr. Drake had accumulated a fine collection of nativity sets from a number of Latin American and European countries. This collection of first-class nativity sets came into the possession of the Marian Library when George Drake decided to move on to other projects. The Drake collection of around 600 artifacts constitutes the base and core of the Marian Library's nativity collection.

During the following years other collections were donated to the Marian Library, for example the Coleman Collection from Minneapolis, the Larish Collection from Rochester, New York, the Elisabeth van Mullekom Collection from Australia, the Judy and Bob Davis Collection from California, the LaCasse Santons Collection from Michigan, and several smaller collections of generous gifts from estates. Each one of them would deserve a special story, and so does the collaboration with collectors and donors, in a special way that with Bill and Annie Baker and their collection of exquisite nativity sets.

Home and Outreach

Instrumental in the beginning, not only for the expansion for our crèche activities but also for the possibility to build settings, was the fruitful and fraternal collaboration with Gallery St. John and the Marianist artists at Mount St. John. Our first public exhibit was at Gallery St. John in 1997, and we have exhibited there ever since. It is at Gallery St. John that we had our first workshop and storage space before moving to the University of Dayton's College Park Center building. The generosity of the Marianists, especially the Marianist artists, and later that of the University of Dayton was crucial for the development and success of our crèche tradition.

It is thanks to the publicity given to the Gallery St. John exhibits that our collaboration with the Dayton Art Institute began in 1999. Other venues developed over the years, taking our displays across the University of Dayton campus, to schools and parishes in town, to St. Peter in Chains, Cincinnati, and to other venues and museums such as Akron/Ohio, New Haven/ Connecticut, and the University of Notre Dame, Indiana.

A Year-round Nativity Museum

Important events gave further prominence to the Marian Library Crèche Collection and related activities. We were able, beginning in 2001, to have our own year-round nativity museum thanks to a reconfiguration of the Marian Library. The nativity sets on display are changed once a year at the beginning of the Advent season.

The Mirror of Hope

To commemorate the Christian Millennium in 2000, Kevin Hanna built for us the *Mirror of Hope* with 24 scenes depicting important stages in salvation history beginning with creation, and concluding with the return of humanity to the "City on the Mount." The *Mirror of Hope* is on permanent display in Roesch Library Gallery, and highlights the Marianist and Catholic character of the University of Dayton. The *Mirror of Hope* remains the centerpiece of our Crèche Collection.

Foundation of "Friends of the Crèche"

In December 1999, thanks to the initiative of Rita Bocher and Fr. Johann Roten, Friends of the Crèche [FOTC], a national society dedicated to the Christmas nativity was launched and saw a rapid expansion. It now counts over 400 members, and every other year a popular and successful annual convention is organized. The Marian Library Crèche Collection is represented in this society founded to promote knowledge and love of the Christmas tradition in the USA.

A Strong Support Group

The next major development for this outreach to spread the beauty and truth of the Incarnation – Jesus Christ brought to birth among us – began in 2006. Recognizing the ever growing number of requests to share the nativities, particularly in their state of the art museum quality settings, the original support group began to campaign for volunteers who would assist the outreach in a variety of ways – everything from preparing settings, wrapping and unwrapping figures for travel, to publicity, fundraising, and schooling of docents.

At the Manger

Upon receipt of the Elisabeth van Mullekom Collection from Australia, Dean Kathleen Webb initiated a yearly open house on the Saturday after Thanksgiving. Free and open to the public, *At the Manger* encompasses three floors of the Roesch and Marian libraries. The displays on each floor have their own theme and focus. In addition to the themes and reflections, there is a nativity related Seek and Find treasure hunt for children, activities and crafts, live Christmas-centered musical entertainment, and an elegant array of cookie treats and beverages.

At the Manger is on display till late January. Over the years, it has proven to bring one of the largest turnouts of any free University of Dayton campus activities. Groups can arrange for guided tours geared to explain in some depth the yearly educational focus.

Brick and Mortar

Ideas and projects inspire. Sometimes they materialize in a beautiful design and a successful display. But there is no design or display that is not built on brick and mortar. An original design, a breathtaking setting can be displayed and admired. Not so the brick-and-mortar work. It remains hidden away in a workroom, and involves hours of cleaning and patching; planning, setting up and shipping; constant updating of an inventory allowing immediate access to country and artist of nativity sets. These are only some of the countless tasks that need to be performed to make a show happen. The first Christmas began as a hidden and lonely feast. It was all brick and mortar. Celebrating now Christmas with pomp and circumstance we do not forget it all began with brick and mortar.

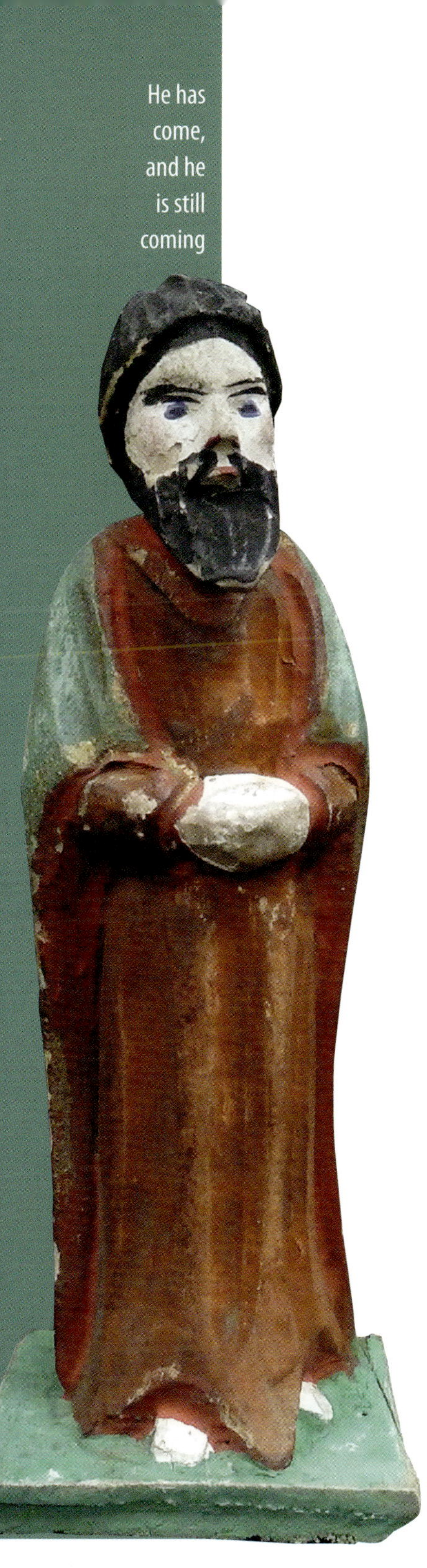

Christmas and No End?

We all measure the distance between us and God. We make it our life's goal to reduce this distance. While we desperately try to close the gap that separates us from God, we forget that God has already built the bridge of our encounter with him. He has come, and he is still coming. He has caught up with us, and still does it! He approaches us from behind like at Emmaus, puts his hand on our shoulder and whispers: "Do not fear, I am with you." His presence reminds us of the many ways in which he has approached humanity in the past. There has always been purpose and direction in God's coming, a sense of progression and holy pedagogy. God's love is that of a teacher and a lover. He knows that we are slow to understand, difficult to move, and of limited faith capacity. His ultimate aim is to conquer our heart with his love. Here is how he did it in the past, and how he continues to do it in the present.

Herald figure announcing the Christmas season: sometimes a hermit, Capuchin or St. Jerome. Grulich tradition.

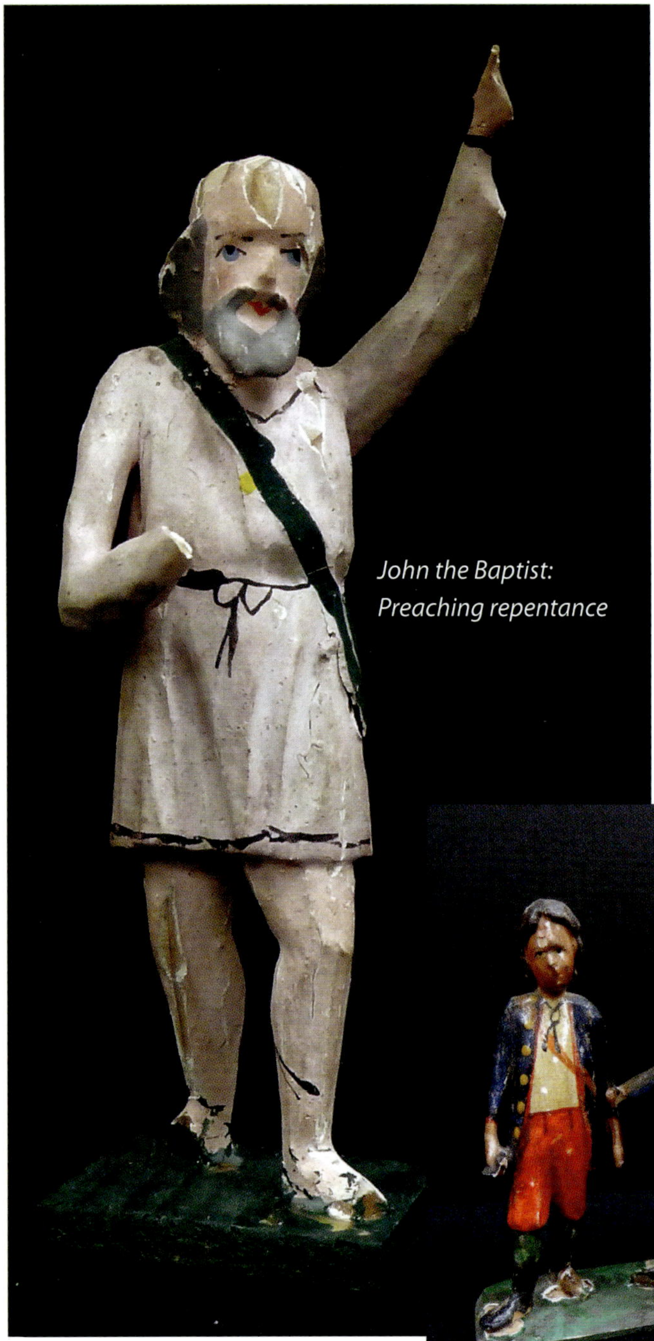

A Love Story

Advent means coming: Advent is not first a time of waiting. Advent means coming; the Advent season symbolizes the long history in which God meets the world, makes his way toward us, and begs to be accepted.

God comes: God's unstoppable coming into the world begins with God himself. God is presented as a living Trinity. He is the overflowing fullness of life. He is the uninterrupted love story symbolized in the unity of Father, Son and Spirit. God is giving, unending, inexhaustible, as Creator, Redeemer and Spirit. And this God is at the beginning of the boundless Christmas mystery. He has left the throne of his apparently unapproachable glory and has made his way into time. His love enters into human history in order to write with us the most beautiful love story of all.

John the Baptist: Preaching repentance

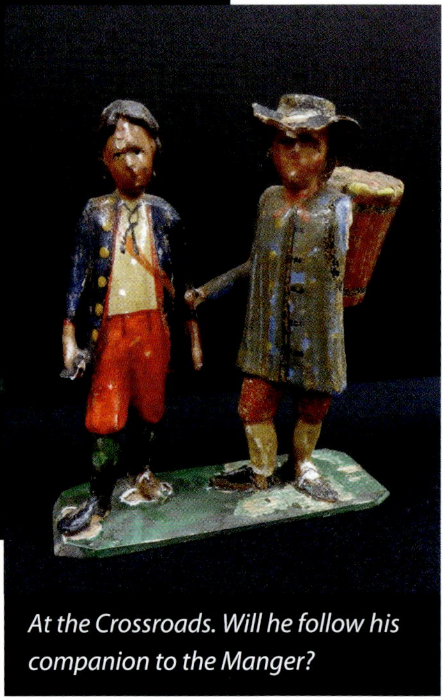

God's coming is progressive: This love story is a long journey which leads over countless epochs, long barren periods and not a few stumbling stones, right to the door of our hearts. A story that is told in many languages, and makes its habitat at the crossroads and service areas of many cultures. God's love can not fail. His descent is sheer goodness of heart with no limitations.

God's coming is continuous: The Crèche culture begins with God. It represents in the first place God's coming as triune Love. Father, Son, and Spirit embody promise, beginning and continuance of God's coming.

At the Crossroads. Will he follow his companion to the Manger?

The nativity figures represented alongside the meditation on Christmas and No End are part of our Nativity Mountain, a Grulich crèche dated back to the mid-nineteenth century, and originally from the East Moravian region of what is now the Czech Republic.

The figures convey various reactions and attitudes of people challenged by the message of Christmas. Some announce it, some resist it, some hail and adore it. Included are also symbols of Christ and of his message.

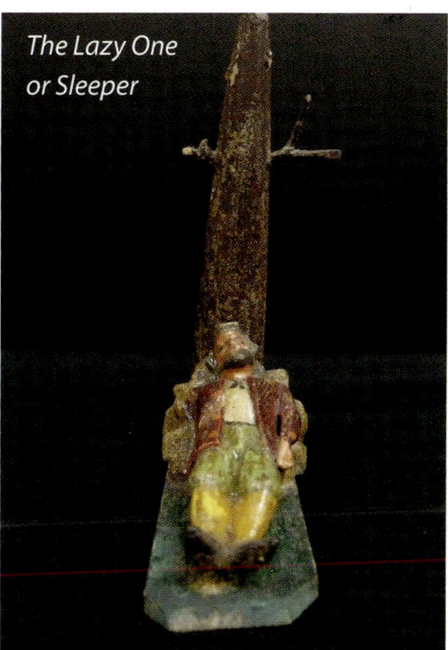
The Lazy One or Sleeper

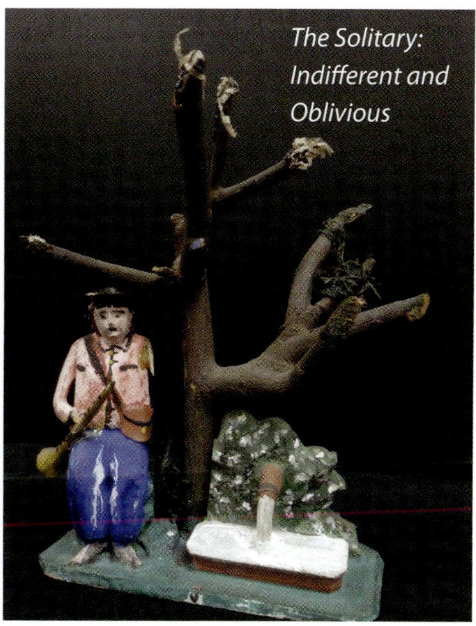
The Solitary: Indifferent and Oblivious

The Tent

In Genesis 3:18, Abraham leaves Egypt. He and Sarah strike their tent, move, and dwell in Hebron. In Hebron, Abraham plants his tent, and builds an altar. Hence, the word Tabernacle is symbolized by the tent. Tents are the dwelling of nomads. In Genesis 18, Abraham hosts visitors at this tent camp in Hebron.

To be a pilgrim: God's first and preferred dwelling among people was the tent. At God's command, Abraham left his solidly built townhouse in Ur. He exchanged the sophisticated way of life of a well-to-do city dweller with the unprotected and uncertain existence of a homeless nomad. His dwelling was a tent; his home, the long lonely road. With no permanent place to stay, tent poles and ropes now secured his shelter instead of protective walls and sturdy beams. Household supplies were reduced to the bare essentials: a string of earthernware hanging on the tentpole, water jugs and cooking utensils, a scale, the loom, the hand-mill, the camel's saddle, the flute.

A symbol of faith: It is here, in the tent, that God lived with Abraham and his family, the God who commanded Abraham's departure. God intended the people to internalize the biorhythm of faith as it is concretely expressed in putting up and taking down the tent. The tent represents a place to stay without a place to stay. Movable and breakable, the tent repeatedly urges its dwellers toward departure. The tent points to the road. To be a pilgrim is our first God-given vocation.

Path and goal: The tent image stands for the beginning of our God experience. God approaches the people as call, promise and miracle. God's call is a persistent urge and restless drive. The God of the tent is experienced as path and journey, as constant movement toward a goal. In associating with God, the people learn the meaning and the demands of loosening and binding, of putting up and taking down our security and comfort. Hence, the God of the tent became the God of freedom: freedom from all that is not freedom for God.

The Land

In Genesis 12: 6-7, Abraham is told by God of an unknown land that will be for his descendents. Canaan, the promised land, is called God's property in Leviticus 25:23.

Moses is told in Exodus 3:17 of God's promise to deliver the Israelites from bondage in Egypt. The Israelites depart from Egypt in Exodus 12:37. They travel through the Red Sea, and into the desert. But their faithlessness prevents a direct entry into the land of Canaan (Numbers 14, 26:63-65, and 32:6-15). Moses is able to see Canaan from afar (Deuteronomy 34:1-5). In Numbers chapter 20, Moses dies at Mount Nebo without entering the promised land of Canaan.

God holds and nourishes: The God who called Abraham into radical discipleship also listens to human needs and whims. The story of Abraham introduces and unfolds a second image: the land.

At first glance, the land stands in opposition to the tent. Did God entice the people out of the city in order to make them settle in a new place? The land is not the property of the people. The land is God's land. The earth is God's. It holds us and nourishes us. The earth, or the land, indicates a new way in God's journey to and with the people. It took form in the life and experiences of Moses.

Holy ground: Thanks to God's kindness and the ruse of two women, Moses was saved from the waters of the Nile. He was given back to the earth. Moses followed the call of blood, he placed himself on the side of his people, and answered the call of Israel's God. Where God spoke to Moses in the burning thornbush, there is holy ground. Here the restless pilgrim has rest. His sandals are loosened. Deeply embedded in Moses' consciousness is the conviction: God is the gloriously-mighty Lord to whom heaven and earth belong.

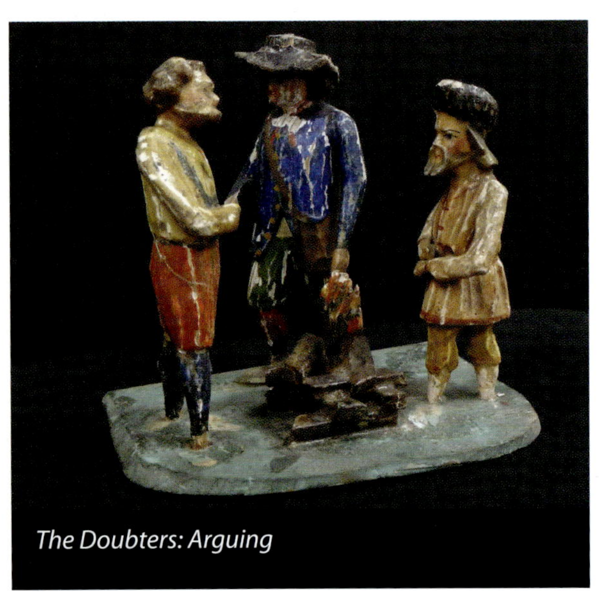

The Doubters: Arguing

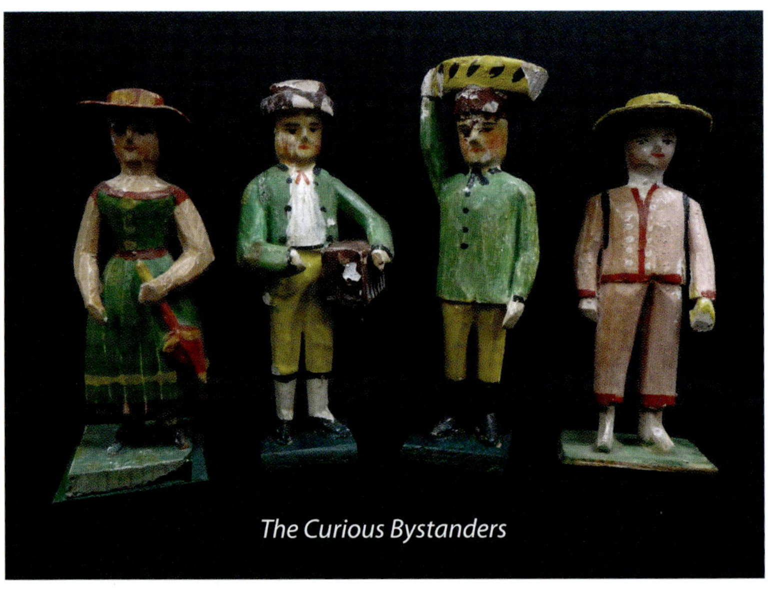

The Curious Bystanders

The promised land: God let Moses' people share in his kindness: the water of life from the rock, quail and manna for nourishment. He came down on Sinai's peak in order to endow Moses with heaven's law for the earth. At the end of Moses' journey, God led him to the battle which opened the door to the promised land. Moses did not taste the honey of the promised land nor did he drink its milk. He saw it with his arms outstretched in prayer, supported by two companions. In God's time, not sooner, the people were allowed to cross the borders to the new homeland.

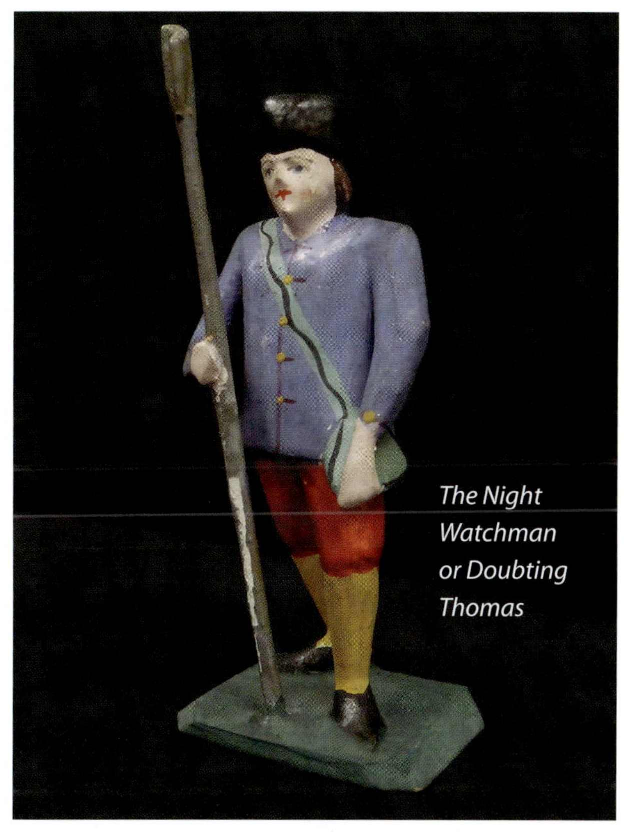

The Night Watchman or Doubting Thomas

A new creation: God has wedded himself to the earth. Henceforth, its name in the words of Scripture is that of bride and partner. The fruitful land flowing with milk and honey (Exodus 3, 17) is only a pale premonition of that new earth which God, maker and redeemer, intended to create (Isaiah 65, 17). The seer of Patmos saw it in a spectacular vision of the future (Revelation 21, 1).

God is a faithful God: If the tent was an expression of the challenge to loosen and bind, so the land, the soil and the earth are an image of God's constancy. God is a faithful God. His love lasts forever. His presence is constant in the city, on the road and in the desert. Life in God is a hidden life. It obeys the laws of dying and becoming. Fruits ripen only in trust and patience. Life in God is fruitful. His goodness is constant.

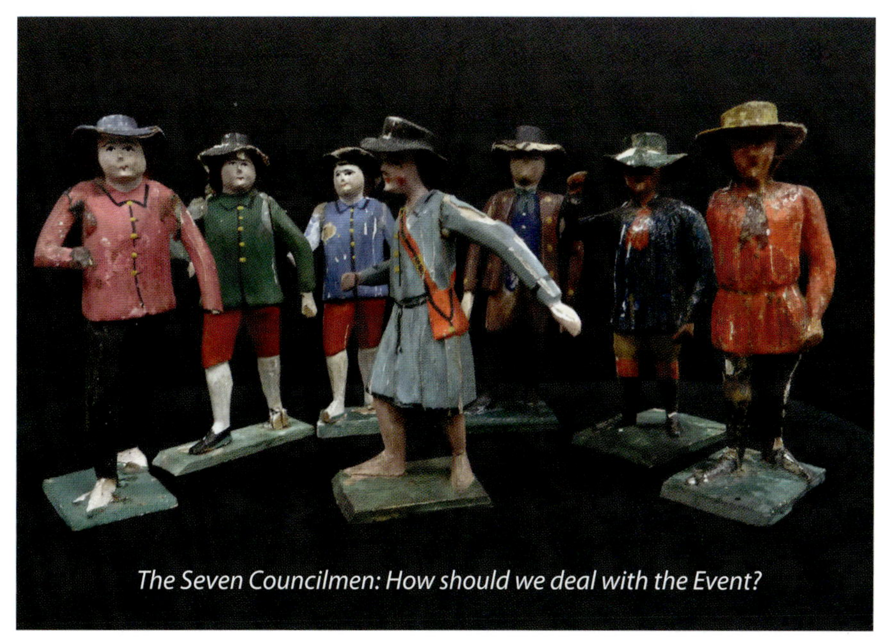

The Seven Councilmen: How should we deal with the Event?

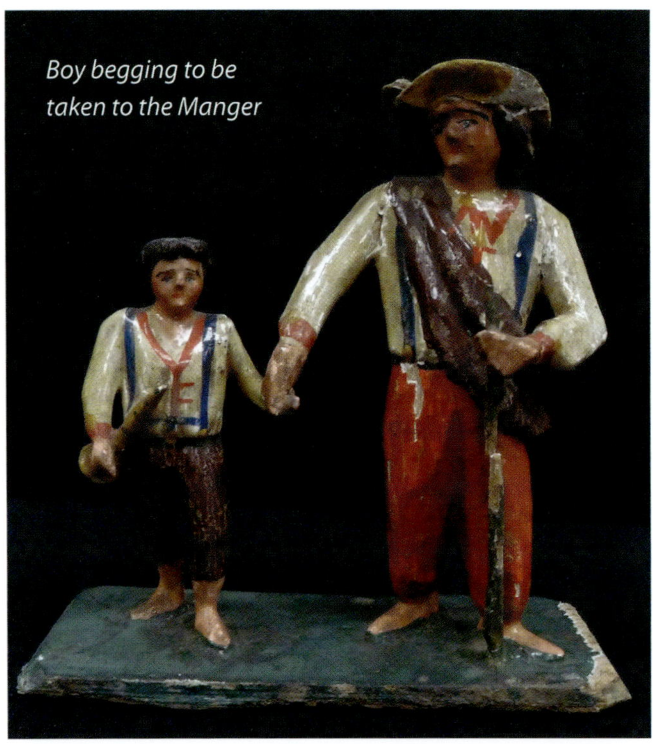
Boy begging to be taken to the Manger

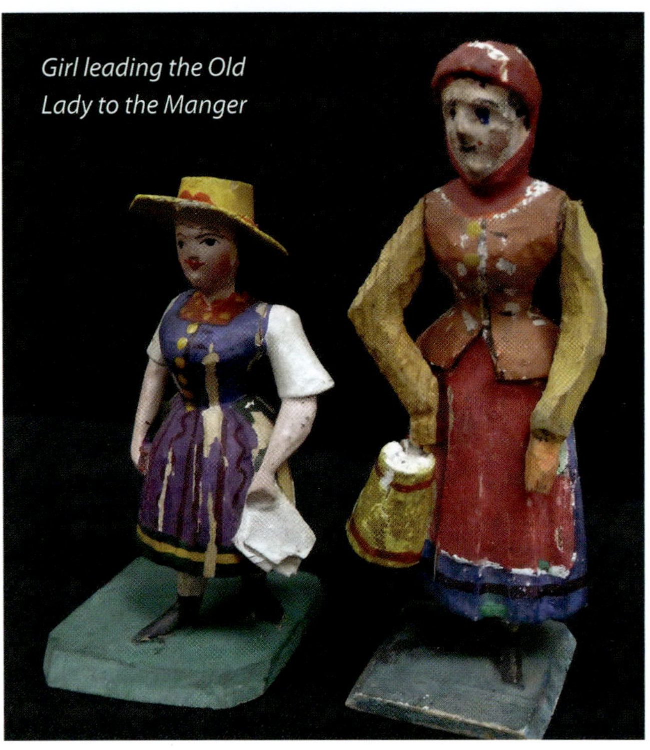
Girl leading the Old Lady to the Manger

The Temple

The Temple is a symbol of God's residence and presence with Israel. In 1 Chronicles 22: 2-5, David brought the Ark to Jerusalem. He assembled stone, metal, and wood in order to build the Temple. Solomon began the actual construction. There are descriptions of the construction in 1 Kings 27-32 and 2 Chronicles 17-18. A fourteen-day-long ceremony of dedication is described in 1 Kings 8: 1-2, 65. The Temple is the heart of Israel's empire (1 Kings 8:65). The Temple is a fortress (1 Kings 7:51, 14:25-26, 15:18, 2 Kings 11:10, 12:4).

God among humans: David belongs to the eminent figures of Advent. God entrusted himself more and more to the hands of his people and their leaders. David became the custodian of God's presence among the people.

David's story marks another step that God takes into the inner spheres of creation and humanity. God's journey to the depths of our heart takes so long because his redemption must penetrate every dimension of reality. If God's presence in the tent and the land was the expression of a cosmological self-manifestation, in David's time God turns to the city and its people. He takes up his dwelling in a temple built by human hands.

The God of the city: David's life led to the threshold of the temple. Only his son and successor Solomon will be allowed to build the marvel, and the glory of God will fill it. God made himself more and more dependent on the people. God accompanied his people in all situations of their personal and social development. He did not recoil from becoming the God of the polis, that is, of the political union, of the temple and of the cult. As partner to human beings, he lived among them. He sealed a covenant with them for time and eternity. In the over-abundance of his love, God's glory entered Solomon's temple (Ezekiel 43, 4) although the train of his mantle would have been enough to fill the great halls of God's house (Isaiah 6, 1). Later, the human body will be elevated to be the temple of the living God (2 Corinthians 6, 16; Hebrews 3,6).

Referee and prisoner of love: God lives in the temple. The Invisible allows himself to be experienced in visible ways. He is within reach at any time; the Untouchable placed himself at the disposal of the people. This manifestation and availability is symbolized in the temple. Out of love, God allowed himself to be domesticated. The city became a holy city in whose midst God dwelt.

The Womb

Sarah was a barren woman we are told in Genesis 11:30 and 16:1. In Genesis 18: 1-15, there is a prophecy that Abraham and Sarah will conceive a son (Isaac). Samuel's mother, Hannah, prays for a child in 1 Samuel 1:11. In 1 Samuel 1:19, Elkanah and Hannah conceive Samuel. An angel tells Zechariah that Elizabeth will have a son in Luke 1:13. In Luke 1:24, the text states that Elizabeth conceived a child (John the Baptist). Mary's virginal conception of Jesus is foretold in Luke 1:31, and restated in Luke 2:21. Jesus is called the "fruit of Mary's womb" in Luke 1:42. In Luke 11:27, a woman tells Jesus that blessed is the womb that bore you.

Bearers of the promise: Abraham, Moses, David – the main actors of the Advent story were men. In reality, the history of the great promise was filled with great women. They often stood in the shadows of the men, but they were not their inferiors when it came to loving faith. Our thoughts turn to the women who were the bearers of God's advent in a physical sense. Without them God's love story with the chosen people would have failed. Above all, without them the singular event that happened to the woman Mary would remain even more puzzling.

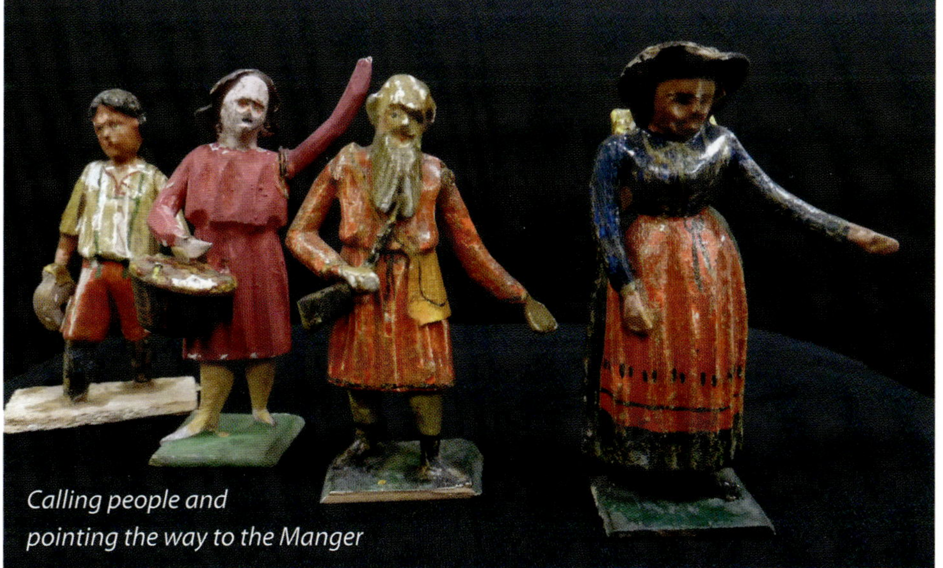

Calling people and pointing the way to the Manger

The tent, the land and the temple were thresholds and anticipations of a still more intimate relationship between God and human beings. Again and again, in the course of the Old Testament, God visited the womb of women in a miraculous way until finally he himself became a human being in the body of a woman.

With God nothing is impossible: In the Old Testament, the bearing of the most beautiful mysteries of encounter with God was often reserved to women who were apparently overlooked in life. One was too old to give birth, another was sterile, and the third was terrified that her newborn would be torn from her and murdered. Still, the miracle happened. God gave and sustained life, contrary to reason, contrary to nature, and contrary to all expectation. Ancient Sarah fell into fits of laughter when she learned of the coming child. She gave birth to Isaac. Jochebed's son, Moses, who must die according to Egyptian law, became the protector and liberator of the enslaved people. God showed mercy through Hannah's humiliating barrenness. From her body came the prophet Samuel. And who does not know the story

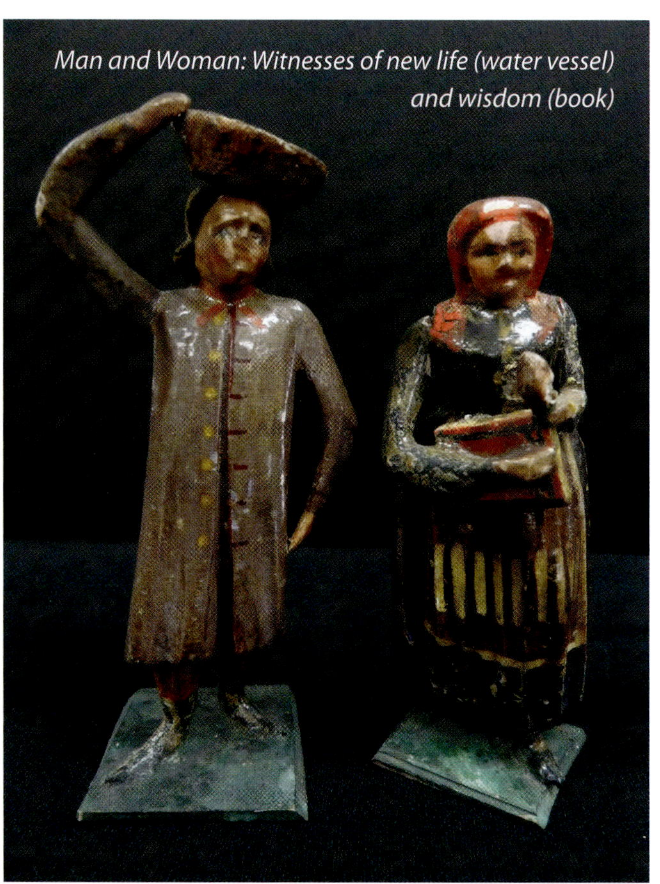
Man and Woman: Witnesses of new life (water vessel) and wisdom (book)

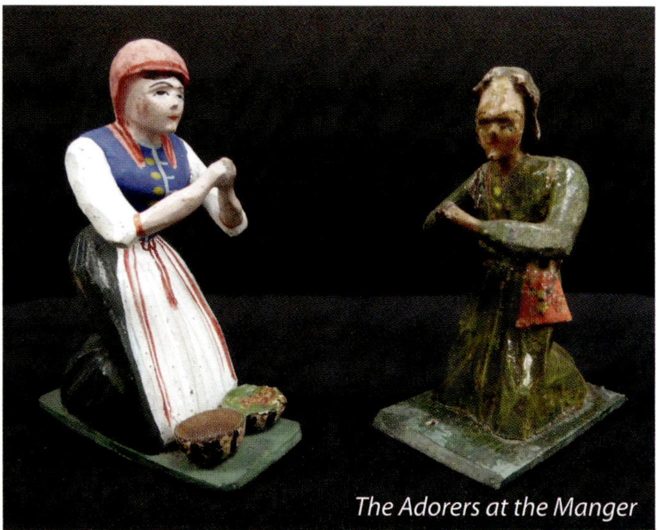
The Adorers at the Manger

of Mary's mysterious conception and birth, which begins with the meeting of the elderly couple, Joachim and Anna, at the golden gate? John the Baptizer! He is the living answer to a long-buried expectation. But here, too, the incredible took place, and the child leapt for joy in the womb of his mother, Elizabeth.

With God nothing is impossible. The laws of neither nature nor logic are unconquerable boundaries for God. The power of his love moves past all hindrances. It transforms contradictions into loving readiness. When the fullness of time was reached, that is when all other forms of his presence in and among people had played out, God became man in his Son from the woman Mary. He became the God-man.

God in the womb and in life: In Mary's womb began the final and most profound God experience of a human being, an experience that was in God's hands alone. Jesus grew and gained strength in and through a human person up to the point where the laws of growth were reversed, and Mary grew ever more intimately close to God. After Mary participated in the fully human development of her Son, she matured in Christ's school to the fullness of her own faith. She became the ever-present figure and model of the Church. We, too, become Christ-bearers as Christ's life increases in us.

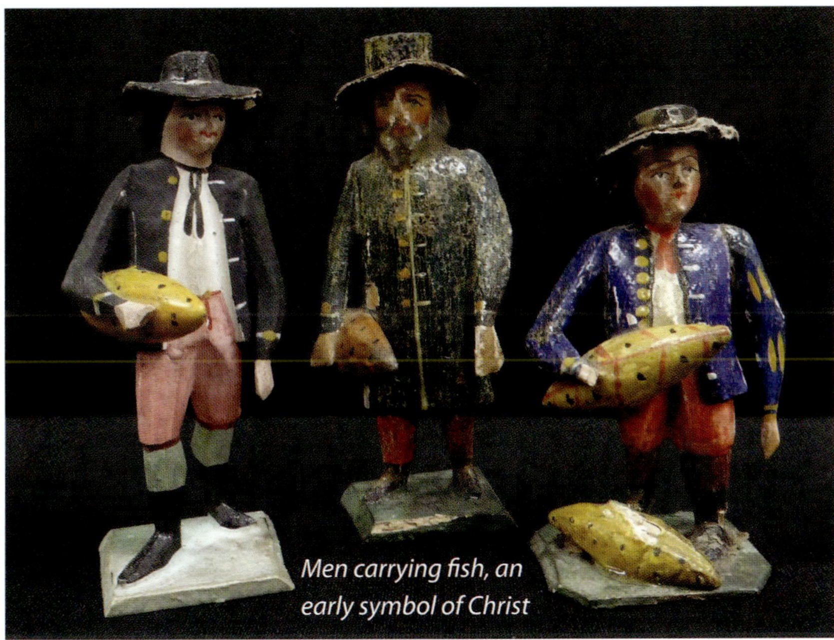
Men carrying fish, an early symbol of Christ

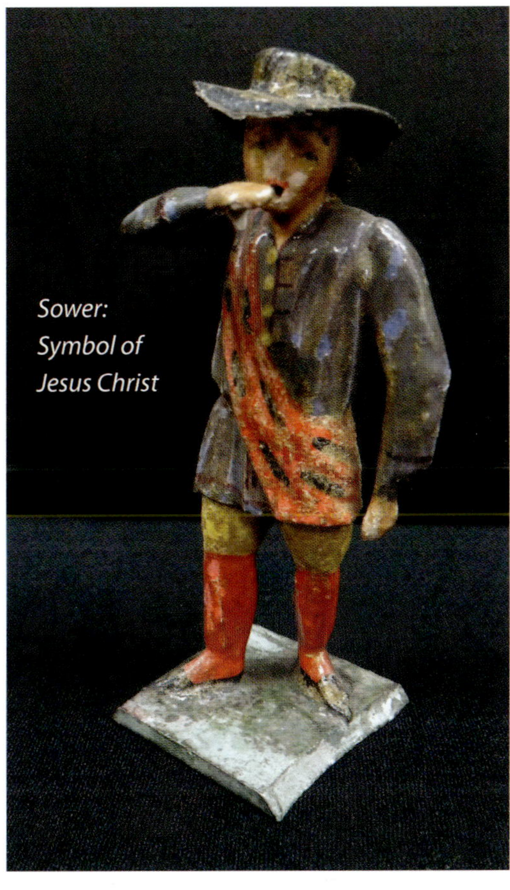
Sower: Symbol of Jesus Christ

The Heart

The heart is the place where conversion to Christ takes place. This is explained in Acts 2:37, Psalm 51:10, and Joel 2:12. In 1 John 5:10, the reader is told that the testimony of God is in the believer's heart. In Revelation 2:23, God is called the searcher of hearts and minds. In Ephesians 3:17, we read: "May Christ dwell in your heart through faith and may charity be the foundation of your life." In Galatians 4:6, we are told that God sent forth into our hearts the Holy Spirit.

God's final destination: On Christmas Eve the actual crèche festival begins. God comes. He is there. He is visibly there. He has allowed himself to be caught in the net of human destiny. He shares the helplessness of the child and the homelessness of the refugee. He experiences in his own body the laws of becoming and growth. He endures the anxieties of the soul, and tastes the joys of the spirit. He is thrown into a maelstrom of human existence which will carry him, test him, and finally crush him.

We celebrate the feast of God's presence. For all times, this moment has been preserved in a multitude of images and memories. The message is one, and one only: "The old reign came to an end because God in human form appeared for the new age of eternal life. And it had its beginning with what had been prepared by God." (Ignatius of Antioch).

The Crèche, symbol of the heart: The crèche symbolizes the historical reality of God's presence. It is also a symbol that points to our hearts. The heart is the final destination of God's coming, your heart, my heart, and the hearts of everyone, because God has come to all people and for all people. Crèche and heart have many things in common. They both stand for faith's poverty and love's wealth. The fragile crèche guards the covenant of love, as it is embodied in the Holy Family. In a similar way, a new covenant is sealed in the hearts of the people, a covenant which in its own way is an image of the Trinity and of the Holy Family.

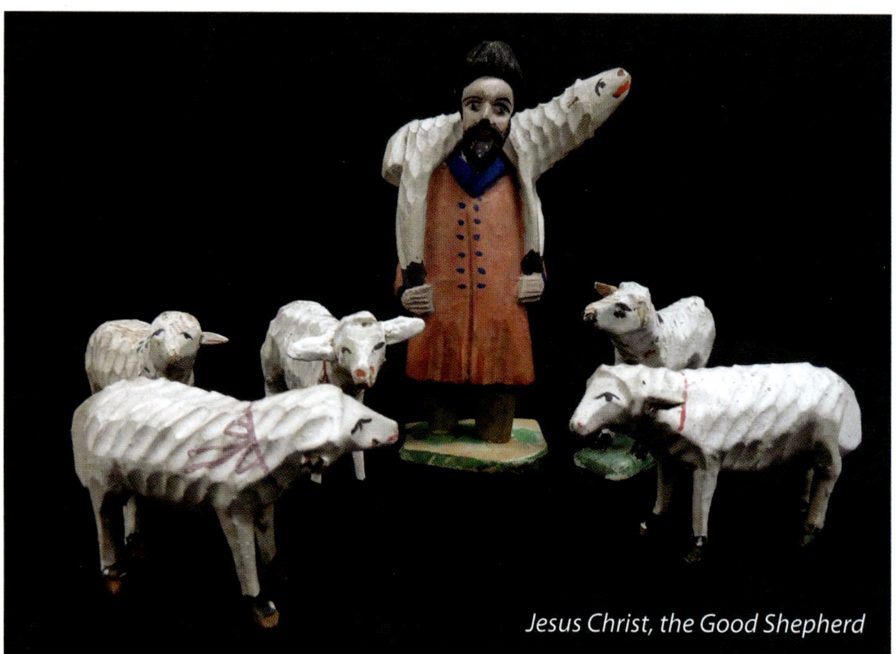

Jesus Christ, the Good Shepherd

Christmas and No End

Even more than 2,000 years after Christ's birth, Incarnation has not come to an end. Incarnation is an ongoing event, personal as well as collective. God's coming is offered to all peoples at all times. This is the deeper meaning of the nativity sets in our collection. They are an expression of the many ways in which Christ has been sought and found.

Christmas and no end. There is an old legend about seeking and finding Christ. The wise man Artaban in his pursuit of the star misses his three friends. He misses the Christchild, too, because his pilgrimage to Bethlehem leads to strange encounters with dying soldiers, ailing beggars, and poor mothers. He gives them two of his three diamonds saved for the child in the manger. After thirty-three years and many adventures he arrives in Jerusalem. There, he still diligently searches for the newborn king. Artaban, now an old man, notes an unusual commotion. Inquiring about its cause he learns that they are taking Jesus of Nazareth, who calls himself King of the Jews, to Golgotha and his death. Artaban knows instinctively that this is the king for whom he has been searching. He rushes to the scene. Alas, once again, he is sidetracked. On his way he meets a young girl being sold into slavery. His heart is moved, and he gives away his last diamond for her ransom. Just then, darkness falls over the city, and Artaban knows that his king is dead. Inconsolable, he cries out: "Thirty-three years I looked for you. Lord, but I have never seen your face or ministered to you." But then a voice comes from heaven and says: "What you did to the least of my brothers and sisters, you did it to me." Artaban's restlessness is gone. His heart grows calm and his soul is peaceful. His long journey is ended. He has found his king. Meanwhile, the story goes on — for each one of us is Artaban.

The blueprint of our nativity sets is the Sacred Page

Sacred Page and Blueprint

Where do we find the blueprint for our manger scenes? Where does the typical representation of the Nativity of Jesus, the Christ, come from? The story of Christmas is embedded in the gospel accounts of the evangelists Matthew and Luke. These accounts have a special name. We call them the infancy narratives. They are found in the first chapters of each of the two gospels mentioned.

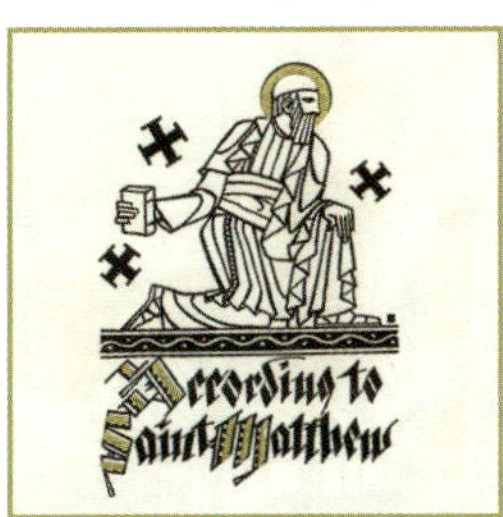

Matthew (80-85 C.E.) tells the story from the perspective of Joseph and the Old Testament. The birth of Christ is the fulfillment of the old covenant (chapter 1). The new covenant is open to the whole world. That is why in Matthew the magi, the wise men from the Orient play an important role (chapter 2).

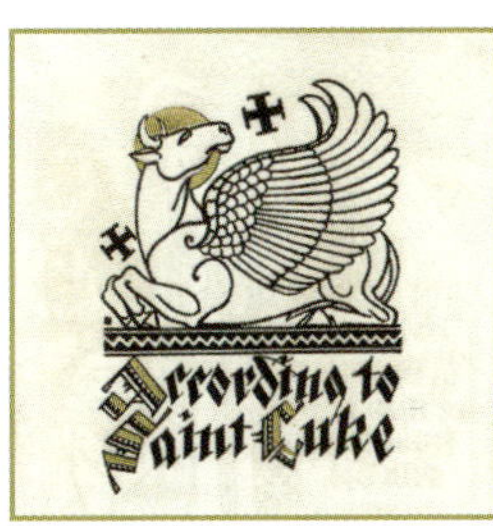

Luke (ar. 85 C.E.) represents the point of view of Mary, of her call and vocation to be the mother of Jesus (chapter 1). The birth of Jesus involves angels and shepherds. Not alone the whole world as in Matthew, but both heaven and earth take part in proclaiming the good news of salvation (chapter 2).

The blueprint of our nativity sets is first and foremost the Sacred Page, a page from the Book of Books. The Book of Books is sacred ground for Christians. It deserves loving respect and attention as highlighted here in the calligraphed reproduction of the sacred texts. The calligraphed rendering of the infancy narratives in Matthew and Luke serves as a memorial of beauty and reverence. Penned and drawn by Chester B. Falls as the *Story of the Birth of Jesus*, it was published in 1929 as one of a thousand copies by the Marchbanks Press, New York.

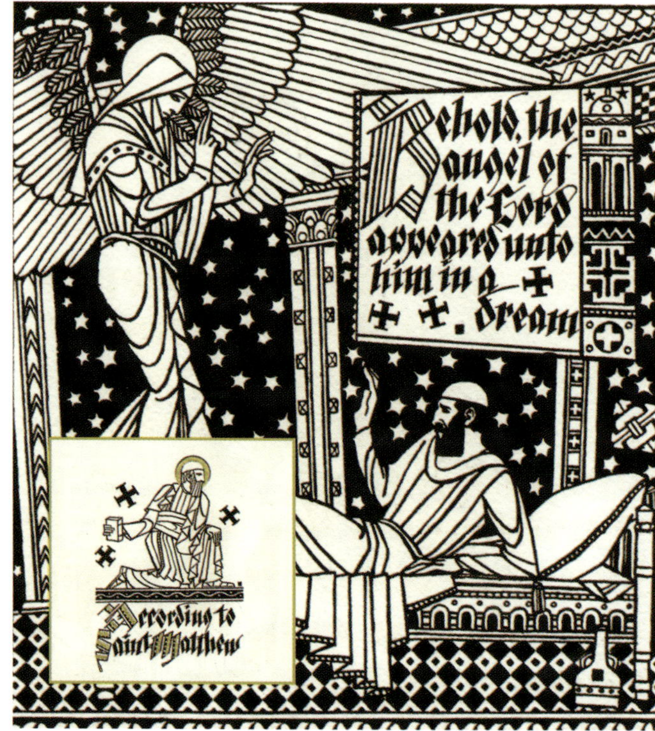

Now the birth of Jesus Christ was on this wise: When as his mother Mary was espoused to Joseph, before they came together, she was found with child of the Holy Ghost. Then Joseph her husband, being a just man, and not willing to make her a publick example, was minded to put her away ✠ privily: but while he thought on these things, behold, the angel of the Lord appeared unto him in a dream, saying, Joseph, thou son of David, fear not to take unto thee Mary thy wife: for that which is conceived in her is of the Holy Ghost. And she shall bring forth a son, and thou shalt call his name Jesus: for he shall save his people from their sins. ✠ Now all this was done, that it might be fulfilled which was spoken of the Lord by the prophet, saying, behold, a virgin shall be with child, and shall bring forth a son, and they shall call his name Emmanuel which being interpreted is God with us. Then Joseph being raised from sleep did as the angel of the Lord had bidden him, and took unto him his wife: and knew her not till she had brought forth her firstborn son: and he called his name Jesus ✠ ✠ ✠

Now when Jesus was born in Bethlehem of Judæa in the days of Herod the king, behold, there came wise men from the

east to Jerusalem, saying, Where
is he that is born King of the ✠ ✠
Jews? for we have seen his star
in the east, and are come to worship him. When Herod the king
had heard these things, he was
troubled, and all Jerusalem with
him. And when he had gathered
all the chief priests and scribes
of the people together, he demand-
ed of them where Christ should
be born. ✠ And they said unto
him, In Bethlehem of Judæa:
for thus it is written by the prophet, and thou Bethlehem, in the

land of Juda, art not the least
among the princes of Juda: for
out of thee shall come a Governor, that shall rule my people
Israel. Then Herod, when he had
privily called the wise men, inquired of them diligently what
time the star appeared. And he
sent them to Bethlehem, and
said, Go and search diligently
for the young child; and when
ye have found him, bring me
word again, that I may come and
worship him also. ✠ When they
had heard the king, they depart-

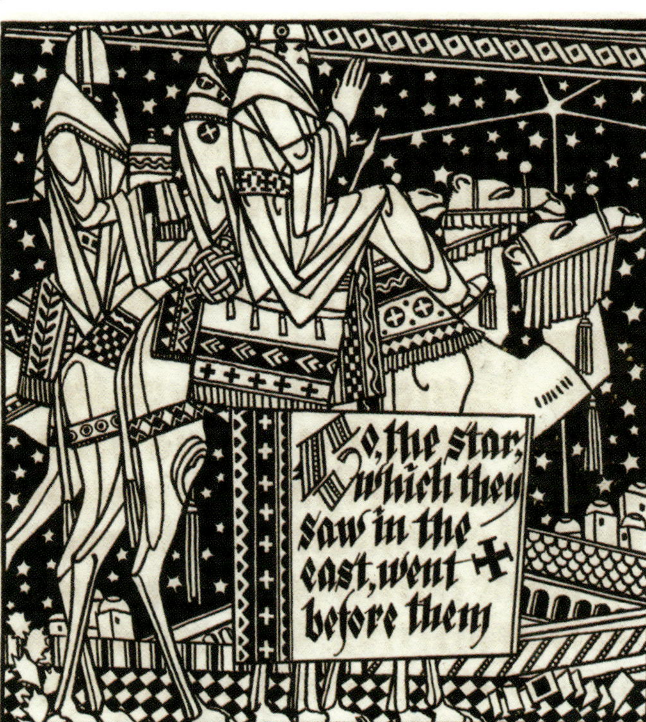

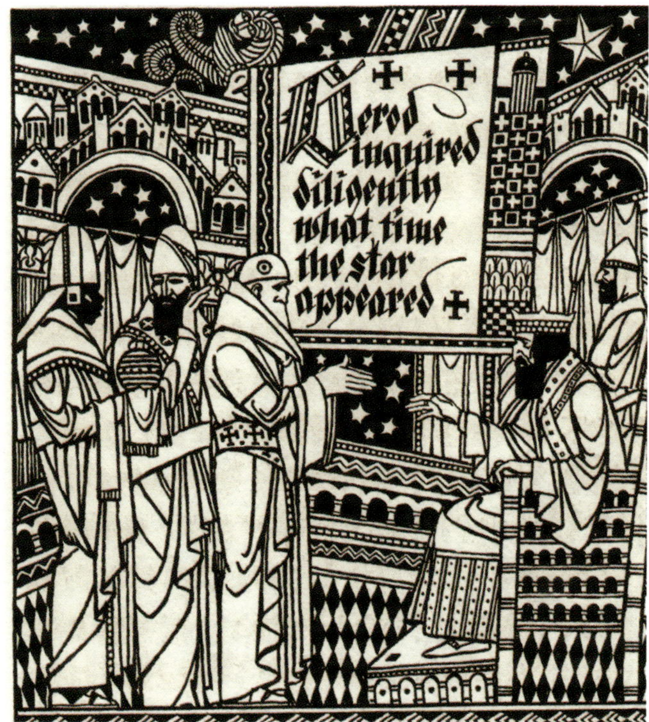

ed; and, lo, the star, which they saw in the east, went before them, till it came and stood over where the young child was. When they saw the star, they rejoiced with exceeding great joy. ✠ ✠ ✠ ✠ ✠

And when they were come into the house, they saw the young child with Mary his mother, and fell down, and worshipped him: and when they had opened their treasures, they presented unto him gifts; gold, and frankincense, and myrrh. And being

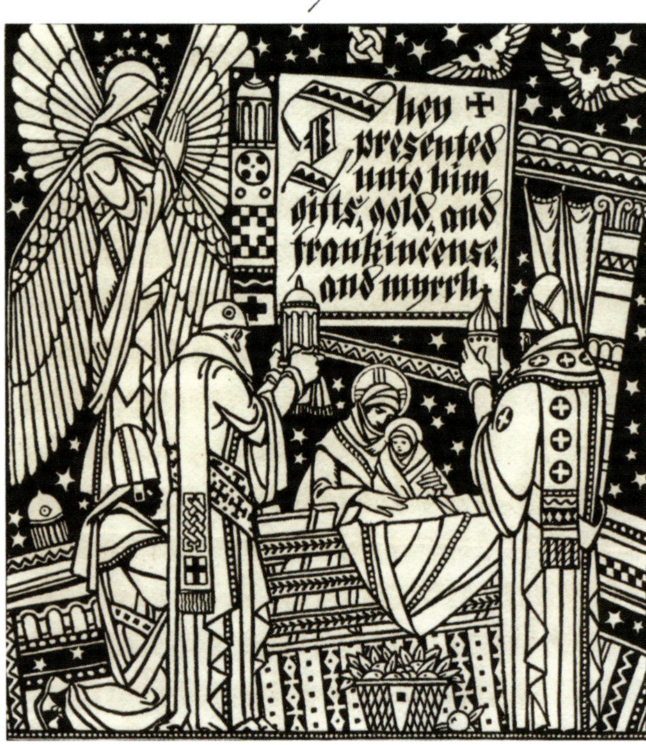

warned of God in a dream that they should not return to Herod, they departed into their own country another way. And when they were departed, behold the angel of the Lord appeareth to Joseph in a dream, saying, ✠ Arise, and take the young child and his mother, and flee into Egypt, and be thou there until I bring thee word: for Herod will seek the young child to destroy him. When he arose, he took the young child and his mother by night, and departed into Egypt.

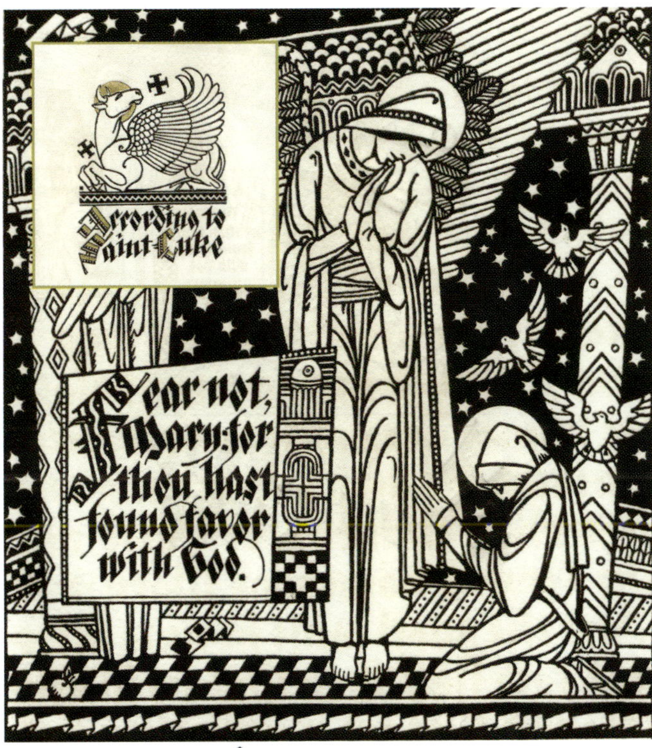

And in the sixth month the angel Gabriel was sent from God unto a city of Galilee, named Nazareth, to a virgin espoused to a man whose name was Joseph, of the house of David; and the virgin's name was Mary. And the angel came in unto her, and said, Hail, thou that art highly favoured, the Lord is with thee:

blessed art thou among women. And when she saw him, she was troubled at his saying, and cast in her mind what manner of salutation this should be. And the angel said unto her, Fear not, Mary: for thou hast found favor with God. And, behold, thou shalt conceive in thy womb, and bring forth a son, and shalt call his name Jesus. He shall be great, and shall be called the Son of the Highest: and the Lord God shall give unto him the throne of his Father David: And he shall reign over the house of Jacob for ever; and of his kingdom there shall be no end. Then said Mary unto the angel, How shall this be, seeing I know not a man?

And the angel answered and said unto her, The Holy Ghost shall come upon thee, and the power of the Highest shall overshadow thee: therefore also that holy thing which shall be born of thee shall be called the Son of God. And, behold, thy cousin Elisabeth, she hath also conceived a son in her old age: and this is the sixth month with her, who was called barren. For with God nothing shall be impossible. ✠ And Mary said, Behold the handmaid of the Lord; be it unto me according to thy word. And the angel departed from her. ✠ ✠ ✠ And it came to pass in those days, that there went out a decree ✠ from Cæsar Augustus, that all the world should be taxed. ✠

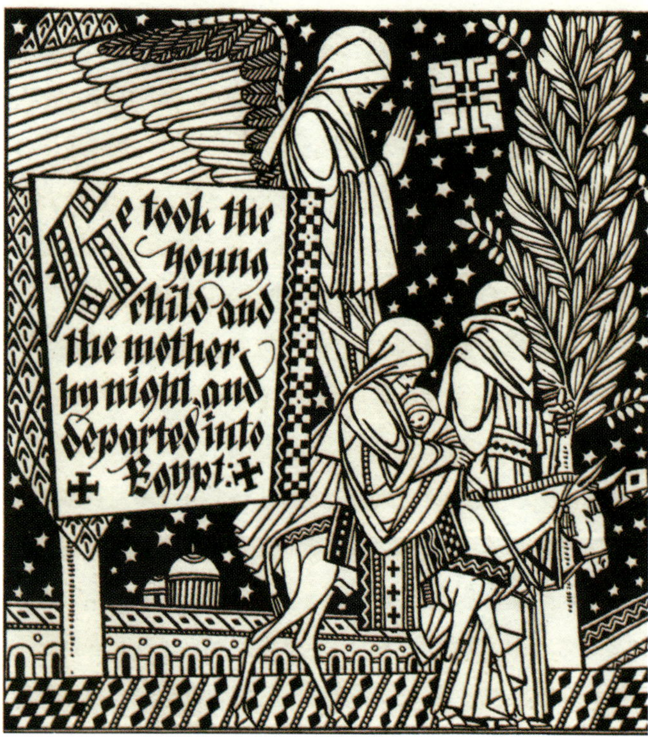

(And this taxing was first made when Cyrenius was governor of Syria.) And all went to be taxed, every one into his own city. ✠ ✠ And Joseph also went up from Galilee, out of the city of Nazareth, into Judaea, unto the city of David, which is called Bethlehem; (because he was of the ✠ house and lineage of David:) to be taxed with Mary his espoused wife, being great with child. ✠ And so it was, that, while they were there, the days were accomplished that she should be delivered. And she brought forth her firstborn son, and wrapped ✠ him in swaddling clothes, and laid him in a manger; because there was no room for them in the inn. And there were in the same country shepherds abiding in the field, keeping watch over their flock by night. ✠ ✠ ✠ ✠

And, lo, the angel of the Lord came upon them, and the glory of the Lord shone round about ✠ them: and they were sore afraid. And the angel said unto them,

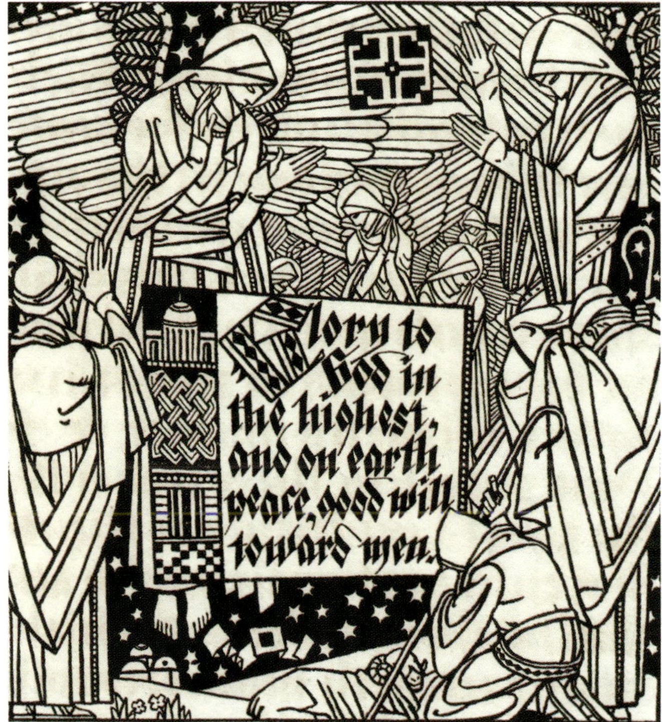

Fear not: for, behold, I bring you good tidings of great joy, which shall be to all people. For unto you is born this day in the city of David a Saviour, which is Christ the Lord. And this shall be a sign unto you; Ye shall find the babe wrapped in swaddling clothes, lying in a manger. And suddenly there was with the angel a multitude of the heavenly host praising God, and saying, Glory to God in the highest, and on earth peace, good will toward men. And it came to pass, as the angels were gone away from them into heaven, the shepherds said one to another; Let us now go even unto Bethlehem, and see this thing which is come to pass, which the Lord hath made known unto us.

And they came with haste, and found Mary, and Joseph, and the babe lying in a manger. And when they had seen it, they made known abroad the saying which was told them concerning this child. And all they that heard it wondered at those things which were told them by the shepherds. But Mary kept all these things, and pondered them in her heart. And the shepherds returned, glorifying and praising God for all the things that they had heard and seen, as it was told unto them.

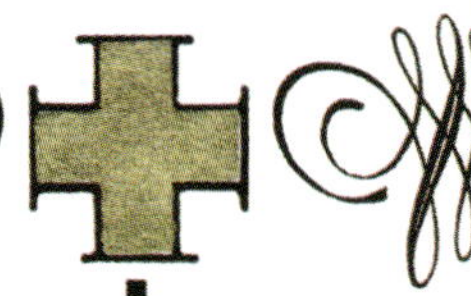

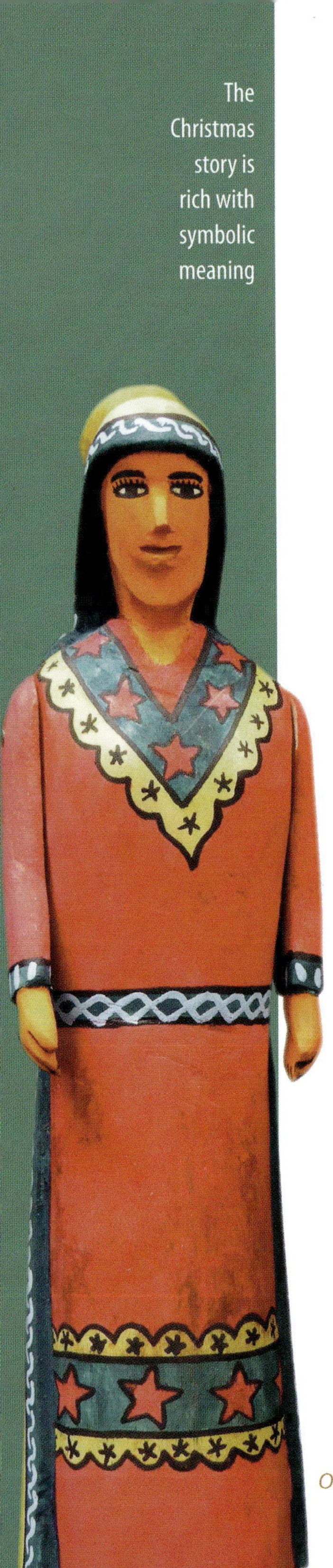

The Christmas story is rich with symbolic meaning

The Bible and Beyond

Actors and actresses of the Nativity story, and important symbols have their origin in the Bible. Tradition and various cultures will adopt and adapt them. However, some popular elements of the Nativity are found in apocryphal writings, and are not part of the Bible as we know it. The first bath of the baby is a purely cultural ingredient; neither the Gospels nor the apocryphal writings tell about it.

The Christmas story is rich with symbolic meaning. The figures are not meaningless figures. They carry a message of theological significance. A message which safeguards both the heavenly origin and the truly human reality of the Incarnation. The Christchild is Jesus Christ, human and divine. He is a challenge for the mind as can be seen in the story of Joseph, but also the beginning of a love story conquering the heart of Mary, the enchantment of the shepherds, and the intrepid pursuit of truth by the wise men.

Octaviano Santiago, Mexico

The Child

Luke 2:12
"And this will be a sign for you: you will find an infant wrapped in swaddling clothes and lying in a manger."

Until the beginning of the 14th century, the child is heavily "bandaged," wrapped in swaddling clothes. Usually only his face is uncovered and visible, a sign that his divine origin remains hidden. For a time, mainly during the Renaissance period, the tendency in the Western tradition was to show him naked. He is a true human baby. Later, ways to indicate both humanity and divinity are sought.

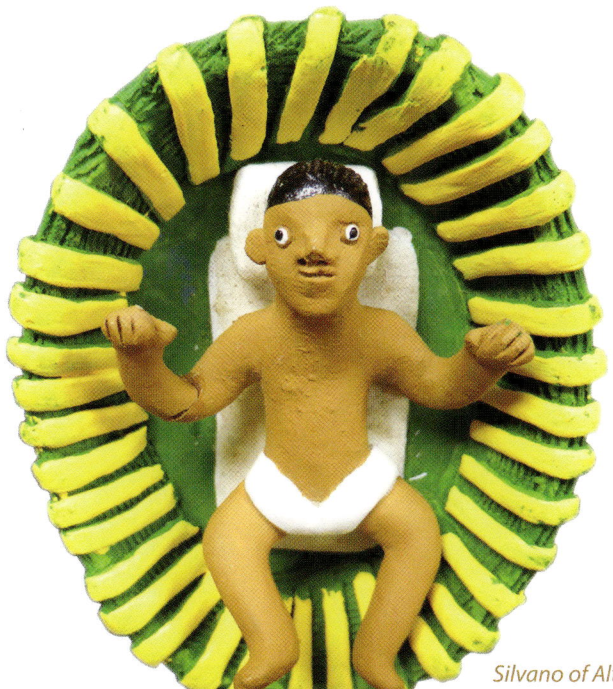

Silvano of Alto do Moura, Brazil

The Manger

Luke 2:12
"And this will be a sign for you: you will find an infant wrapped in swaddling clothes and lying in a manger."

Mentioned several times, scripture is silent about the place where the manger stood: in a stable, a cave, a hut, or in the ruins of a palace?

In the icon tradition, the manger simultaneously symbolizes the bed of the child, the tomb of the Redeemer, and the altar upon which the Eucharist is celebrated.

In the Western tradition, the manger is mostly a trough to feed animals. Renaissance art frequently placed the Christchild on a bed of "straw" made of golden rays symbolizing his divine origin.

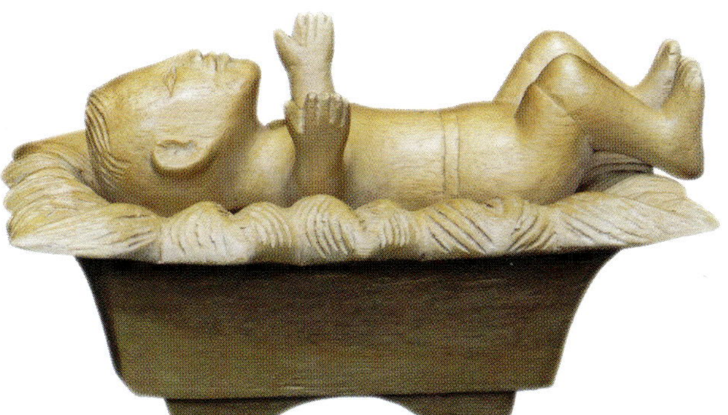

Sardjano E. Tribandi, Indonesia

Mary and Joseph

Luke 2:16

"So they went in haste and found Mary and Joseph, and the infant lying in the manger."

Cultural tradition presents Mary in various postures. As the early rock mother she is sitting on a stone and musing. Demonstrative of her child she is the enthroned mother. She is also depicted as the nursing mother. Iconography shows her exhausted and reclining after birth. Beginning in late medieval times Mary kneels and adores the Christchild. Modern representations feature her as the hugging and cuddling mother. The contemporary Mary relies more heavily on Joseph as husband and father of adoption.

Early on Joseph is frequently depicted as a marginal figure separated from the manger, sleeping, expressing doubt (Matthew 1:18), or tempted by the devil. He is more prominently featured in modern times, sometimes as the caring Joseph preparing food for the baby.

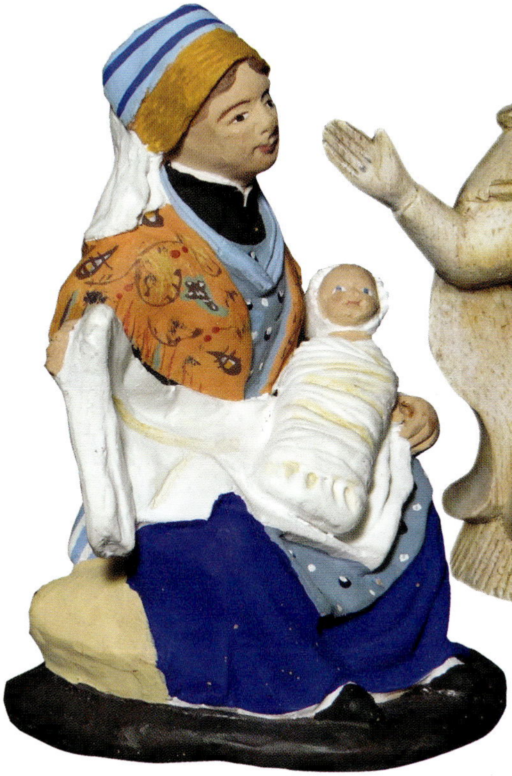

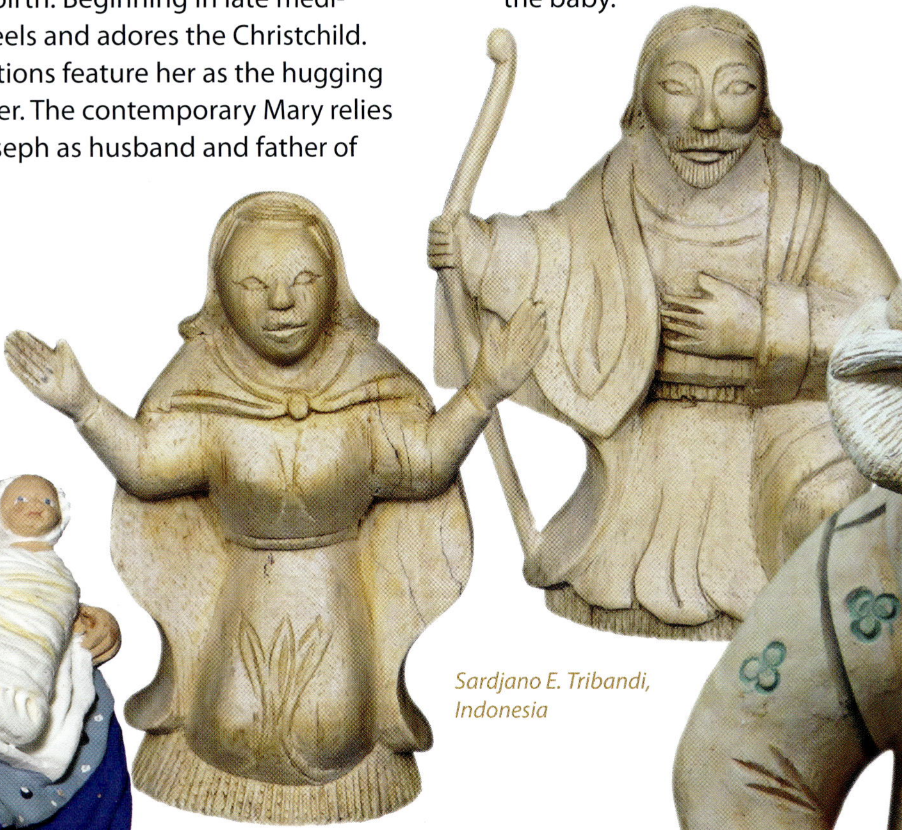

Sardjano E. Tribandi, Indonesia

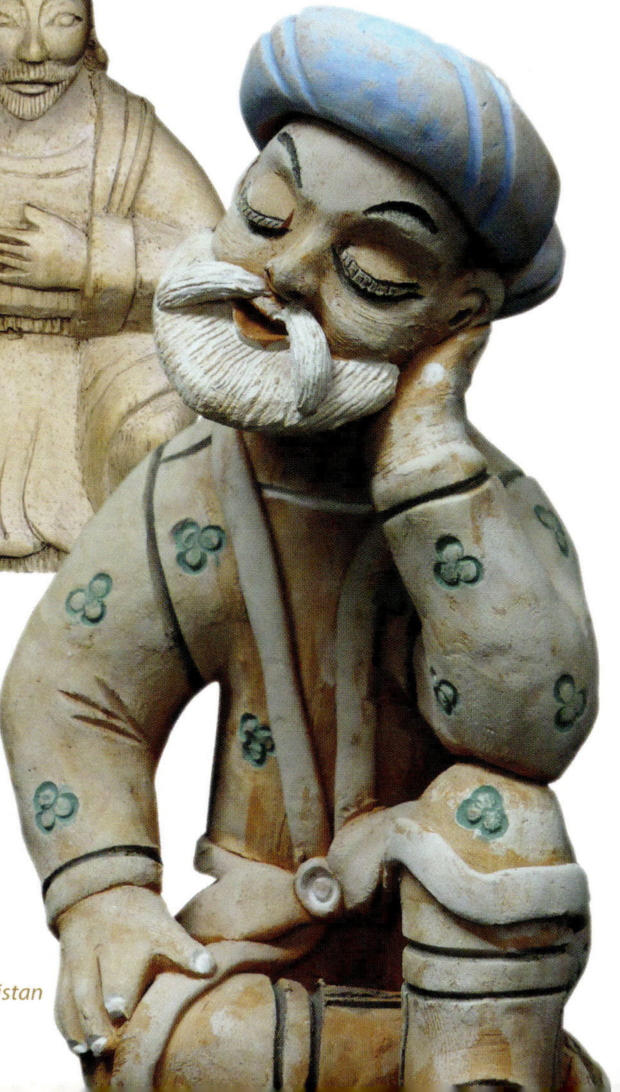

Michel Vincent, Belgium

The Registan, Samarkand, Uzbekistan

The Shepherds

Luke 2:8

"Now there were shepherds in that region living in the fields and keeping the night watch over their flock."

They are promised by the angel "to find an infant wrapped in swaddling clothes" (2:12) who is "Messiah and Lord" (2:11). They found the infant, and "they made known the message that had been told them about this child (2:17). They returned, "glorifying and praising God…" (2:20).

The number of shepherds is not mentioned in the Bible. Art took great liberty in numbering and representing them. We usually distinguish between shepherds in the field and shepherds at the manger. Shepherds frequently represent moral behavior and psychological dispositions, f.ex. watchfulness and laziness, joy and generosity, poverty and humility, piety and indifference. Some traditions depict the three ages of the human person: the old, the middle-aged, and the young shepherd.

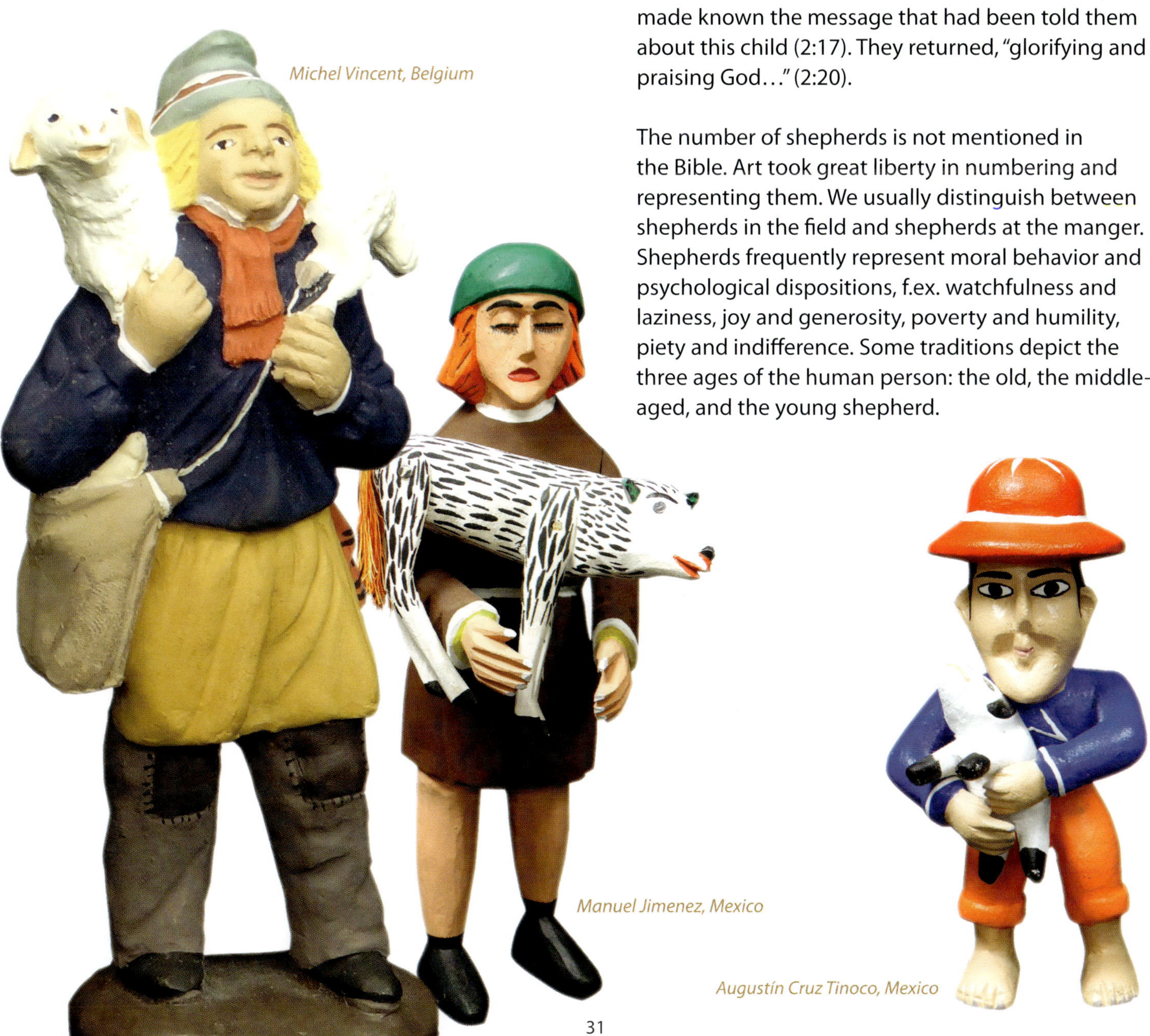

Michel Vincent, Belgium

Manuel Jimenez, Mexico

Augustín Cruz Tinoco, Mexico

The Angels

Luke 2:9-14

"The angel of the Lord appeared to them (scil. shepherds) and the glory of the Lord appeared to them."

He (the angel of the Lord) proclaims "good news of great joy." (2:10) "Suddenly there was a multitude of the heavenly host with the angel, praising God and saying; 'Glory to God in the highest, and on earth peace to those on whom his favor rests.'" (2:13-14)

Both the "angel of the Lord" and a "multitude of the heavenly host" are mentioned. The single angel is the angel of the announcement, the heavenly host goes by the name of Alleluja Angels. Sometimes a critical voice from heaven is heard: the angels questioning the wisdom of the Incarnation. The presence of angels at the Nativity goes from sober and simple to representations of great sophistication, as can be found on the Isenheim Altar by M. Grünewald.

Octaviano Santiago, Mexico

Convento de Jesus Maria, Huelva, Spain

The Magi

Matthew 2:1

"When Jesus was born in Bethlehem of Judea, in the days of King Herod, behold, magi from the east arrived in Jerusalem."

They will find "the child with Mary his mother," do him homage, and offer him gifts of "gold, frankincense, and myrrh." (2:11).

The number of magi is not mentioned in the Bible. Early church fathers concluded from the three gifts mentioned that there were three magi. Present early on in representations of the Nativity to illustrate the universal character of the Christian message, the episode of the magi carries a rich symbolism highlighting eternal truth illuminating creation, the three ages of the human person, or the three regions of the world, Europe, Africa, and Asia.

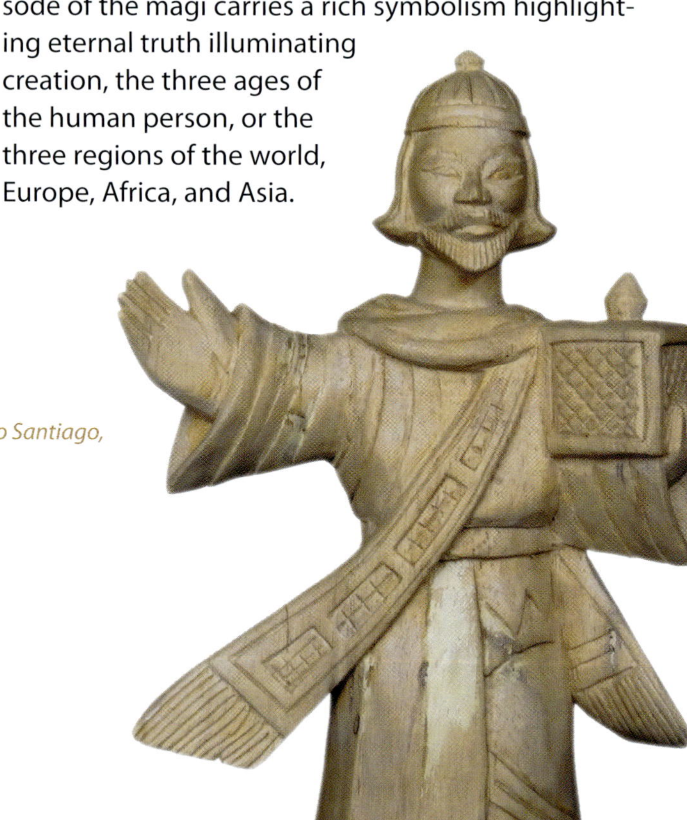

Sardjano E. Tribandi, Indonesia

Kathy Andrews Fincher, United States

The Star

Matthew 2:2

The magi inquired: "Where is the newborn king of the Jews? We saw his star at its rising and have come to do him homage."

The star has been represented and interpreted in various ways. It is first and foremost a star of orientation and guidance for he magi. It also has he role of ascertaining God's presence and Christ's divinity. In a special way, the star may be understood as the "Sun of Justice" symbolizing Christ himself.

Convento de Jesus Maria, Huelva, Spain

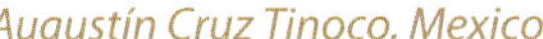

Augustín Cruz Tinoco, Mexico

From Scripture to Apocryphals

Important elements of the Nativity representation are not in Scripture. They are found in so-called apocryphal writings, in two of them, mainly: the Protevangelium of James and the Gospel of Pseudo-Matthew. The Apocrypha are, to a degree, illustrations embellishing the canonical gospels. They are telling stories where the gospels relate crucial teachings and events of salvation history. Many of the apocryphal writings neither contradict nor deny the binding character of the gospel text. They are not invested with the authority of the Church, but frequently refer to biblical sources to comment and expand on.

Among the most popular and informative writings about the Christmas tradition are the Protevangelium of James and the Gospel of Pseudo-Matthew. The Protevangelium of James is the oldest (ar. 150 C.E.) and most influential apocryphal writing regarding the early life of Mary and the Nativity of Jesus Christ. The traditional Christmas story borrowed the reference to the cave and the episode of the midwife from the Protevangelium of James.

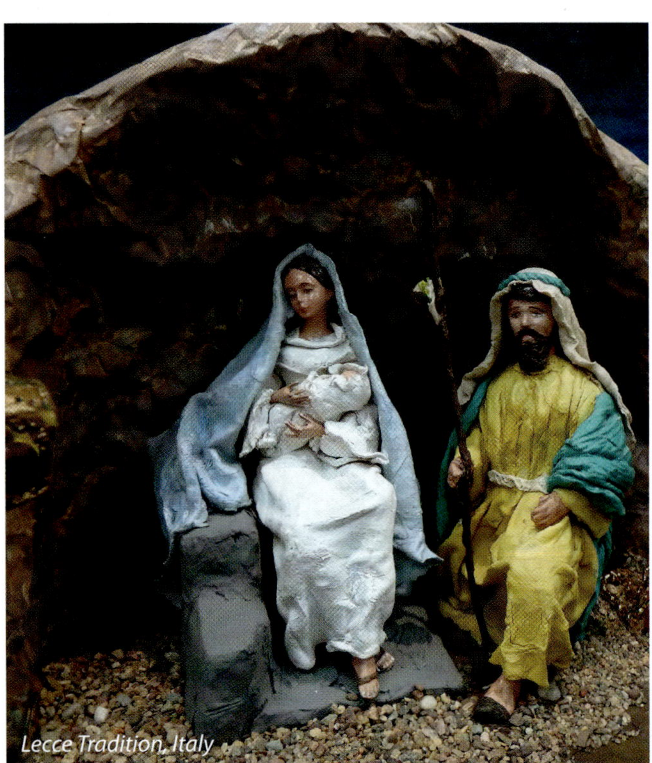

Lecce Tradition, Italy

The Cave

Protevangelium of James 17 and 18

"... Mary said to him: 'Joseph, take me down from the ass, for the child within me presses me, to come forth'. And he took her down there and said to her: 'Where shall I take you and hide your shame? For the place is desert'. (17)

And he found a cave there and brought her into it, and left her in the care of his sons..." (18)

Eastern iconography represents the cave as a black gaping hole in the mountain. It is reminiscent of death and evil. Mother and Christchild in the manger are placed in front of the cave to suggest protection against evil and salvation.

On the third day after the birth of Jesus – according to Pseudo-Matthew 14 – Mary takes the child and moves to a stable. Cave and stable are among the classical habitats of the Christmas story.

Ox and Ass

The Gospel of Pseudo-Matthew which is of later origin (8/9th c.), and of composite nature, reflects and partially reproduces the Protevangelium of James in its first part (1-17), and dedicates its second part (18-24) to the flight to Egypt.

This apocryphal Christian writing makes mention of the two ever present animals.

Gospel of Pseudo-Matthew

"On the third day after the birth of Our Lord Jesus Christ, Holy Mary went out from the cave, and went into a stable and put her child in a manger, and an ox and an ass worshipped him.' (14)

Ox and ass are mentioned in Isaiah 1:3 where their fidelity contrasts with the disloyalty and inconstancy of God's people: "An ox knows its owner, and an ass, its master's manger. But Israel does not know, my people has not understood."

Perennial and essential for the representation of the Nativity and is tradition, the two animals come with a rich symbolism regarding Christ's person and future mission, as we will see.

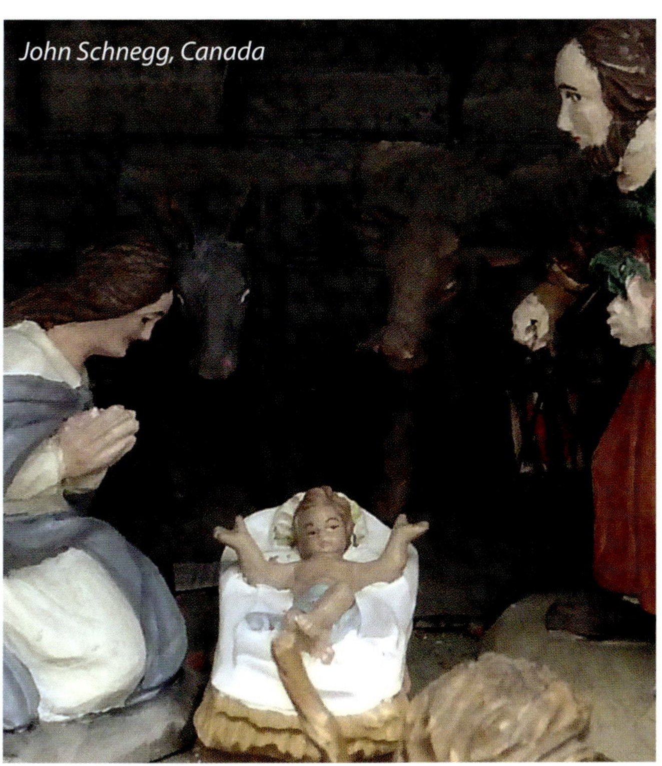
John Schnegg, Canada

The Midwife (Zelome and her friend Salome)

Protevangelium of James 18 and 19

... [Joseph] went out to seek for a Hebrew midwife in the region of Bethlehem. (18)

... And he found one who was just coming down from the hill country, and he took her with him, and said to the midwife: 'Mary is betrothed to me; but she conceived of the Holy Spirit after she had been brought up in the temple of the Lord.'" (19)

"The midwife came out of the cave and Salome met her." (19)

The midwife Zelome witnesses the birth of Christ. Meeting her friend Salome in front of the cave, she tells her: "I have a new sight to tell you; a virgin has brought forth." (19) Salome remains skeptical. She is allowed to test Mary's virginity. Her hand withers and she cries out: "Woe for my wickedness and my unbelief." (20)

Art shows the two women in a secondary scene of the Nativity, Zelome holding her friend's withered hand. Salome's hand is healed by the Christchild. (21) This scene highlights the virgin birth and the divine origin of Jesus Christ.

The First Bath of the Baby

Another secondary scene of the Nativity, the episode of the first bath of the Christchild, sometimes replaces the scene with the midwife and Salome. The intent is to show the true humanity of Jesus Christ. Inspired by the bath of the baby Mary in icons depicting the birth of the Virgin, this iconographical motif, common in representations of the birth of famous people, is neither of biblical nor apocryphal origin.

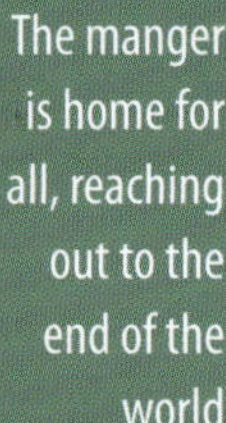

The manger is home for all, reaching out to the end of the world

Sacred Space and Time

The Sacred Page is the blueprint, the scenario or script of the Nativity representation. But a script without a stage is useless. The same is true for the Incarnation. There is no Incarnation without space and time – without a place and moment in time we can pinpoint and say: Here and now the Son of God became man.

Space and time play an important role in the representation of the Incarnation. The scenario evolves and changes with time, cultural adaptations, and artistic sensitivity. However, these changes revolve around a fixed point, the manger. The manger with the Christchild directs and orchestrates the Nativity play. Here, they all come together: the shepherds and magi, and the many anonymous characters which eventually entered the crèche to become the familiar figures of the Neapolitan pizza baker, the Provençal cobbler, and the German night watchman.

The manger is home for all (village), reaching out to the end of the world (landscape), but in the end it remains a home away from home. The real home is the place where the Christchild came from, and where he wants to lead us – to the City on the Mount, symbol of eternal life (mountain).

It should also be remembered that the journey to the manger is a time of decision for or against the message of Christmas. Not all want to belong. Some will decide to remain outside the sacred space shared by the Holy Family and their trusted friends; others will not even be tempted to enter. They may be ignorant or indifferent. Thus, the space of the Christmas story is divided between *fanum* (sacred space) and *profanum,* the space outside and separated from the manger. This is one way of organizing the crèche space. There is another, different way. It makes of the sacred space the stage of a liturgical event, as will be shown.

The representation of the Christmas story is replete with symbolisms. One of the most important is space. Here is the reason why it is called *sacred* space – It hides, and at the same time discloses part of the mystery of the Nativity, and therefore, also of the Incarnation.

Jar, Spain

A Name and Its Meaning

The generic designation *nativity set* does not capture the deeper meaning of Nativity representations. It designates a group or ensemble of figures which constitute the Nativity scene. Tradition and various cultures have been more explicit and enlightening when describing the scenario of Christ's birth. Summarized in a single word or appellation these descriptions open a variety of insights about the Nativity event.

The most common of these names and cultural expressions are *manger* and *crib* in English, *Krippe* in German, *crèche* in French, *presepe* or *presepio* in Italian, and *Belén* in Spanish and Portuguese. Their common origin is the Bible and Jerome's use in the Vulgate of the word *praesepium* for manger. Some cultures go their own way, and coin a special name for the Nativity. The Moravian *Putz*, from the German *herausputzen* or decorating, designates a whole landscape including scenes such as the Annunciation, the Visitation, the Shepherd's field, the flight into Egypt, the presentation in the Temple, and others. The Polish culture uses *Szopka* for the Nativity scene. Dating back to the 19th century Kraków, it sets the Nativity of Jesus in historical buildings, most of them splendid church façades. The Maltese *Maxtura* has the meaning of manger but designates primarily a low stone wall separating a section of the stable from the rest. The Czech *Betlemy* from the town of Bethlehem can be used generically to designate a nativity set, but it also characterizes the typical Bohemian paper crèches.

As culture adopts a particular name it slowly but surely fills it with a secondary or new meaning. Limiting ourselves to some of the more current names for nativity sets, their cast and display, we discover four specific meanings highlighting significant aspects of the spirituality of the Incarnation.

Words such as manger, crib, and Krippe point to the cave or stable, and call attention to the poverty of the event. The child and his parents are placed in a situation not only of physical indigence and want, they are characterized as outcasts from society forced to share a trough with animals. Simultaneously, the manger represents a focal point of attention. It is both signpost and magnet. There may be many ways to the manger but there is only one manger. Those who approach the crib, and all are invited, have to assume a degree of solidarity with the child and his parents.

At the same time, the crib can be a crèche. The extended meaning of crèche includes the idea of home away from home. The association with security and protection comes to mind. The crèche is a place of rest and new vision as the sanscrit word *sumatanga* suggests. The Christchild is our *sumatanga*,we find peace at the manger but also a new vision of ourselves, the world and God.

The etymological explanation of *praesepium, presepe* or *presepio* point in a different direction. Presepe designates an enclosed space and its surroundings, the place in front or beyond the enclosure. The extended meaning is one of separation, or of the classical distinction between *sacrum* and *profanum.* The latter *profanum* posits the visitor to the manger outside the sacred space, and suggests that there are those who belong and those who do not belong as frequently shown in Nativity scenes.

Belén, the Spanish and Portuguese word for the crèche scene, not only takes us back to the purported birthplace of Jesus and to biblical geography. The name of this town has a deeper meaning, and strong associations with the Nativity. According to the prophet Micah (5:2) Bethlehem is "too little to be among the clans of Judah," and so a geographical confirmation of the humble and poor birth of Christ, largely unknown and hidden from the world. But Bethlehem is also the *House of Bread,* a place not only of weeping but also of blessing, anointing, and refreshment. The association with the house of bread recognizes in Jesus the bread from heaven, and the coming into the flesh a symbol of his eucharistic presence.

A name and its meaning is always more than just a name. Religious culture appropriates the name and plants a seed of love and devotion in it. Manger, crib, crèche; belén and presepe – their meaning grows and blossoms into a little spirituality of the Nativity.

As it was in the Beginning

No, the manger is no longer as it was in the beginning of its artistic and spiritual history. It evolved with time and cultural changes. Message and essential visual expressions remain, but the composition of the scene and the importance of some of the figures mutated. This is particularly true for the composition of the Nativity representation.

Among the earliest visual testimonies about the Nativity of Jesus Christ are sarcophagi of the 3/4th centuries. Their primary meaning is not to feature the birth of Christ but the revelation of salvation. On the lid of the sarcophagus of Severa (4th century, Museo Pio Cristiano, Rome), who seems to have been a Roman woman intellectual of the late second century, the inscription reads, "May you live in God, Severa." The scene that accompanies the portrait of Severa shows the adoration of the magi.

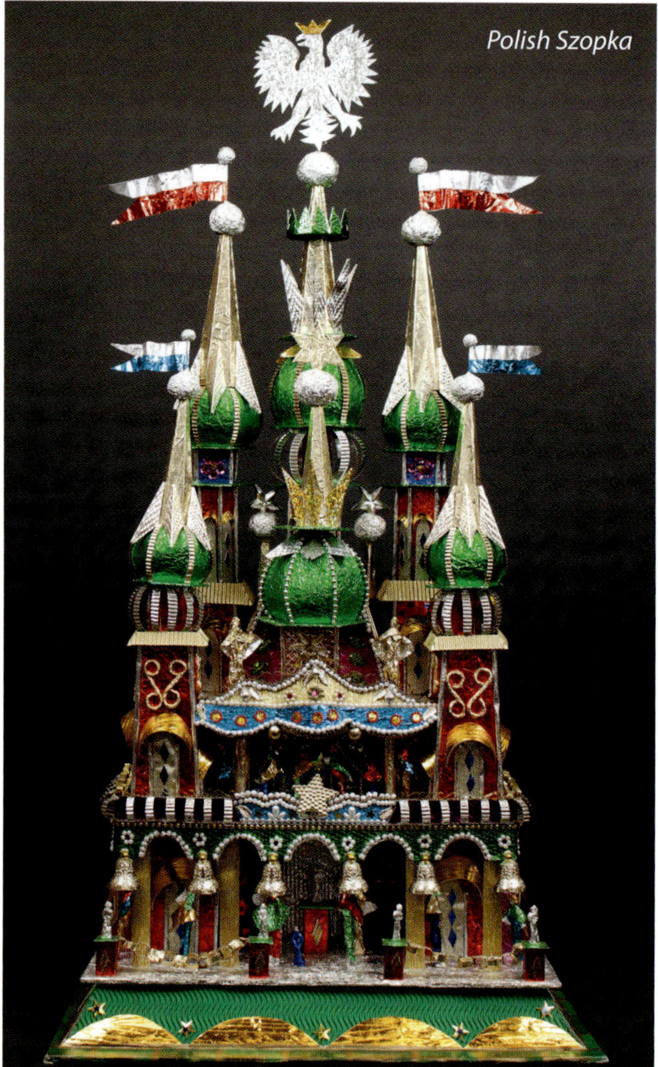
Polish Szopka

The Incarnation is made visible – the Epiphany! – to all those who seek God like the magi and Severa. Salvation awaits them in the person of the child with outstretched arms sitting on the knees of his mother. The mother's gesture of presenting the child to the visitors underscores and reinforces the Christchild's welcome.

Thus, what we call the manger scene is in fact the revelation of salvation symbolized in the magi approaching the light of the world with eager pace and fluttering mantles.

A highly structured and comprehensive composition of the manger scene will appear in the 5th century and conquer East and West for many centuries. Based on the iconographical method of unity and simultaneity of time and space, this new composition unites in one and the same representation animals and humans, angels and shepherds, central actors of the Nativity like the magi, and peripheral figures such as Joseph and the midwife Zelome and her friend. In front of the cave, in the center of the scene, we are met by the reclining figure of the mother, the child wrapped in swaddling clothes, and the two animals. The representation is horizontally and vertically structured. We usually distinguish three symmetrically arranged vertical levels with at the lowest level the marginal figures (Joseph, the servant woman), in the center the mother and baby, and angels and magi at the top. The overall underlying structure is reminiscent of a mountain peaking toward the top, suggesting the unity between heaven and earth.

The transition from a predominantly symbolical rendering of the Nativity scene to a more figurative and anthropomorphic style occurred around 1290 with the inauguration of what is believed to be the oldest extant nativity set located in the Sistine Chapel of the Roman Basilica of Maria Maggiore, formerly *S. Maria ad praesepe*. The 50cm alabaster figures of the enthroned Madonna and Child (replaced in the 16th century), Joseph, the animals, kings, and two prophets were fashioned by Arnolfo di Cambio (c. 1240-1300/10), a noted Tuscan architect and sculptor. In the Gothic style of his time, these moveable figures announced a new vision of the human person, and thus a new crèche culture. The nativity figures are no longer only the anonymous representatives of a pre-ordained script. They have their own personality and individual bearing. Though a product of their specific culture, they can be moved, positioned and removed inspired by the whim and taste of the moment. This means that the sacred story encapsulated permanently and protectively in the icon will be, from now on, a human story and a never ending quest for the invisible.

Pious imagination and artistic inspiration will forthwith be the driving force behind the crèche culture. The visions of mystics, changing cultural patterns, attempts to make the Christmas story into a morality play or vanity fair have fashioned the manger scene for centuries. New figures were added to the cast, old figures endowed with new meaning and physical expression, and the overall message was regularly adapted to the needs of the time. The *Adoration of the Child* (1520) by Hans Baldung is a classic example of continuity in discontinuity, of both pious imagination and artistic inspiration. Dwarfed by the crumbling walls of the palazzo-like stable, the Nativity is bathed in a double source of light: light from above – Christ, the sun of justice? – and light emanating from the Christchild himself transfiguring the holy couple immersed in adoration, and the little angels adding playfulness to the whole scene. Immovable and protective, the animals convey a sense of placid and peaceful stability, while outside the stable, in the field, the angel prepares the shepherds for their visit to the Christchild. Baldung's painting is a variant among thousand others which all have tried to capture the essential message, disclose its miraculous character, and to give it its own cultural hallmark. The motif of the crumbling palace is a symbol of the culture of death replaced by the culture of life in Jesus Christ. The little angels and the intense light are a reminder of the miraculous core of the Nativity story.

There is no common denominator to characterize the nativity set of the present. The cultural expansion of the crèche tradition is ongoing and includes mentally and culturally far-away countries like Uzbekistan and Kyrgistan. Meanwhile, the nativity set has conquered cooperatives and associations of artisans all over the world, and has joined them in the fight against poverty. The classical names and traditions are as present as ever: the Oberammergau crib, the Provençal crèche, the Neapolitan presepe, and many, many others. The one observation which seems to lead like a red thread through all or most of these traditions is a new sense of simplicity, a quest for authenticity, and for the essential message as we find it in Rose-Anne Monna's four-figure manger scene. Her set (Montreal, 1993) is of natural and reverent simplicity. From the confident abandon of the baby to the tender look on Joseph's face; from the caring hands and bare feet of Mary to the wobbly joy of the newborn lamb, there is great peace in this set, the peace that comes when joy is in the soul.

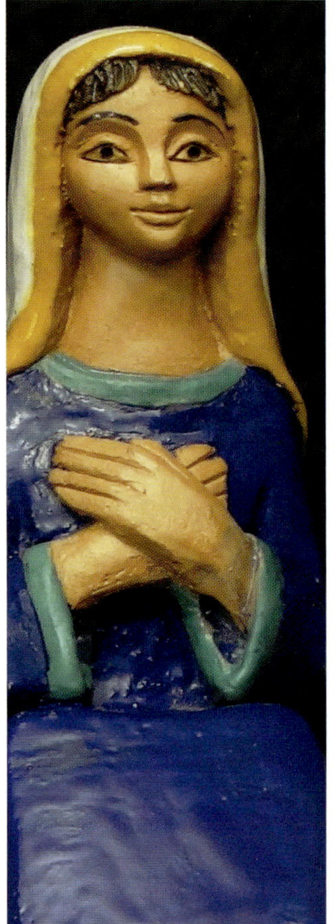

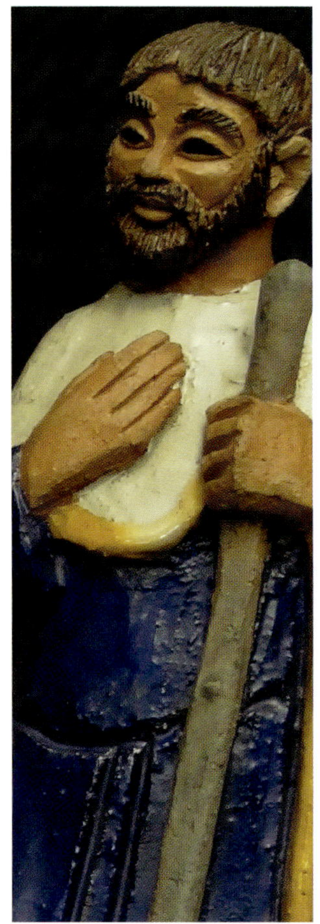

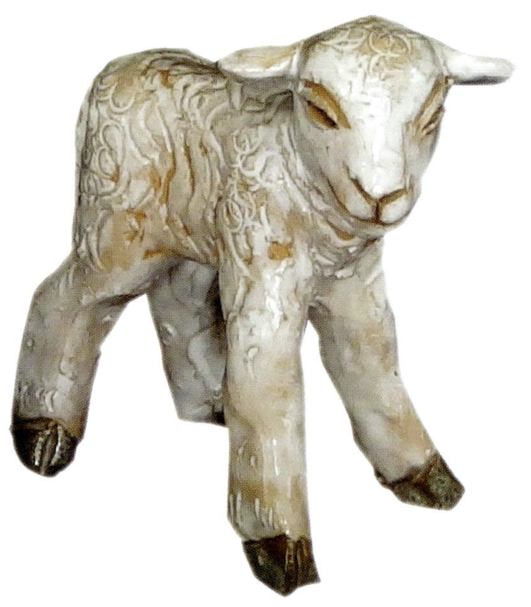

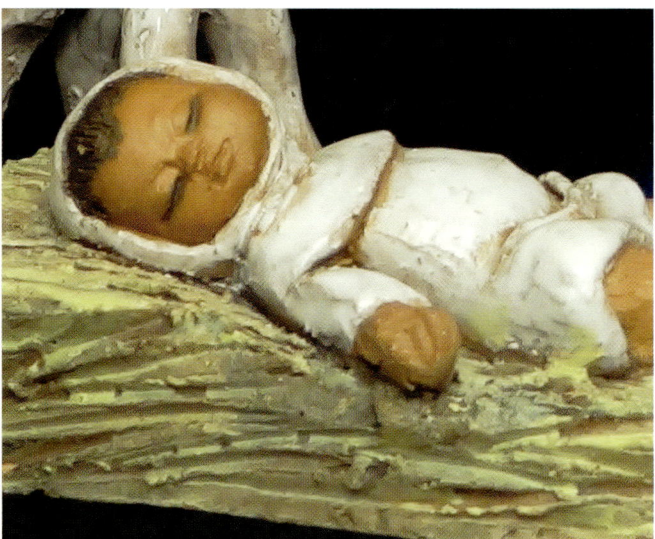

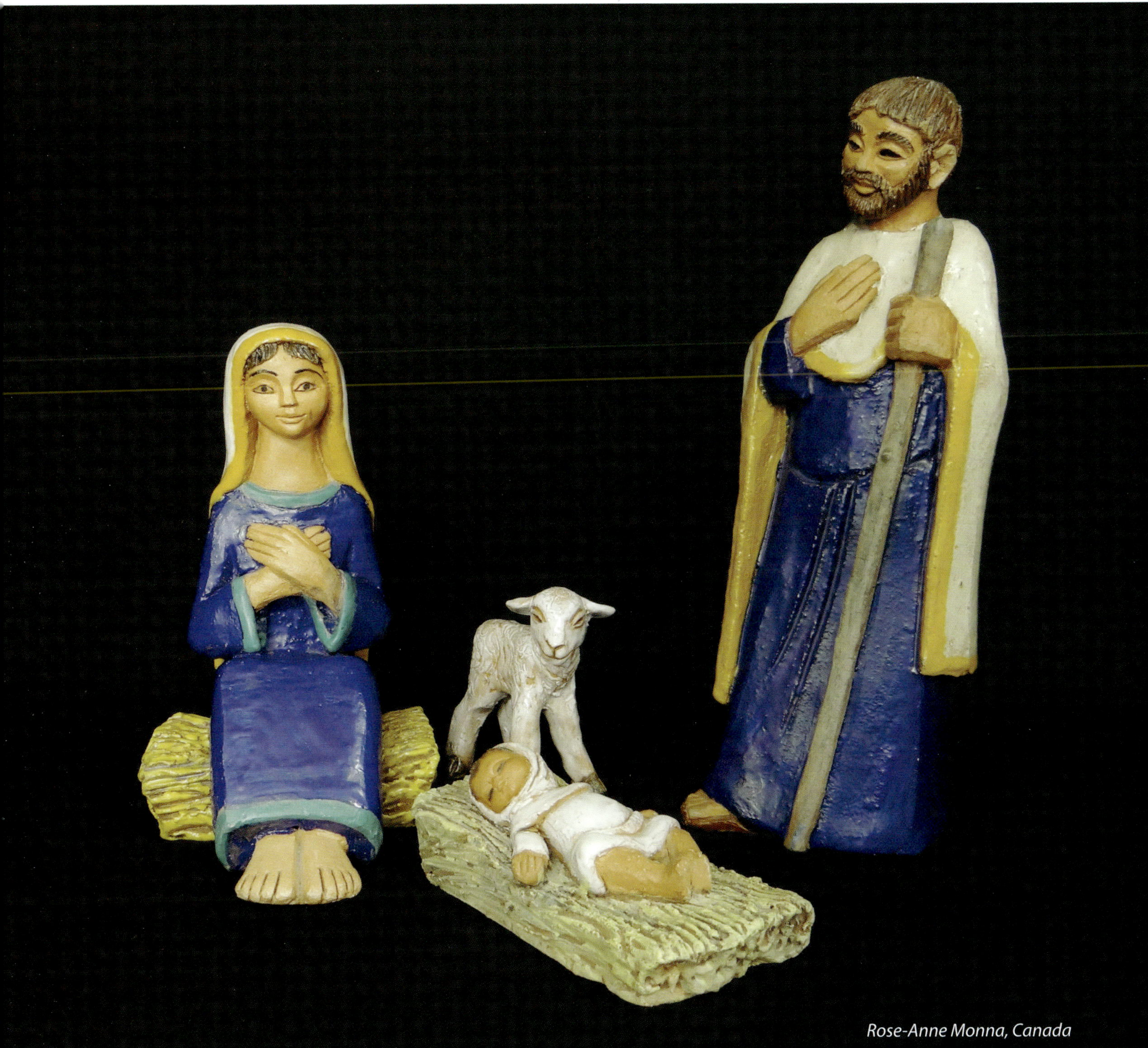

Rose-Anne Monna, Canada

To the Center of the Earth — The Mountain

Crèche figures and their arrangement around the manger with the Christchild re-enact and symbolize the Christmas story. Their role is to spin the story, to give meaning to time, to link beginning and end. They are the actors of the drama played out before us. But there is another dimension to the Christmas narrative. The figures evolve in a given space. Crèche space is sacred space. It makes its own and important contribution to the whole story.

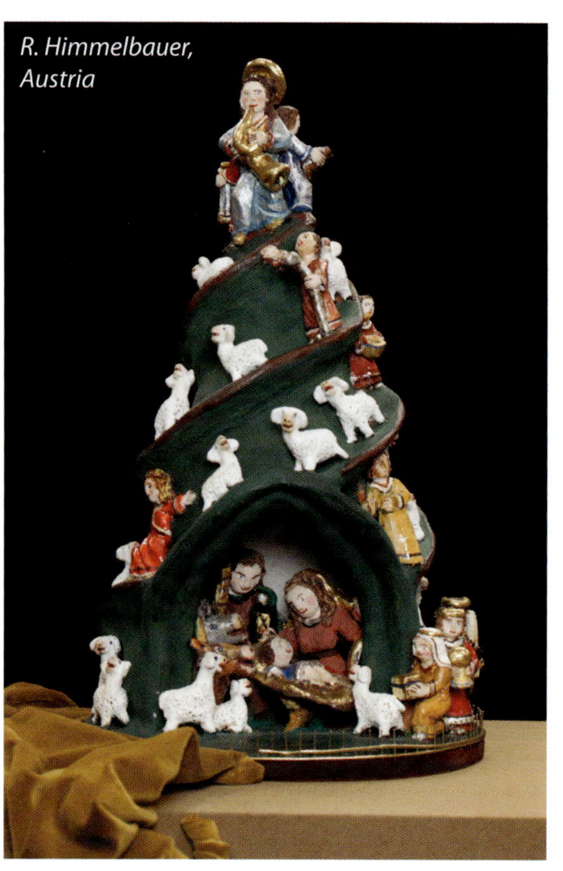
R. Himmelbauer, Austria

One of the classical representations of sacred space is the mountain. The mountain is a universal religious symbol. Prophets and mystics climb the mountain of God. The mountain at its highest elevation is the point of junction between heaven and earth, the place of encounter with God, the site of new revelation. On top of Mount Sinai Moses received the tablets of the ten commandments; at the term of the *Ascent of Mount Carmel* – a symbol of the ascetical life – the soul, according to Saint John of the Cross, finds mystical union with Christ. The ascent to the top highlights human effort and commitment to the spiritual life. Salvation beckons at the top after much trial and hardship. However, in the story of the Nativity the ascent of the mountain is reversed. Ascent becomes descent. It is not the human person who ascends the mountain, but God who descends from its top to meet humanity at the foot of the mountain. In the Nativity tradition the mountain stands for God's willingness to lose himself in order to find each one of us where we are. The mountain is a beautiful symbol of God's unconditional love as it is witnessed in the Incarnation, the Passion, and Death of Jesus Christ. There is an ancient theological tradition which says that only what has been assumed can be redeemed. Here is the reason why representations of the Nativity built on a mountain show a cave at the bottom of the mostly triangular space. The cave holds the Christchild and his faithful companions, the animals and the holy couple. The meaning, again, is obvious. God wants to accept human reality in its entirety, from top to bottom, assuming it completely in order to be able to redeem it. Symbolically speaking, he left his station at the top of the mountain to hunt us to the center of the earth. The cave, a symbol of the center of the earth, is not a simple rest-stop or checkpoint. The cave, symbolically again, is God's dwelling place among us, making him the God with us, in all like us, save sin.

The tradition to include a mountain in the Nativity presentation goes back to icon painting.

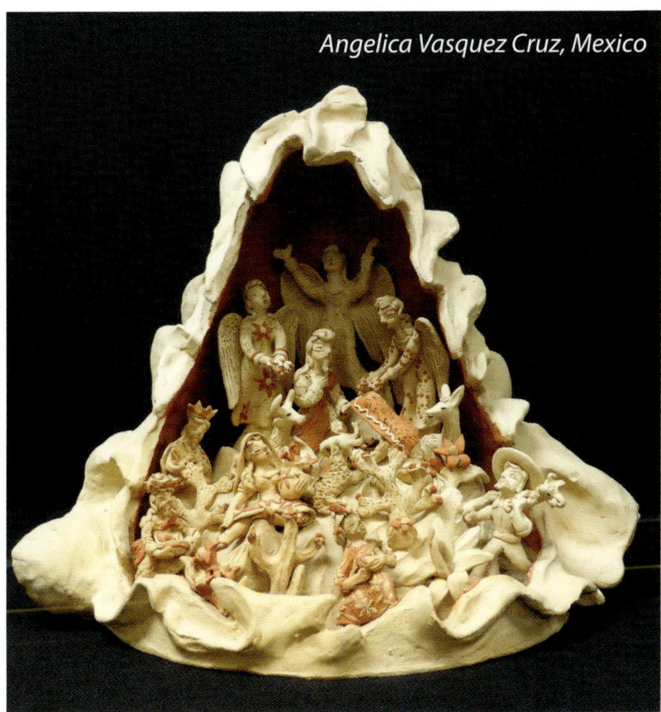

Angelica Vasquez Cruz, Mexico

Mirror of Hope (detail)

Obscured by the prominence given to the many figures, the shape of the mountain in icons of the Nativity may sometimes be difficult to make out. Careful observation, however, discovers the vertical structure and organization of the Nativity pointing to the origin of the event in God enthroned and invisible beyond the peak of the jagged mountain. The opening of the cave is barricaded by the manger and the child, by the reclined shape of his mother, and the two animals. The mountain as sacred space of the Nativity can be observed in various cultures and forms. The symbol of the mountain is present in the nested dolls of the Russian Matryoshka nativity set, in the Polish Szopka, the German nativity tower, the Italian *Torre di Natale,* the Spanish Nativity jar, and the Peruvian nicho nativity. The *Mirror of Hope* of the Marian Library Collection is built according to the model of the mountain, triangular in shape, with the origin and fulfillment of salvation history at its top, and the stable of the Nativity at its base.

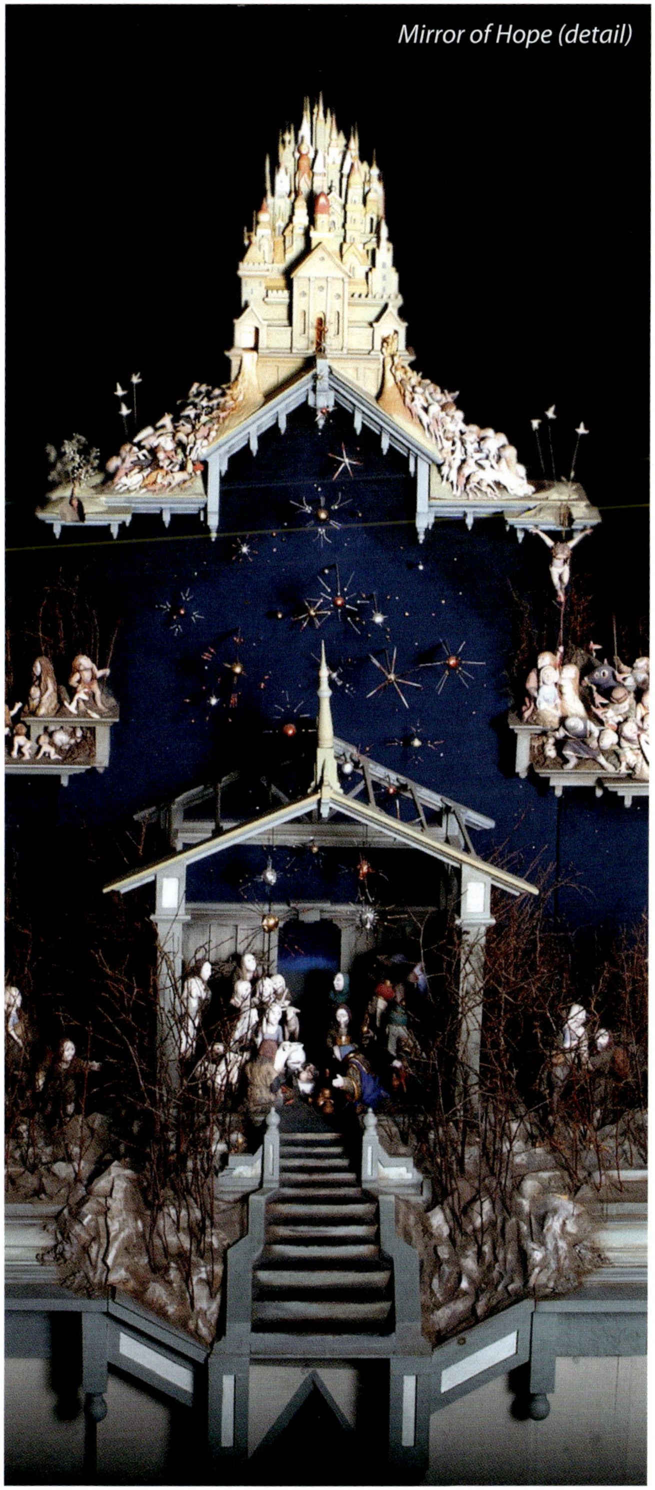

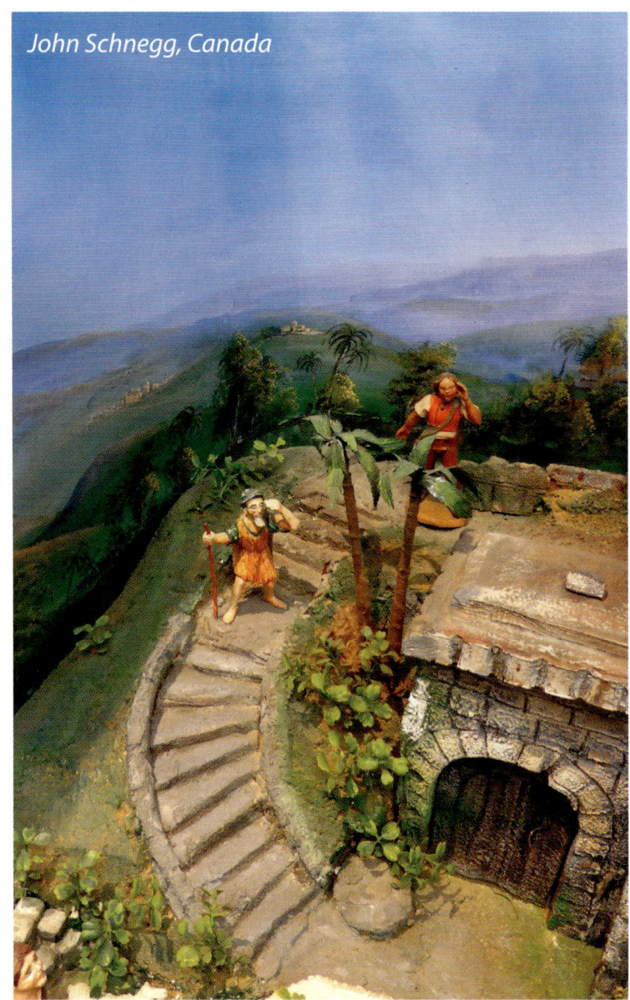

John Schnegg, Canada

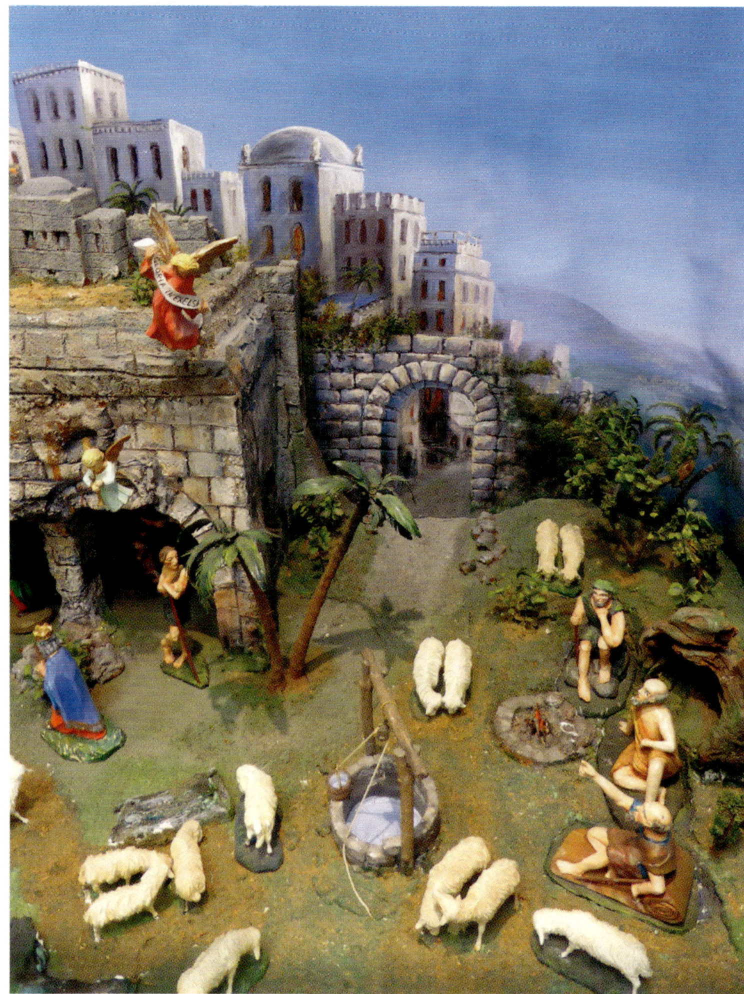

From Center to Periphery — The Landscape

The landscape is an integral part of the deeper meaning of Nativity representations. It establishes a relationship between the Christchild in the manger and his surroundings: The immediate surroundings are those of his parents and the ever present ox and ass, frequently closer to the baby than Mary and Joseph, but also of shepherds and magi usually positioned at some distance from the manger. Only after these figures have been placed, do accessory personages, so the many gift-bringers and other cultural witnesses find their station in the crèche landscape.

The first meaning of the Nativity landscape is to establish the importance of the different groups of people by drawing concentric circles around the Christchild. The second and more extensive meaning is to highlight the universality of the Incarnation. What happened in the cave of Bethlehem is destined to reach the ends of the world. In fact, the landscape of the crèche is a symbol of the world with Christ at its center. But, the world is not only the world of people. It includes nature, and nature includes the universe of sun, moon, and stars. Simultaneously, the landscape frequently carries a message of wonder and magic: the carnation blooming on the night of Christ's birth, the apple tree laden with big red apples, and Madelon, the poor shepherd girl, decorating the manger with an armful of Christmas roses which sprang from the frozen ground thanks to the magic of the angel Gabriel's staff. The legends about the wonders of nature at Christmas are legion.

The representation of the landscape takes on many forms. It can be the painted backdrop of snow-covered mountains, or a widespread scenery dotted with important episodes or stages of the Nativity story. The illusion of a landscape can be conveyed in the gifts and costumes of the figures. The woman bringing a basket filled with mushrooms to the manger points to a wooded area and rural origin, whereas the fishmonger represents people of lake and sea.

The magi-kings represent the three regions of the time: Europe, Africa, and Asia. They wear the typical costumes and trappings of their region. The Polish shepherds and mountaineers of the Tatra Mountains wear the white *Ciucha* thrown over their shoulder, whereas the city folk of Kraców parade in jackets and pants of blue and red colors. Costumes and colors, fruit and flowers, woods and deserts are as many different ways as it takes to remember the colorful and meandering roads along which the Incarnation moved, and still moves, to link its center to the farthest ends of the earth.

Of One Mind and Heart — The Village

Aside from mountain and landscape there is a third structural element destined to organize and build the crèche scene. It is the village, its people, buildings, and customs. The village projects a semblance of realism, picturing everyday life, with its joys and pains, with poor and rich, with those who have power, and those who would like to have it. In the village virtue and vice coexist, but in the end the thief repents and amends, and the village fool will be the first to sense and hail the wondrous character of the Nativity event.

The village of the Nativity is a popular version of the *theatrum mundi* as it is found in the baroque dramas of Calderón de la Barca and Pierre Corneille. A zesty mixture of tragedy and comedy, the world theatre includes everything and everybody, and leaves out nothing and nobody, neither saint nor sinner. The leading idea of the Christmas village is to bring together people from all walks of life, and to gather them around the manger. The intent is to show the diversity of life in its many expressions in order to demonstrate the transforming and unifying power of the Christchild. Indeed, in the end these colorful and checkered village people will be kneeling together at the manger, mayor and parish priest, the tramp and *Arlatenco*, the noble woman from Arles in Provence. Never left to themselves, to their prejudice and idiosyncrasies, the manger becomes for a holy night – or for life – the great equalizer of class, race, reputation, and merit for all of these crèche figures. The village is a global village. It suggests the beginning

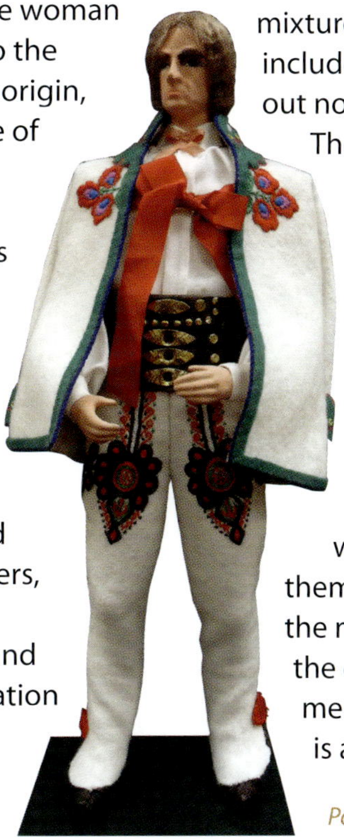

Polish shepherd wearing a white ciucha

of salvation offered to the whole world. And there is love in the air: a God made man, the poor God to heal hardened hearts.

The Nativity is not always a whole village. Frequently the village is limited to a street scene, a tavern, a marketplace, the contrast between palace and hut. What counts are the many people engaged in some form of exchange and interaction. Contrast, passion, and drama are a distinctive characteristic of the Neapolitan nativity. The figures are known for their sculpted faces and dramatic expression, for the ravages of vice, age, and sickness, and the intensity of eyes and gestures. The Neapolitan nativity is a combination of street theatre and courtly etiquette, the former a colorful explosion of human passions, the latter a script for a heavenly ballet celebrated in one of the *palazzi* of Naples. It is in one of these palaces that the Neapolitan nativity was born, a prime example of courtly baroque art and, by the same token, an expression of contrast between rich and poor.

The Provençal village is of a more popular and rural character. The figures are numerous, but they are the "little saints," the humble santons, and each of them has its own story, a story that invariably ends at the manger with everybody else. This form of crèche culture, which finds expression in the village is not limited to the Neapolitan and Provençal tradition. In general, the African nativity culture has a pronounced social profile which can also be observed in some of the Latin-American countries. A feast is always the feast of the community, and not alone of the individual. Announced with song and music, the feast progresses in the common procession to the manger, and finds its culmination in common praise and the presenting of gifts to the Christchild.

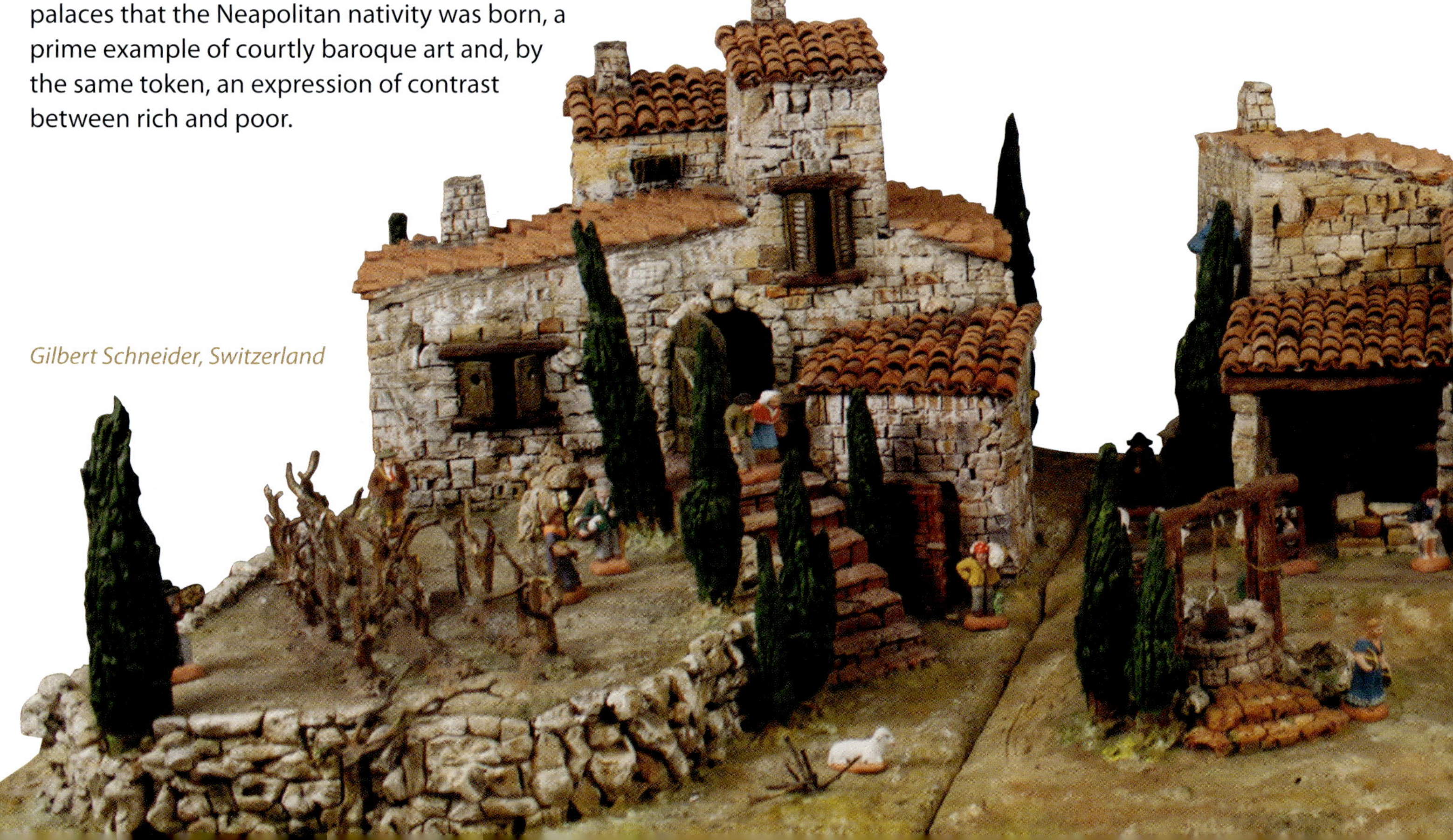

Gilbert Schneider, Switzerland

Between Sacred and Secular

The Nativity remains a challenge. For some it may be a challenge for the mind. Did the Nativity happen as we know it? Did God come to meet us in his Son? Is the miraculous conception and birth palatable to the modern mind? These questions have been asked and answered many times. As faith queries intelligence, we find comfort and assurance in the historical and theological data of a two thousand year tradition.

There is a more frequently voiced challenge; a challenge of moral nature. It can be summarized with these questions: What does it take to belong? Who will side with the Christchild? What is the price to pay to be part of the circle of believers? Representations of the Nativity have been, and still are highly inventive in featuring this moral dilemma. There are in nativity sets the sleepers and indifferent ones; the curious bystanders and the arguing doubters; the people at the crossroads unable to make up their mind whether to take the road for the manger or not. The night watchman may be a symbol of the unbelieving Thomas, the young shepherd playing the flute and lost in his own world a way to picture self-centeredness and the lack of attention to the greater things in life. The message seems obvious. There exists a line of demarcation between the secular and the sacred which needs to be crossed if we want to join the Christchild in the manger. Sometimes, this line of demarcation is marked by a fence, a trellis, a bridge, or a gate.

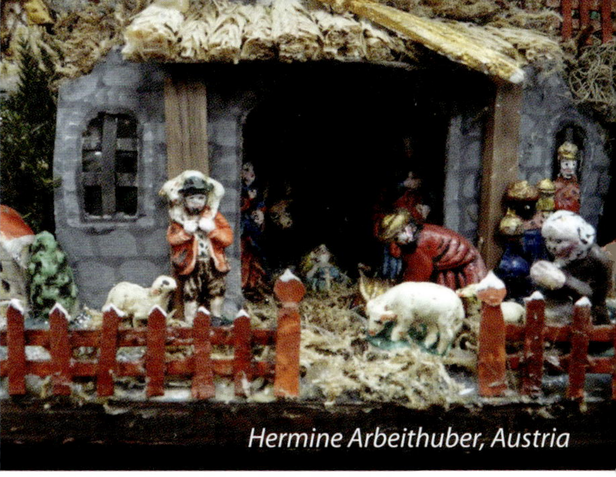

Hermine Arbeithuber, Austria

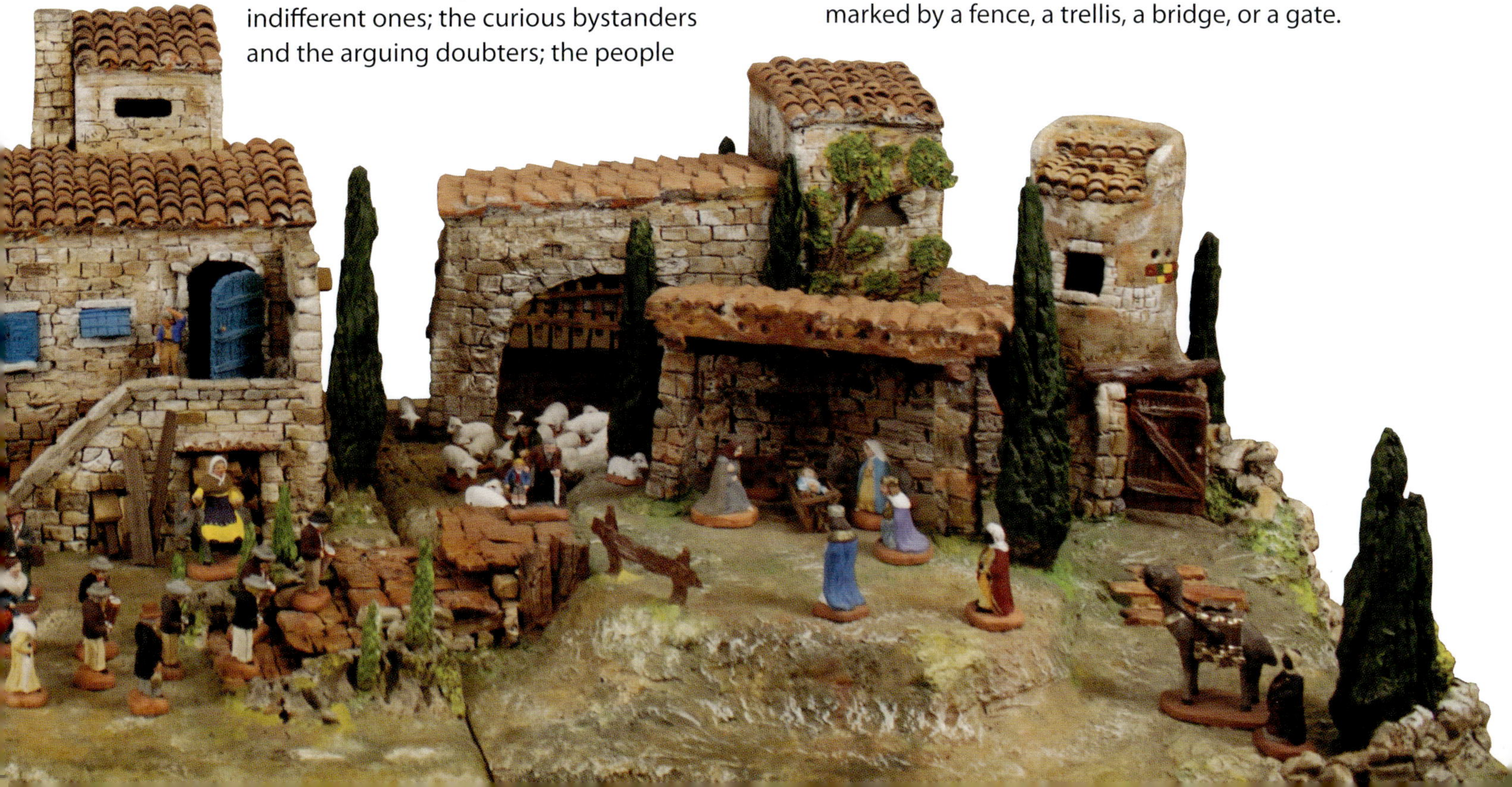

The nativity presentation sets warning signs for those who do not pay attention: the rooster, a symbol of treason, the poor soul in purgatory, or Saint Michael, the angel of judgment. Especially frightful is the figure of the devil, watchful and hidden, the ultimate symbol of opposition to the Christchild, and of the ongoing war between good and evil. We have in our collection a monumental representation of the Christian story from Creation to the end of time which highlights the tension between the secular world and sacred space and time. Called *Mirror of Hope,* and fashioned by Kevin Hanna, the artwork has four structural elements. Two of them represent sacred space. They are the *City on the Mount* and the *Stable of the Nativity*. The *City on the Mount* is a symbol of life in its fullness. Here is the origin of life from which Creation springs, and here life finds fulfillment in the One who is the source of all life. The *Stable of the Nativity* is the cradle of new life in Jesus Christ. Open on all sides, the stable reaches out to the whole world. It is a standing invitation to celebrate the fullness of time and life in Christ together with shepherds and kings. The other two structural elements of the *Mirror*

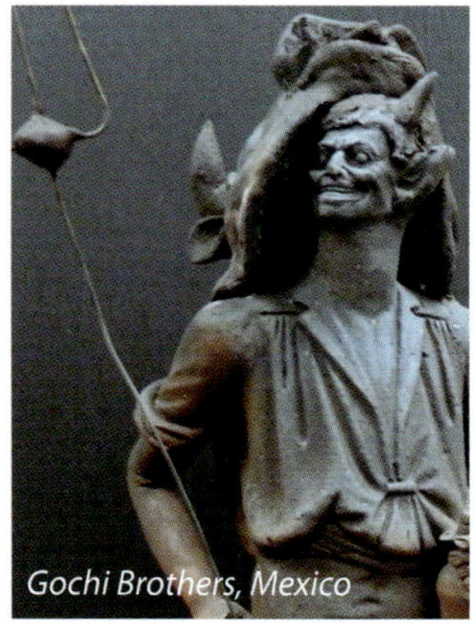
Gochi Brothers, Mexico

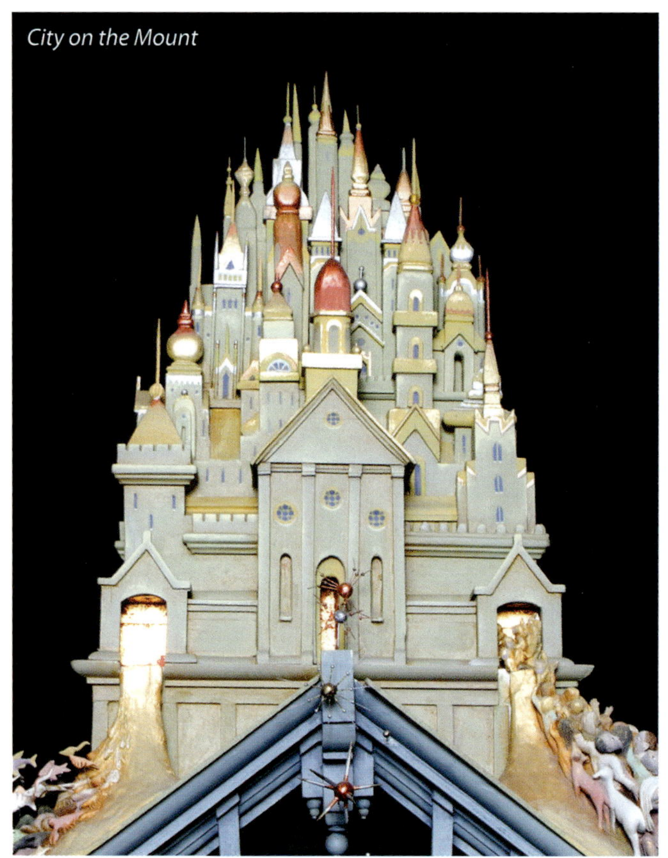
City on the Mount

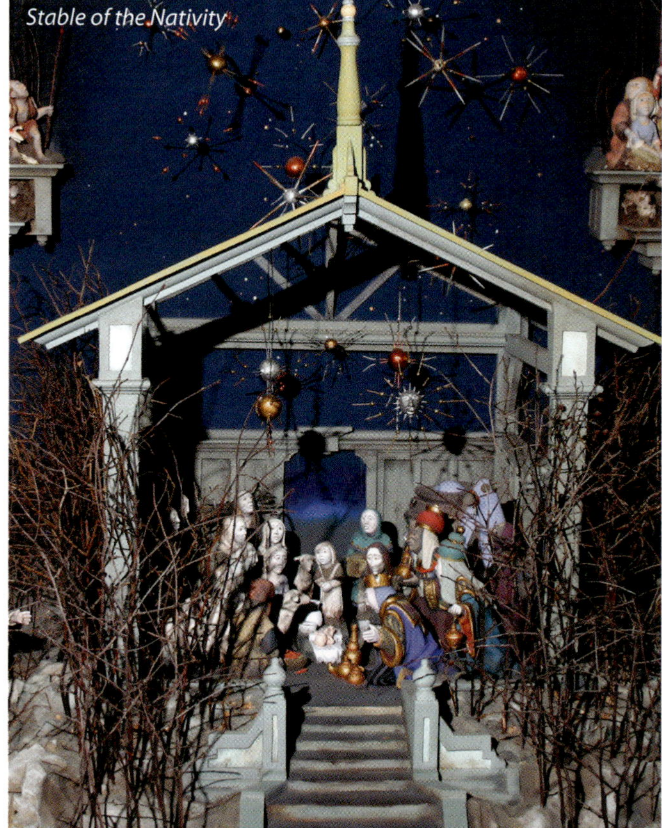
Stable of the Nativity

of Hope stand for the secular world and some of its imperatives. They are meant to raise questions, and to challenge the visitor. As counterpoints of the *City on the Mount* and the *Stable of the Nativity* they mark a potential opposition to the message of the Nativity and its authentic meaning. The *Tower of Babel* to one side of the *City on the Mount* is an imposing symbol of human inventiveness and ambition. It has been stylized as sign of contradiction between humanity and God, and expresses human self-sufficiency and hybris. It is a reminder that completion and fulfillment of life is the work of God. If the *Tower of Babel* signifies the rejection of God, the *House of God*, on the other side of the *City on the Mount* signals the danger of appropriating God. Temple or cathedral, the *House of God* is a sign of God's permanent dwelling place among his people. It may also reflect the temptation to make God a prisoner of human expectation and design. We are faced with this personal question: is the *House of God* a monument to human pride, or does it invite a humble but festive worship of the newborn king?

Nativity sets in their more elaborate form or expression frequently convey a not so subtle hint that the event of the Nativity is part of a much larger drama or *theatrum mundi*. The forces of good and evil are intuited and thematized, the need for a moral commitment is alluded at, and thus the world of the Nativity is pictured as divided in sacred and secular.

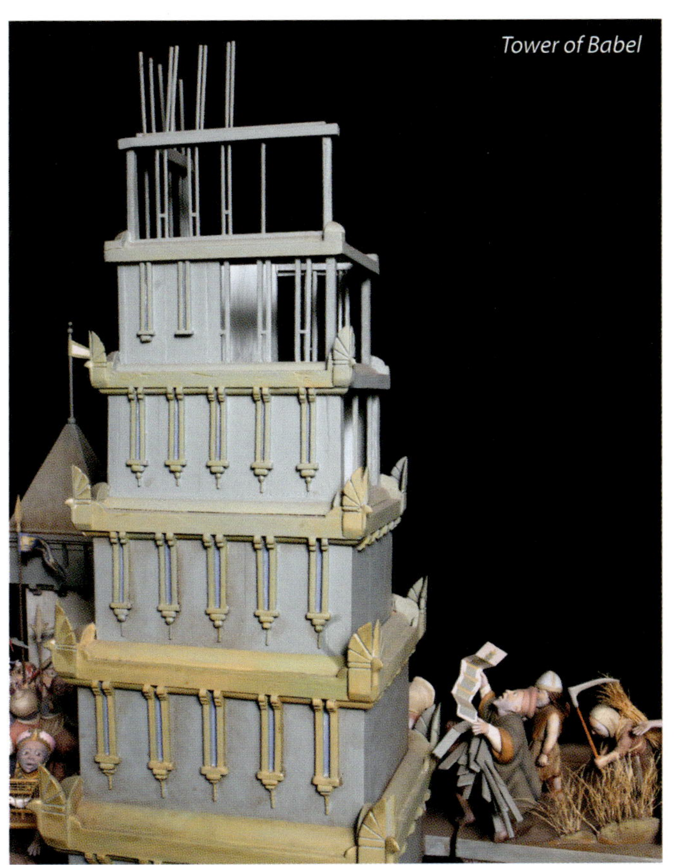
Tower of Babel

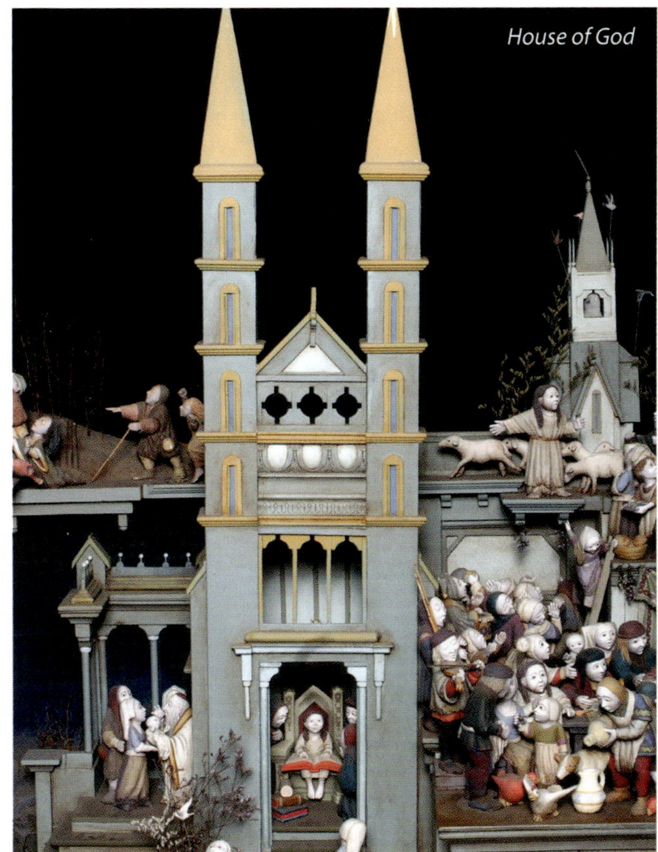
House of God

From Beginning to End

To be a true story, the Christmas story, like all stories, has to have a beginning and an end. The Nativity is not the complete story but it points to beginning and end of the whole story. Indeed, the Incarnation points backwards to the divine origin of Christ, to the beginning of Creation, to a Father-God and Holy Spirit. Pointing to the future, the Nativity is the beginning of what we call salvation history, leading to Christ's Passion, Death, and Resurrection, and into the Christian story preparing the end of time and the eternal present for all. The Christmas tradition attributes the role of visualizing beginning and end of salvation history to the *City on the Mount*.

Name and meaning are of biblical origin. In the book of Revelation, the seer of Patmos "saw the holy city, a new Jerusalem, coming down out of heaven from God." (Revelation 21:2). This heavenly city is a manifestation of God's truth and love. The city is powerfully built. It has massive walls, twelve gates, is square, and "its radiance was like that of precious stone, like jasper clear as crystal." (Revelation 21:11). This powerful image is a reminder of the "things above," a visual promise of life eternal. Paradise was lost at the Fall, but the *Heavenly Jerusalem* or *City on the Mount* is now and will always be the symbol of paradise retrieved. Scripture sees in the *Heavenly Jerusalem* a symbol of eternal fulfillment for both Israel and the Church, for both Old and New Testament.

Art has frequently been inspired by this new vision of paradise. We find the *Heavenly Jerusalem* or *City on the Mount* featured in the famous mosaics of San Vitale in Ravenna/Italy (5th century), in illuminations (Lambertus, *Liber Floridus*, c. 1448), icons (Russian School, 16th century), and in paintings (*The vision of Saint Peter Nolascus*, Zurbaran, 1629). In the late Baroque period, the *City on the Mount* made its appearance in the Nativity culture. Representations of the Nativity were frequently topped and decorated with impressive renderings of city walls, fortresses, castles, and spires. Triangular constructions of the Nativity scene, so-called crèche mountains featured at their top a replica of the *City on the Mount*.

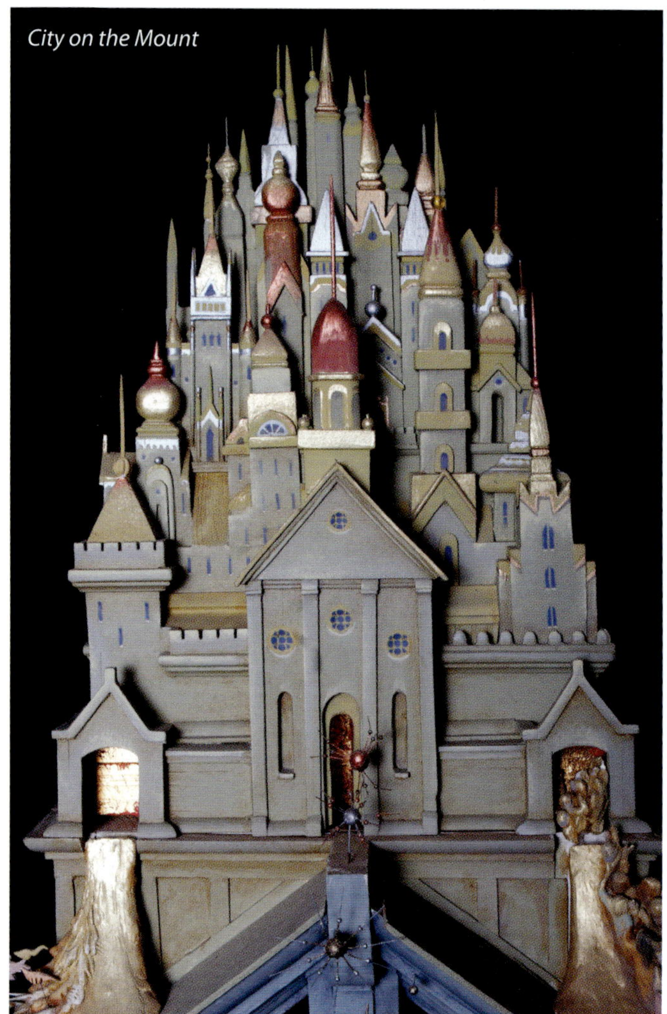

City on the Mount

In time a new tradition developed according to which the silhouette of the city reflected some familiar features of local landmarks or geography.

A Roman nativity showed at its top the feature of Santa Maria in Aracoeli, that of Jerusalem the Church of the Nativity. The deeper meaning of the new tradition was to prepare the *Heavenly Jerusalem* – our eternal life – by "being local" and committed to the task at hand. Eternity is not built on empty dreams or wishful thinking. It is made in time. To achieve eternal merit and value Christian life needs to be in the likeness of a God made human.

The Marian Library included the symbol of the *City on the Mount* in its *Mirror of Hope* or representation of salvation history. It represents all the meanings mentioned. It reminds us of the true beginning of the Nativity story and its ultimate significance. The *City on the Mount* is the symbol of Creation and Redemption, but it also puts salvation where it can be achieved: in the here and now. Thus, the *City on the Mount* of the *Mirror of Hope* features in its frontal section the silhouette of the Immaculate Conception Chapel situated at the center of the University of Dayton campus. Its façade and adjacent portals are open to give and receive life. We contemplate in the façade of this chapel the symbol of the earthly Jerusalem, the place and time where eternity is fashioned. The university's landmark chapel or *City on the Mount* mirrors time and eternity, their unity and challenge.

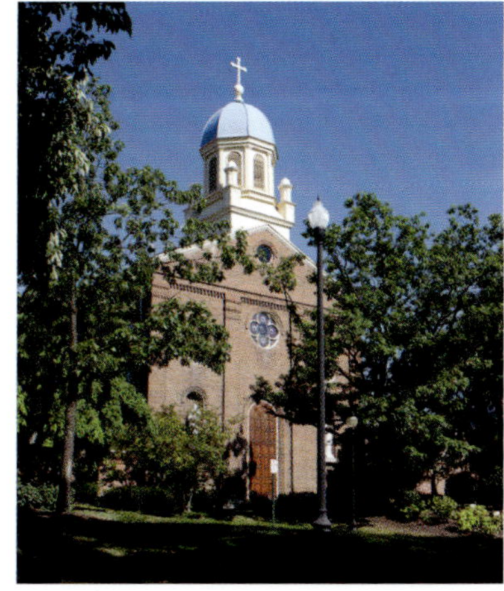

Where Liturgy and Culture Meet

Should the Christchild always be placed in the center of the manger scene? Where is Mary's place? Is she on the right or the left of the baby? What about the position of shepherds and magi? These and other questions are frequently asked by those who, on the eve of Christmas, set up the manger scene in churches, schools, and homes. They would like to do it right. Luckily, there are no rules hewn in stone. There are, however, traditions which offer guidance.

Eastern iconography follows set patterns. Some of these patterns, the wrapped body of the baby, the posture of the mother, the marginal position of Joseph, to name some, found a way into Romanesque and Gothic art. The Renaissance artist , on the other hand, enjoyed great freedom in imagining and positioning the Christmas scene and its many figures. It is during the Baroque period that crèche builders remember the close relationship between church and Christmas tradition. Medieval mystery plays of the Nativity were staged in front of the church. After the play actors and faithful were led in procession inside the church to celebrate the liturgy of the Nativity. The manger was set in front of the altar, sometimes placed on the altar. At the same time, representations of the Nativity were limited to churches. It is only at the end of the 18th century that the crèche culture moved to individual homes, and became the nativity set with its growing appetite for popular culture as we know it today.

The home nativity set inherited the memory of its former close affinity with the liturgy. Liturgical space and ceremonies are carefully organized and orchestrated. Their purpose is to proclaim the word of God, and to celebrate the memorial of Christ's Passion, Death, and Resurrection in the holy

Eucharist. Accordingly, sacred space, the sanctuary of the church, was subdivided in altar and lectern or ambo, meaning the sacred space of proclamation and celebration. The traditional organization of the sanctuary situates the altar in the center. It is flanked by two lecterns, one for the first reading(s) taken habitually from the Old Testament, the other destined to the proclamation of the gospel reading from the New Testament.

There exists an intimate connection between the three objects. The first lectern, on the left of the altar, sometimes called the lectern of the epistle, stands for the announcement and promise of the Good News. The reading from this lectern intuits, anticipates, and prepares the reading from the second or gospel lectern on the right side of the altar. The gospel in turn speaks the language of reality and presence. It proclaims what has happened, and therefore now is, the Good News. The gospel points to the altar in the center of the sanctuary, the symbol of the whole Christ, his Incarnation, Redemption, and sacramental presence.

The Nativity tradition was inspired by the organization of the liturgical space and its deeper meaning; it

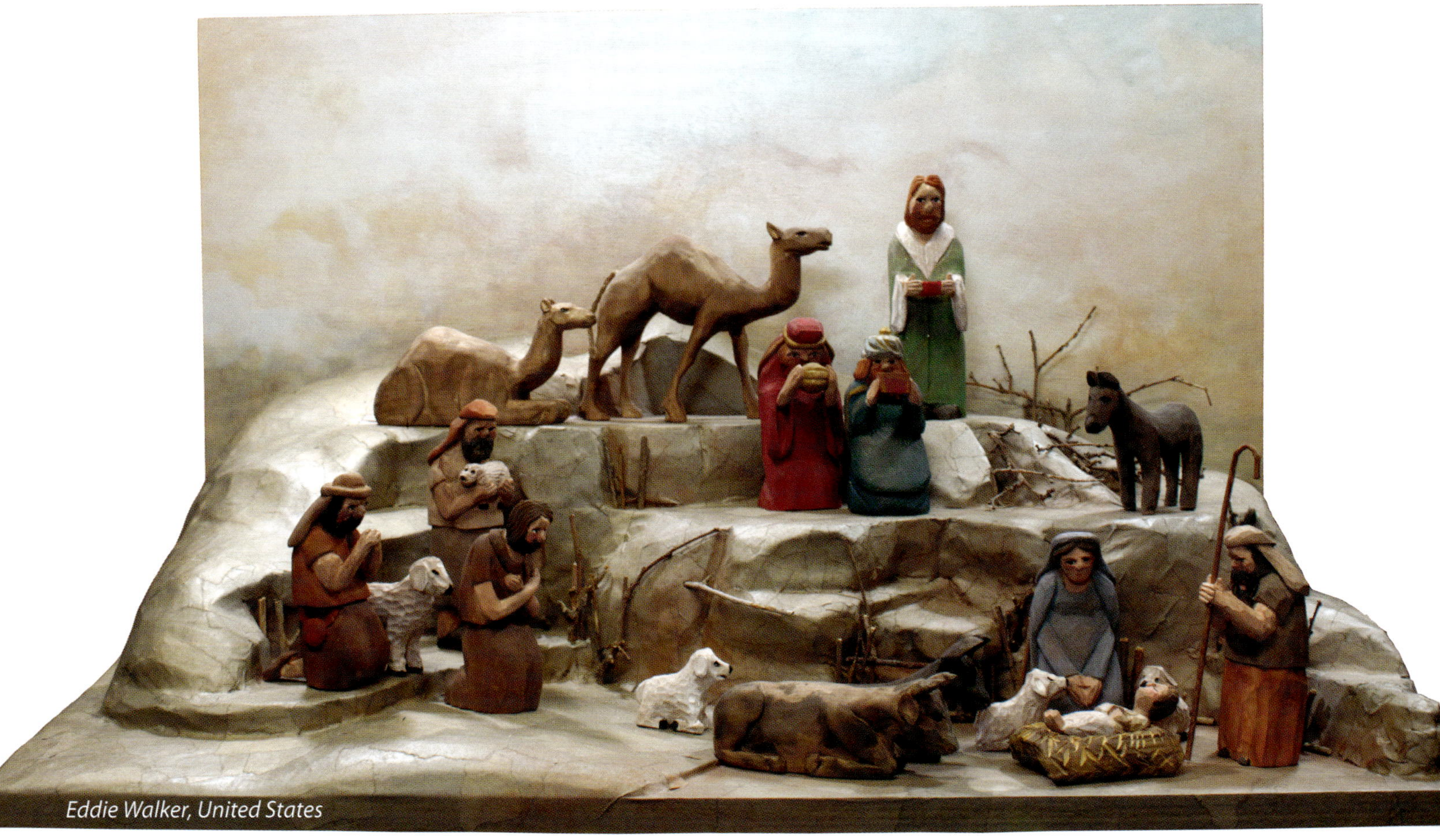

Eddie Walker, United States

adopted it, and frequently used it to set up and group the figures of the nativity scene. Obviously, the center belongs to the Christchild. To his left we find the figures which prepared his coming, sometimes after personal struggle (Joseph), after seeking and finding (magi), or filled with feelings of nostalgia for a better world (ox). The ox has the role of representing the pre-Christian culture and peoples; sometimes, this animal symbolizes Christ himself who was offered in sacrifice for redemption. The figures on the gospel side, Mary, the donkey, and the shepherds proclaim the reality of Christ's coming. Mary brings him into the world, and presents him to all faithful believers, the shepherds adore him, whereas the donkey, a symbol of Christ himself, proclaims his meekness, obedience to the Father, and patient suffering.

Liturgy and culture meet at the manger, and the nativity set assumes the role of a humble messenger of the gospel. Nothing human is left out: neither quest nor struggle, but the story culminates in the adoration of those who find and found the Christchild.

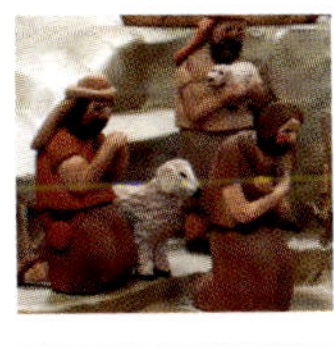

Shepherd
Adoration

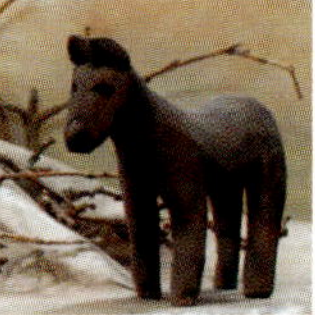

Donkey
Christ's meekness, obedience, patience and suffering

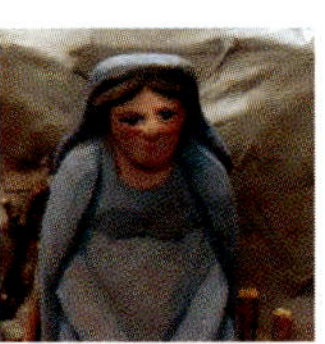

Mary
Gives Christ life and shows him to the world

Christchild

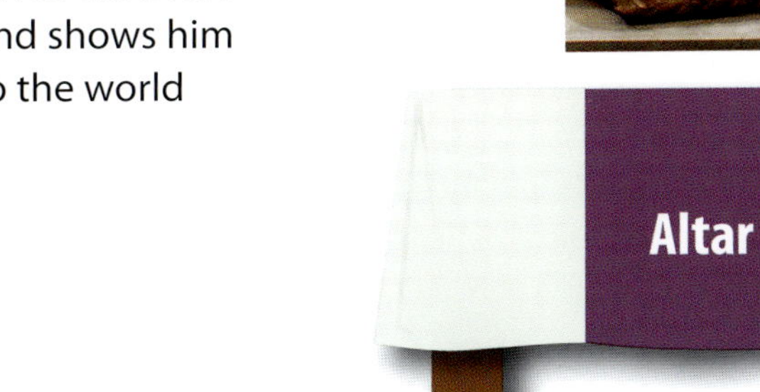

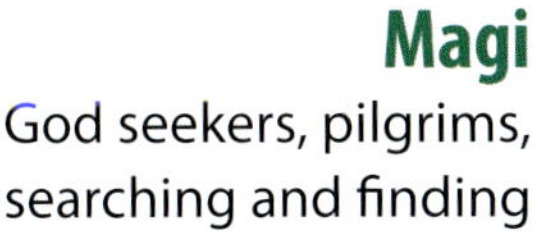

Magi
God seekers, pilgrims, searching and finding

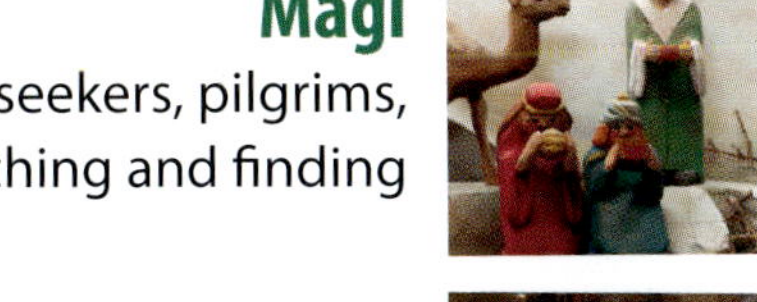

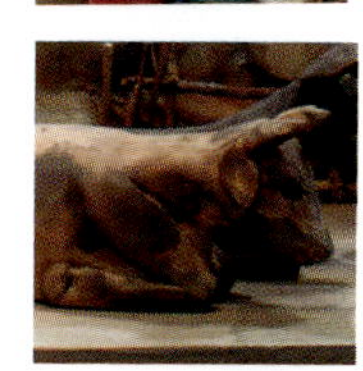

Ox
Nostalgia and hopeful anticipation

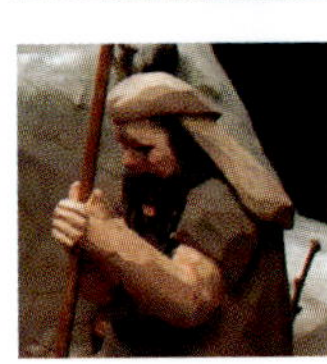

Joseph
Personal struggle, practical faith

Gospel
Proclamation of Christ's historical reality

Epistle (First Reading)
Preparation of Christ's coming

The Sacred Image

Illustration and Exploration

There is no end to Christmas. The Sacred Page as we called it harbors a promise which outlasts time and space. Sacred Space prepares the stage to cast the story, but it takes the Sacred Image to make the message come alive. The following pages are an illustration and exploration of the many themes pondered, articulated, and celebrated in the event of the Nativity.

The representation of the Nativity is more than a matter of figures and sets. Nativity sets convey a message. They come with a special intent, sometimes obvious and clearly stated, at other times the message is wrapped in symbols, colors, or cultural ingredients. The central message will always be that of the Incarnation of Jesus Christ. Every single Nativity representation is a sacred image of God's coming into the world. From this sacred image other and related themes develop. Presenting in the following pages a number of nativity sets from our collection, we would like to explore and illustrate the rich meaning of the Nativity, and display for the reader the manifold and colorful creations of human imagination and religious culture.

We would like to show that the Nativity invites community. It reaches out to the whole world. The message is couched in matter, the materials which constitute the stuff of everyday life, wood and clay, and many others. The story comes alive in the costumes and customs of regions and seasons, and in the style and shapes of buildings and figures. In a very special way, the Nativity is a hymn to life from seed to cosmos, and on to the promise of eternal life with God. Nativity sets invite a celebration of beauty as only the many and great cultures of the world are able to generate. From the vast and grandiose world of culture we move to magic and mystery! The representation of the Nativity leads to the heart of children where magic and mystery commingle in a beautiful puzzle. There is joy in nativity sets, but also humor to lighten the burden of the mystery. Psychologists and moralists, not to forget politically minded people, have explored and illustrated the meaning and importance of the Nativity culture. They use nativity sets to characterize the meaning of human existence, the reality of good and evil, and the challenge of poverty and injustice.

Illustration and exploration of the many expressions of the Nativity as we find them in our crèche collection point out that even if the story and its essential representation do not vary, there is always room for creativity and a new look at tradition.

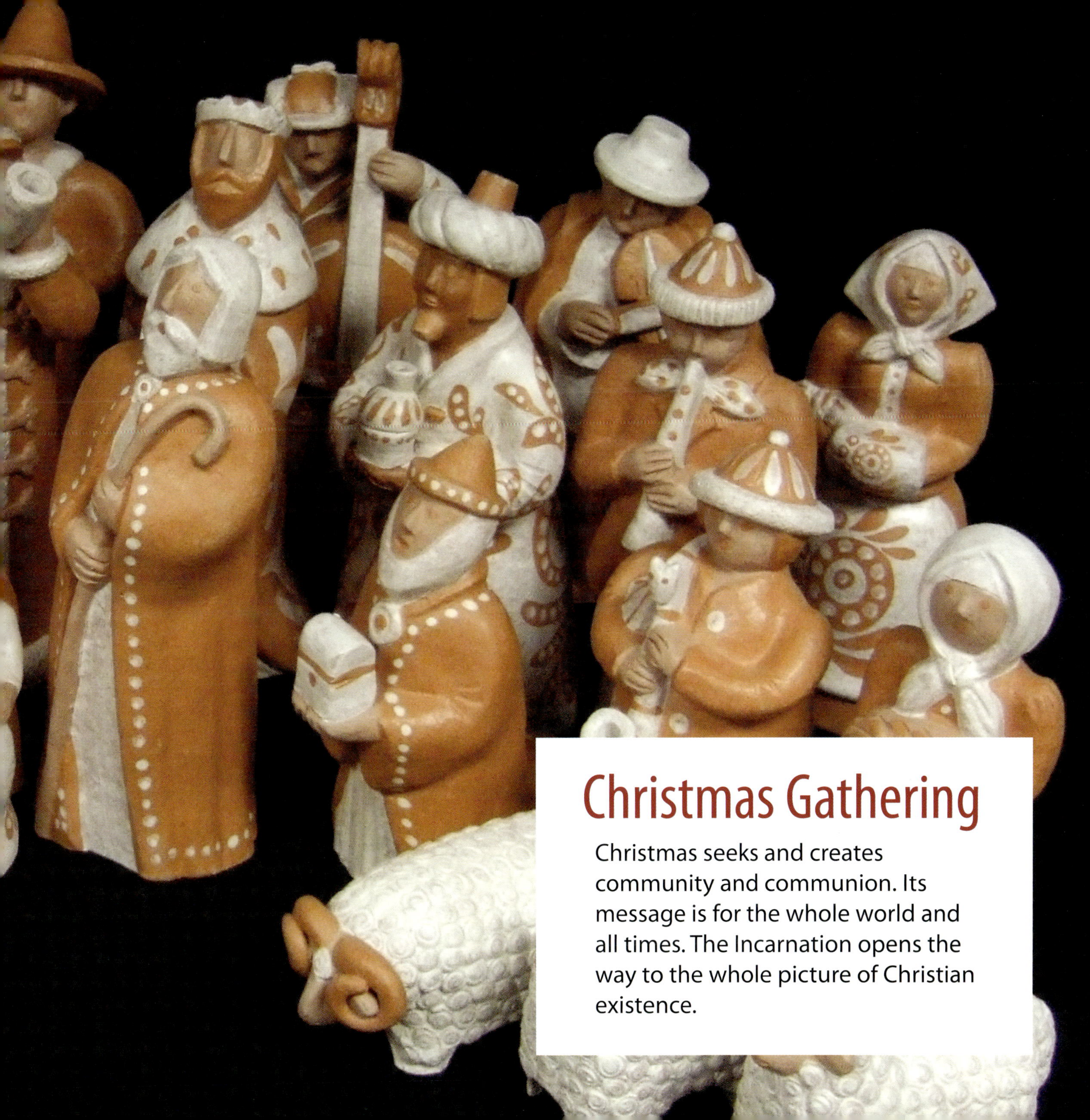

Christmas Gathering

Christmas seeks and creates community and communion. Its message is for the whole world and all times. The Incarnation opens the way to the whole picture of Christian existence.

Christmas Gathering

Many Nativity traditions put emphasis on the social dimension of Christmas. The Nativity is not a solitary feast. It brings together those "who spontaneously congregate, those who are family, or those who share similar affinities. There are those who share neither affinity nor communality. Their only common ground is in the one who calls them together. So they gather around the manger in search of a new commonality, developing new affinities of sharing and belonging. Different cultures share different social sensitivities, and thus highlight common history or activity, uniformity or common experience.

A Common Center

The foremost reason for the Christmas gathering is the Christchild in the manger. He creates communality, even community.

Feast for the Many

Uniformity and a certain anonymity among the manger figures are not, in some cultures, without a deeper social significance. Uniformity highlights a degree of communality, and the anonymous character may attempt to exorcise exaggerated individualism.

Common History

Common tradition and common history are some of the building blocks upon which to create the Christmas village. History creates tradition, and tradition strengthens community.

Unity in Action

Common purpose constitutes a solid foundation for the pursuit of the common good and well-being. It takes the concert of many to achieve unity.

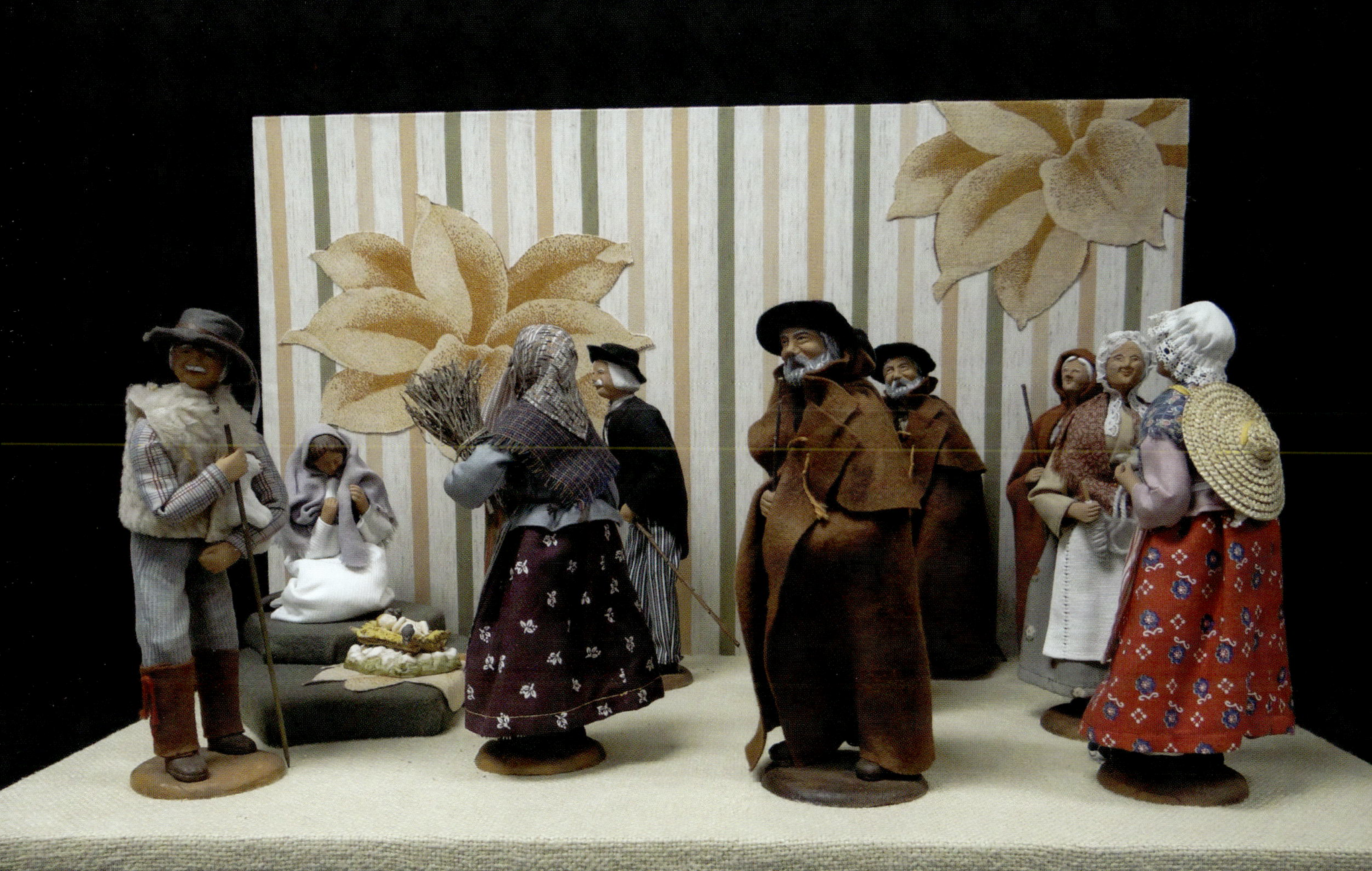

J. Peyron, France

A Common Center

In the French tradition of Provence the Holy Family comes to the village, and eventually the whole village will gather around the manger. Provençal Santons — the so-called "little saints" — are most gregarious. And when Christmas comes, the whole village from the mayor down to the village fool is mobilized. Now have you ever seen a congregation of Frenchmen and women who do not engage in some lively discussion and dispute? This nativity scene could have been called "The Dispute." From the running commentary by the farmer on the left — to the two ladies engrossed in conversation on the right, the whole scene is bristling with a mixture of curiosity and enthusiasm. Not even Joseph escapes the quizzing of Professor Boniface. Meanwhile, Mary holds silent watch, and the "Bous-quae-tiero, " the woman with the bundle of wood, delivers her modest gift.

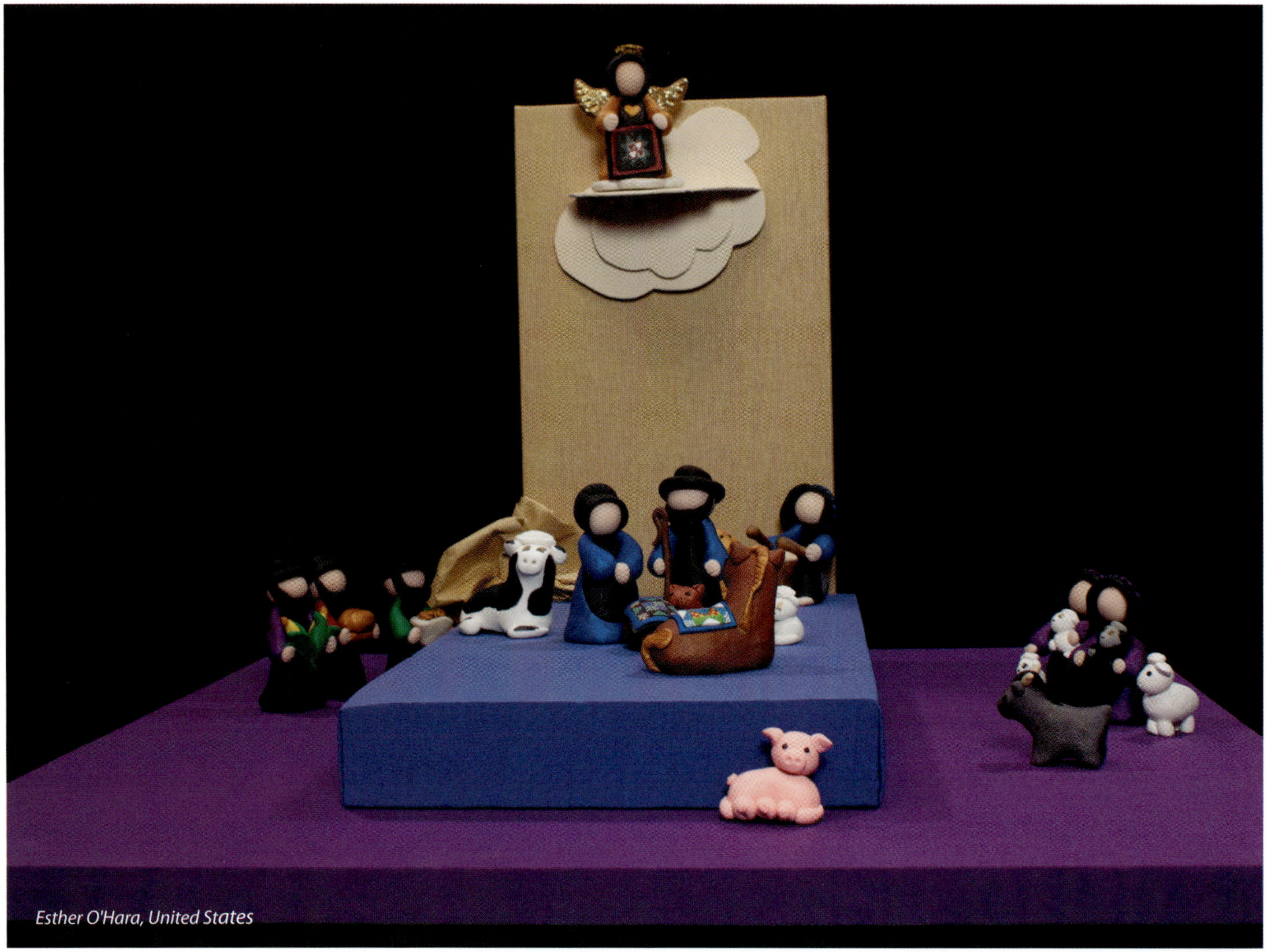

Esther O'Hara, United States

Feast for the Many

Amish life style and clothing express separation from the world. Not the individual person, but family, community, and church are essential. The faceless people of this set point to the spiritual dimension of our lives. We need the eye of the soul to understand the grandeur of Christmas.

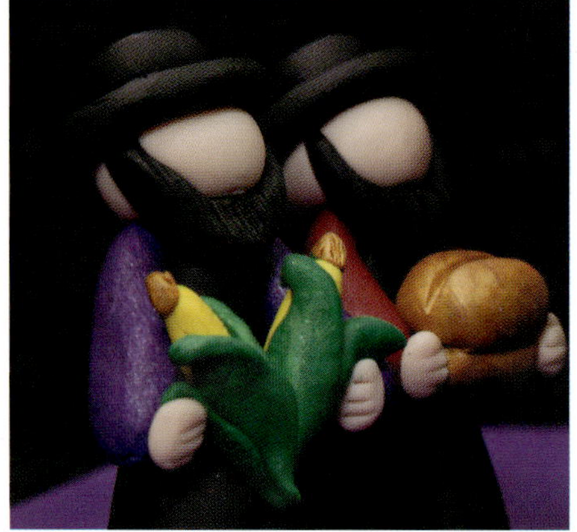

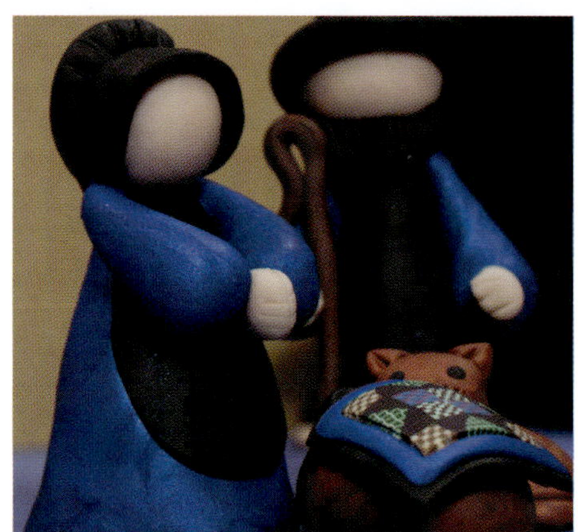

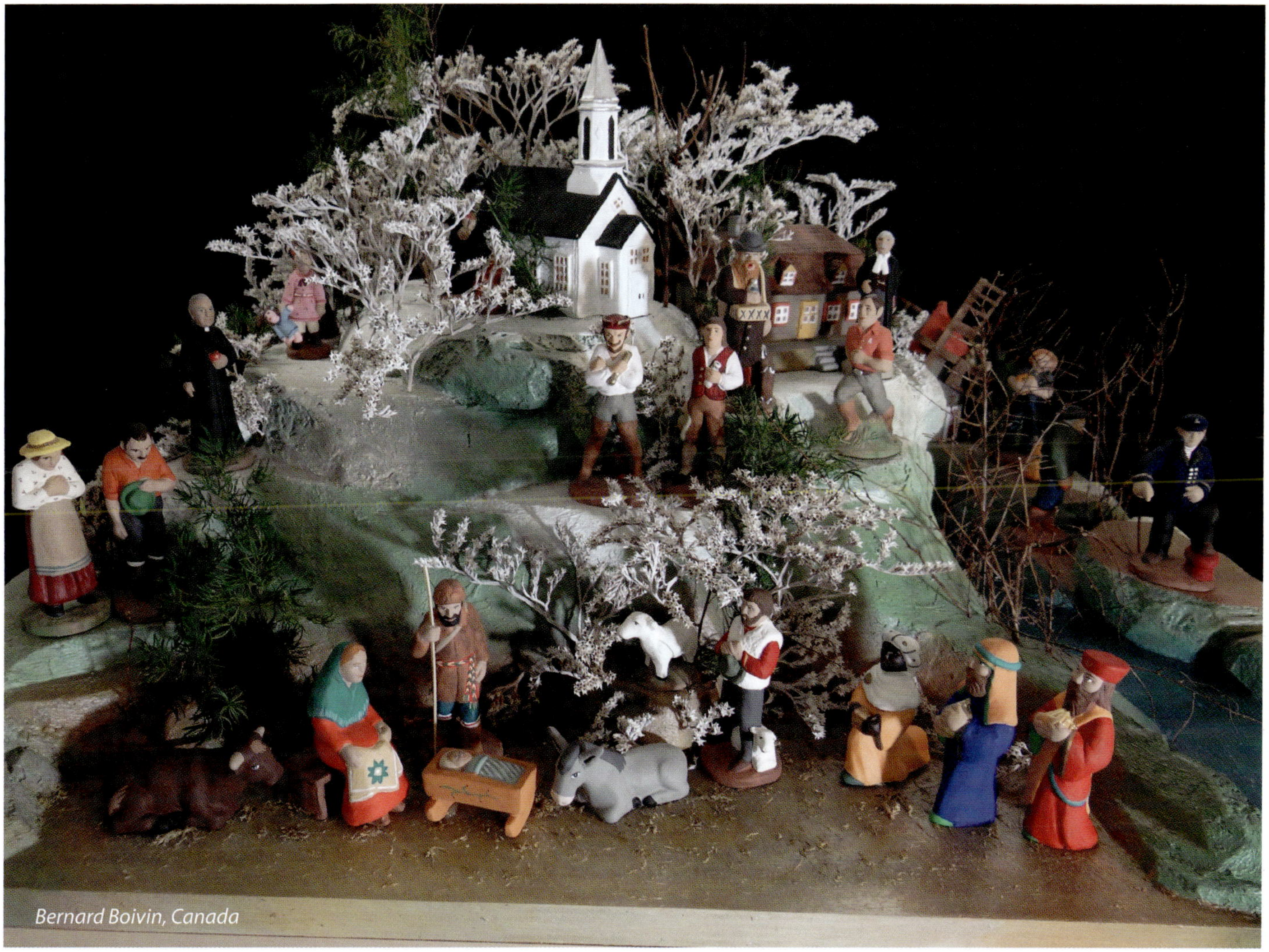

Bernard Boivin, Canada

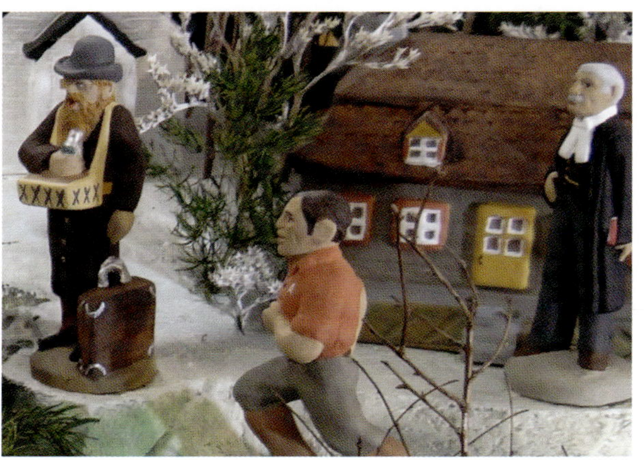

A Common History

Charlevoix in French-speaking Canada has its own collection of terra cotta figurines depicting a typical Québécois nativity scene. Its colorful characters bring back the memory of traditional activities and historical events of old Charlevoix. Scenes of farming, logging, and shipbuilding alternate with brightly colored houses and chapels. Our nativity set presents historical personages, animals, folkloric and legendary characters, and of course, a beautiful local rendering of the Nativity.

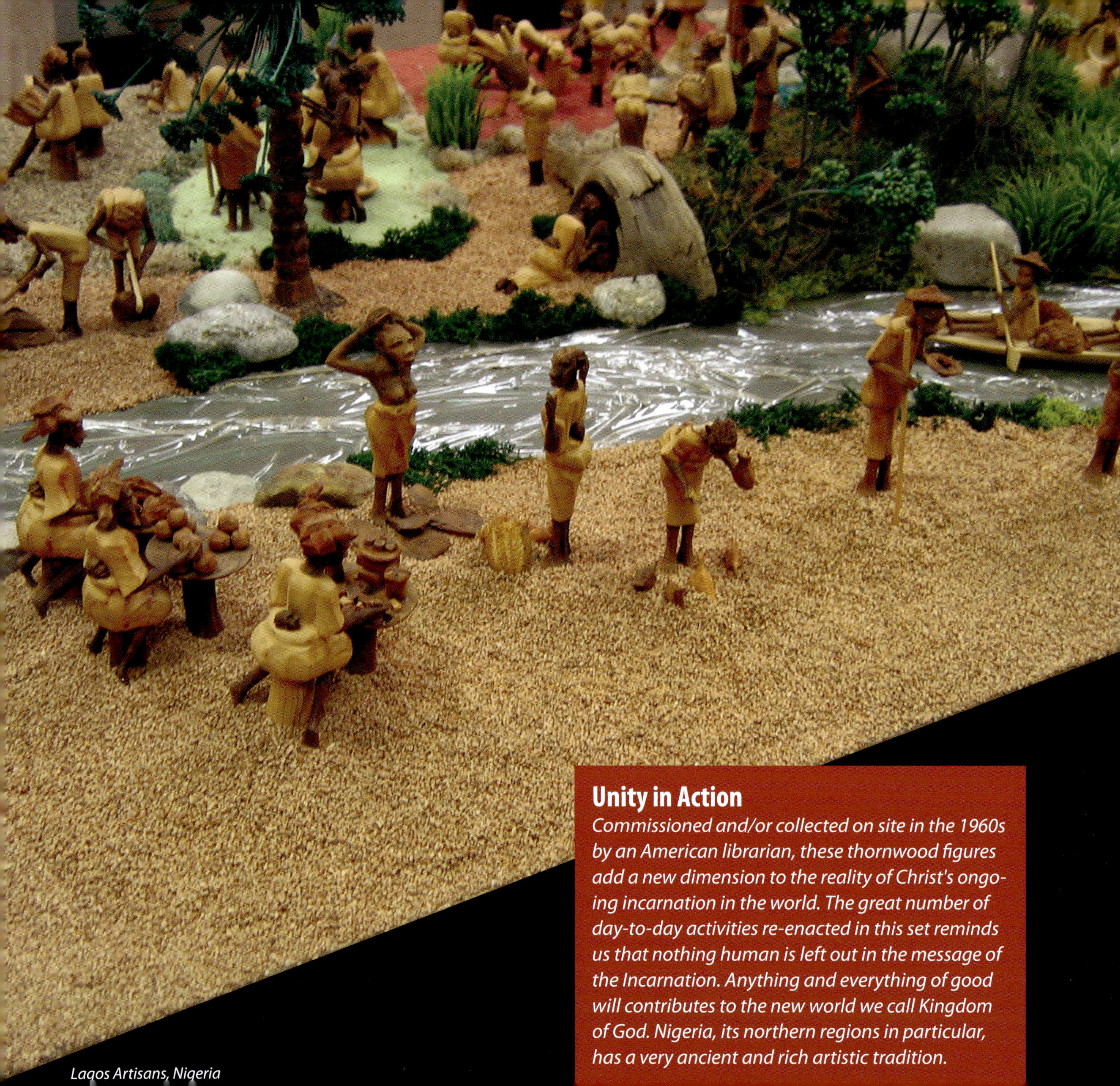

Unity in Action

Commissioned and/or collected on site in the 1960s by an American librarian, these thornwood figures add a new dimension to the reality of Christ's ongoing incarnation in the world. The great number of day-to-day activities re-enacted in this set reminds us that nothing human is left out in the message of the Incarnation. Anything and everything of good will contributes to the new world we call Kingdom of God. Nigeria, its northern regions in particular, has a very ancient and rich artistic tradition.

Lagos Artisans, Nigeria

For the Whole World
By all Means
Among the People
He Comes Our Way

The Whole World

Traditional nativity sets stress the movement of the whole crèche toward its center, the manger. Shepherds prompted by the angel, magi on horseback or in haste with flying robes – as can be seen in Nativity representations on sarcophagi – they all are on their way or have already arrived at the manger. Contemporary representations seem to find joy in altering direction. The movement seeks no longer the center only, but the center seeks the world. Indeed, God still comes! That is the message, and it reaches out to the world.

For the Whole World

Whatever the culture, whichever the religion, they are no obstacle for the coming of the harbinger of the Good News.

By all Means

In search of the world and all peoples, the Holy Family uses whatever means at their disposal.

Among the People

The Holy Family may be only passing through but so do we all, pilgrims of the earth. They have reached the marketplace to be with the people, among the people, and for the people.

He Comes Our Way

There is a new concentric movement. The new center and goal is now the heart of the visitor or spectator. The Christchild always comes our way … with all his friends.

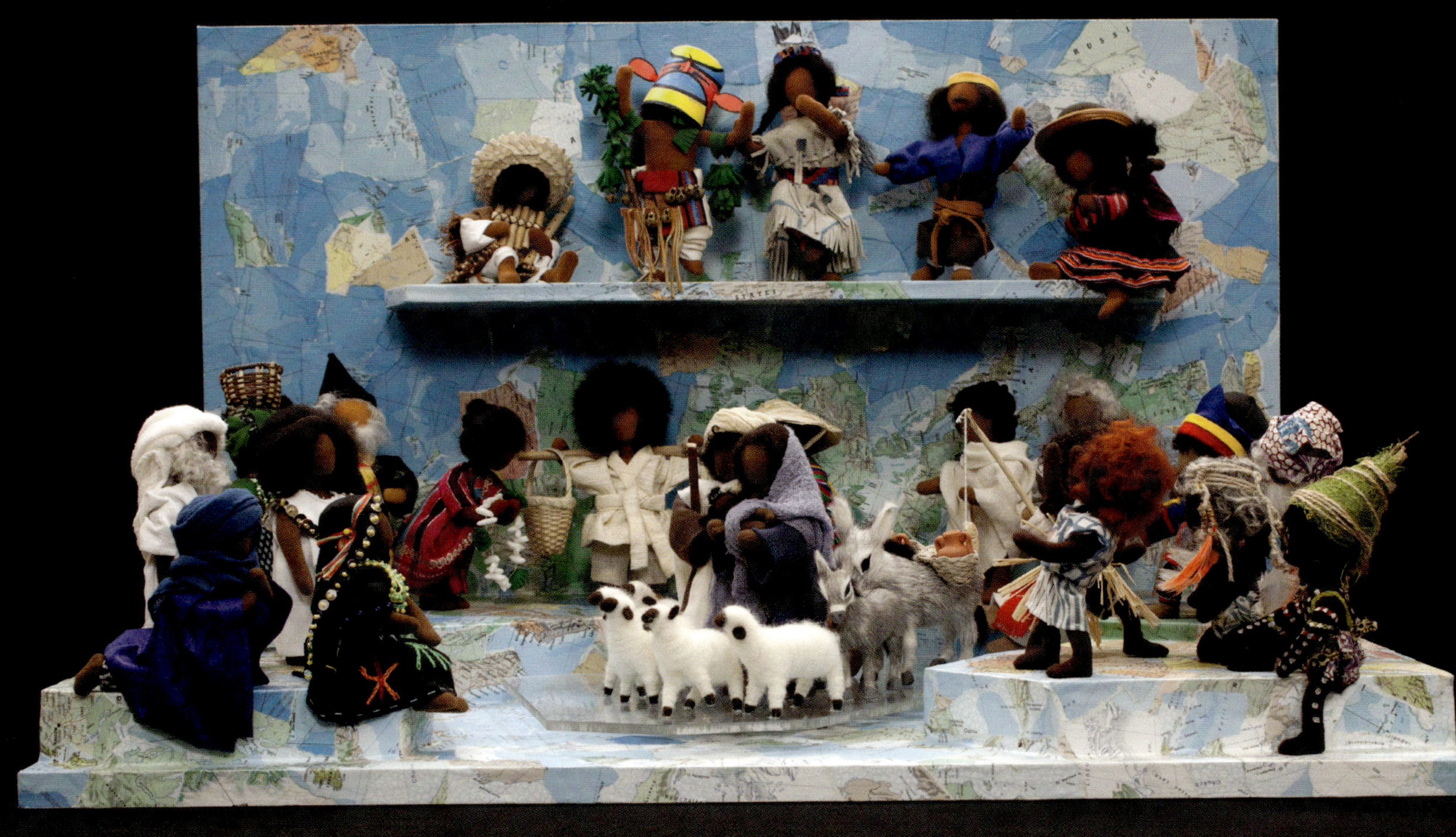

Bernadette Roten-Kaufmann, Switzerland

For the Whole World

The Holy Family accompanied by sheep and donkeys is on the move again. Their travel is no longer the flight to Egypt or the shelter-seeking in Bethlehem. The journey takes them to the ends of the world, to North and South, East and West; to the five continents of this world. Each of the continents is represented with five figures illustrating history and culture, beauty and poverty; those who made history and those left behind.

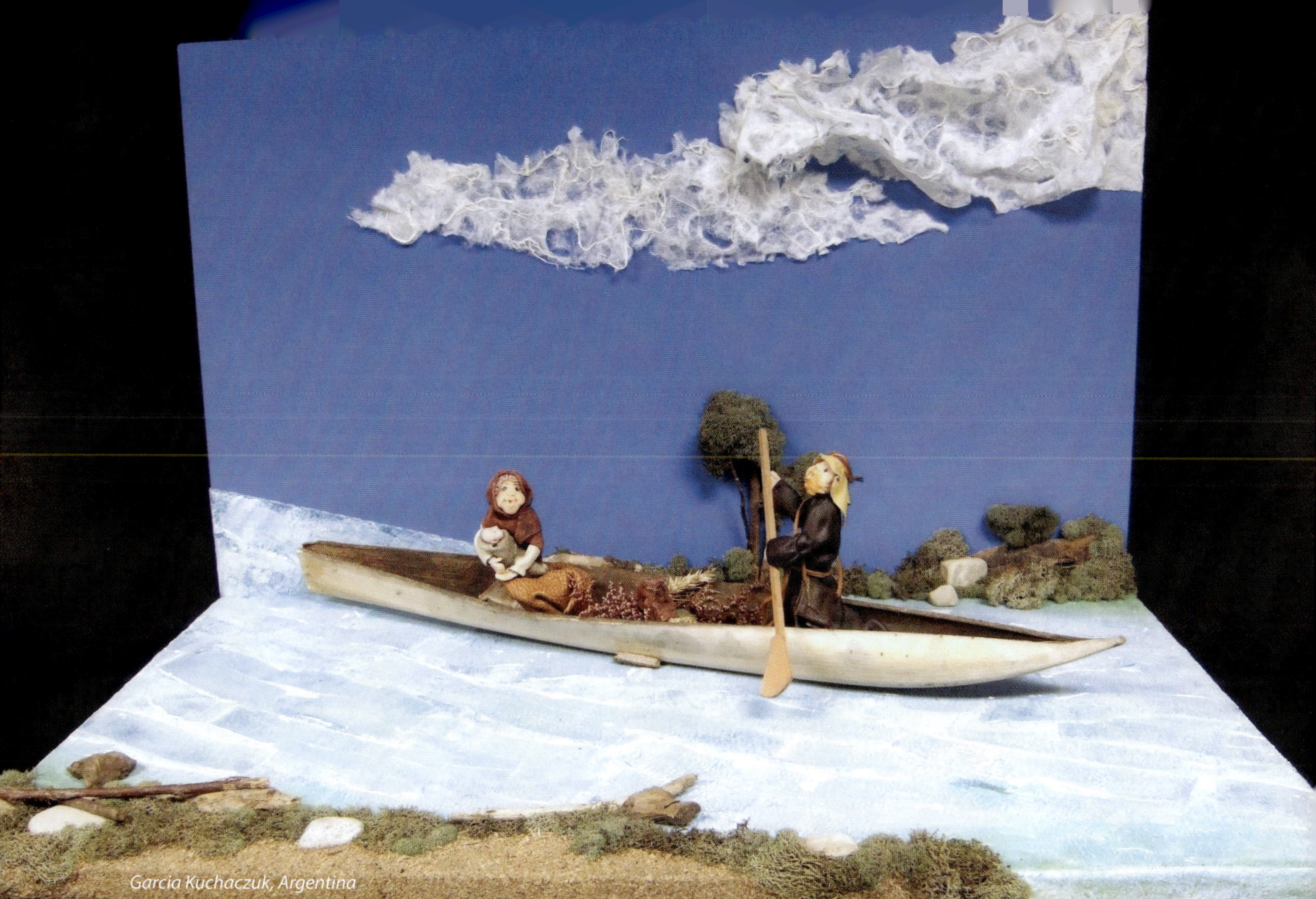

Garcia Kuchaczuk, Argentina

By All Means

This set, in the style of Arte Isleño, shows the Holy Family in open space limited only by a distant horizon separating water and sky. We don't know where their boat—made from leather—will take them. The sheer limitless space seems like an unfair challenge for the humble couple and their child. But there lingers a confident joy on their faces. The mission is engaged. It must continue. This set is reminiscent of a different boat ride and a different river. Apocryphal presentations of the flight to Egypt has the Holy Family riding the river Nile. The banks of the river are infested with wild animals, lions, and dragons. Threatening first, they eventually follow the Holy Family subdued and subservient. Again and again, the message of Christmas travels the world.

Among the People

People with hats are on the way; they are pilgrims or simply busy moving around. Even Joseph in this set wears a hat and carries a basket on his back. Indeed, the holy family is only passing through. They stopped for a moment at one of the street corners of the marketplace. Soon they will disappear among the multicolored robes, scarves, shawls, veils, and, of course, hats of many shades. There is little physical and vestimentary difference between Mary, Joseph, the baby, and everybody else. God does not make waves when he comes. The marketplace or street corner will do. What counts is attentiveness, the ability to find him, the redeemer, among the many hats.

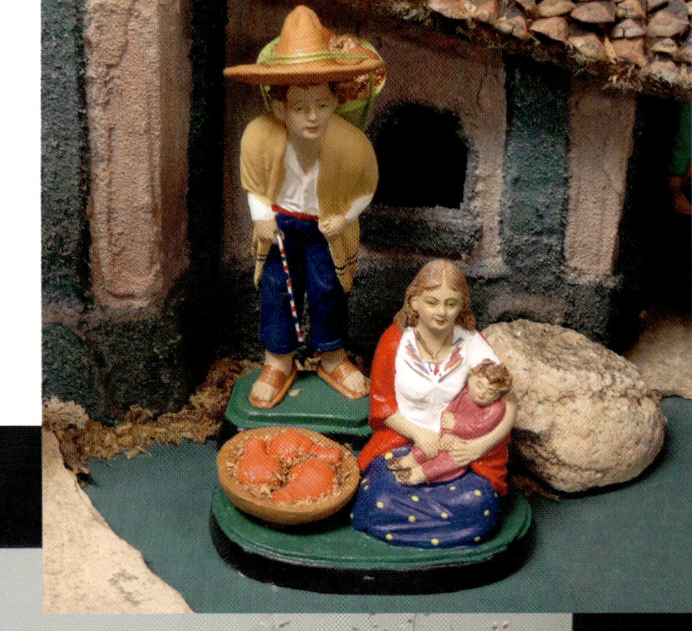

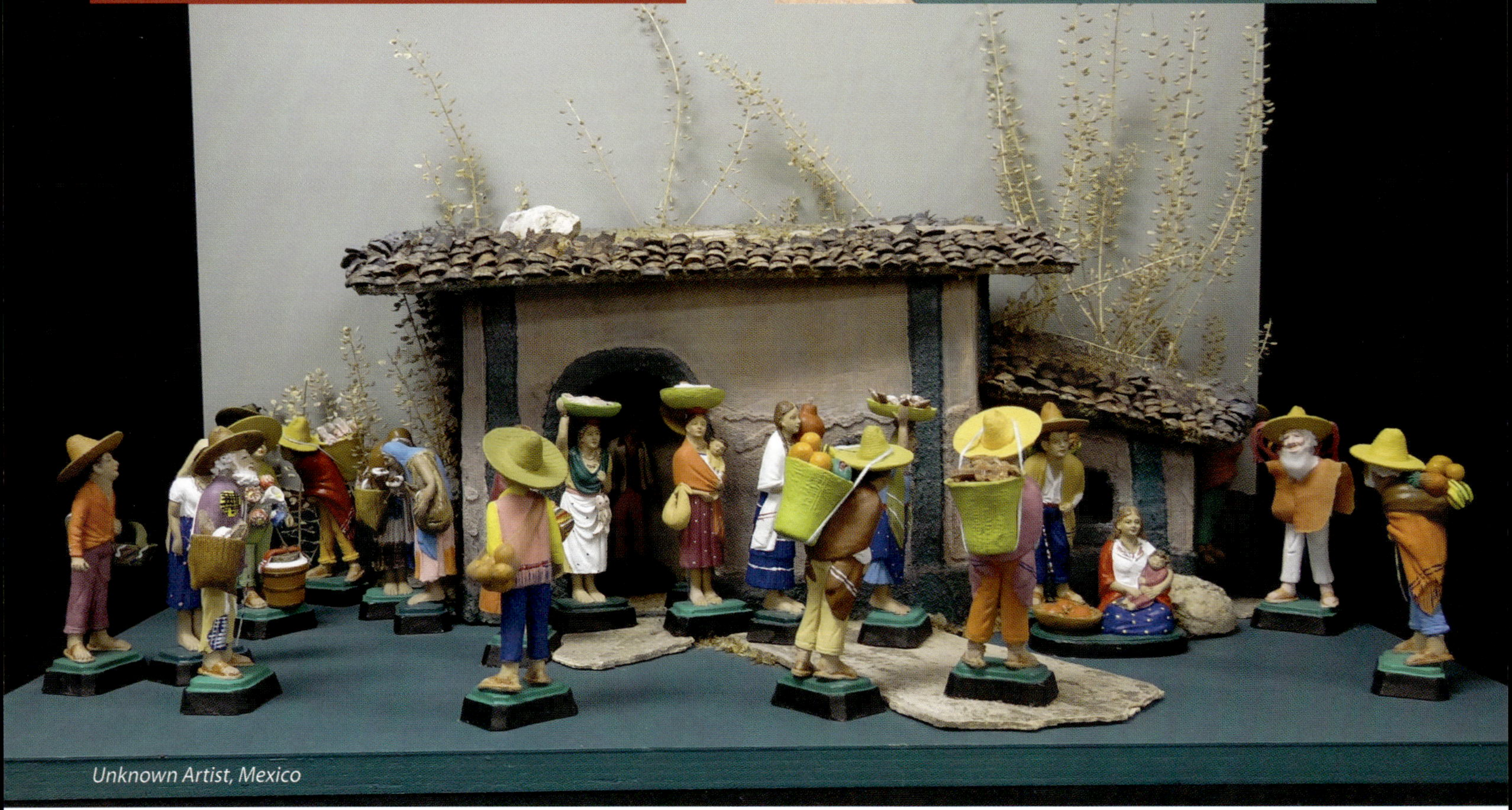

Unknown Artist, Mexico

He Comes Our Way

This is an important part of the Christmas message. Jesus came, and always comes our way. And he is not alone. With him come all those he once met and drew to himself. Together they form a long and age-old procession, the people of God on the march. This nativity set would like to express the idea of the pilgrim people of God. At first glance no more than a beautiful mass of orange and white colors, familiar figures reveal themselves gradually to those who take a closer look. There is Mary holding the Child and sitting in the first row, Joseph slightly behind them, the night watchman announcing with his horn the hour of salvation, the lady with the goose, one making butter, others carrying a variety of delicious breads, not to forget the many musicians.

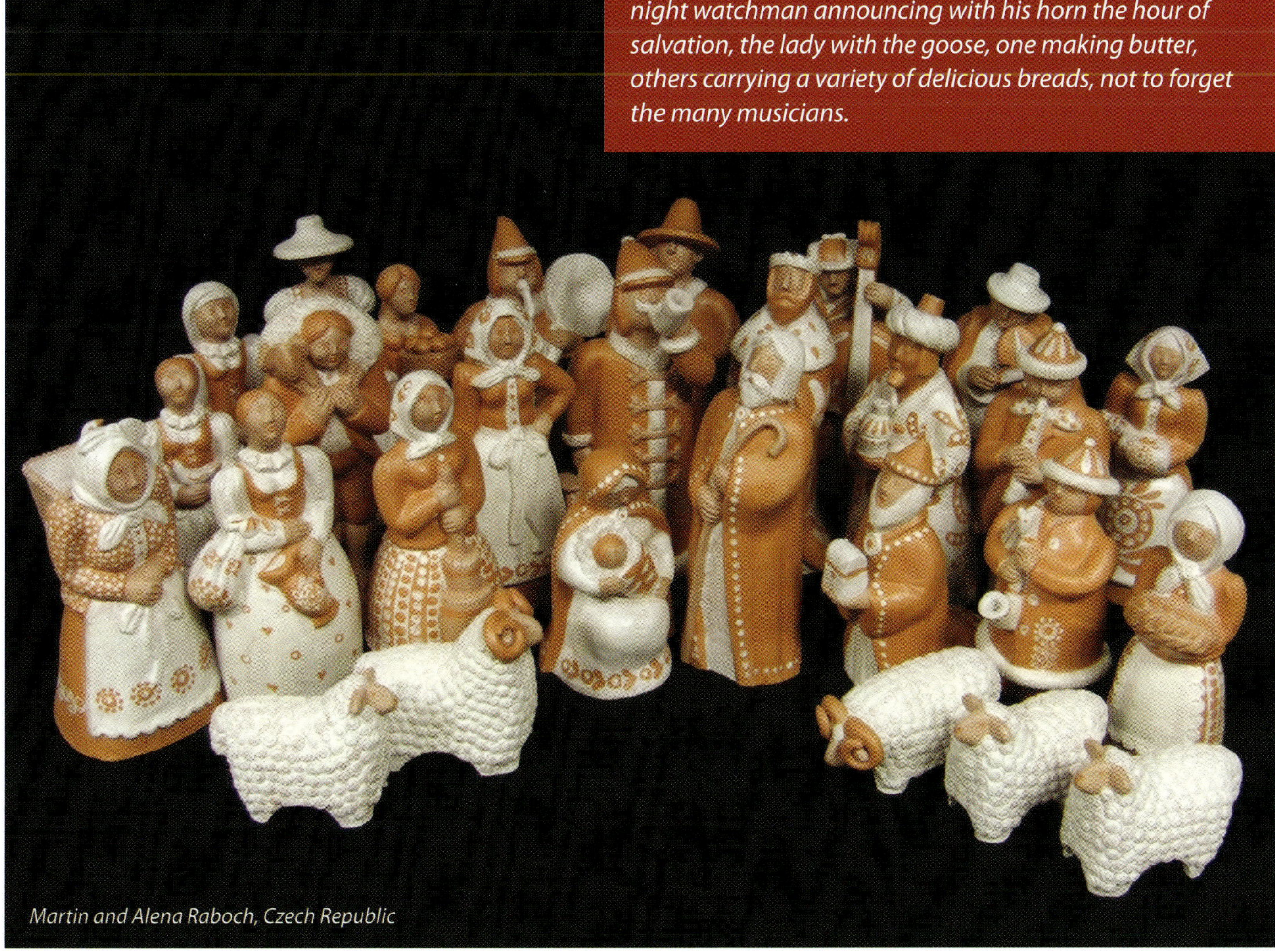

Martin and Alena Raboch, Czech Republic

The Whole Picture

The Nativity is not an isolated event. It forms an integral part with the whole message of the Bible, and explains the history not only of the Christchild in the manger, his origin and mission, but also the promised destiny for those who enter the Christmas story. There are many ways to capture the whole picture.

Genealogy

The Christchild enters genealogy in order to highlight his humanity. He is part of the human family, and a human descendant from Joachim and Anne, the Virgin Mary, and the line and house of Joseph.

Life and Mission

Some Nativity traditions, foremost the German one, include stations of Christ's life and mission in the Christmas narrative, highlighting especially the Annunciation, and Jesus's death and Resurrection.

Time of the Church

The Nativity leads beyond the life of Jesus Christ, and enters the time of his Church. He remains present to his followers in the Holy Eucharist.

From Beginning to End

The representation of the Nativity may reach out and picture a full panorama of human history as it is seen by the Bible. In this case, the whole picture begins with Creation and ends with the end of time and the beginning of eternity.

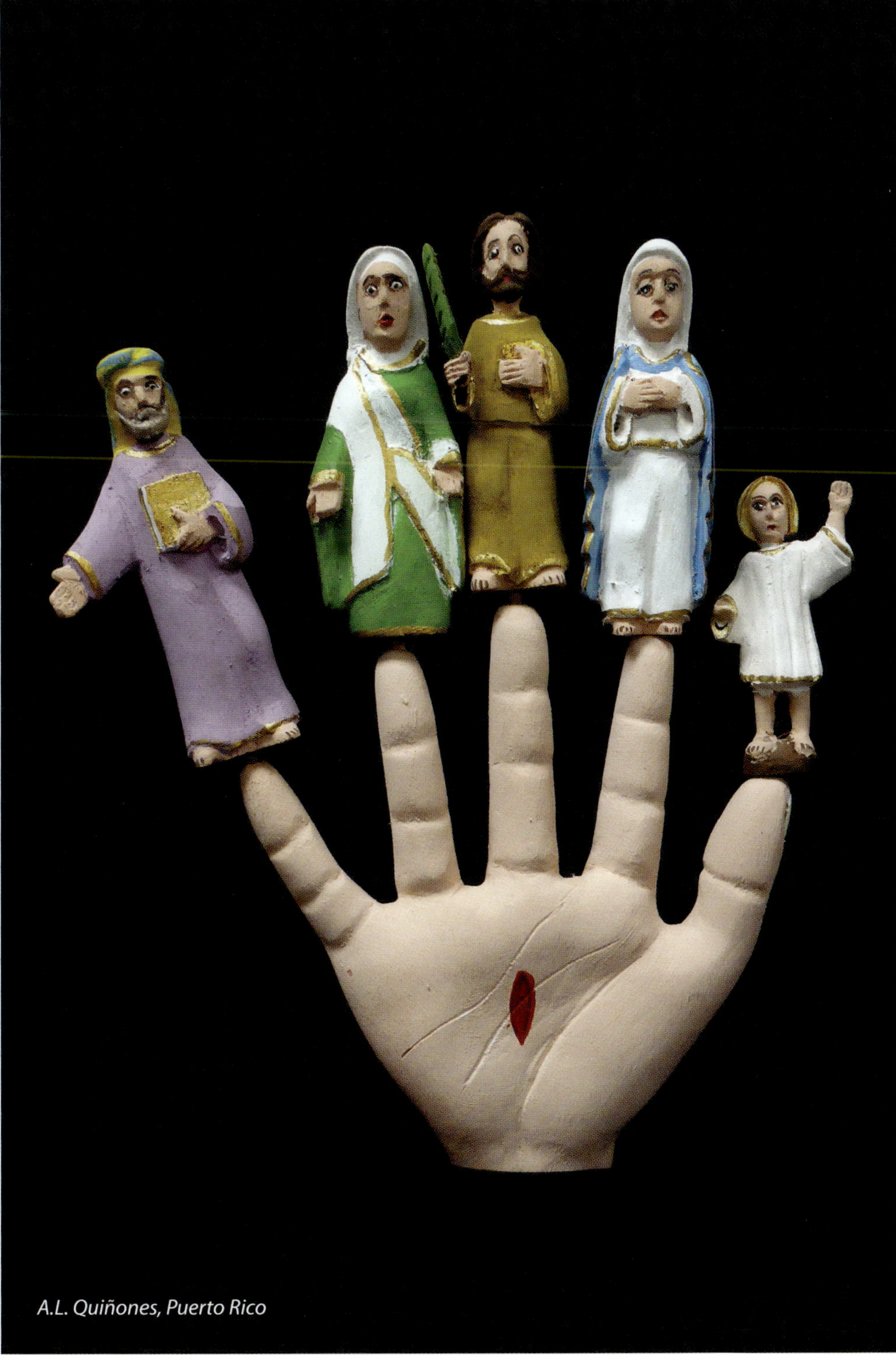

A.L. Quiñones, Puerto Rico

Genealogy

This unusual "Nativity Set" conveys a rich and poignant message. Incarnation and redemption, life and death are in the hand of God. The hand of God is a very ancient iconographical motif. The invisible God manifests his active presence in this world through his visible hand, as can be seen in many icons. In a special way, God's hand is the hand marked by the stigma of the Passion of Christ, the redeeming hand. It is also a hand that does not work in solitude. Each one of the fingers of this hand is topped and crowned by one of five saintly figures. The Mighty Hand, a typically Hispanic tradition, is a genealogical tree. It shows, from left to right, Joachim and Anne, Mary's parents, and Joseph and Mary with Jesus. The Mighty Hand has the meaning of an abbreviated Tree of Jesse, signaling that God is a God of history and human generation.

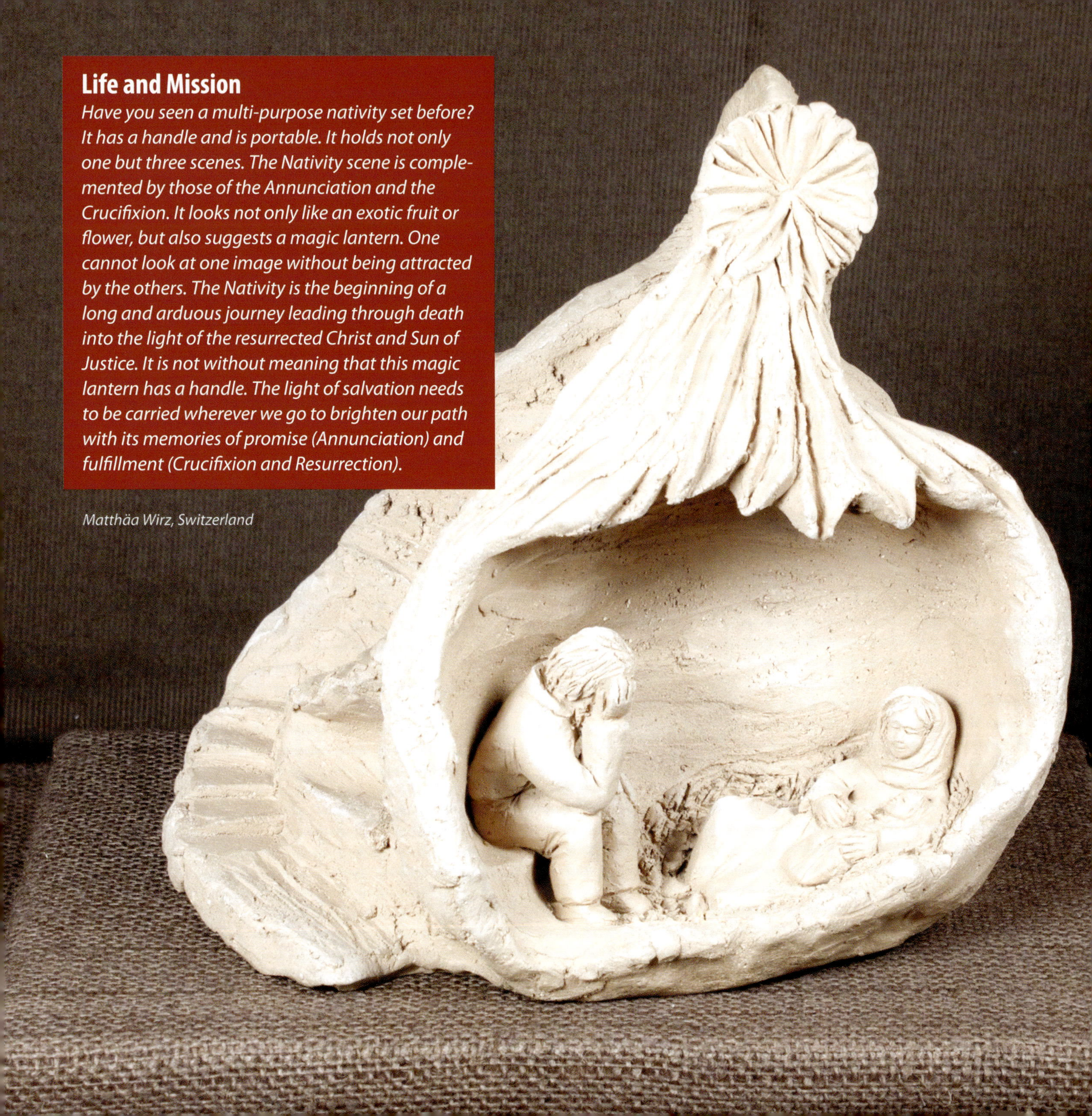

Life and Mission

Have you seen a multi-purpose nativity set before? It has a handle and is portable. It holds not only one but three scenes. The Nativity scene is complemented by those of the Annunciation and the Crucifixion. It looks not only like an exotic fruit or flower, but also suggests a magic lantern. One cannot look at one image without being attracted by the others. The Nativity is the beginning of a long and arduous journey leading through death into the light of the resurrected Christ and Sun of Justice. It is not without meaning that this magic lantern has a handle. The light of salvation needs to be carried wherever we go to brighten our path with its memories of promise (Annunciation) and fulfillment (Crucifixion and Resurrection).

Matthäa Wirz, Switzerland

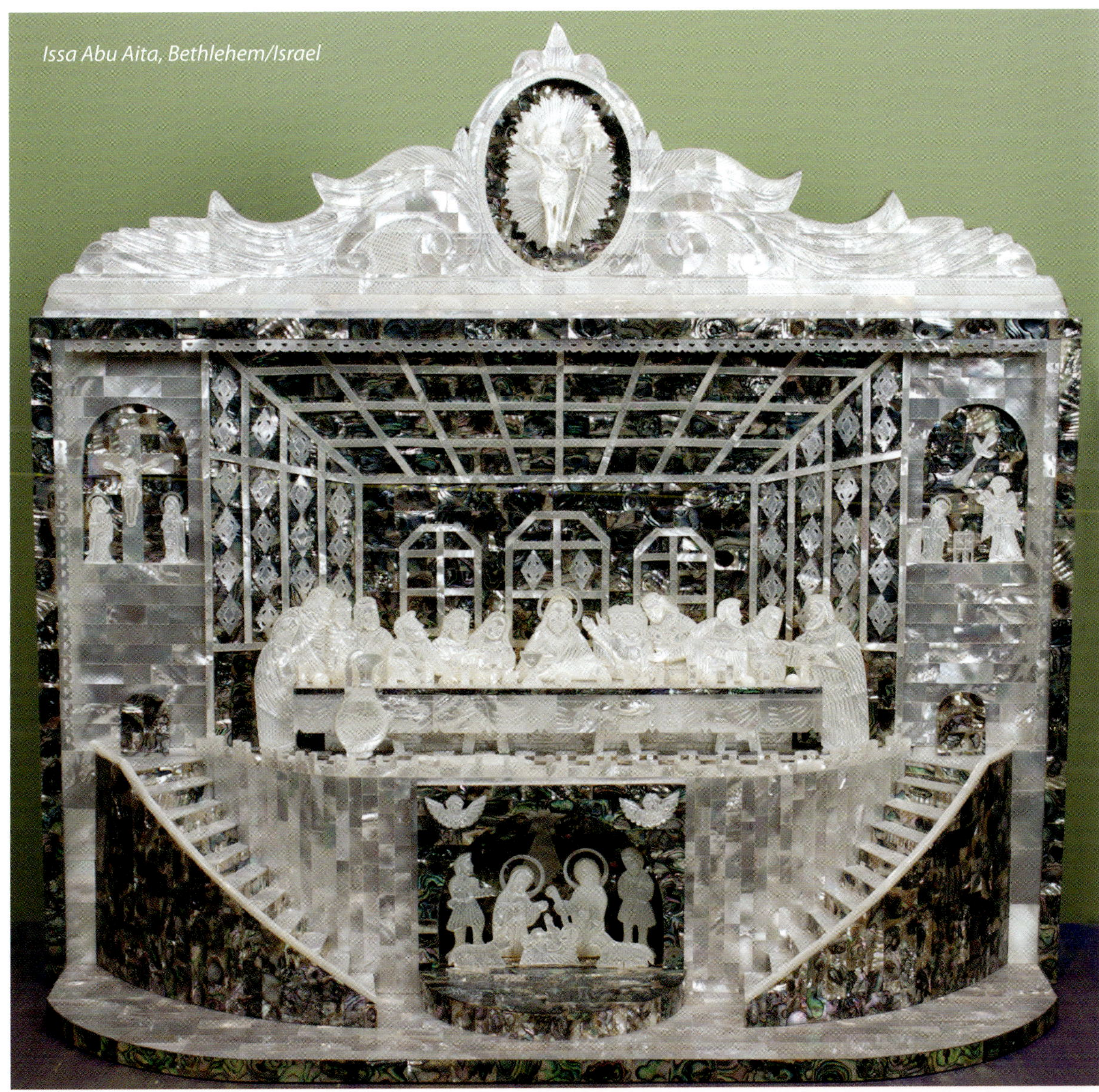

Time of the Church

This artwork is more than a nativity set. It is a little synthesis of the Christian faith. Linking the Nativity with a monumental staircase leading to the Last Supper and the Eucharist, it highlights the lasting presence of Jesus Christ among us. We are reminded that the Incarnation would not have become reality without the Annunciation (upper right), and its meaning would not have been complete without Crucifixion and Redemption (upper left). The resurrecting and ascending Christ makes this artwork a promise of eternal life (top center). All of the events depicted in this abbreviated diorama of Christian life remind us that there exists a staircase to Heaven.

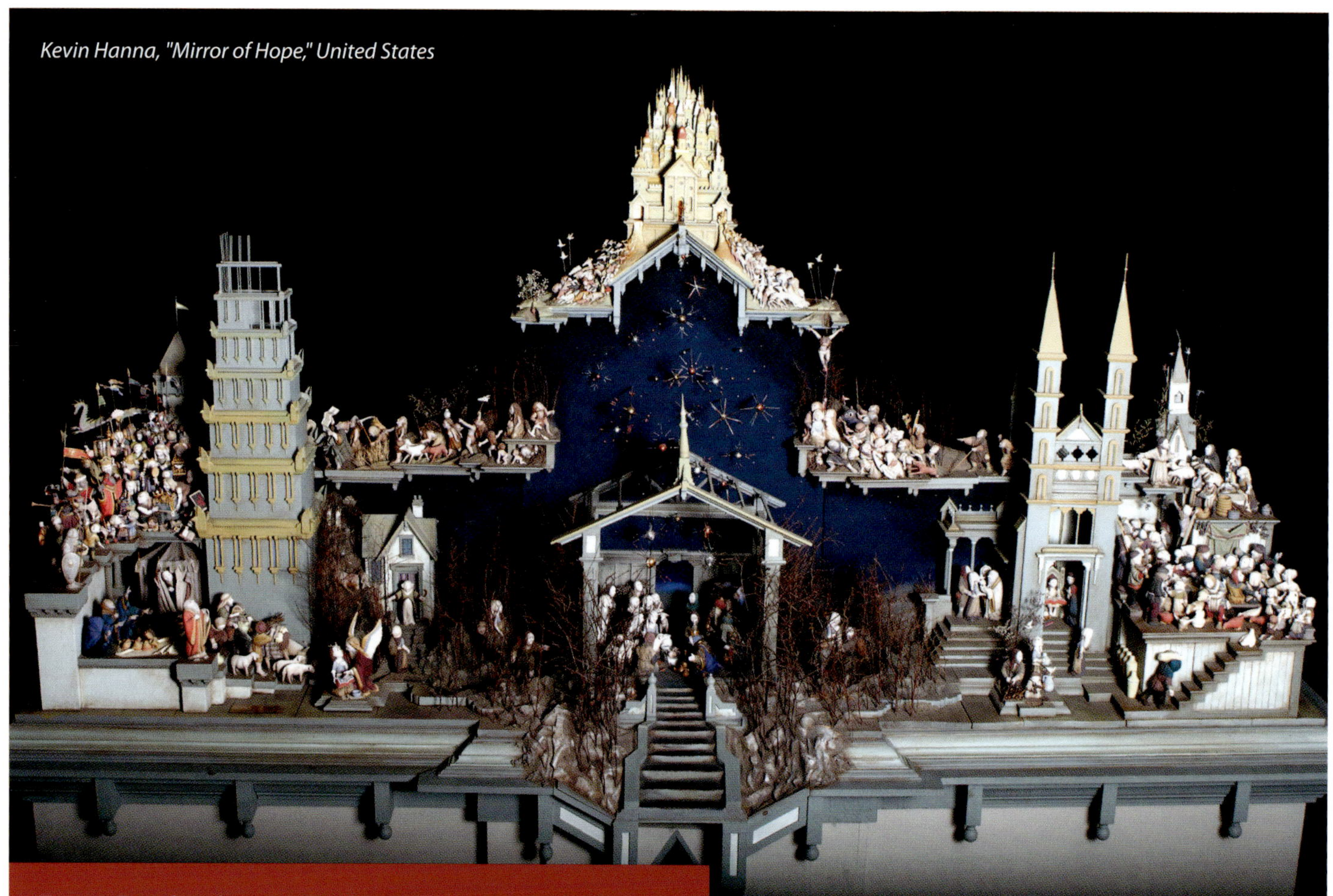

Kevin Hanna, "Mirror of Hope," United States

From Beginning to End

The love of God for his creation is expressed in a circular movement. Indeed, it begins with Creation, penetrates civilization and culture, culminates in a new covenant with humanity in the Incarnation and Redemption of the God-man, and finds fulfillment in the ultimate re-unification between God and his people. The golden City on the Mount is a symbol of God's love from beginning to end.

Matter Matters

The Nativity accepts and assimilates everything human. It enters the material world, too, and creates its manifold expressions with the matter and materials typical of the geographies of the world.

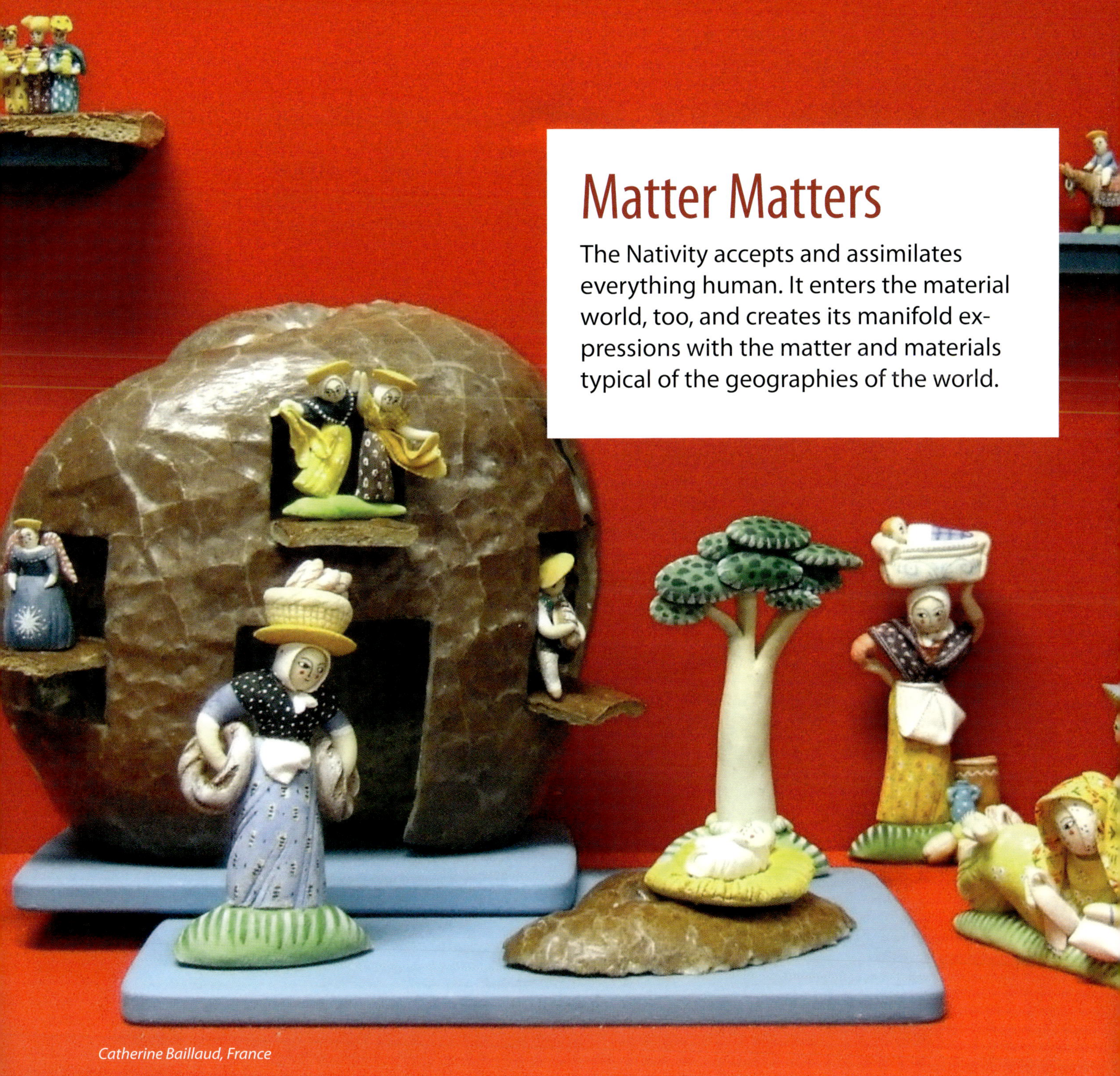

Catherine Baillaud, France

Wood
Burlap
Straw
Wax
Horns
Fennel
Dough
Paper
Faience
Auto Parts

Matter Matters

Medium or matter of which the figures of the nativity sets are made tends to be both typical and common. Matter matters because it represents local culture, the stuff of everyday life, and therefore is the stuff which contributes to make a culture typical. Matter matters because in many cases it represents the livelihood of people. Lastly, and not to be ignored, matter matters because it lends body, shape, and visibility to the Incarnation.

The materials from which to carve, cut, fashion, or knit a crèche figure are amazingly varied, and often of great originality. It is true that the ordinary and mass-produced set is of plastic, plaster, polymer and resin, but where creativity has the upperhand we find the bamboo set from Taiwan, the Singapore nativity made of *pâte d'encens*, banana leaves for crèches from Africa and Latin America, crèches carved in bone or soapstone, nativities fashioned from clay and wood. However, it is the artistic touch which transforms matter and gives it genius. Here are samples of how matter matters.

Wood is not just Wood

The barn is Walnut, the manger Rosewood (India), but guess which woods were used to make Jesus, Mary and Joseph? The Holy Family was crafted with a variety of woods: Robe-Buckeye, Halo-Satinwood (Sri Lanka), Blanket-Maple, Flesh-Luan (Philippines), Robe-Zebrawood (Africa) and Hood-Poplar (Brazil). From Africa to Brazil and the Philippines, these wonders of wood are extolling the wonders of creation and its recreation in Christ.

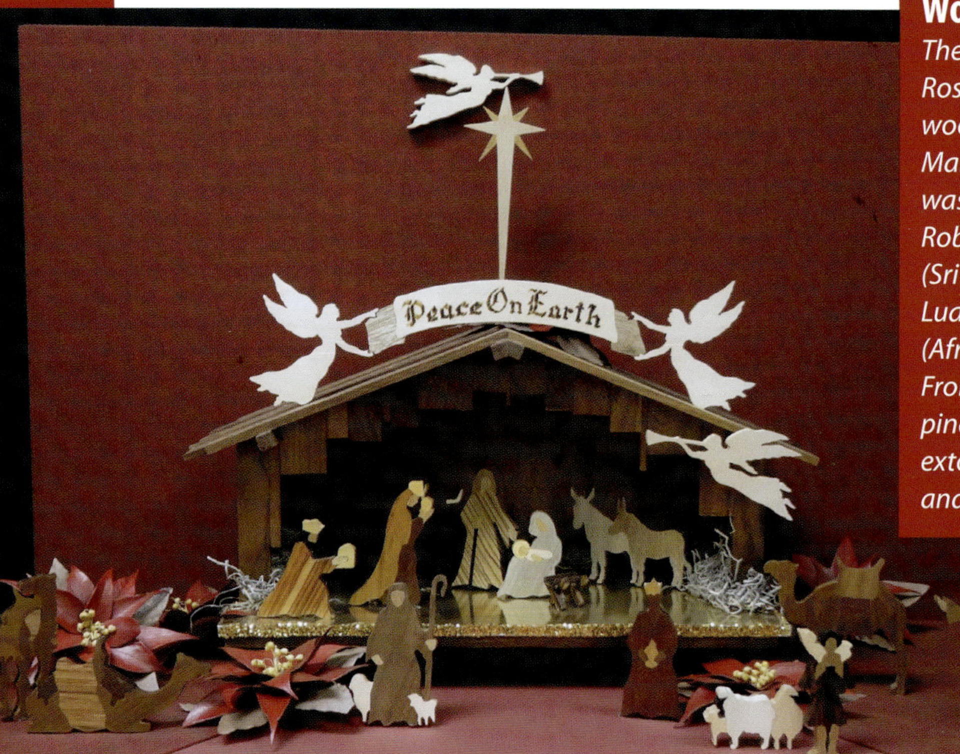

John F. Weber, United States

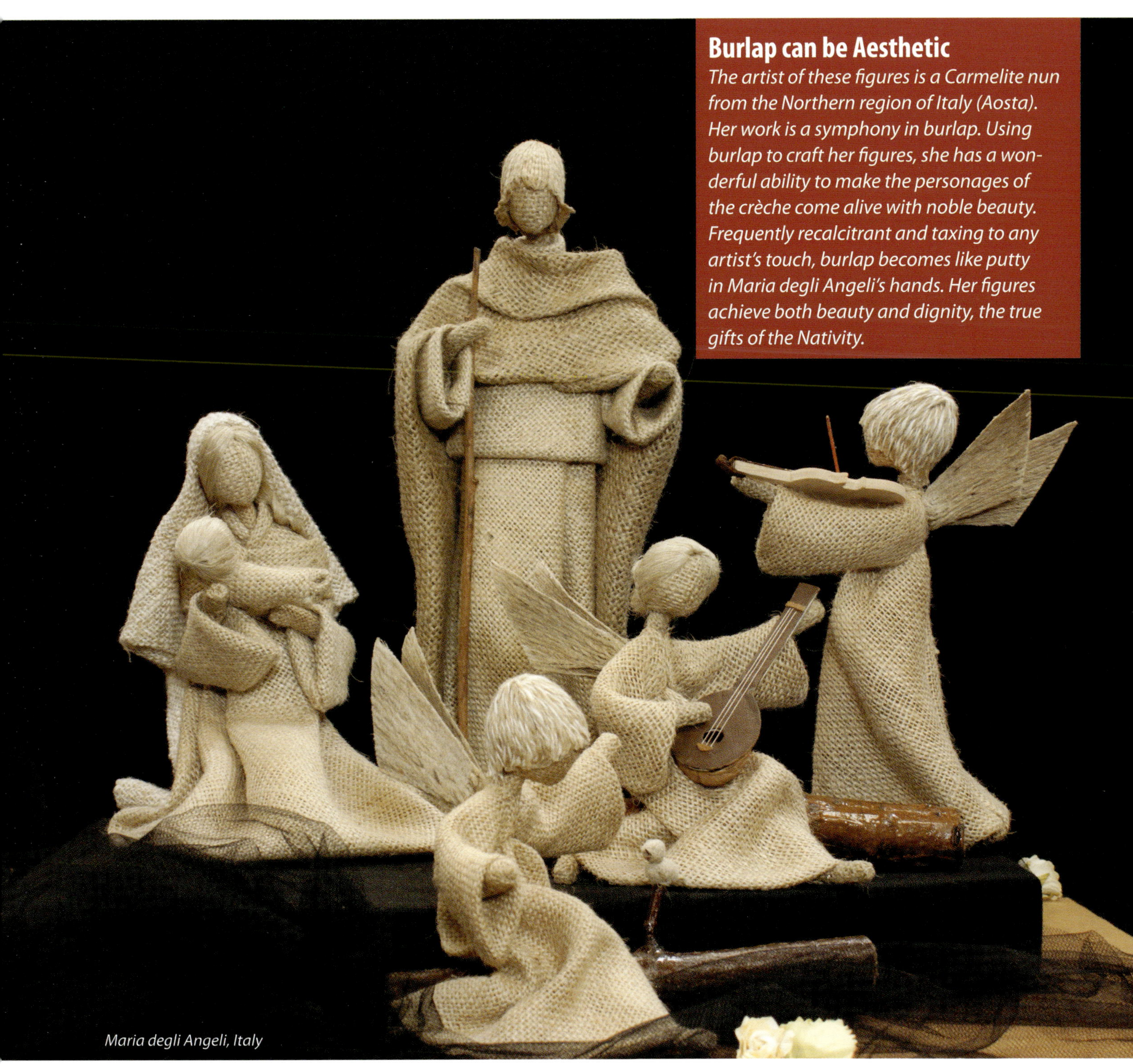

Burlap can be Aesthetic

The artist of these figures is a Carmelite nun from the Northern region of Italy (Aosta). Her work is a symphony in burlap. Using burlap to craft her figures, she has a wonderful ability to make the personages of the crèche come alive with noble beauty. Frequently recalcitrant and taxing to any artist's touch, burlap becomes like putty in Maria degli Angeli's hands. Her figures achieve both beauty and dignity, the true gifts of the Nativity.

Maria degli Angeli, Italy

The Golden Gleam of Straw

When poverty and faith meet, they frequently generate inventiveness and creativity. This is the case for the beautiful straw nativities from the Tzintzuntzan region of Mexico. The artist of this set, Bernardino Marquez, is a master weaver with a magic touch. Decorative on large surfaces and intricate where small features are concerned, the artist's weaving produced figures of great simplicity and dignity. Admire Joseph with his blooming staff, the gourd hanging from its top, a pilgrim's hat on his head. A golden glow emanates from this straw set, as if the ordinary material was ennobled by the noble purpose it serves. As for the meaning of this nativity set, God is able to make beautiful things from humble beginnings.

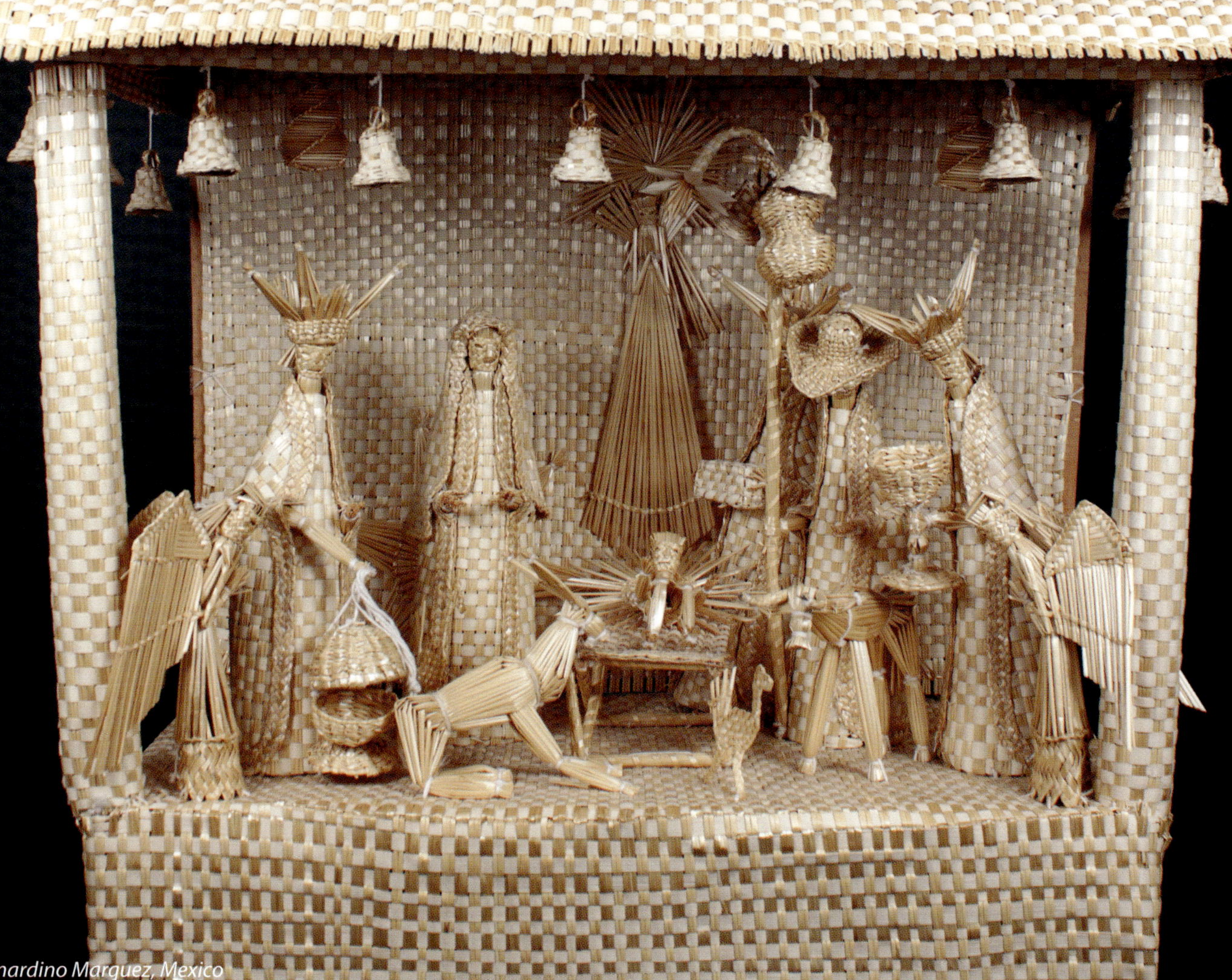

Bernardino Marquez, Mexico

The Fragile Truth of Wax

This set is part of a fifteen-piece nativity from Mexico. The figures are cast in wax and draped in rich and colorful robing. They convey an atmosphere of dignity, peace, and silent prayer. The whole scene is a still life of adoration pressed into wax. Wax is a fragile material. The figures are of fragile and almost translucent beauty. They symbolize the greatness and fragility of our faith in the God made man.

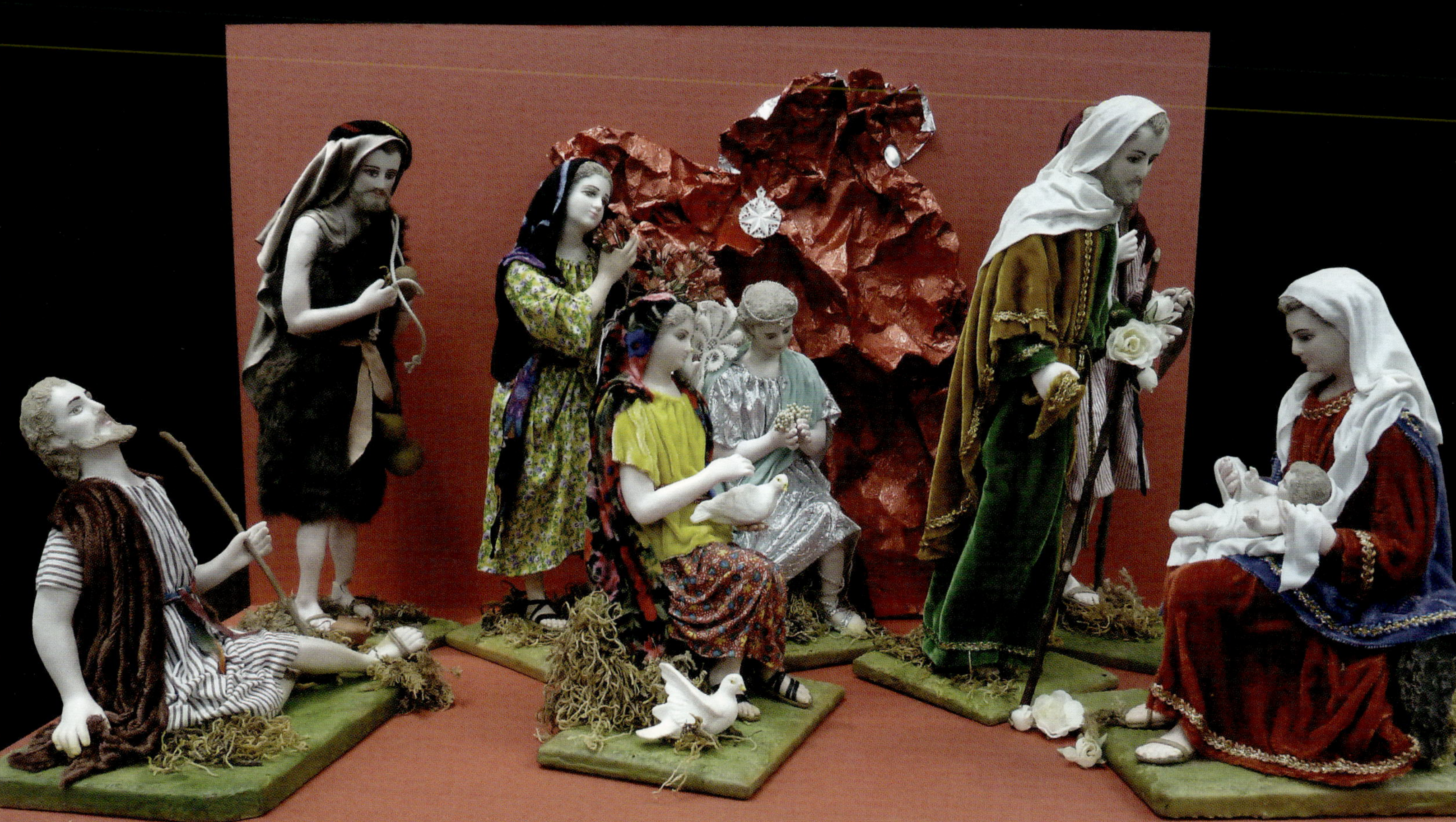

Angelita Gutierrez, Mexico

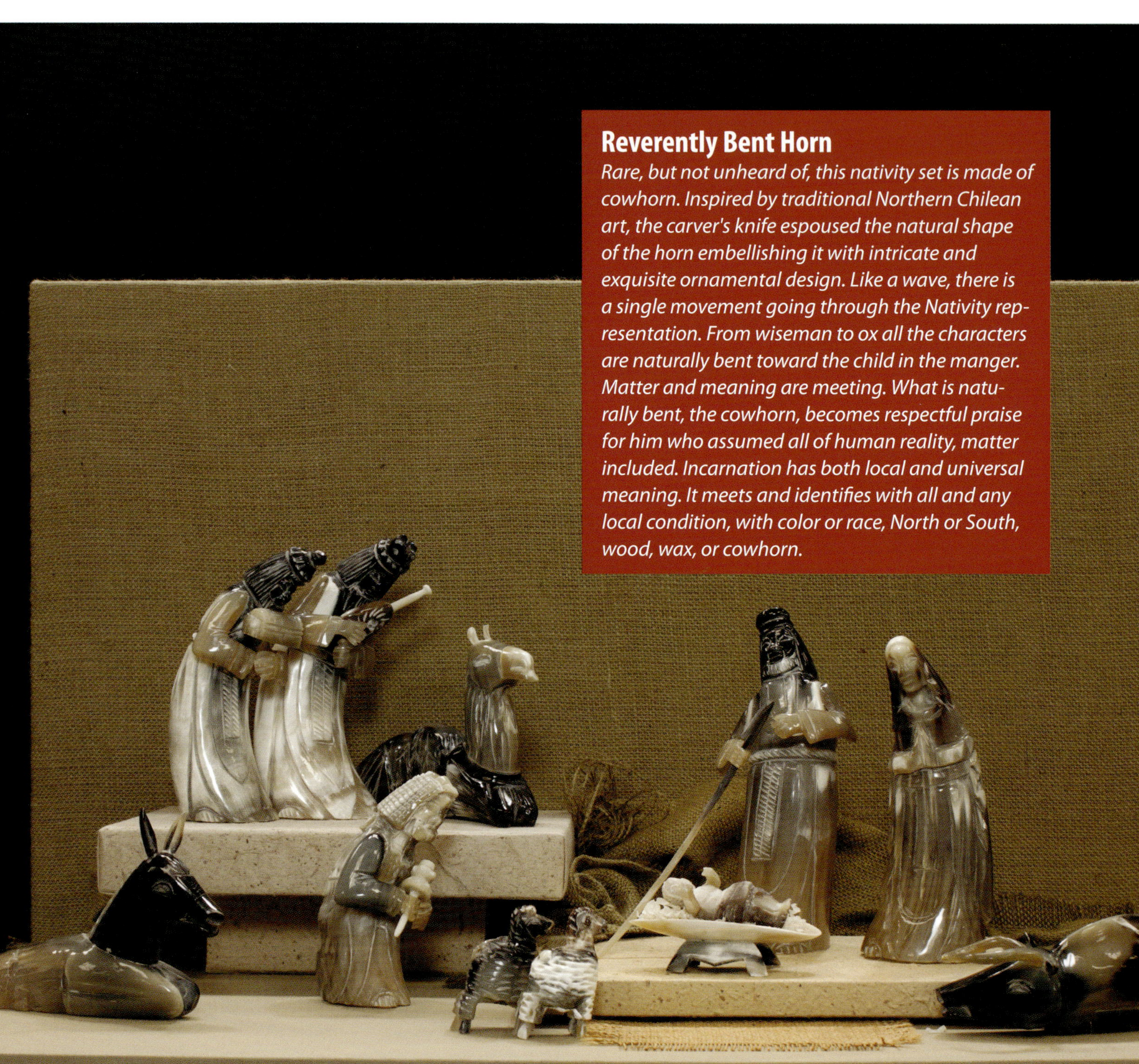

Reverently Bent Horn

Rare, but not unheard of, this nativity set is made of cowhorn. Inspired by traditional Northern Chilean art, the carver's knife espoused the natural shape of the horn embellishing it with intricate and exquisite ornamental design. Like a wave, there is a single movement going through the Nativity representation. From wiseman to ox all the characters are naturally bent toward the child in the manger. Matter and meaning are meeting. What is naturally bent, the cowhorn, becomes respectful praise for him who assumed all of human reality, matter included. Incarnation has both local and universal meaning. It meets and identifies with all and any local condition, with color or race, North or South, wood, wax, or cowhorn.

Carmen and Antonio Jerez y Carevic, Chile

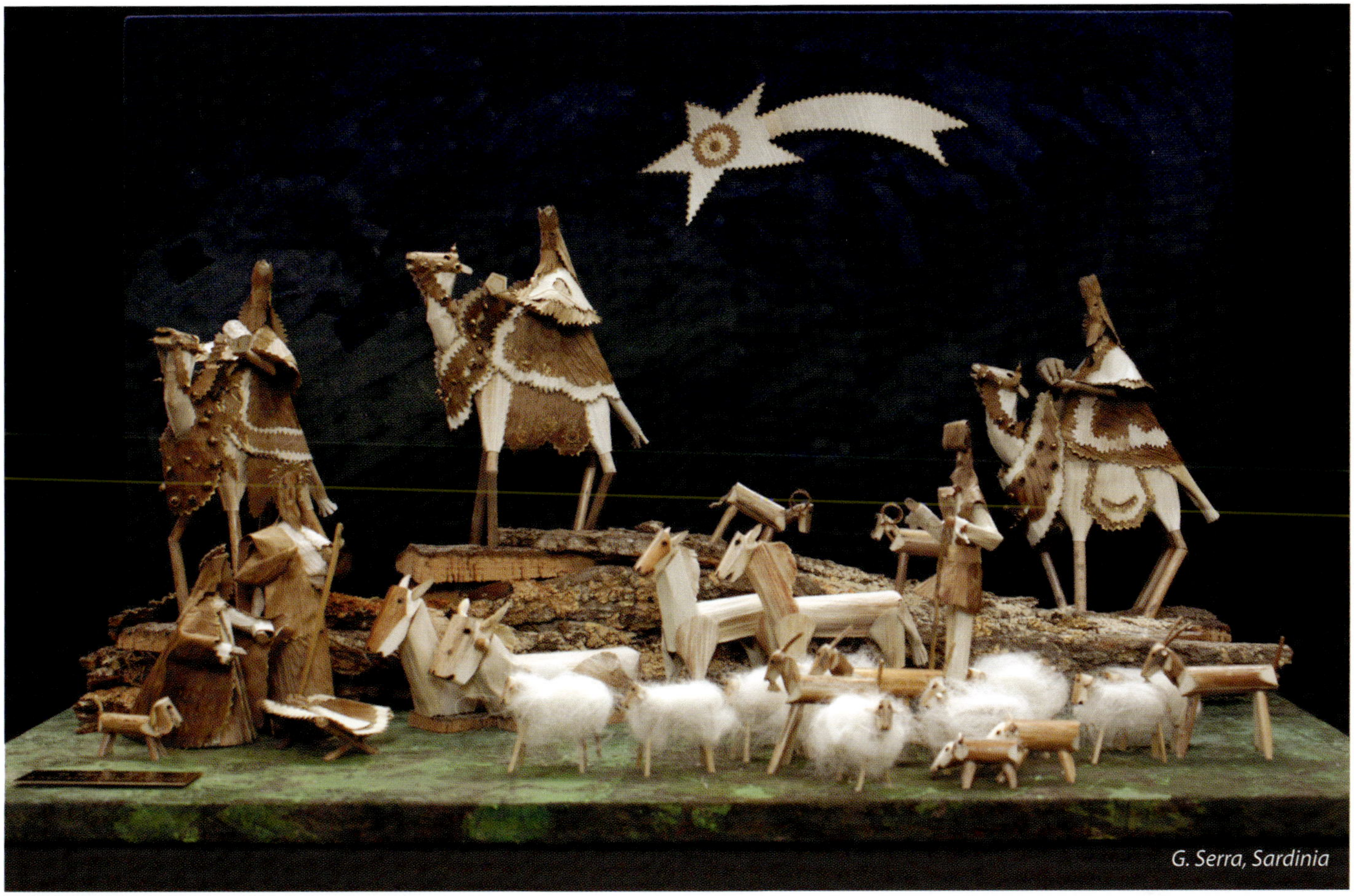

G. Serra, Sardinia

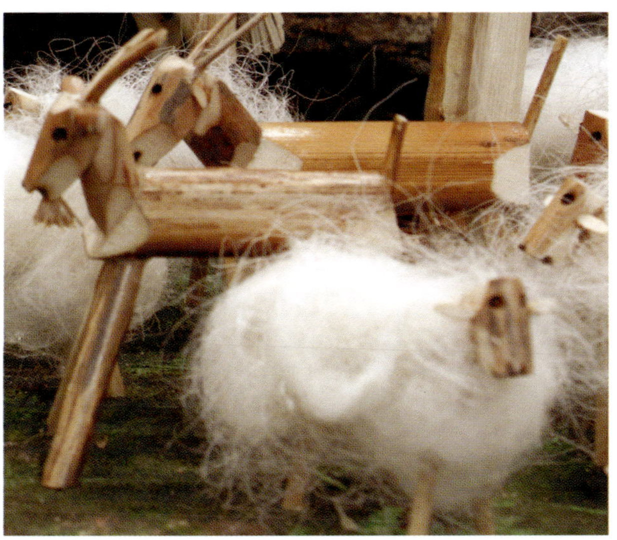

The Soul of Fennel

There are not only crèches made of resin and polymer. Although the more common materials have been wood and clay, we also have Nativity sets made from wax and straw, peat and bone, or, as in this scene, from the leaves, twigs and little branches of the giant fennel (ferulae). Ferula is a genus of stately herbaceous perennials, native to the Mediterranean, Western and Central Asia. Sardinia being an island of the Mediterranean, the giant fennel is one of the typical and common materials used by the natives. It was the genius of the artist which made the giant fennel come alive as gentle piglet, stately horse, and majestic camel.

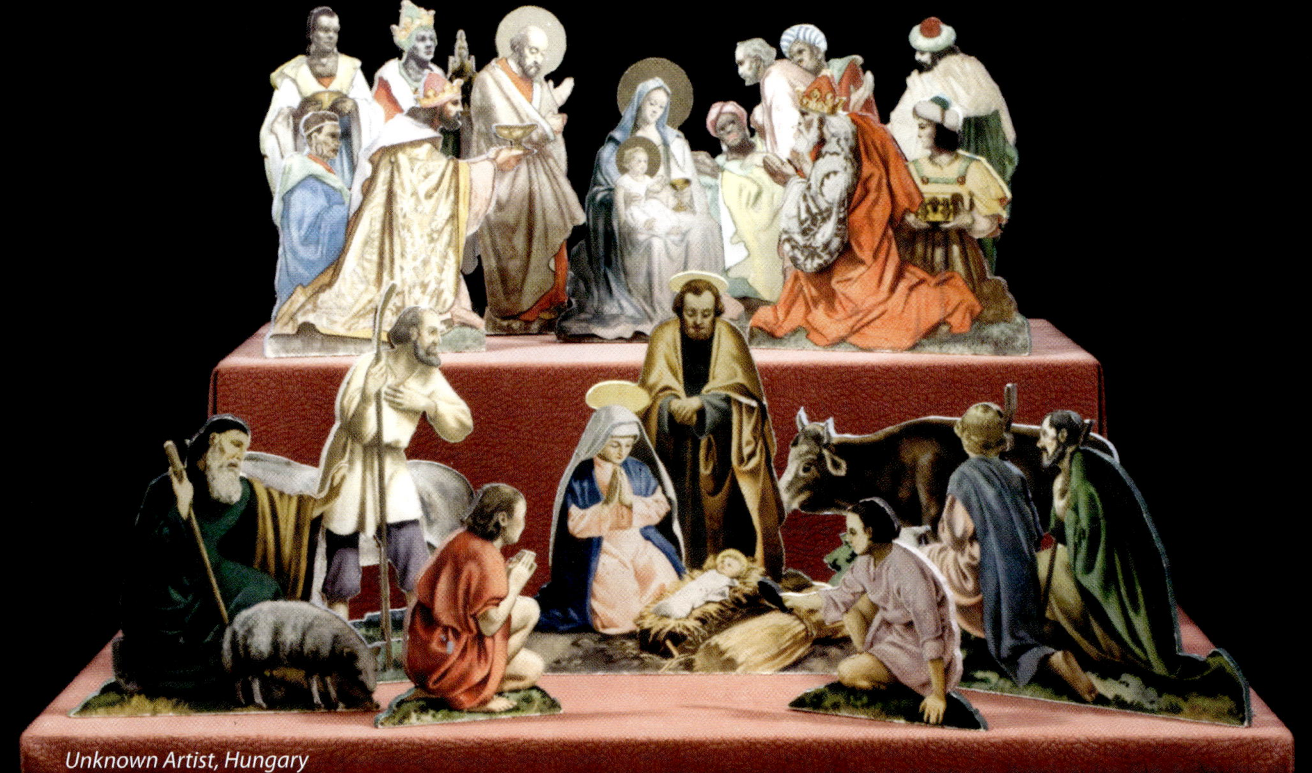
Unknown Artist, Hungary

The Narrative Genius of Paper

Is Jesus twice born? In a way. He was born to his mother, to Joseph and the shepherds, not to forget ox and ass, on December 25. On January 6, he was born, so-to-speak, to the whole world represented by the magi. Latin countries tend to celebrate Christmas on January 6, the feast of Epiphany, which corresponds to the original Christmas tradition. In this nativity set of cut-out figures the two moments of Christ's birth have been combined. Cut-out figures owe their existence to the Jesuit theater tradition originating in the 18th century.

The Glazed Nobility of Faience

A popular name for small and cheap statues of saints in the beginning (1850-1900), the "little saints" or Nativity santons are guardians of the charming, gregarious, and joyful nature of the French soul. In Quimper (Brittany), one of the citadels of French faience creations, they achieve a special patrician look thanks to their intense colored glaze: the white, yellow, and blue colors of the magi, and the greens for the shepherds. Only Mary and Joseph, no doubt to single out their humble station, are clad in colors of grayish green. The Christchild sides with the kingly visitors in regal blue, white, and yellow.

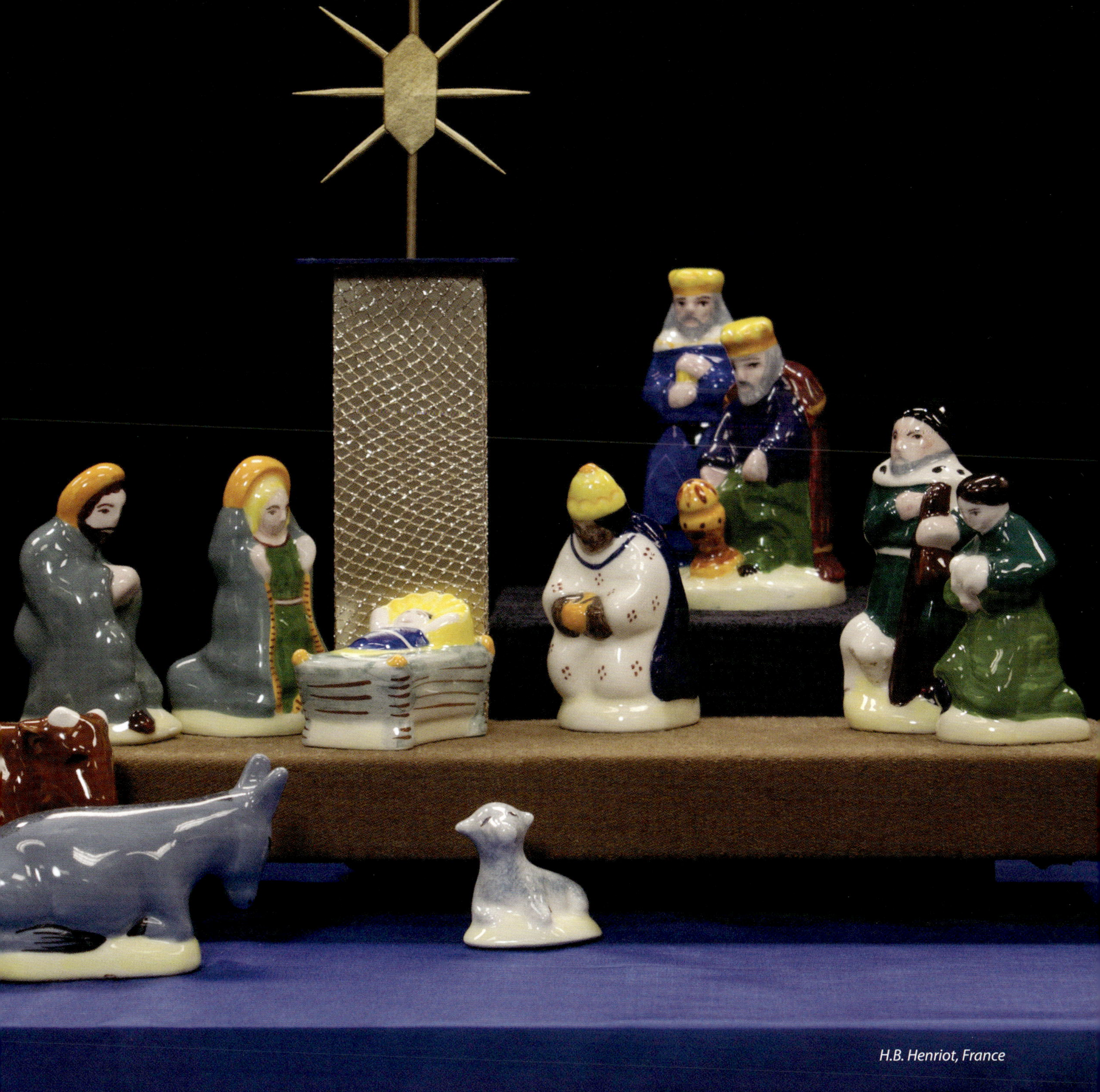

H.B. Henriot, France

The Hidden Charm of Auto Parts

There are times when child's delight and adult inventiveness dovetail and merge. It happened for this nativity set. We discover the adult determination to bring the Nativity into the present age and culture, where sheep are no longer sheep but auto parts. Armando Ramirez's rustic nativity also reflects the delightful playfulness of the child, bringing to life what the adult eye rejects as rubble and wreckage.

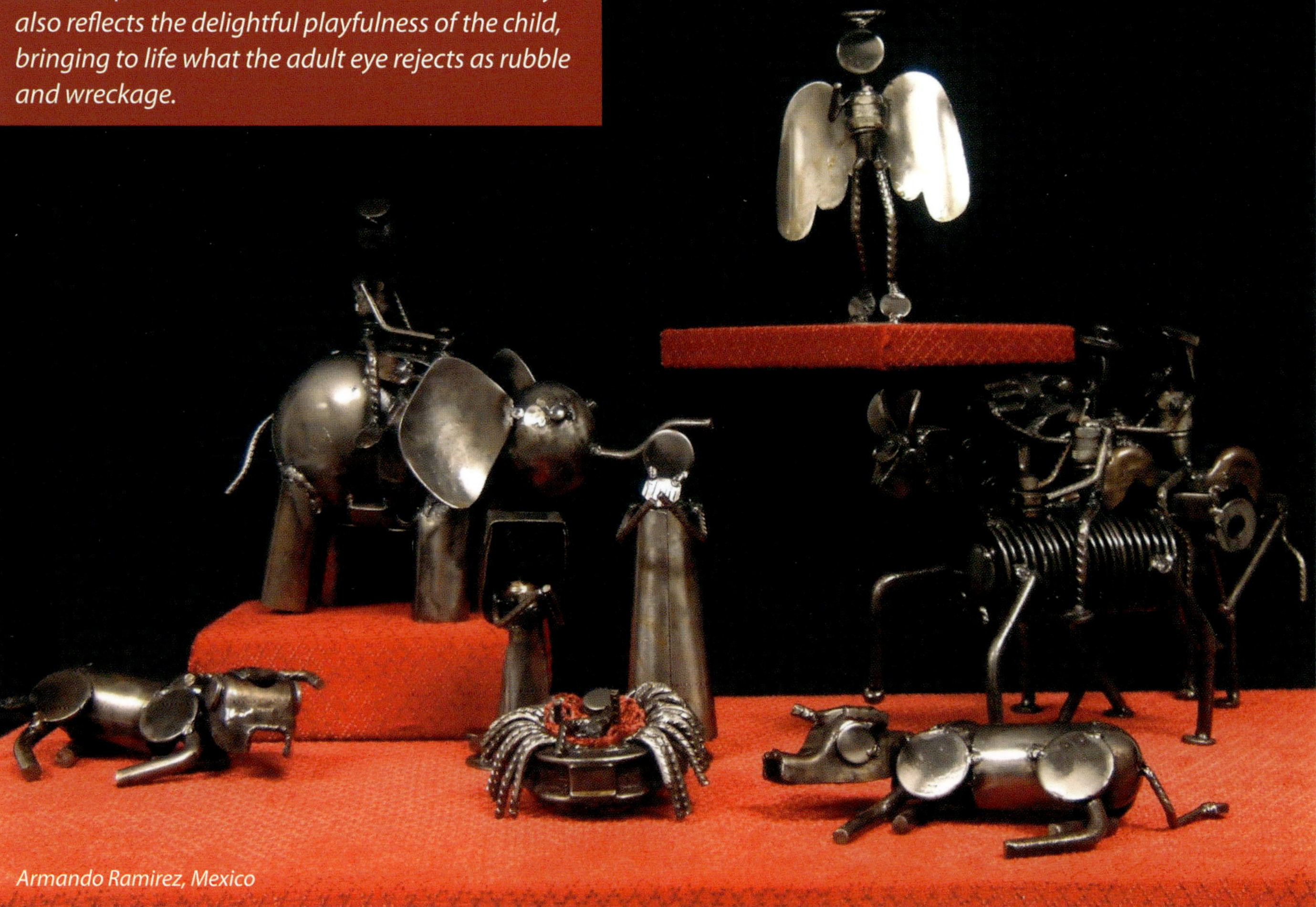

Armando Ramirez, Mexico

A Humble Abode

First in a cave, then in a stable, so tells us the pseudo-Matthew. Pious imagination did not stop at cave or stable. The humble abode becomes a palace, though in ruins, to symbolize the old and pre-Christian culture about to be replaced by Christianity, the new culture of life. The humble abode can also be a jar or gourd. Here as elsewhere in the Nativity tradition the local culture plays an important role. In Kyrgyzstan Jesus is born in a Kyrgyz yurt, in the Brazilian rainforest he is tucked in a hammock. Here are some examples.

Grotto

The Grotto or Cave is the earliest dwelling place of the Christchild. God conquers the world penetrating its very depth.

Szopka

The Church façade is the Cracovian understanding of the humble abode. It unites Christmas culture and Church liturgy.

Jar

The Jar is the Latin and Spanish version of the cave. The birth of Christ is brought home. He is part and parcel of everyday life, present among pots and pans.

Tent

Connecting Old and New Testament, the tent is a reminder of God's promise to Abraham, and of our own pilgrimage in faith. A typical dwelling of nomads all over the world, the tent comes in many forms and shapes.

Chalet

A typical habitat of alpine regions, the chalet is known wherever people are seeking a dwelling protected against flooding and rodents.

Adobe

The Adobe, or any form of habitat, keeps reminding that matter matters, the matter of a particular lieu, the stuff of everyday life. This is what the adobe is for the Pueblo Indians.

Stable

Best known to most lovers of the Nativity, the stable is witness to the rejection and poverty of Christ's birth.

Open House

The deeper meaning of Christ's first dwelling is its total openness on all sides: to grace from above and to people from all walks of life.

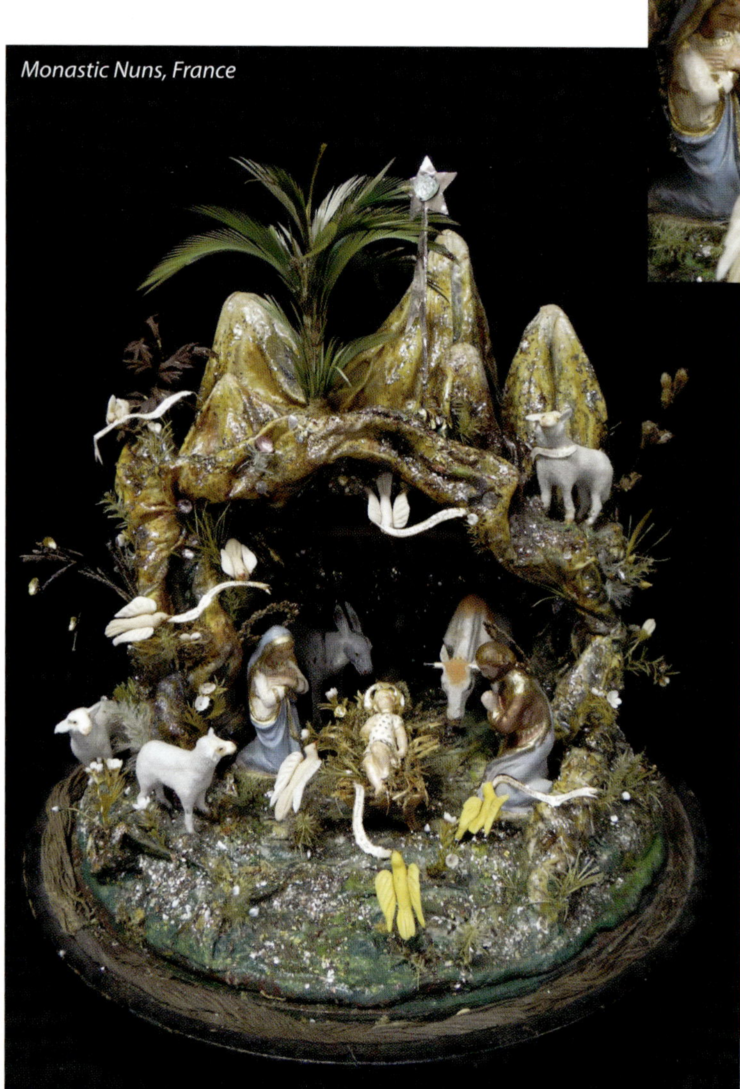

Monastic Nuns, France

Grotto

Monasteries have been for centuries a source of inspiration and support of the nativity tradition. The custom of "Rocking the Baby," Christmas carols such as "In Dulce Jubilo," and crèches of all forms and sizes had their origin in monasteries of nuns. Even now, monasteries of women enrich the crèche tradition with artful and original creations. The very delicate artifact on display here stems from this century-old custom. Created in the late 1800s, it has a very definite feminine touch. Flowers and stars, little birds holding phylacteries with calligraphed prayers, tender lambs and enraptured parents hail the newborn king in his star-strewn shirt. The Nativity grotto is carved into a mountain of papier-mâché. Its peaks and crevasses are sprinkled with glint and glitter glistening in colors of blue and gold.

Szopka

The characteristic feature of the Cracovian Christmas crib or Szopka is a fanciful blend of the Bethlehem miracle and the atmosphere and charm of Krakow's art and architecture. The meticulously detailed and imaginative church façade creates a setting fit for the presentation of the Nativity. Its origins can be traced to early 19th century wandering crib shows, which utilized puppetry to present Gospel stories interspersed with secular scenes. The shape of the Cracovian Christmas crib is tall, slender, multi-leveled, pinnacled, and reminiscent of the city's architecture. The richly ornamented structure is built with a variety of light-weight materials, namely tinfoil and cardboard. Traditionally, the Nativity is placed on the top floor, while below, a combination of biblical stories and Polish legends and history are displayed.

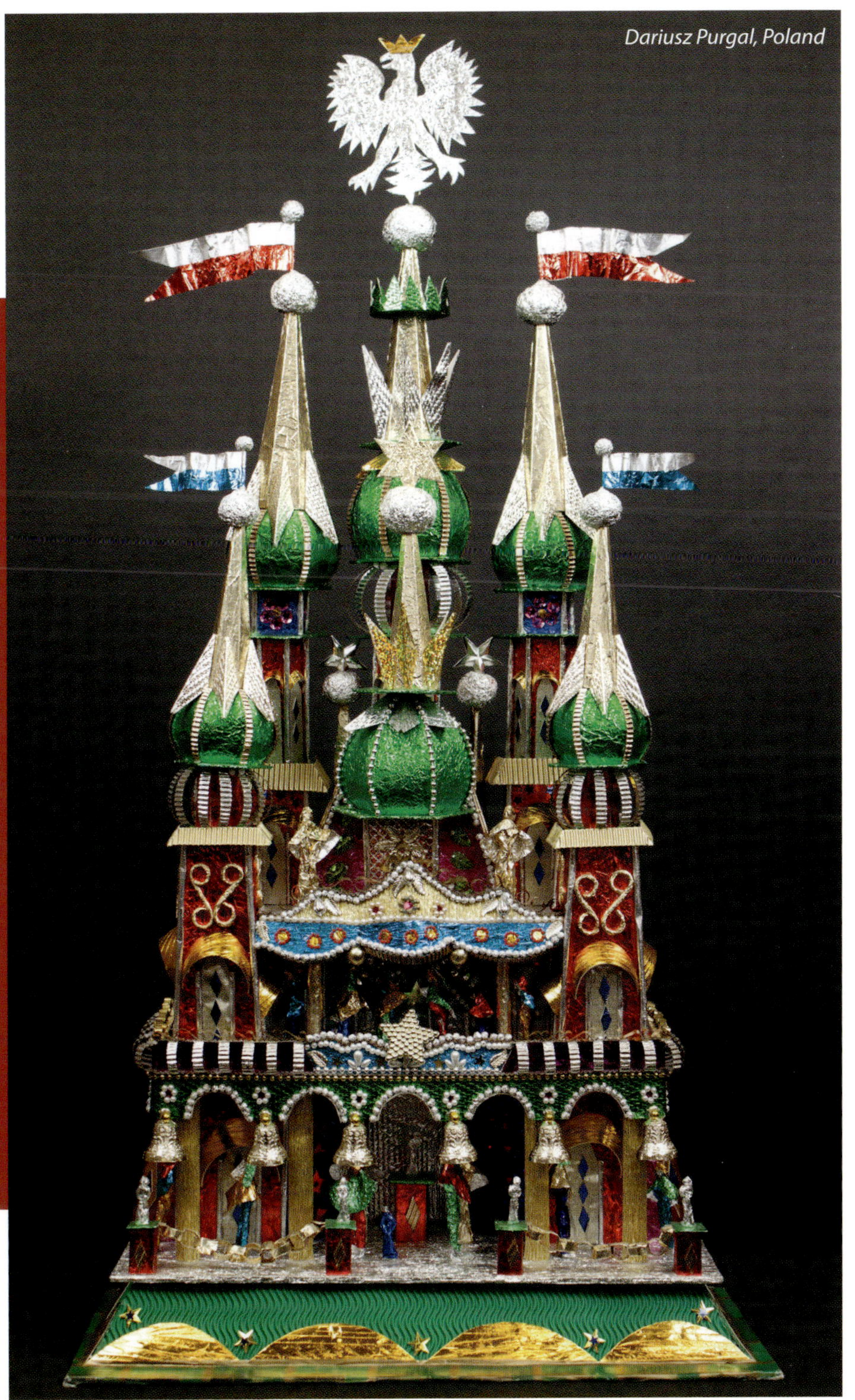

Dariusz Purgal, Poland

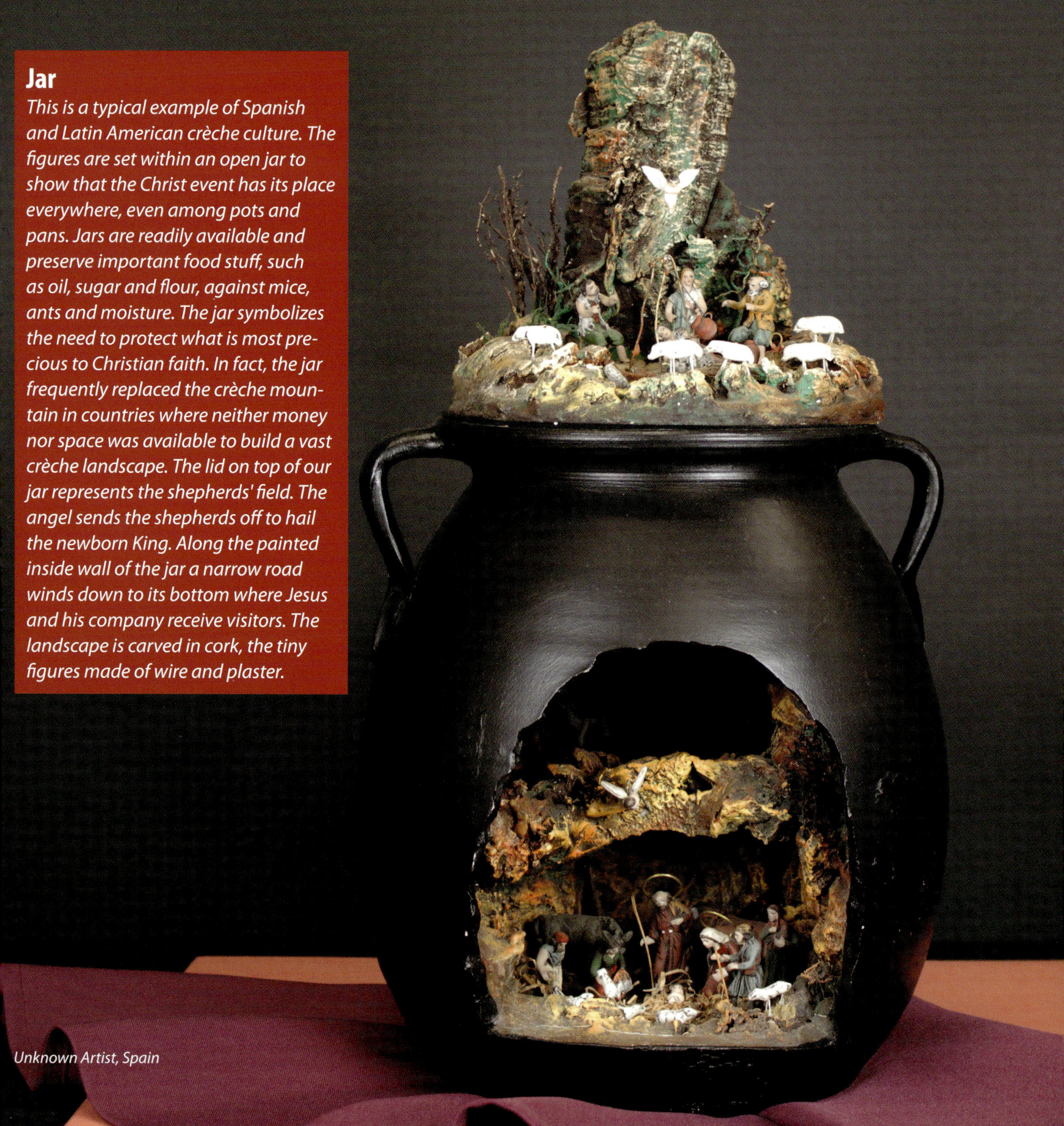

Jar

This is a typical example of Spanish and Latin American crèche culture. The figures are set within an open jar to show that the Christ event has its place everywhere, even among pots and pans. Jars are readily available and preserve important food stuff, such as oil, sugar and flour, against mice, ants and moisture. The jar symbolizes the need to protect what is most precious to Christian faith. In fact, the jar frequently replaced the crèche mountain in countries where neither money nor space was available to build a vast crèche landscape. The lid on top of our jar represents the shepherds' field. The angel sends the shepherds off to hail the newborn King. Along the painted inside wall of the jar a narrow road winds down to its bottom where Jesus and his company receive visitors. The landscape is carved in cork, the tiny figures made of wire and plaster.

Unknown Artist, Spain

Tent

Although designed in Switzerland, this set recreates a Bedouin scene, complete with a square, black tent and household goods. The intent is to show the intimate connection between God's promise and its fulfillment in Christ. Following Yahweh's call and promise, Abraham left his townhouse in Ur and lived in a tent. Ultimately, his journey of faith led to the announcement to Mary and the birth of Jesus. The tent is the symbol of this journey. God lives in a tent, even in churches of stone. He lives in the tent of history and its ever changing face. He lives in the fragile walls of our frequently shaky faith. The figures are left faceless, not to point out anonymity, but universality. We need to give the Christ event a face, our own face, and the face of all those of good will.

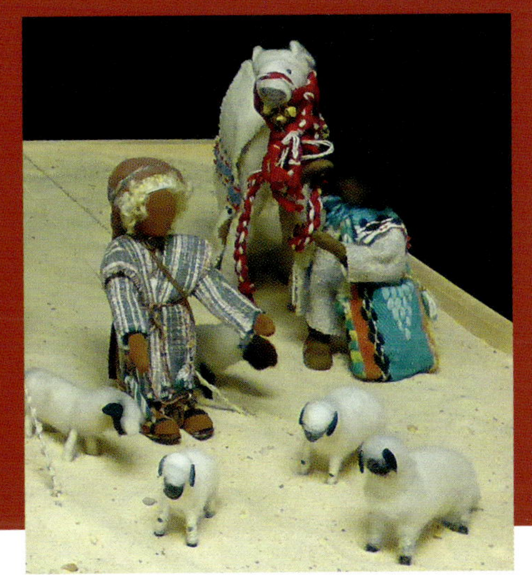

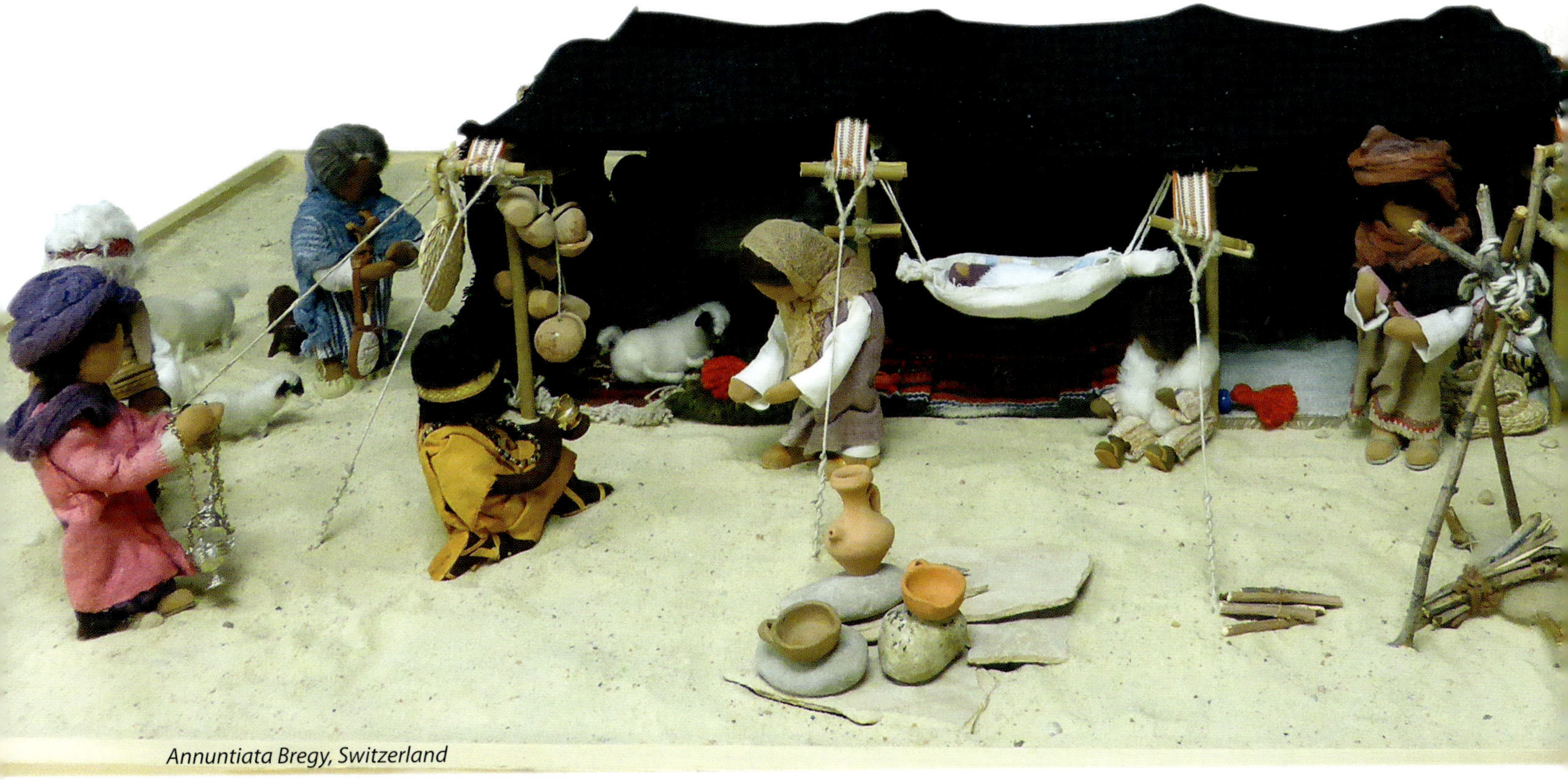

Annuntiata Bregy, Switzerland

Chalet

The central feature of this nativity is the typical habitat of the Alpine regions of Europe. The wooden constructions, burnt a deep brown or black by the sun, are covered with slabs of granite or wooden shingles. They are built on stilts topped by circular slabs of granite to prevent mice from penetrating homes and storage rooms. Similar constructions can be found in Northern Spain and countries of the Pacific rim. The chalets of this nativity are set in the barren landscape of the pre-Alps where grass and trees are sparse, but rocks, sheep, goats and old people, left behind, are many. The Holy Family finds refuge in a shelter used by shepherds and sheep. The birth of the Messiah needs to be proclaimed not only to cities and plains, but also from the mountain tops.

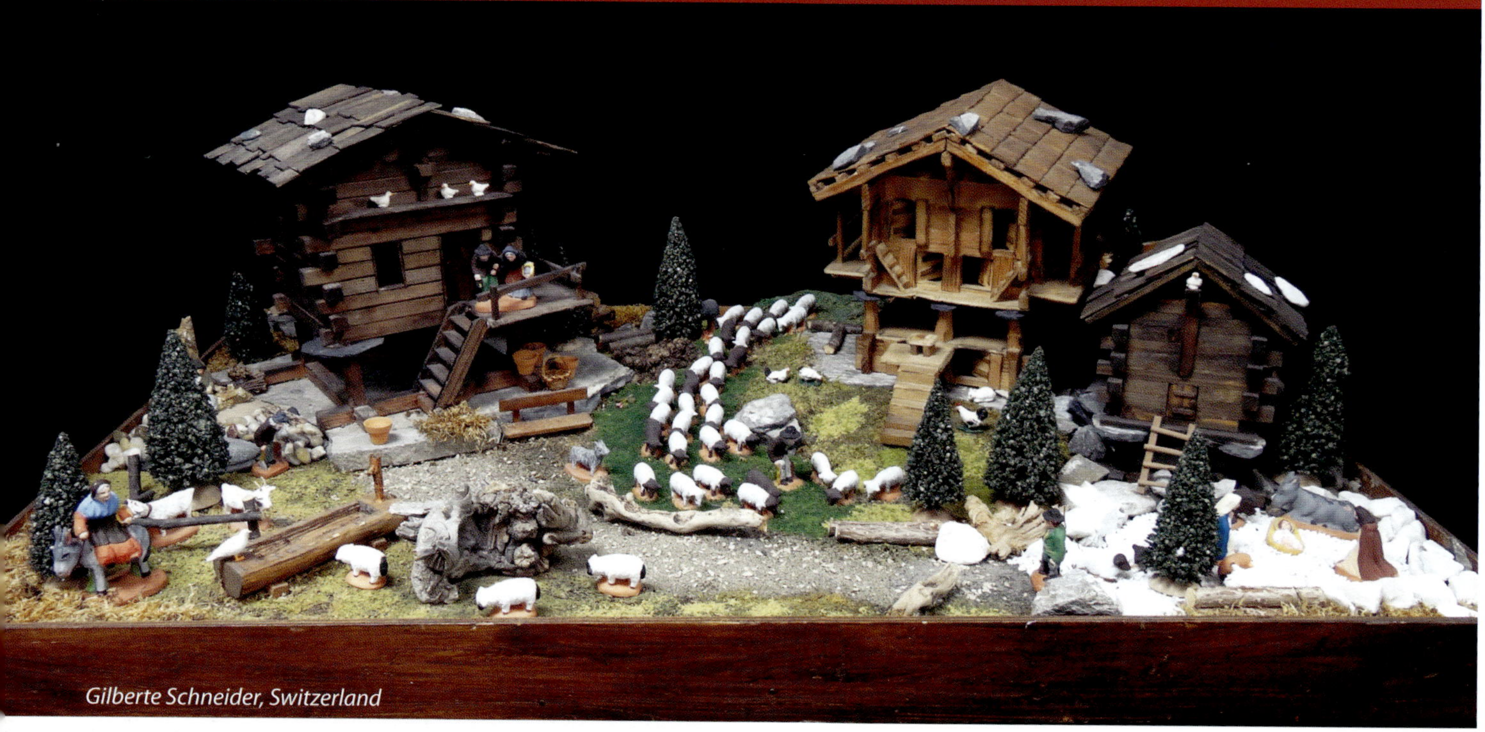

Gilberte Schneider, Switzerland

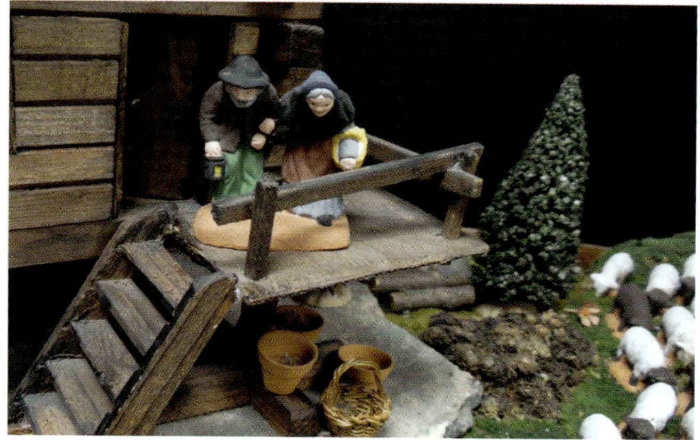

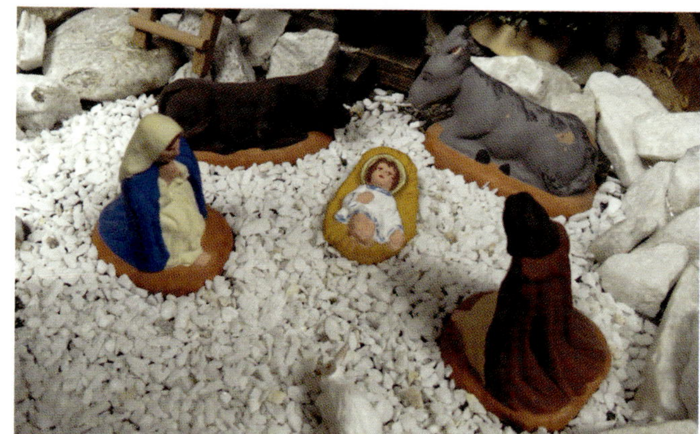

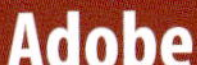

Adobe

The traditional house of Pueblo Indians is the adobe. The adobe is made of clay bricks which are sun-dried, sanded, painted, and fired—a process used by the Pueblo potters to make crèche figures. This set by Jemez artist, Robert Toledo, points to the merging of two cultures: the traditional nativity figures are joined by two rainbow dancers.

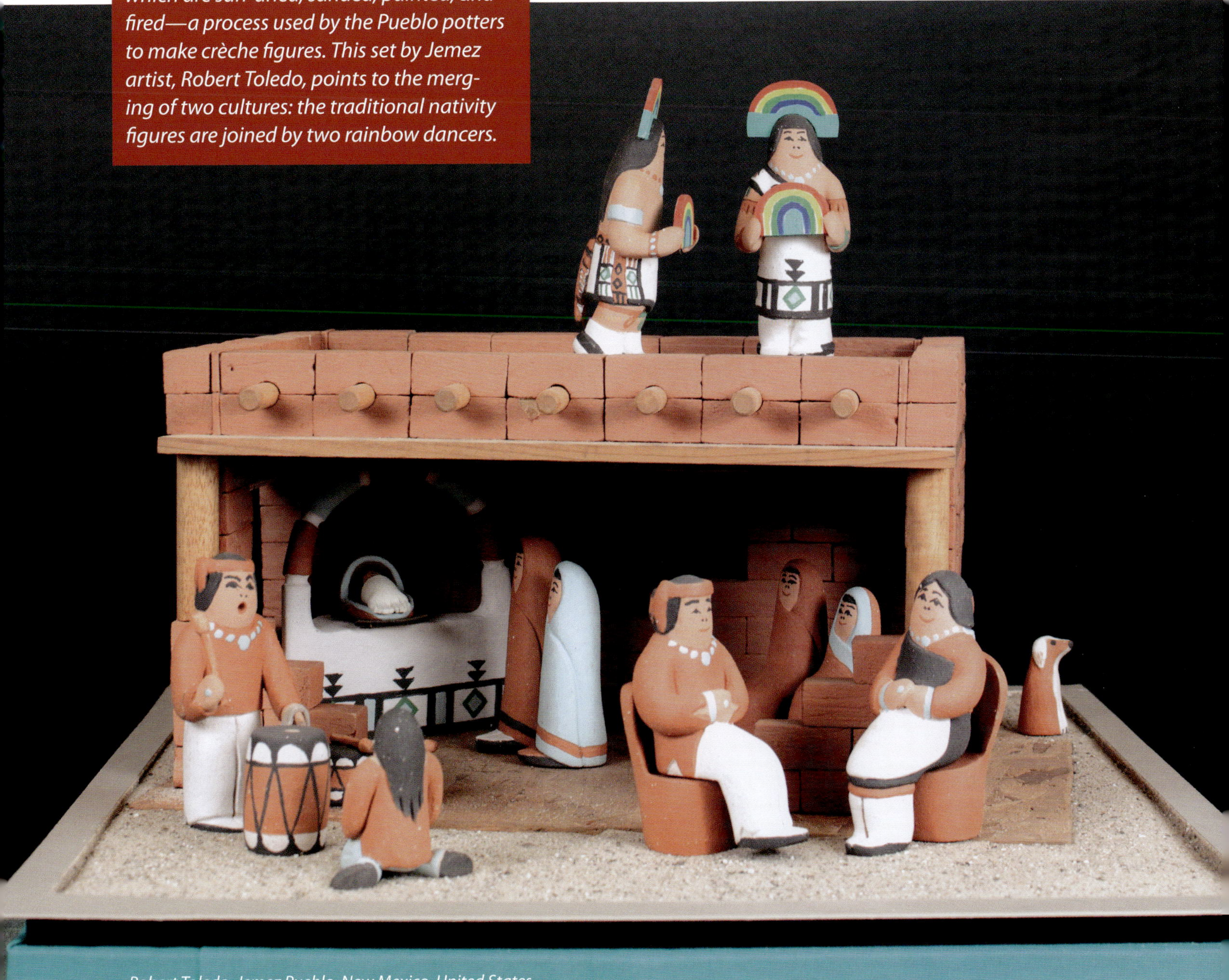

Robert Toledo, Jemez Pueblo, New Mexico, United States

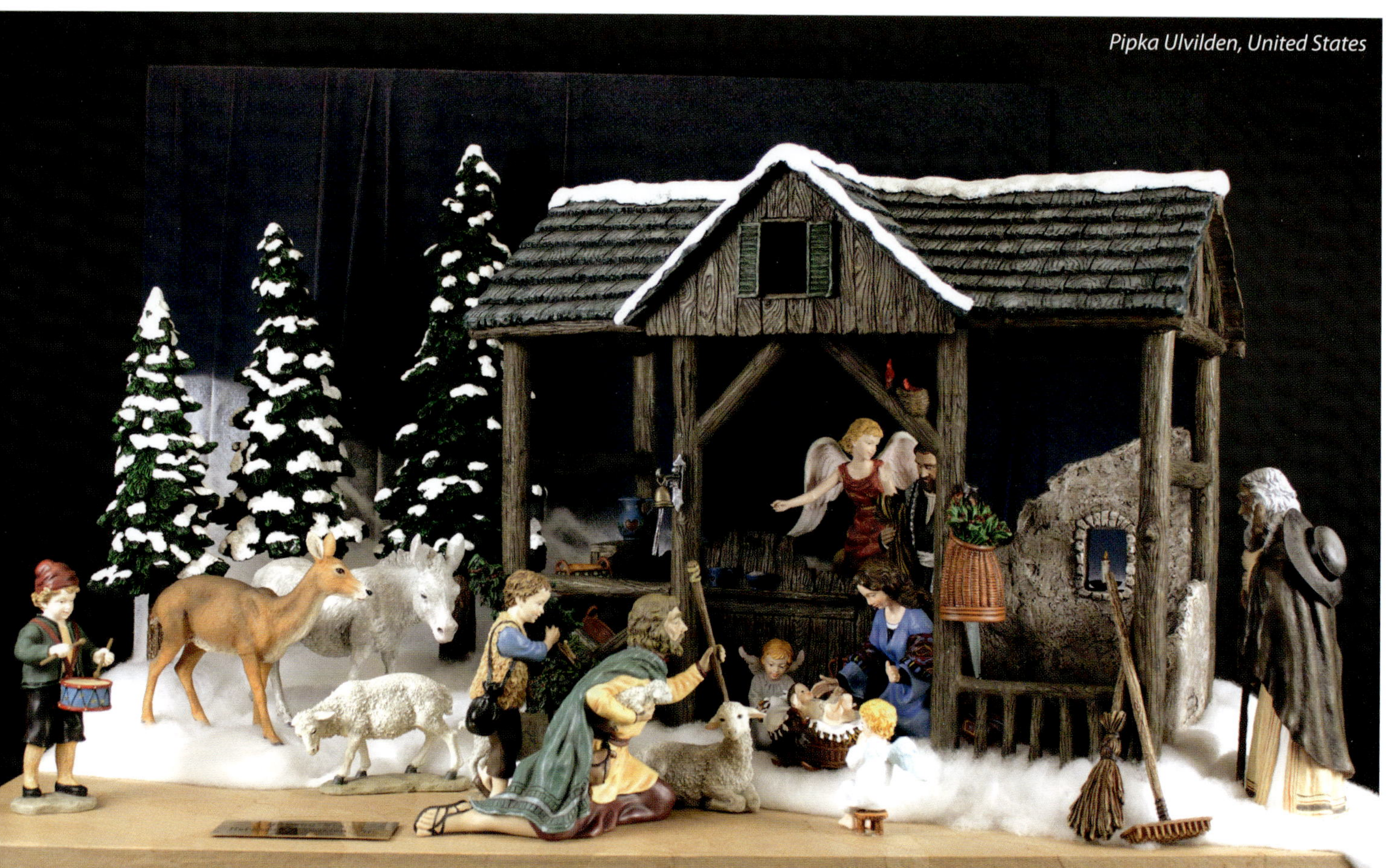

Pipka Ulvilden, United States

Stable

Pipka has created a nativity set which has all the ingredients of sentimental appeal and sweet memories. It suggests a white Christmas. There is the little drummer, the tender fawn and meek donkey, the boy with the lamb, and angels of all ages. The stable is sturdy and drafty, but it presents the essential comforts of home: pots and pans, candle, and house bell, even a wicker basket filled with flowers. Saint Joseph holds the customary lamp, the mother reflects the beauty of a Madonnina by Raphael. Not to forget the elegant flourish of the adult shepherd's sincere tribute to the baby. It all seems to be right; right as it should be, right as it was when we first experienced the Christmas event. First experiences have a lasting effect as they shape our expectations and mark our imagination. Retrieving and purifying them would seem like a salutary challenge.

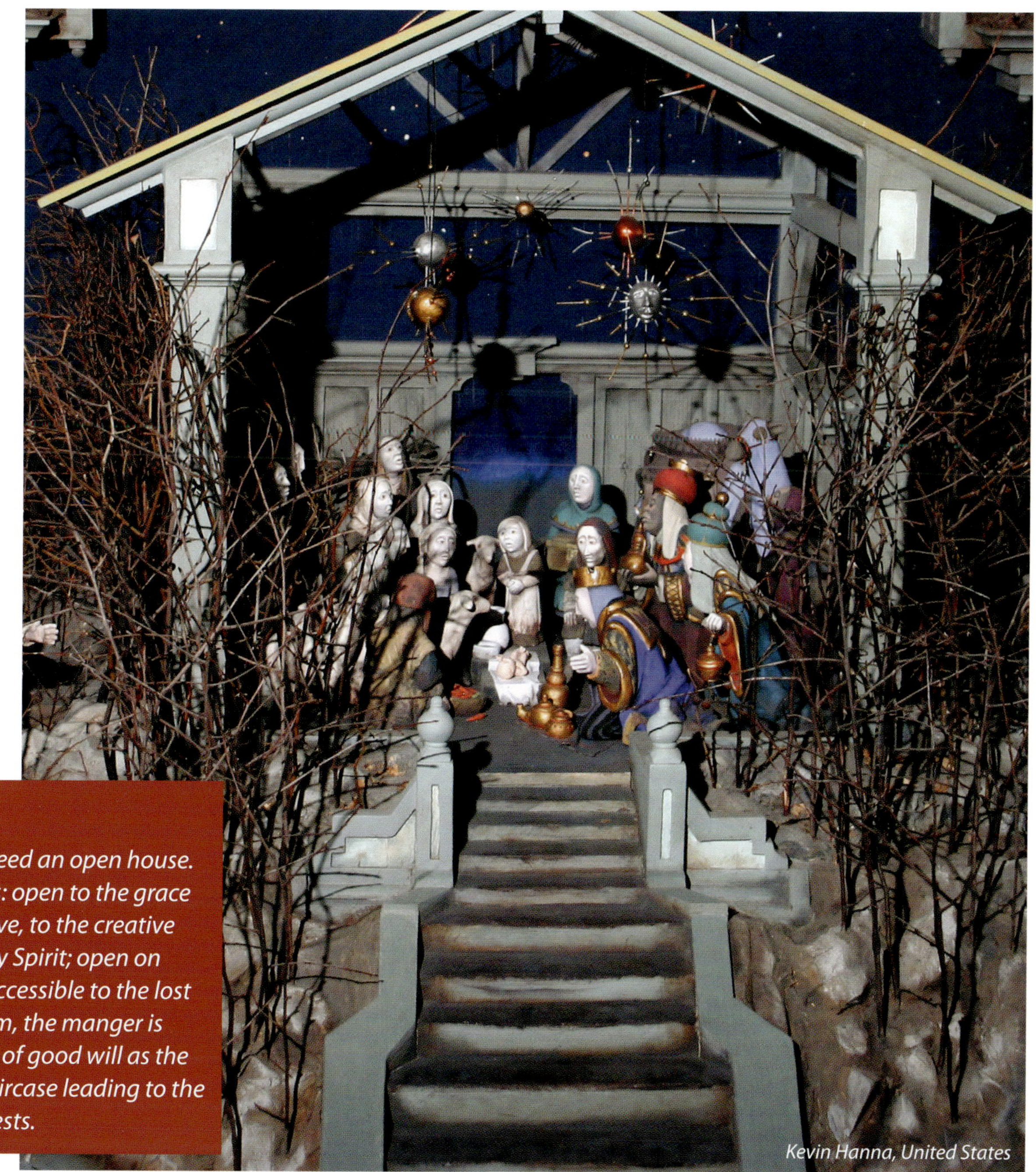

Kevin Hanna, United States

Open House

The crèche is indeed an open house. Open on all sides: open to the grace of God from above, to the creative power of the Holy Spirit; open on both sides and accessible to the lost and found. In sum, the manger is open to all those of good will as the monumental staircase leading to the Christchild suggests.

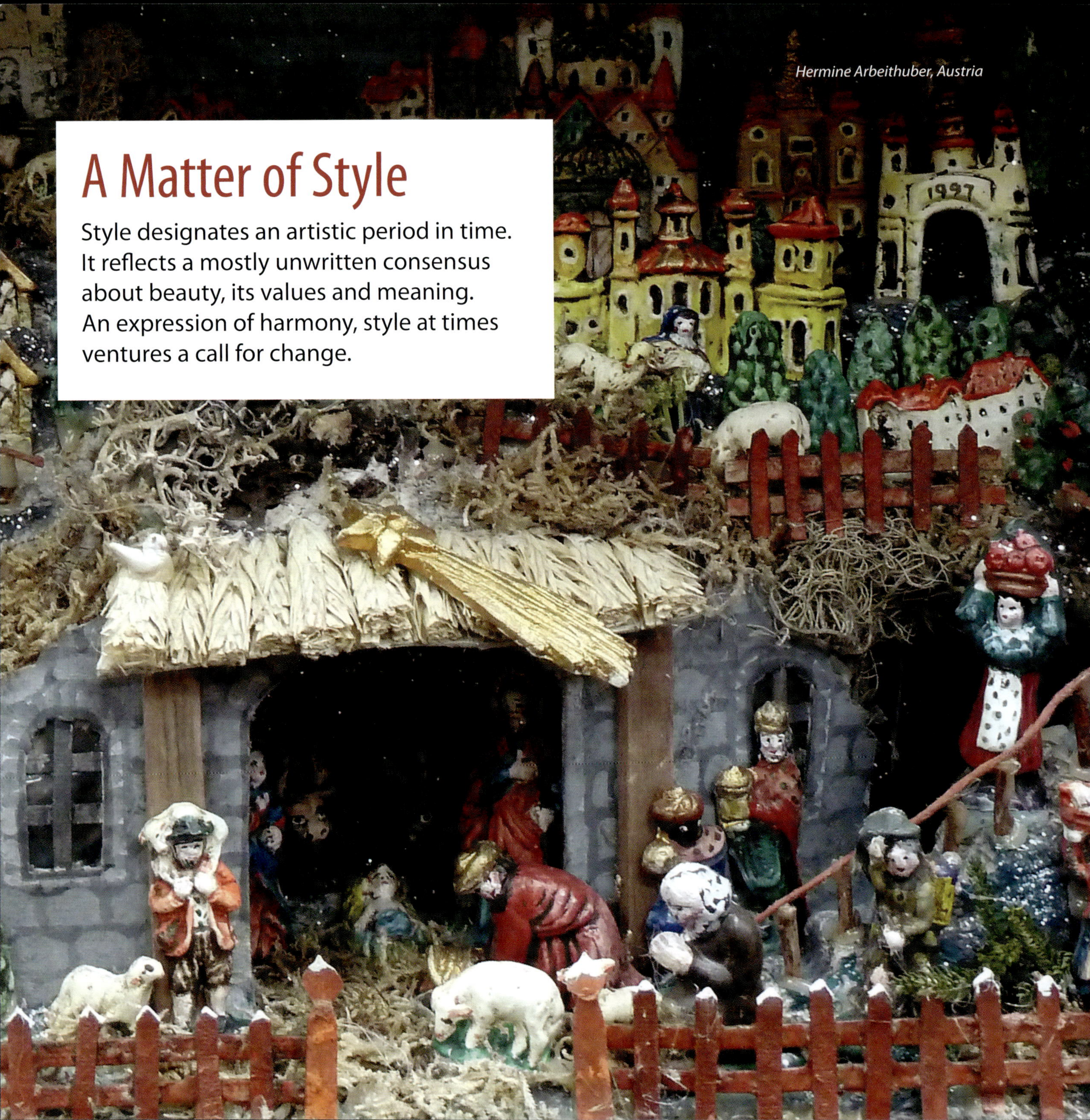

Hermine Arbeithuber, Austria

A Matter of Style

Style designates an artistic period in time. It reflects a mostly unwritten consensus about beauty, its values and meaning. An expression of harmony, style at times ventures a call for change.

Romanesque Style
Peasant Gothic
Northern Renaissance
Rococo of the Poor
Orientalist Art
A Contemporary Look

A Matter of Style

Art history is a matter of styles. Styles designate a period and reflect a collective mood on how to label beauty and its expression. Contemporary crèche culture reaches out and embraces a number of styles, many of them inspired by a special tradition, commercial interests, or a generic cultural atmosphere or feeling. Among the latter we count a certain trivialization of the crèche with its baby faced figures and animal nativities. Special traditions, too, seem to migrate. We find copies of the Provençal style in Brittany, Alsatia, and Quebec. The commercial interest has impacted some of the Latin American styles catering to the taste of their neighbors in the Northern half of the hemisphere.

There is a different, a more artistic sensitivity borrowing into some of the great traditions of the past.

Romanesque Style

The Romanesque style, humble and hieratic, elicits a meditative reverence and a sense of endearing beauty.

Peasant Gothic

Peasant Gothic style endeavors the artistic revival of an endearing and simplified version of Gothic symbolism and symmetry.

Northern Renaissance

Northern Renaissance with its colorful peasant look and worn but soulful faces ambitions to recreate human drama in a Northern style, the replica of a Neapolitan crèche.

Rococo of the Poor

A name attached to the crèche culture of Grulich in Eastern Moravia (Czech Republic), these crèche figures are a curious mixture of Rococo sophistication and sturdy peasant art.

Orientalist Art

Reminiscing the beginning of Christianity in the Holy Land, religious art of the second half of the 19th century attempts to revive life and culture of the time of Jesus, and becomes Orientalist art.

A Contemporary Look

Giving new actuality to the crèche culture, artisans and artists resort to wrapping figures in a contemporary look.

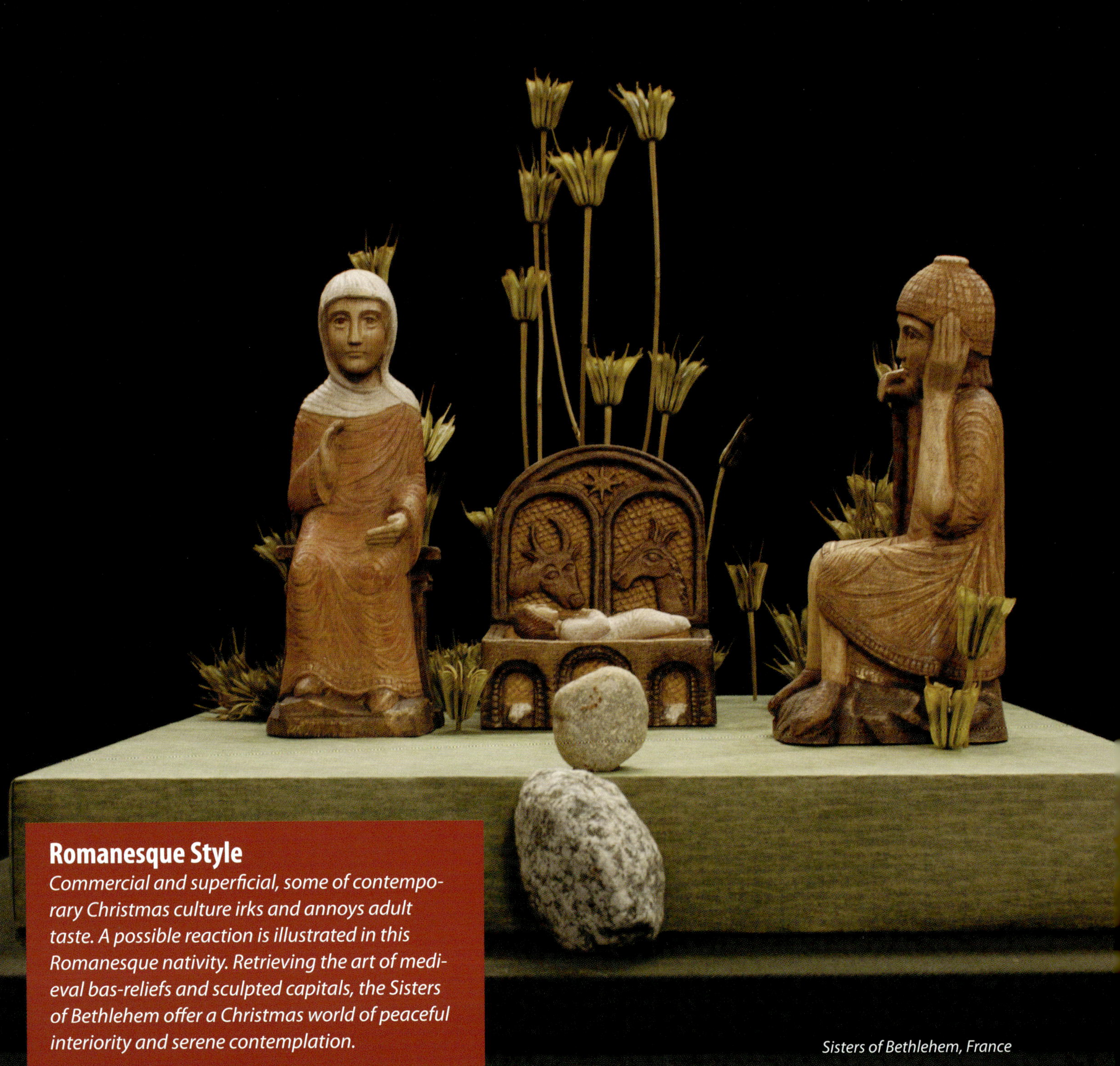

Romanesque Style

Commercial and superficial, some of contemporary Christmas culture irks and annoys adult taste. A possible reaction is illustrated in this Romanesque nativity. Retrieving the art of medieval bas-reliefs and sculpted capitals, the Sisters of Bethlehem offer a Christmas world of peaceful interiority and serene contemplation.

Sisters of Bethlehem, France

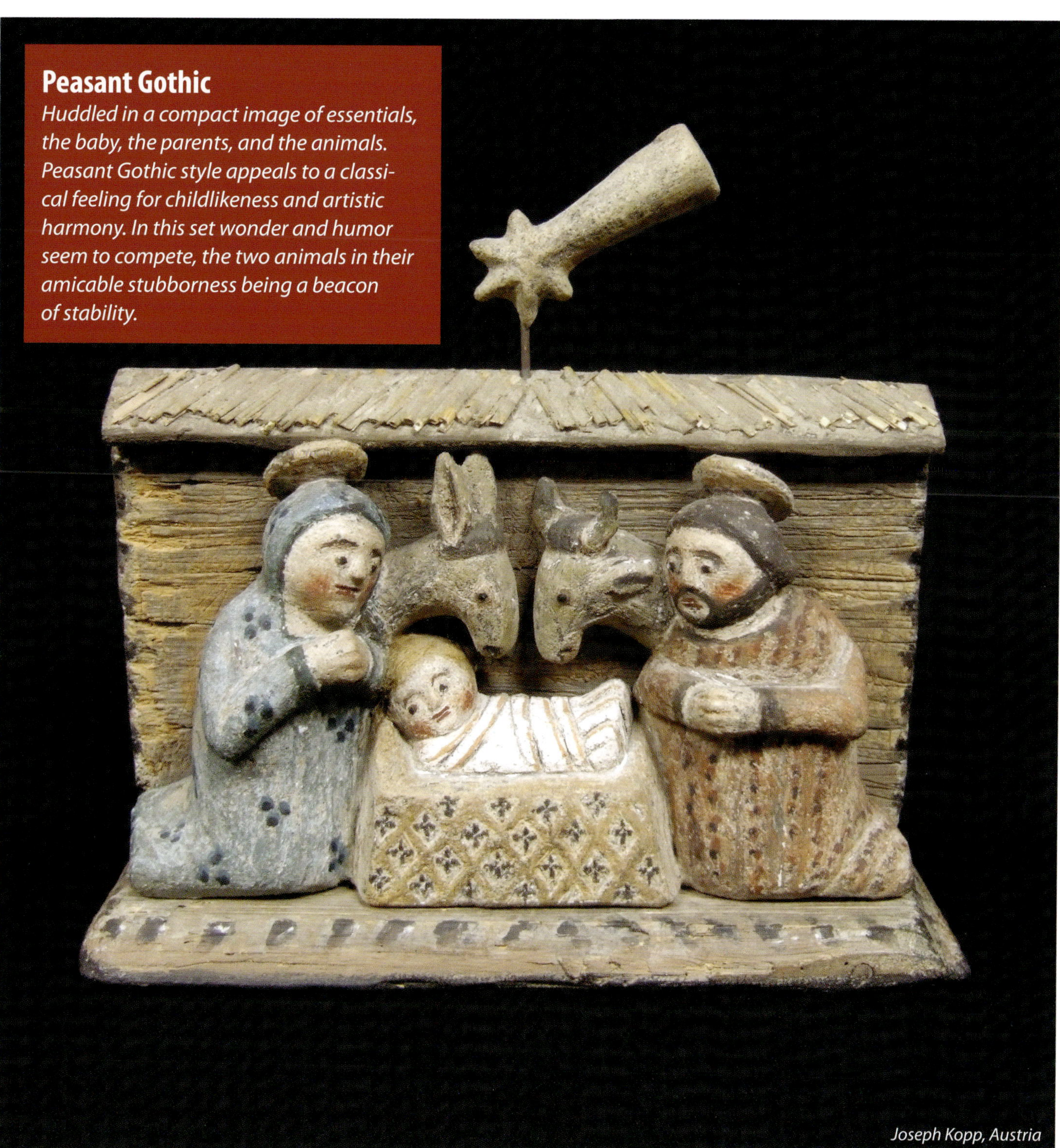

Peasant Gothic

Huddled in a compact image of essentials, the baby, the parents, and the animals. Peasant Gothic style appeals to a classical feeling for childlikeness and artistic harmony. In this set wonder and humor seem to compete, the two animals in their amicable stubborness being a beacon of stability.

Joseph Kopp, Austria

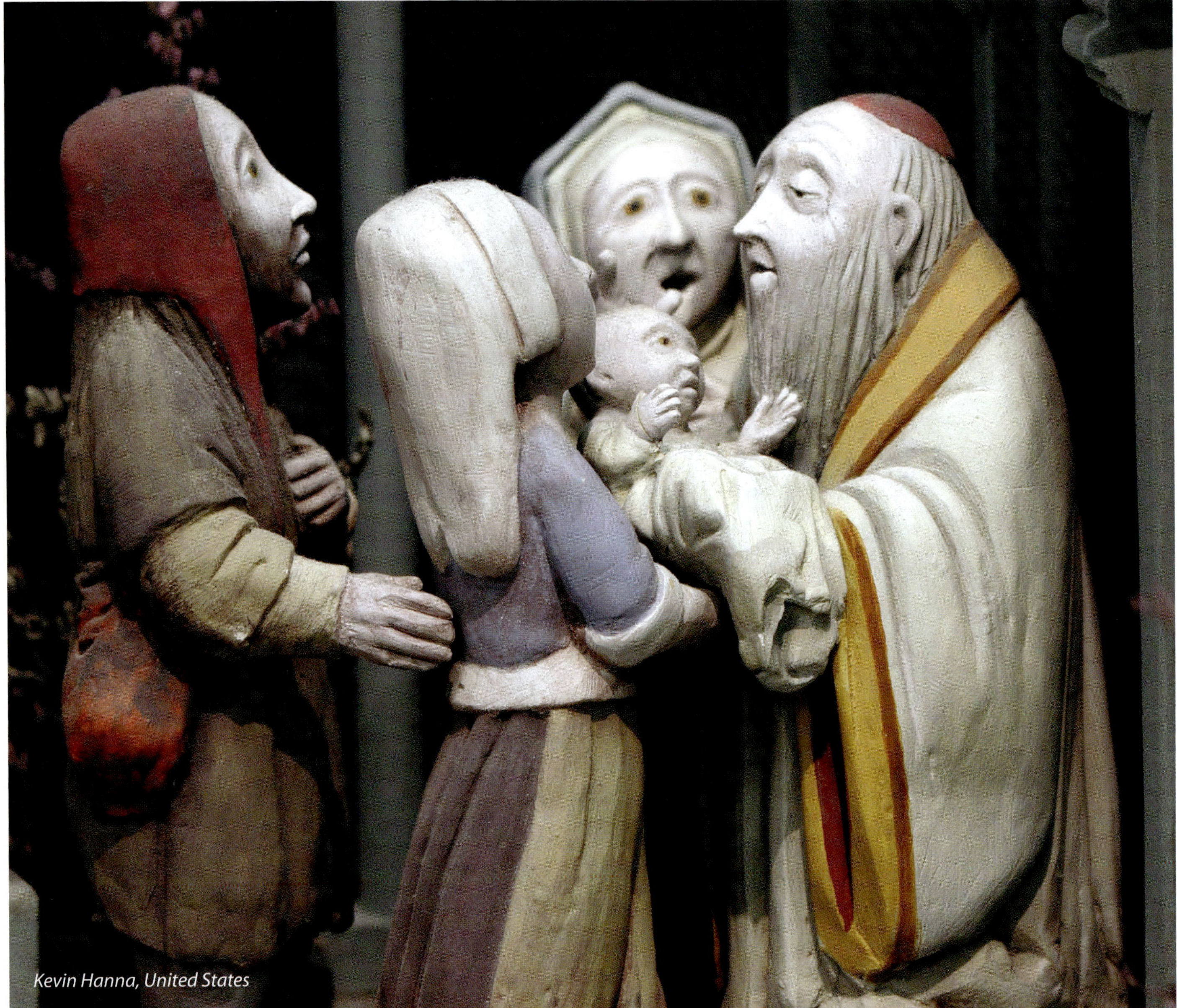

Kevin Hanna, United States

Northern Renaissance

A detail of the "Mirror of Hope" by Kevin Hanna, the Presentation in the Temple remembers the encounter between the Holy Family and the two prophets, Simeon and Anna. The four adults are gathered around a somewhat disoriented baby. Mary and Joseph are pictured in peasant dress typical of Northern Renaissance art. Simeon and Mary form the center of the group. Joseph keeps a respectful distance, while Anna has the inspired look of an age-old Roman sybil. Helplessly extending his little hands, Jesus Christ espouses the whole of human reality, except sin.

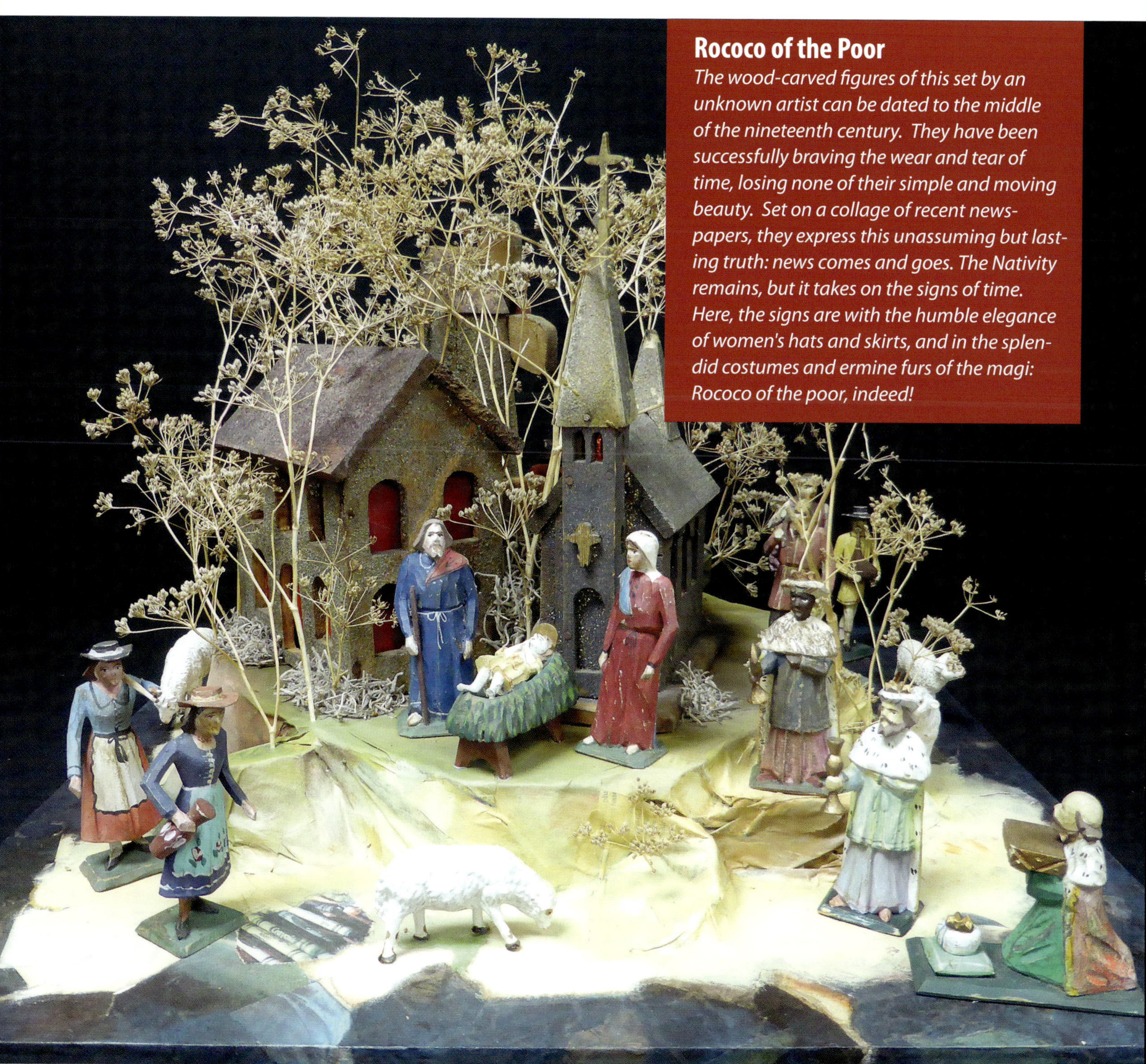

Rococo of the Poor

The wood-carved figures of this set by an unknown artist can be dated to the middle of the nineteenth century. They have been successfully braving the wear and tear of time, losing none of their simple and moving beauty. Set on a collage of recent newspapers, they express this unassuming but lasting truth: news comes and goes. The Nativity remains, but it takes on the signs of time. Here, the signs are with the humble elegance of women's hats and skirts, and in the splendid costumes and ermine furs of the magi: Rococo of the poor, indeed!

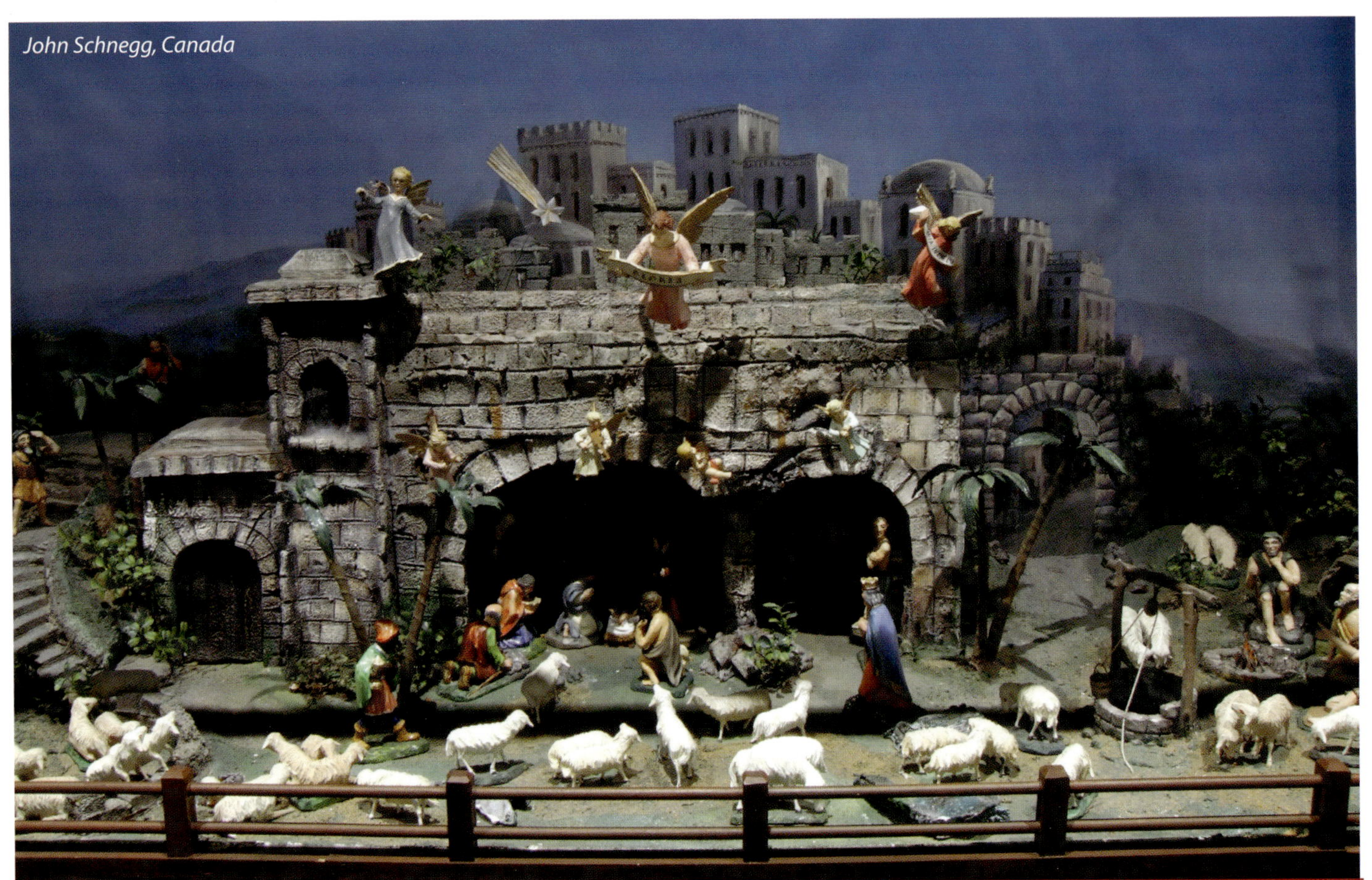
John Schnegg, Canada

Orientalist Art

The style of this crèche follows the so-called Orientalist style, an attempt to reconstruct the Nativity "as it was in the beginning." This tradition, initiated by Austrian artists at the turn of the 19th century, use "oriental" (mid-Eastern) architecture, dress, and other ethnic characteristics. These elements are mixed in with typically Austrian features, in particular the elaborate setting and the painted landscape of the Holy Land.

A Contemporary Look

Joseph wears a denim jacket and Mary's robe and veil appear to be of similar fabric. Did the holy couple finally give in to popular taste and contemporary fashion? Rose-Anne's teachers, it is said, were the humble, anonymous and yet peerless sculptors of the 11th and 12th centuries. Her artistic sense and human experience were marked by the architects and artists of Romanesque churches and cloisters. This is manifest not only in the reclined posture of the mother, but foremost in the simple of the figurines, and in the peaceful spiritual atmosphere they convey.

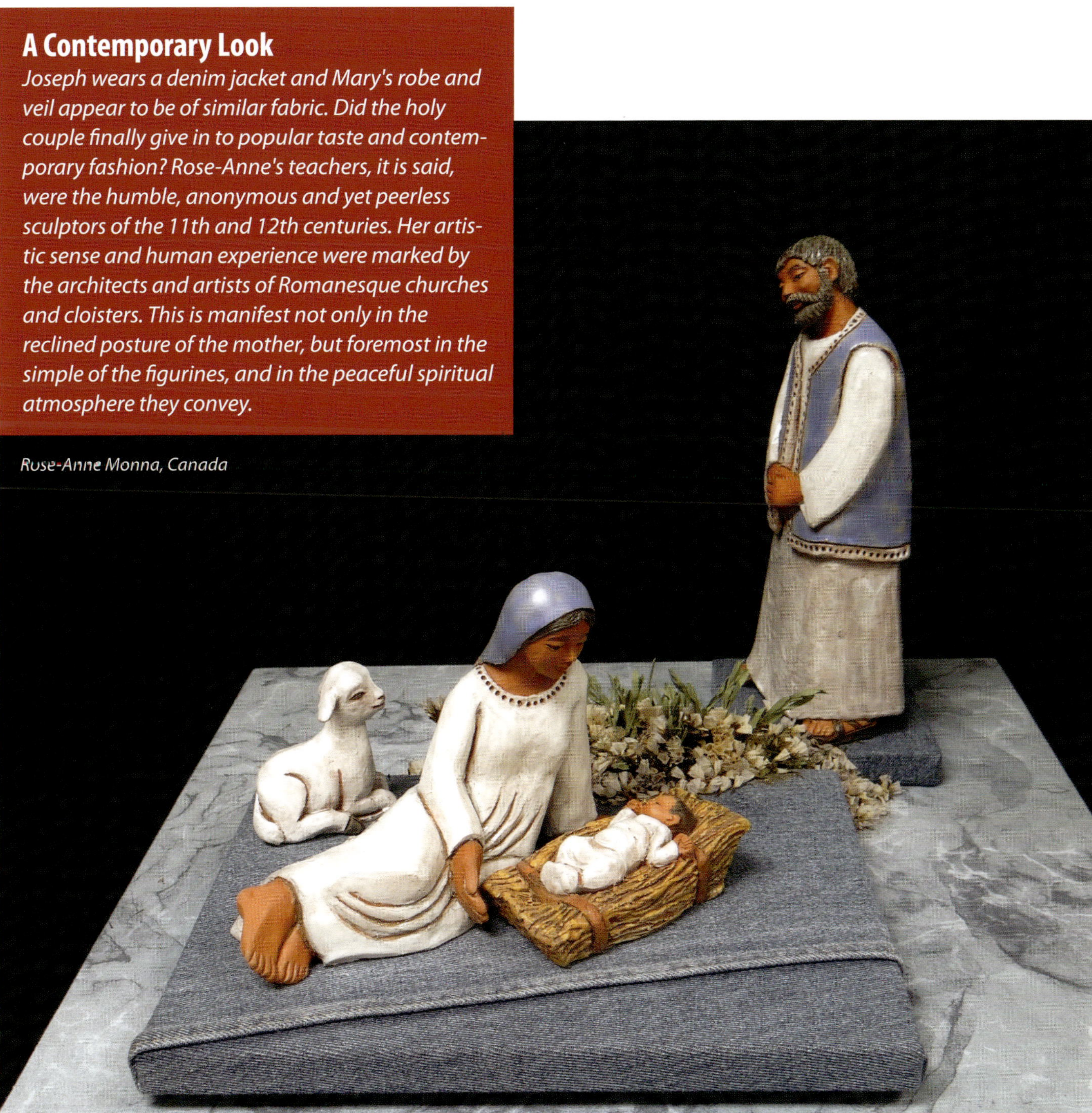

Rose-Anne Monna, Canada

A Portable Feast

There exists a traveling Nativity, a long-standing tradition which originated with various forms of nomadism. Nobility traveling from castle to castle, peasants moving from mountain to plain and back at the mercy of nature and seasons, but also the traveler of the long haul, pilgrims and warriors. They all had in their baggage the occasional portable nativity set. Different types of portable nativity sets developed.

The One-Piece Nativity

Mostly sculpted or in clay the set represents a limited number of figures, ordinarily the Holy Family.

The Nativity Niche

A more elaborate and typically Latin American portable Nativity is the *Nicho*, a colorfully decorated box containing highly imaginative and artful representations of the Nativity.

The Box Nativity

The German tradition has a similar type of portable Nativity. As the liturgical year progresses, the box housing the Nativity may feature a different scene, for example, that of the Crucifixion.

The Nativity Altar

A one-piece Nativity of many and symmetrically ordered figures on three different levels, the Portuguese Nativity tradition seems to have been influenced by the idea of altars erected for religious processions.

The Miniature Nativity

From the nutshell to the miniature clay church hiding a minuscule nativity set, there are countless ways to press the Nativity into reduced and portable space.

The One-Piece Nativity

At first glance, this set of artificial stone gives the impression of a Pop and Mom Crèche. Mary and Joseph radiate the well-fed happiness of people at ease with themselves and the world. Indeed, for some German cultures, physical plentiness is a sure promise of bliss. This holy couple seems happy to present their Child-Savior to the world. Mary's posture, although mama rather than queen, is that of the enthroned Madonna. The figure of Joseph suggests both physical support and a proud husband. His generous stature complements and contrasts the sturdy laurel to Mary's right. Its dense foliage covers mother and child ike a victor's crown.

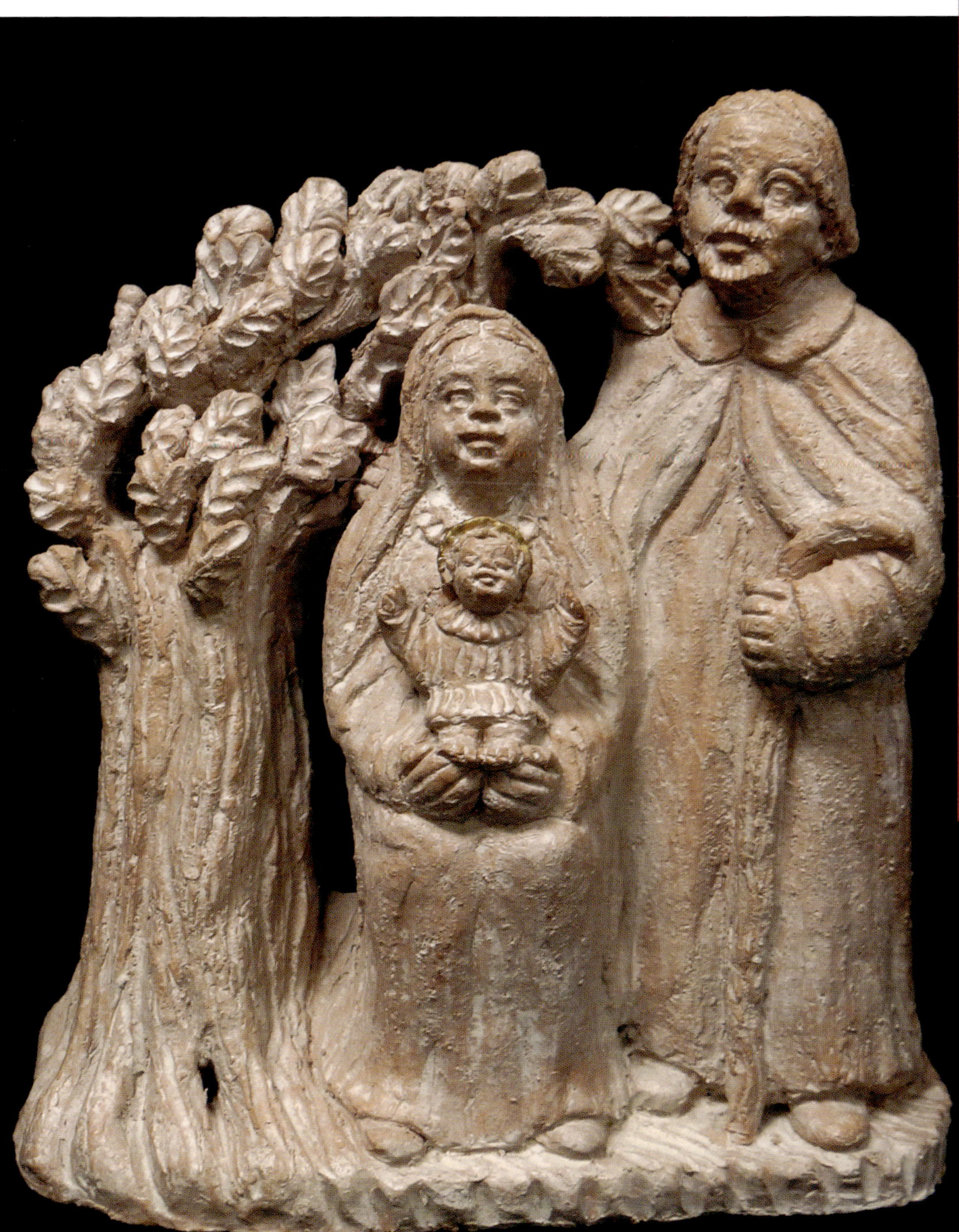

Hermine Arbeithuber, Austria

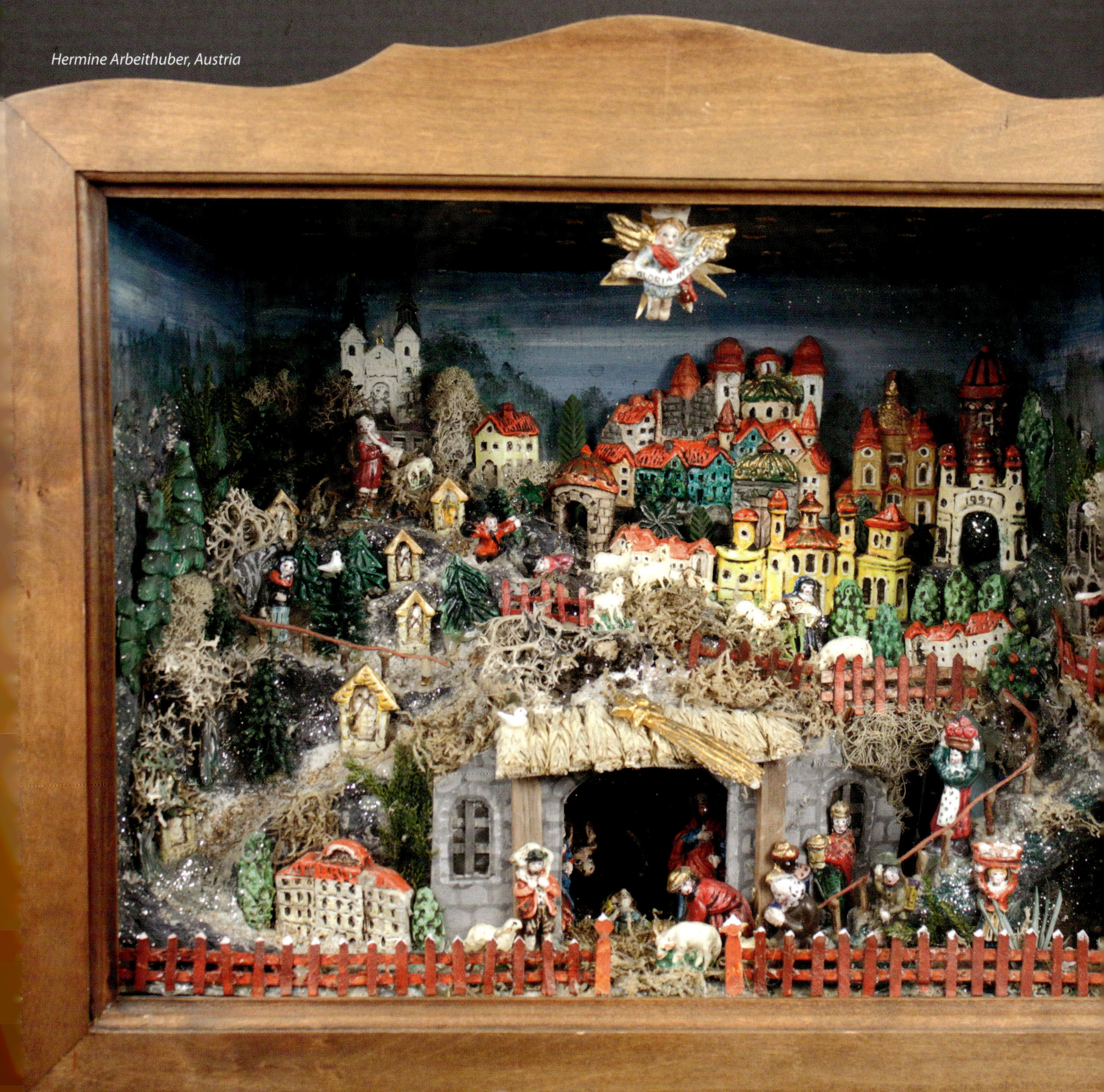

Hermine Arbeithuber, Austria

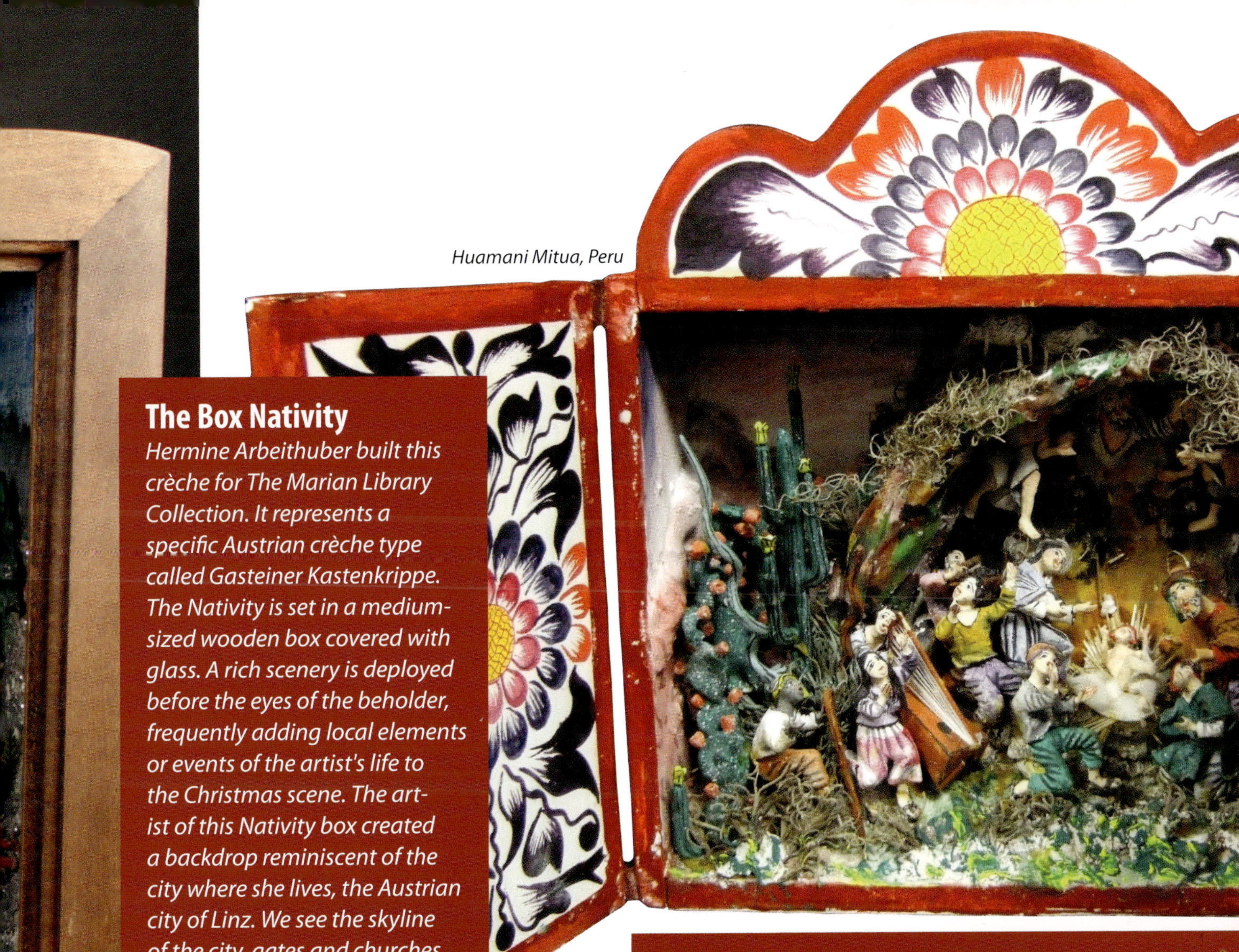

Huamani Mitua, Peru

The Box Nativity

Hermine Arbeithuber built this crèche for The Marian Library Collection. It represents a specific Austrian crèche type called Gasteiner Kastenkrippe. The Nativity is set in a medium-sized wooden box covered with glass. A rich scenery is deployed before the eyes of the beholder, frequently adding local elements or events of the artist's life to the Christmas scene. The artist of this Nativity box created a backdrop reminiscent of the city where she lives, the Austrian city of Linz. We see the skyline of the city, gates and churches, in particular the famous Marian sanctuary of Pöstlingberg. The pilgrim's path leading to the sanctuary is marked with the Stations of the Cross.

The Nativity Niche

Still another of the many Peruvian representations of the Nativity comes in a painted box with doors. Open during the Season and on feastdays, it is meant to be a traveling companion for people who need a portable altar. The expression of this Nativity reenactment in painted plaster is one of pure bliss. A sea of hands is raised in praise of the Messiah, and musical instruments like harp, violin and castañet join in the joyous chorus. The baby with the red cap takes part in the general excitement, and even heaven has opened the curtain to become part of this portable bliss.

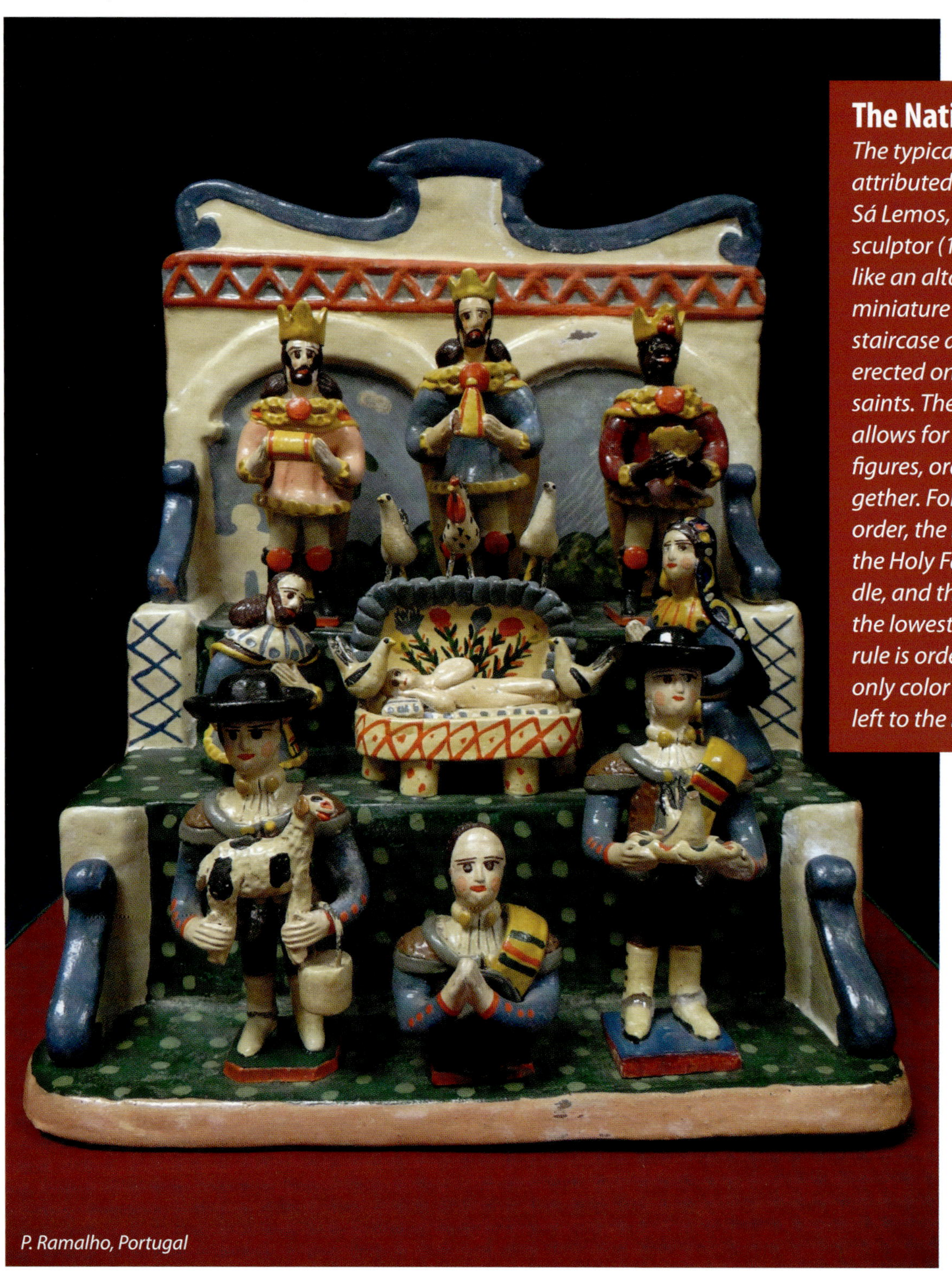

P. Ramalho, Portugal

The Nativity Altar

The typical Estremoz Nativity attributed to José Maria de Sá Lemos, noted Portuguese sculptor (1892-1971), is built like an altar or shrine. It is a miniature version of the large staircase altars or thrones erected on festivals of popular saints. The three-tiered altar allows for a limited number of figures, ordinarily nine altogether. Following a traditional order, the kings are at the top, the Holy Family is in the middle, and the shepherds are on the lowest level. The golden rule is order and symmetry; only color and costumes are left to the imagination.

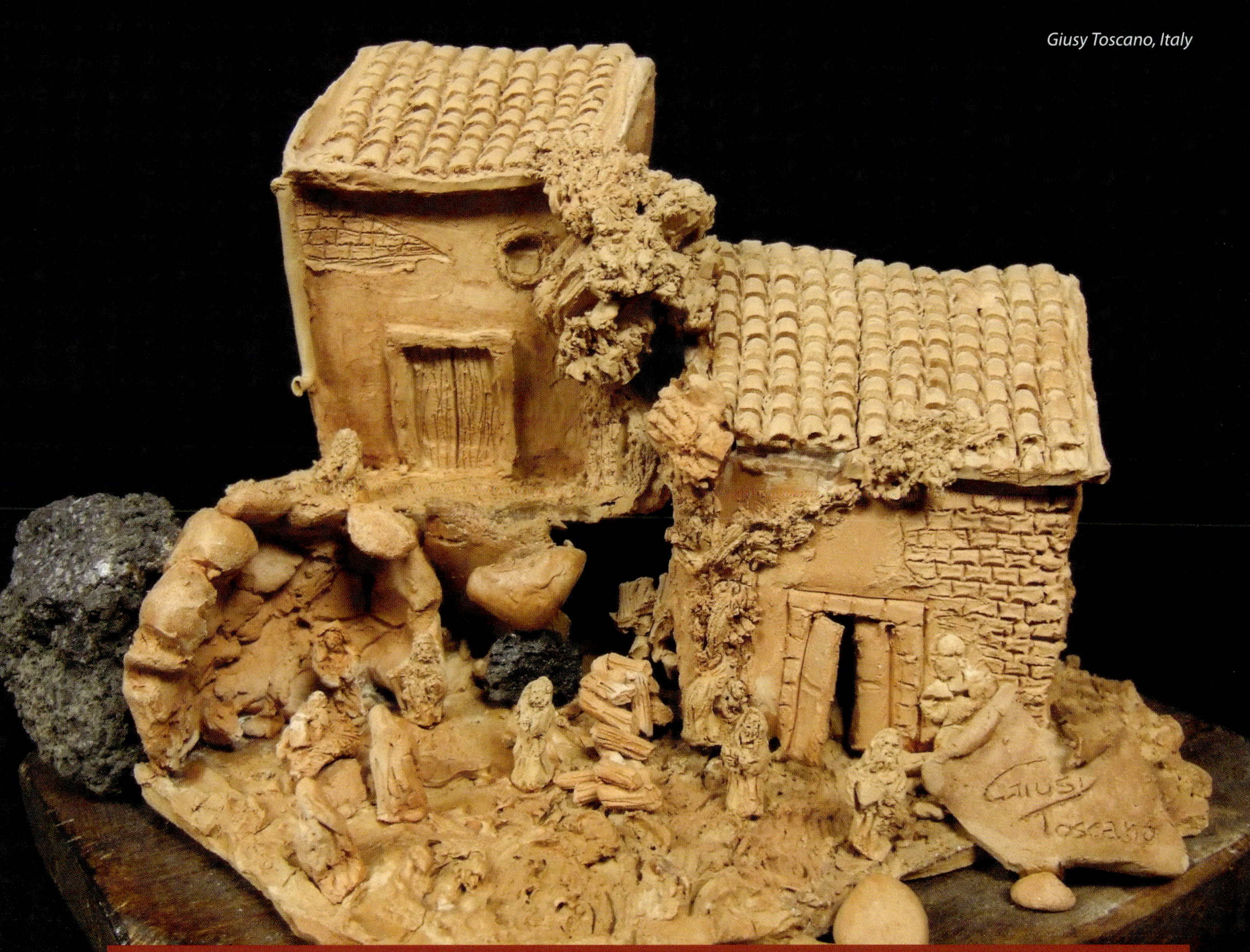

Giusy Toscano, Italy

The Miniature Nativity

Giusy Toscano lives in Rome but is Sicilian of origin. The village of her family lies at the foot of Mount Aetna. Lava, the typical rock of the region is part of Giusy's geographical heritage. The house of her parents is built on ancient rocks of lava. Thus, lava reminds Giusy of home. On her visits to her native Sicily she would take pieces of lava back to Rome and incorporate them into her artwork. The little village in this set is a tribute to home and family. It rests on a rock of lava and remains ensconced in nature. Indeed, the litle crèche figures only painfully extract themselves from the mass of clay. The Holy Family in the cave to the left shares the lot of the many.

Nativity Abstract

Has abstract art entered the Nativity tradition? Abstract art is minimalist art; it reduces elements of design which may be a distraction from what the artist considers central and essential. Following a trend to return to sober and simple forms of expression, abstract art has indeed entered the world of the nativity sets. A reaction in part against Baroque opulence, the new, and specifically European style comes with an artistic, and sometimes with a spiritual or moral agenda.

Invitation to Co-Creation

Abstract art in some of its developments is an invitation to the spectator to complete the work of the artist. The artwork is given a voice begging: Make me as you would like me to be. Give me your eyes, your hands.

Reduction of Matter

The classical expression of abstract art in the Nativity tradition applies a canon of purification and reduction. Eliminating all superfluous details the form is reduced to its essential message as intended by the artist.

The Emerging Form

The artist imitates creation, and shows with his art the slow and painful emerging of form from formless mass. All life is becoming and growth. Allusion is made to the Incarnation, that of Jesus Christ gestating in his mother's womb, but also to the slow understanding and growth of Christ's life in the soul.

"Innocent Art"

Innocent art is poor art. Its abstract character is not so much a style as it is a means. Ordinary, and forgotten or rejected things are used to build the nativity set. These humble materials of everyday life convey the reminiscence of the first, poor and humble nativity.

Invitation to Co-Creation

There is no photo-ID to identify the Holy Family. Puzzled, the adult capitulates and creates faceless figures. Popular in religious art of the 1960s and 1970s, gesture and posture define the actor. Faces remain blank—a standing invitation to paint eyes, nose and mouth of your choice.

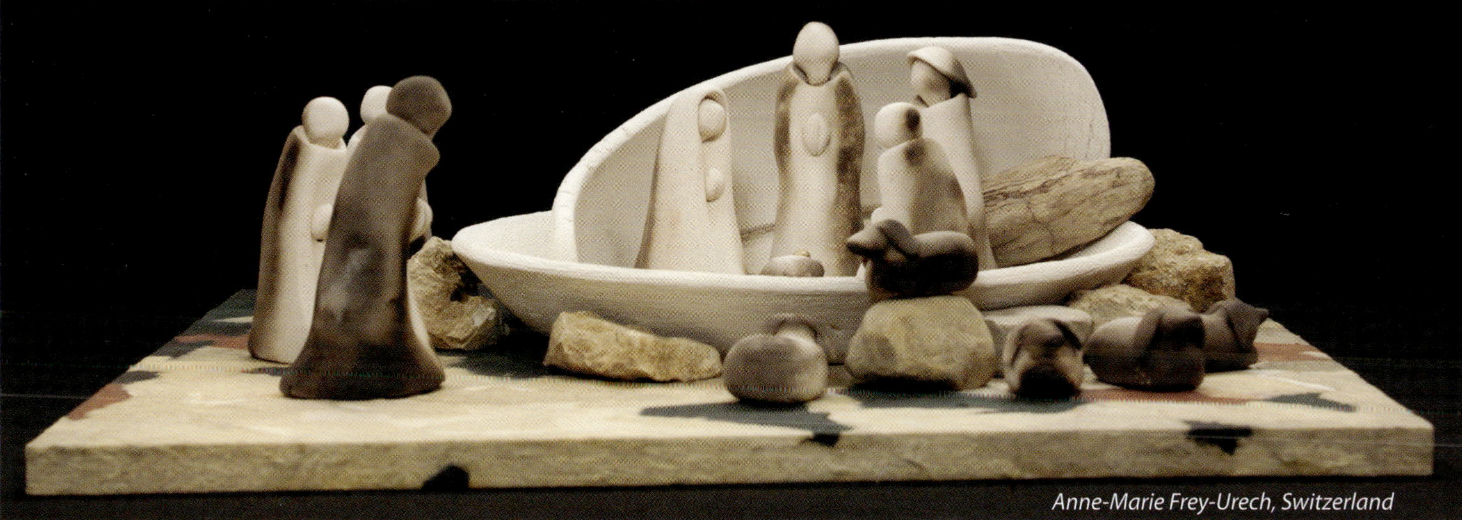

Anne-Marie Frey-Urech, Switzerland

Reduction of Matter

Contemporary nativity sets of Western Europe, which pride themselves of some artistic ambition, have a tendency to avoid figurative representations. It is the conviction of this artist that nativity figures need to avoid familiar patterns and comfortable projections. Resonating with A. Giacometti's artistic creed, Tilde Biner reduced matter to its farthest viable form and to a minimum of movement. The result is one of heightened expressiveness. The tall and lean figures of Mary (with the Child) and Joseph are messengers of a fragile but tender message. The group of the three women is a monument of attention and tension, a lively but equally fragile counterpart to the migrant couple. The women bear gifts to cover the Holy Family's simple needs. Will the exchange take place or not? Will the message of the "Good News" pass? Will the women present their gifts to the Child? In sum, will the "wonderful exchange" -- the ultimate meaning of the Incarnation – become reality?

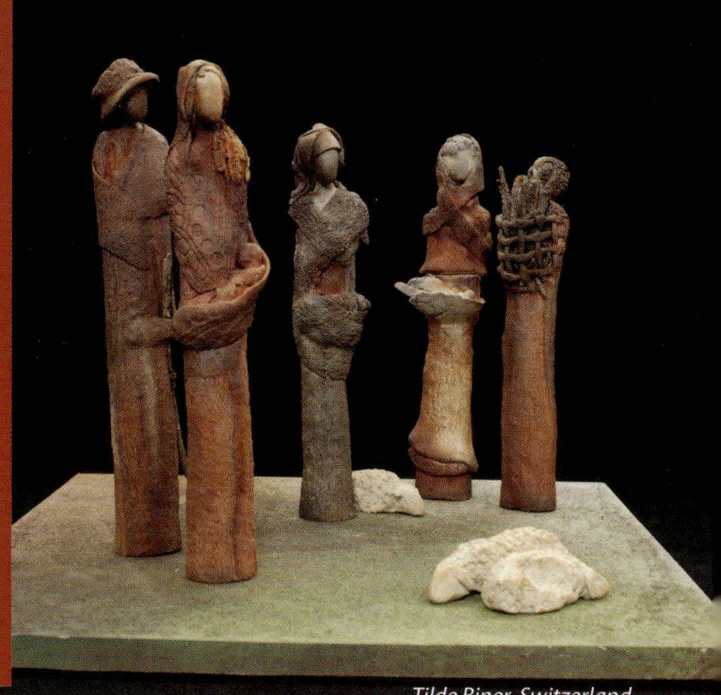

Tilde Biner, Switzerland

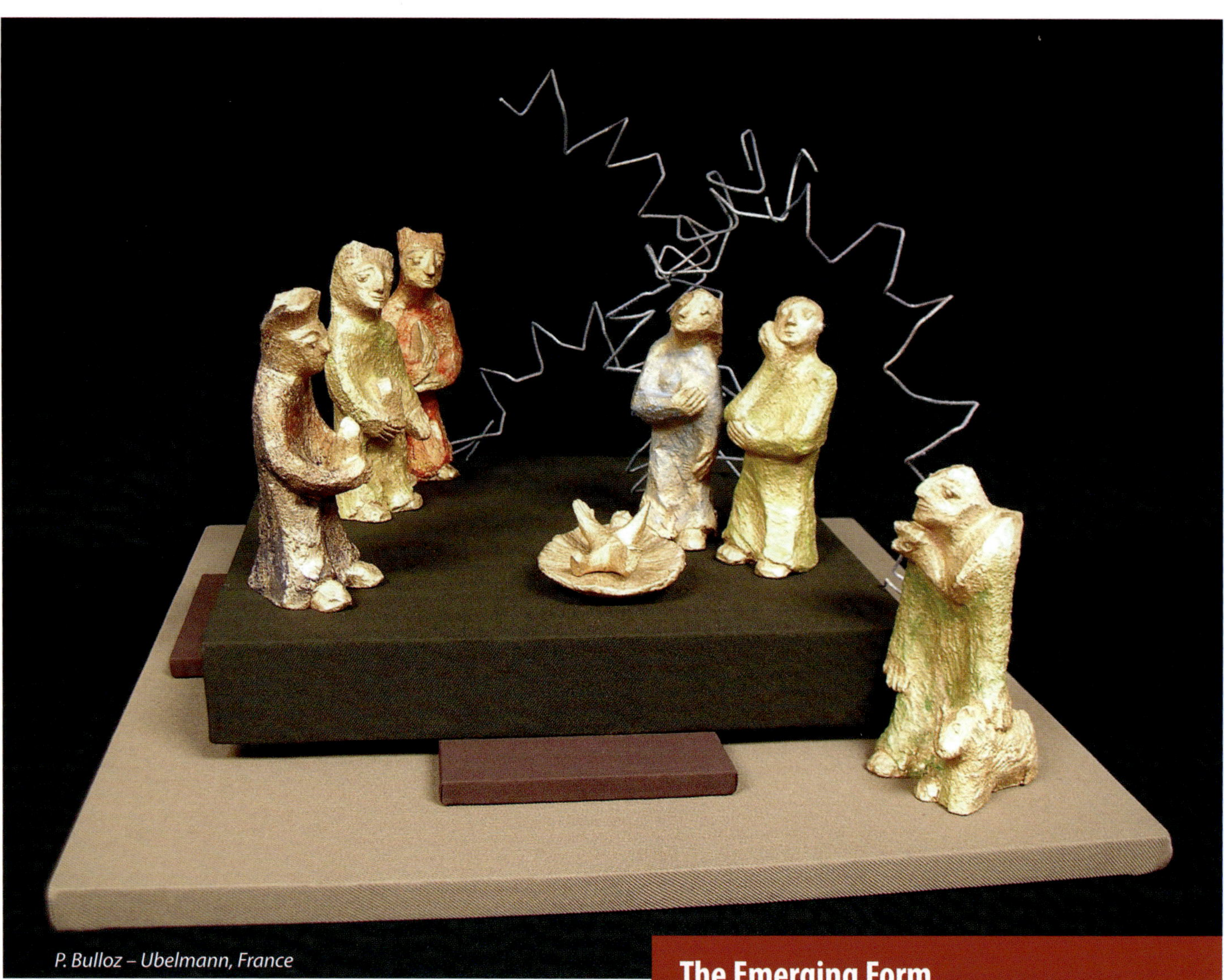

P. Bulloz – Ubelmann, France

The Emerging Form

Christmas closely relates to expectation and new life. Pascale Bulloz's figures are a tribute to new life; of form and character emerging from formless matter. Coated with gold patina this nativity set is a timely reminder of how noble and precious the "stuff of life" is.

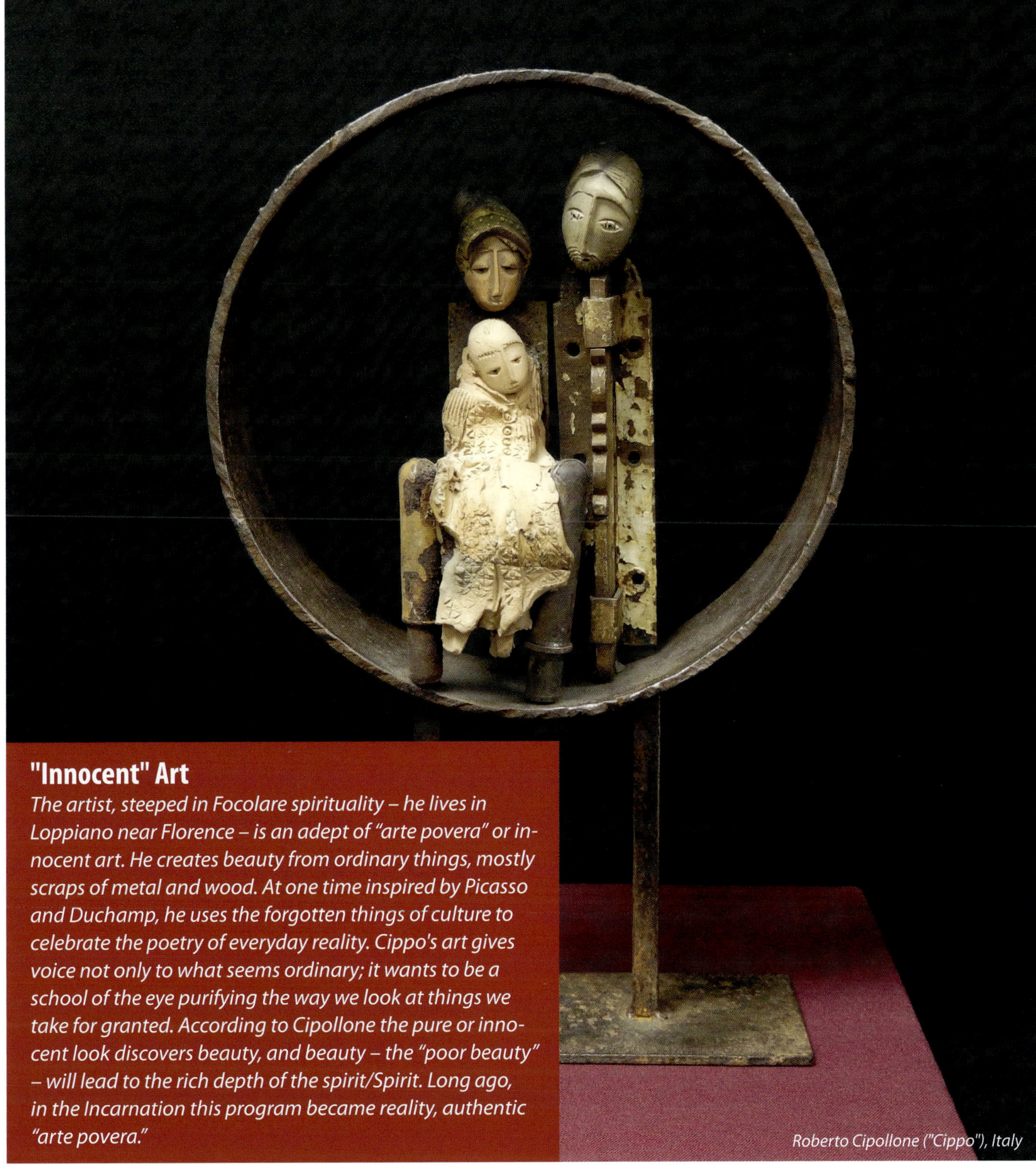

"Innocent" Art

The artist, steeped in Focolare spirituality – he lives in Loppiano near Florence – is an adept of "arte povera" or innocent art. He creates beauty from ordinary things, mostly scraps of metal and wood. At one time inspired by Picasso and Duchamp, he uses the forgotten things of culture to celebrate the poetry of everyday reality. Cippo's art gives voice not only to what seems ordinary; it wants to be a school of the eye purifying the way we look at things we take for granted. According to Cipollone the pure or innocent look discovers beauty, and beauty – the "poor beauty" – will lead to the rich depth of the spirit/Spirit. Long ago, in the Incarnation this program became reality, authentic "arte povera."

Roberto Cipollone ("Cippo"), Italy

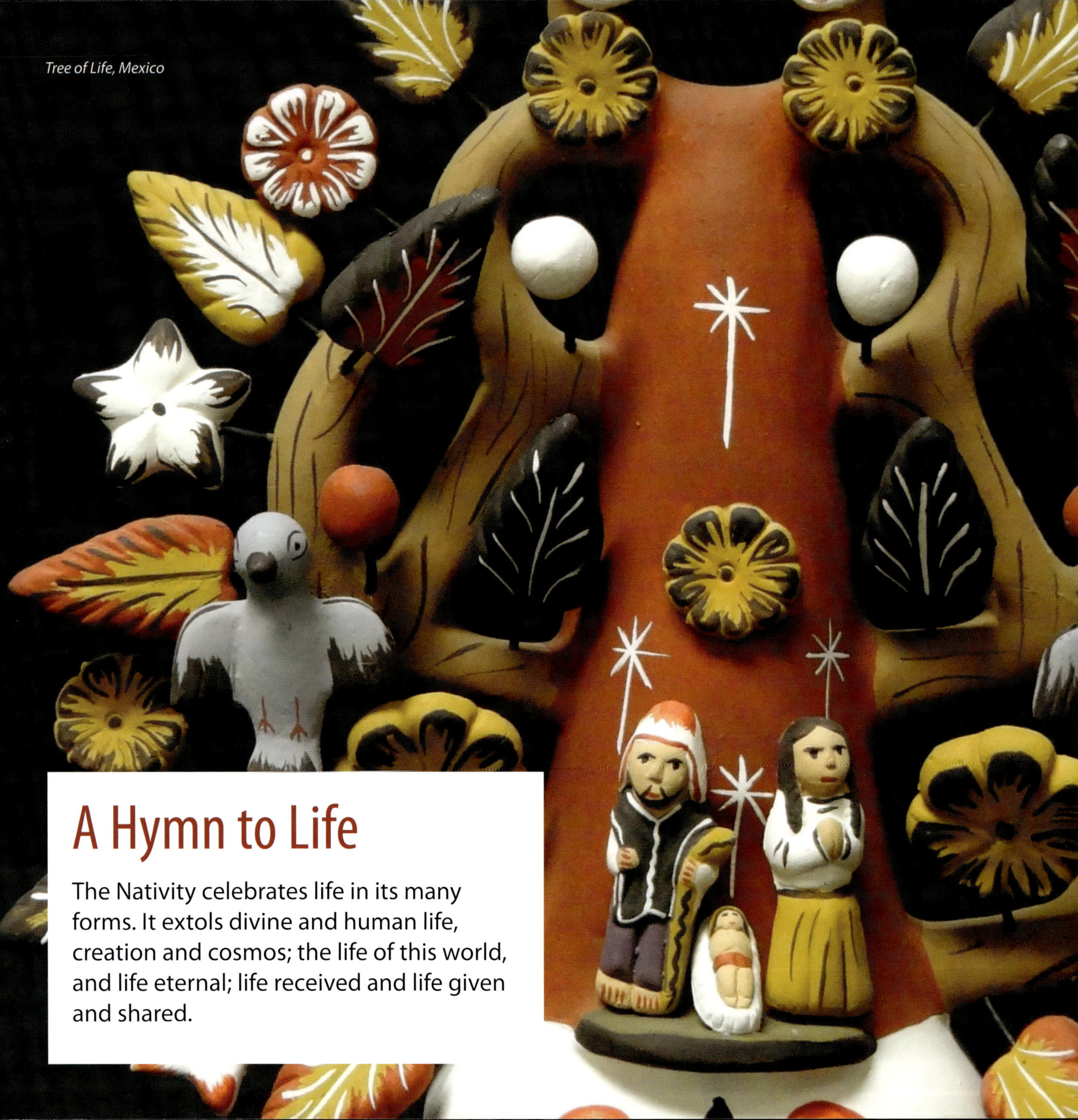

Tree of Life, Mexico

A Hymn to Life

The Nativity celebrates life in its many forms. It extols divine and human life, creation and cosmos; the life of this world, and life eternal; life received and life given and shared.

Abundance of Life
Life as Culture
Life as Gift Given
Life as Gift Returned
Life Everlasting

A Hymn to Life

The word "life" is one of the keywords of the Nativity and its culture. The Nativity is related to new life, to life restored, to new creation, abundance of life, to eternal life; to life in all its forms and expressions, from the life of God, to human life and that of nature. The ultimate meaning of life as suggested by the Incarnation is that of all life in God. Nativity sets have great reverence and respect for life. Their constant attention to mother and child, the central figures of all nativity representations, holds this essential message: the Incarnation celebrates human life in the symbol of the mother, and divine life in the Christchild. Together they symbolize the unity of human and divine life. There exists a wide array of representations to celebrate a hymn to life.

Abundance of Life

The abundance of life is frequently depicted in reference to nature, its luxuriant plenty and pristine beauty. Nature reflects the goodness of both Creator and Creation.

Life as Culture

Culture reflects the many meanings of life: On how to receive and protect it; on how to live and understand it. Life is physical, cultural, and spiritual. In all these forms there lives and acts a watchful mother.

Life as Gift Given

Nativity sets are a reminder that the Incarnation is a gift of God. All life is first and foremost gift. The gift is symbolized in the mother at the manger, and all other mothers.

Life as Gift Returned

It is the nature of life to be received, cherished and developed, in order to be shared and passed on. The midwife of the Nativity is a symbol of those who care for life, and facilitate it.

Life Everlasting

Of all meanings of life conveyed by the meditation on the Nativity the most important is that of life everlasting. It is encapsulized in the memory of the tree of life in paradise (Genesis 2:9) and the tree of life of the world to come (Revelation 22:1-2). The Latin culture has made of the tree of life a cultural and spiritual symbol of the Nativity.

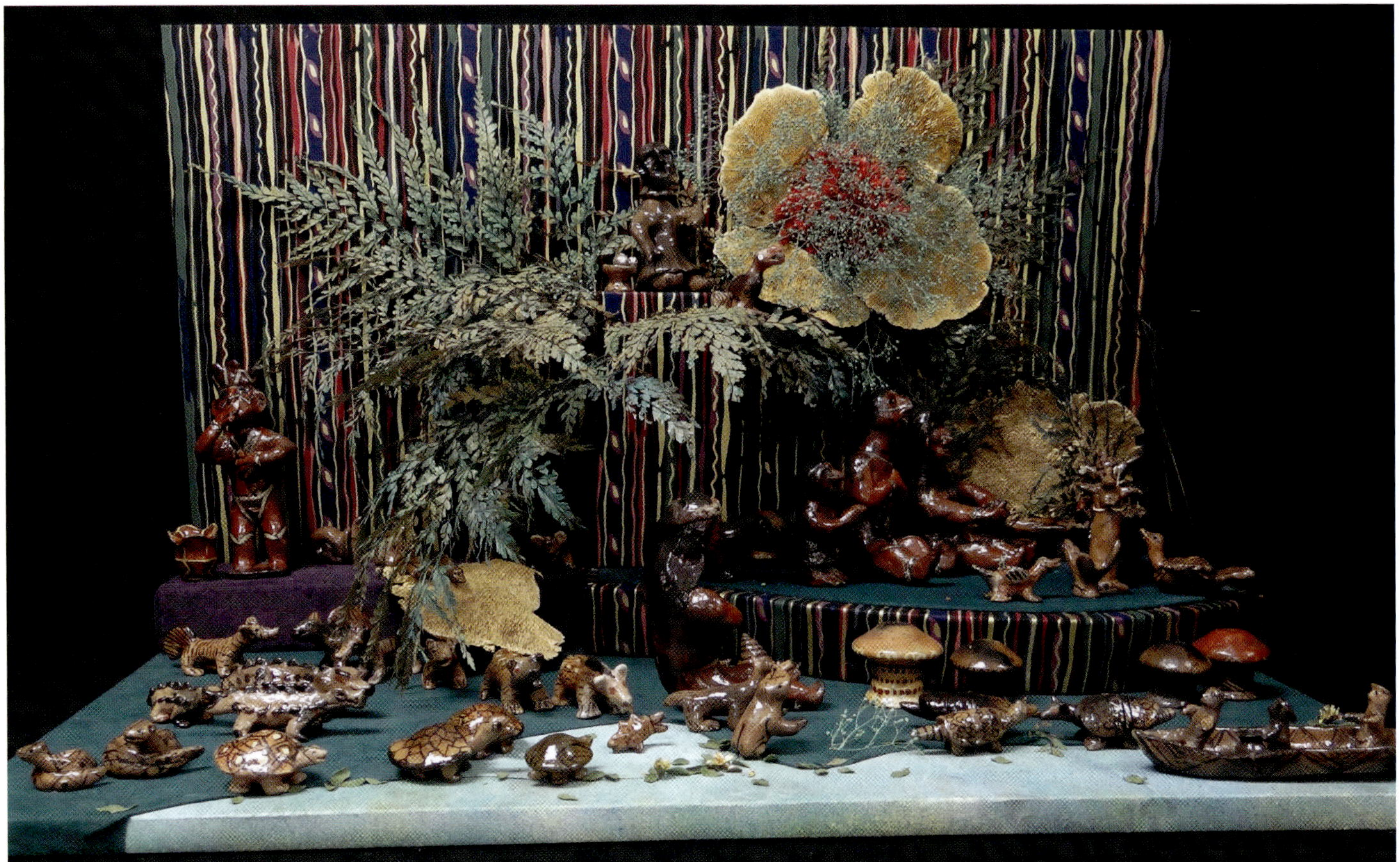

Myra Vargas, Ecuador

Abundance of Life

This nativity representation comes from one of the most remote regions of our globe, the rain forests of the Amazon. Lifting the curtain of dense foliage, which hides a kaleidoscope of luxuriant color and primeval sounds, we discover in a sea of birds and beasts the main actors of the feast of life: a few – in appearance – clumsy and awkwardly heavy figures. But there is a pristine beauty in their raptured faces and painted limbs. Their burnished bodies are like rare jewels glowing in the dark green night of the jungle. One is reminded of Psalm 139: "If I say: Let the darkness hide me and the light around me be night, even darkness is not dark for you, and the night is as clear as the day." Imagining in the orchid-shaped flower a symbol of the Creator's loving presence, echoes of this other canticle come to mind: "Seas and rivers ... all water creatures... all you birds of the air ... all you beasts wild and tame, bless the Lord. You sons of men, bless the Lord" (Daniel 3, 57f).

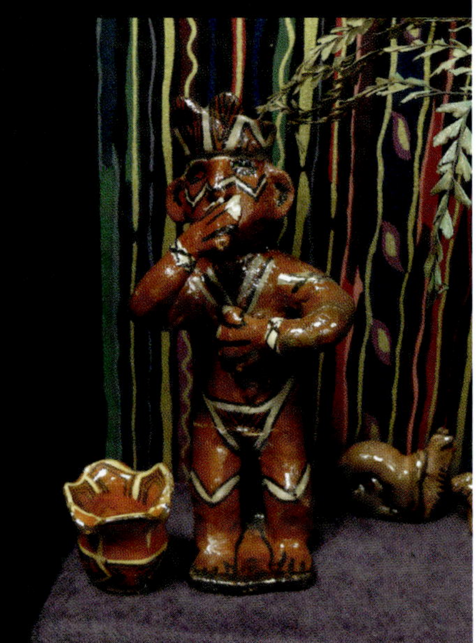

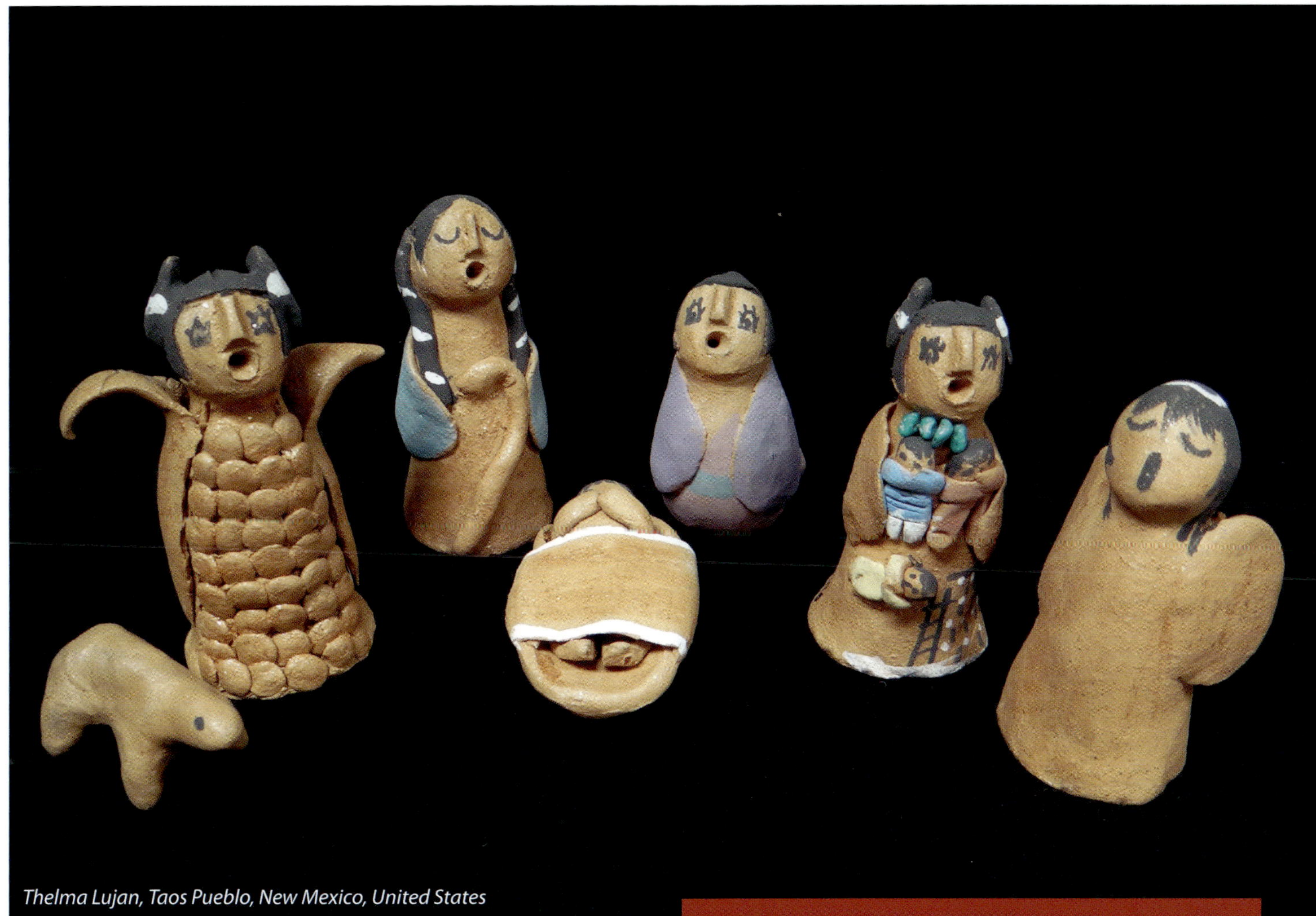

Thelma Lujan, Taos Pueblo, New Mexico, United States

Life as Culture

Thelma Lujan of Taos Pueblo, who calls herself Rain Circle, has contributed a humble nativity set where Indian tradition is represented with the corn mother and the even better known storyteller. Together with Mary, the three women symbolize the various roles of the mother: to give life (Mary), sustain it (corn mother), and give it meaning and direction (storyteller).

Life as Gift Given

This nativity representation emphasizes contrast and similarity. The two dominant mother figures are of pre-Columbian tradition. They represent a birthing mother (right) and a mother nursing her child (left). The nativity scene, dwarfed and traditional in style, suggests a stark but welcome contrast. Each of the figures is a little masterpiece of ornamental design in the pre-Columbian tradition. Most important, the set is in praise of mothers then and now. One of them was Mary, mother of Jesus called Savior.

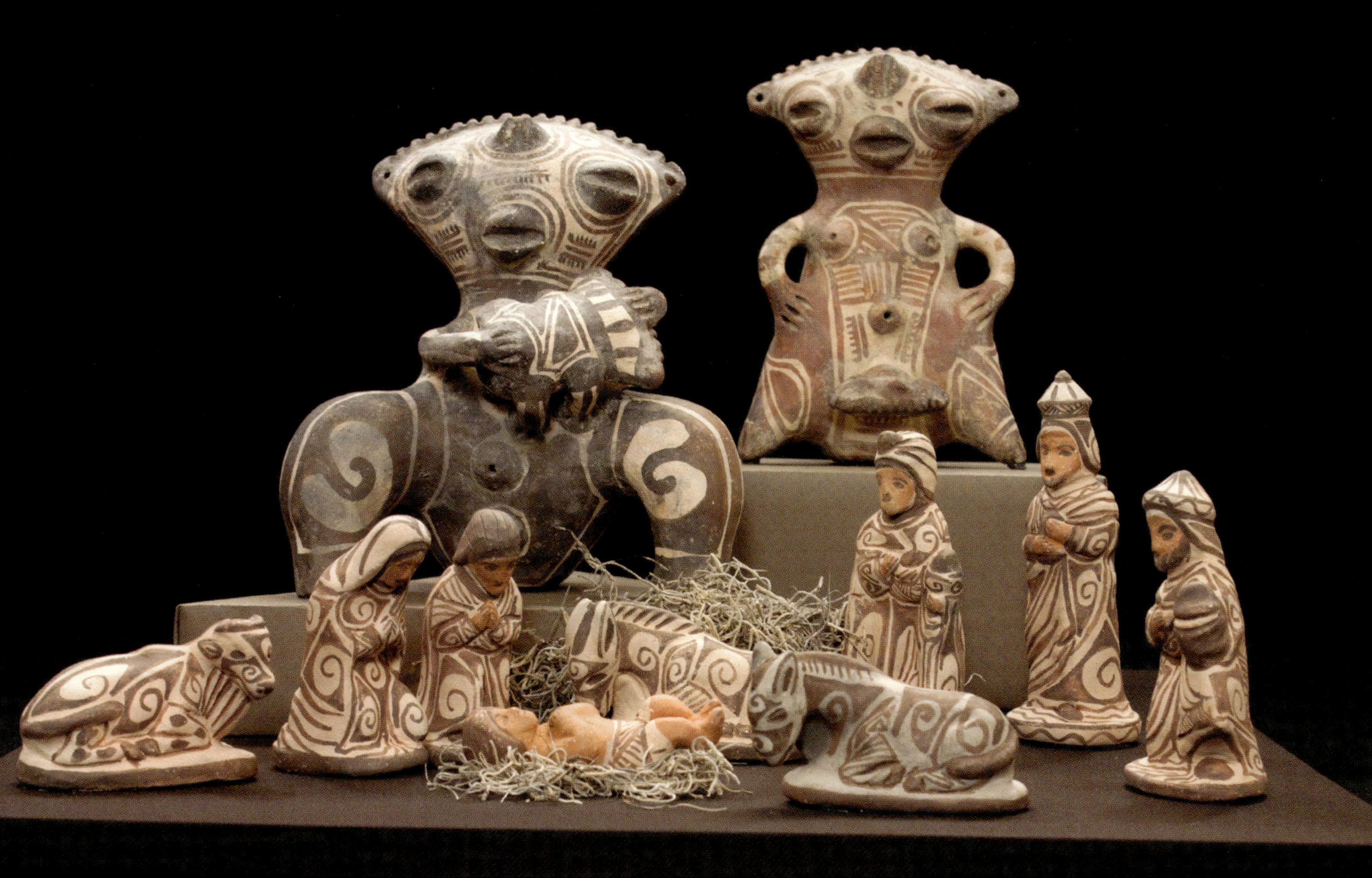

Taller Elmilagio, Venezuela

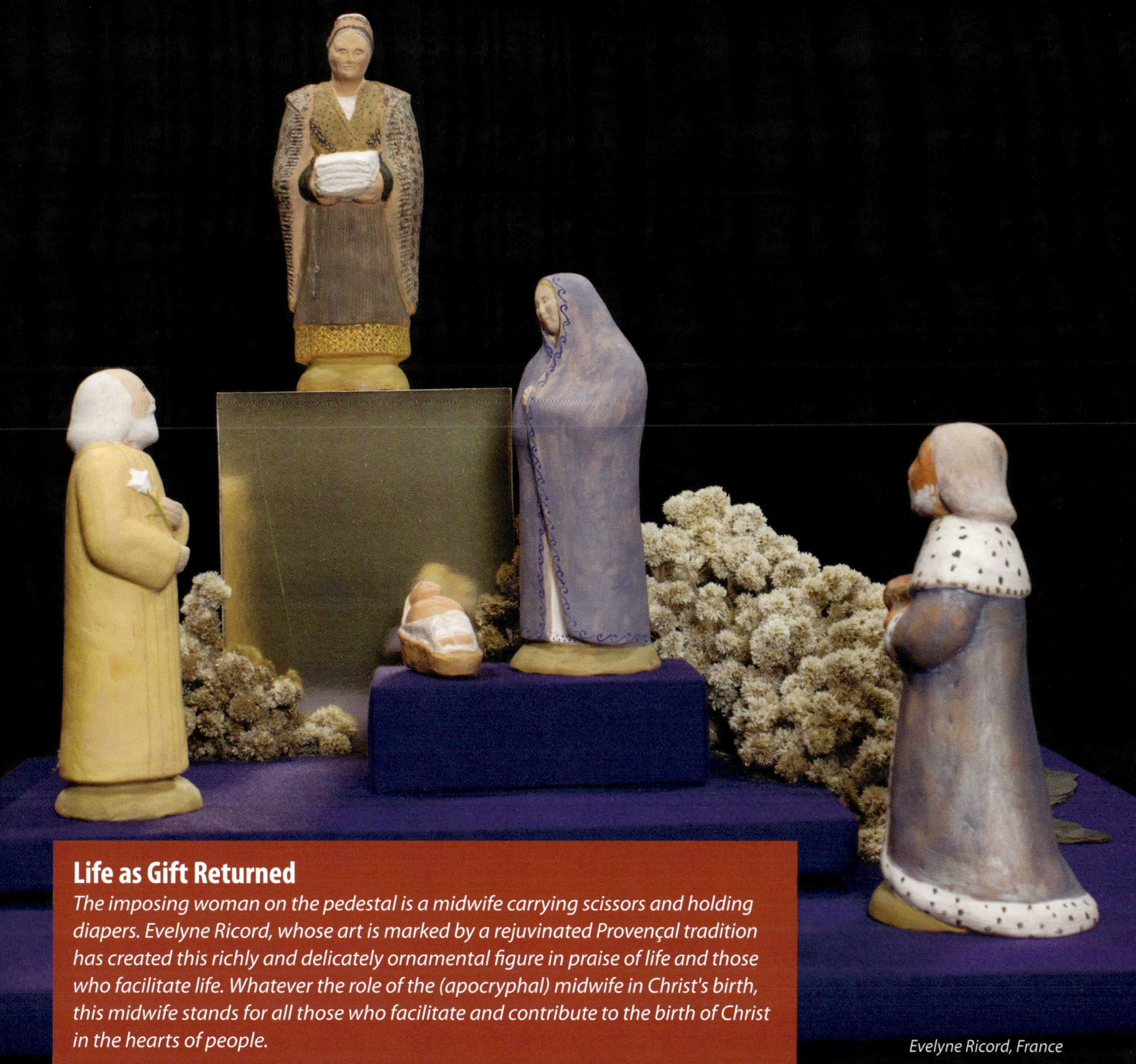

Life as Gift Returned

The imposing woman on the pedestal is a midwife carrying scissors and holding diapers. Evelyne Ricord, whose art is marked by a rejuvinated Provençal tradition has created this richly and delicately ornamental figure in praise of life and those who facilitate life. Whatever the role of the (apocryphal) midwife in Christ's birth, this midwife stands for all those who facilitate and contribute to the birth of Christ in the hearts of people.

Evelyne Ricord, France

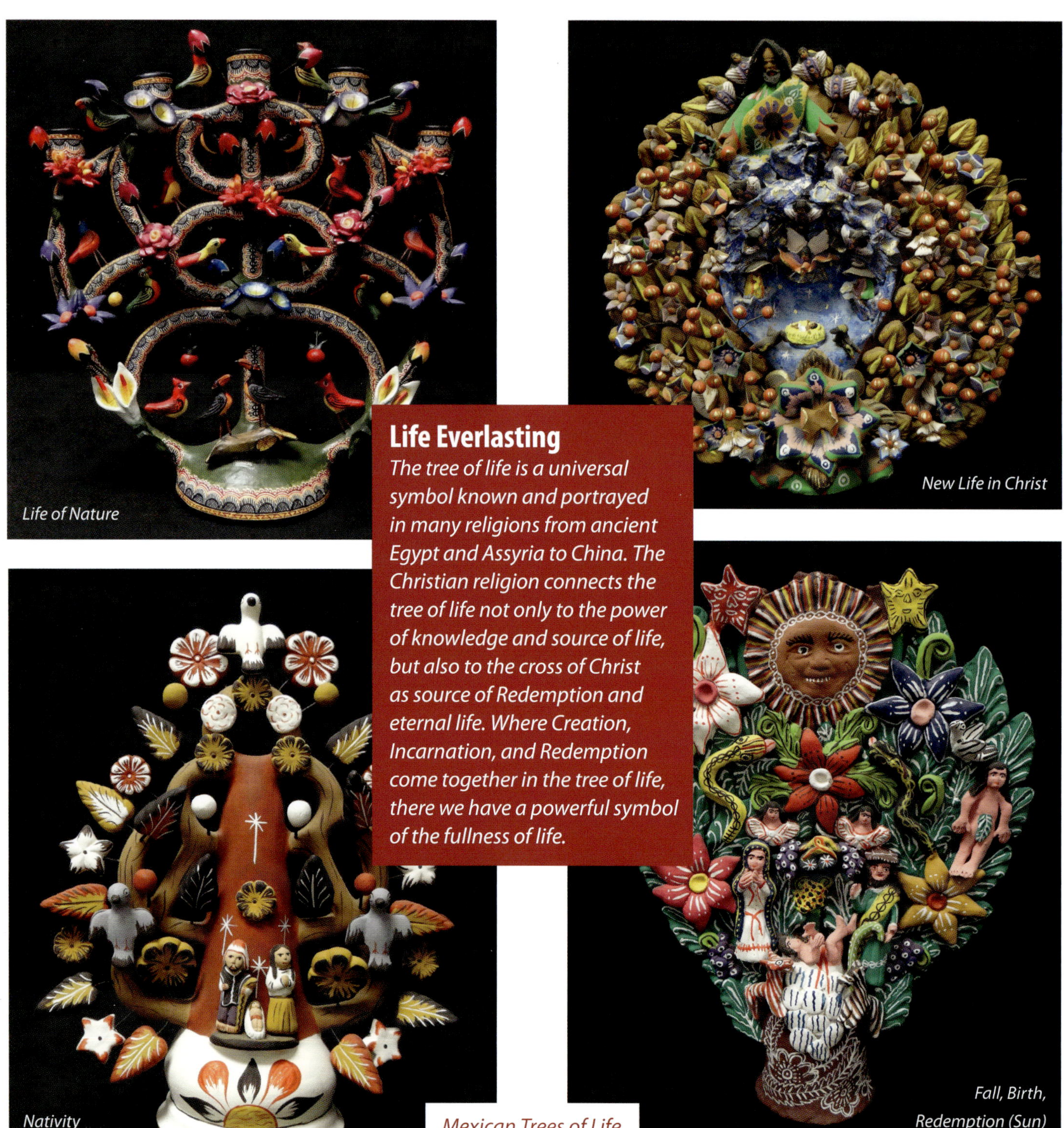

Life of Nature

New Life in Christ

Nativity

Fall, Birth, Redemption (Sun)

Life Everlasting

The tree of life is a universal symbol known and portrayed in many religions from ancient Egypt and Assyria to China. The Christian religion connects the tree of life not only to the power of knowledge and source of life, but also to the cross of Christ as source of Redemption and eternal life. Where Creation, Incarnation, and Redemption come together in the tree of life, there we have a powerful symbol of the fullness of life.

A Cosmic Event

Imagination is boundless when dealing with God's love for all of Creation. Nativity representations are not only looking forward to the accomplishment of the Incarnation in Redemption for humanity. The miracle of the Incarnation, which is the summit of Creation, includes all orders of Creation, the whole cosmos.

Sun, Moon, and Stars

The Star is an important and fixed part of the Nativity story. Sun, moon, and stars are a constant reminder of the place of light in the crèche tradition. It is light that leads, and light that gives life.

Animals of Air, Land, and Sea

Ox and ass may be the faithful and permanent companions of the Christchild, but they are not the only representatives of the animal reign at the manger. Animals are frequently used to represent the whole of nature at the crèche.

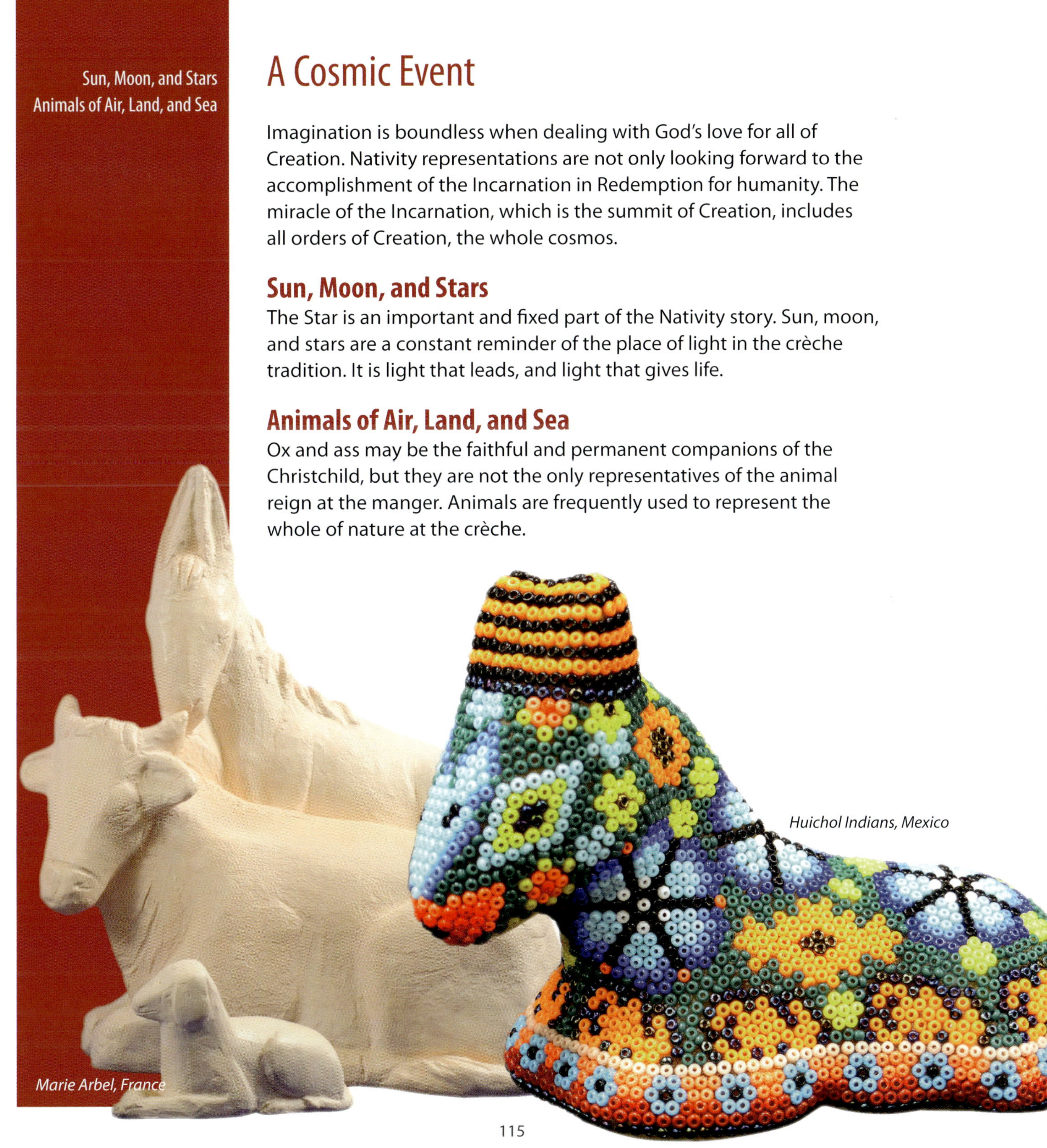

Huichol Indians, Mexico

Marie Arbel, France

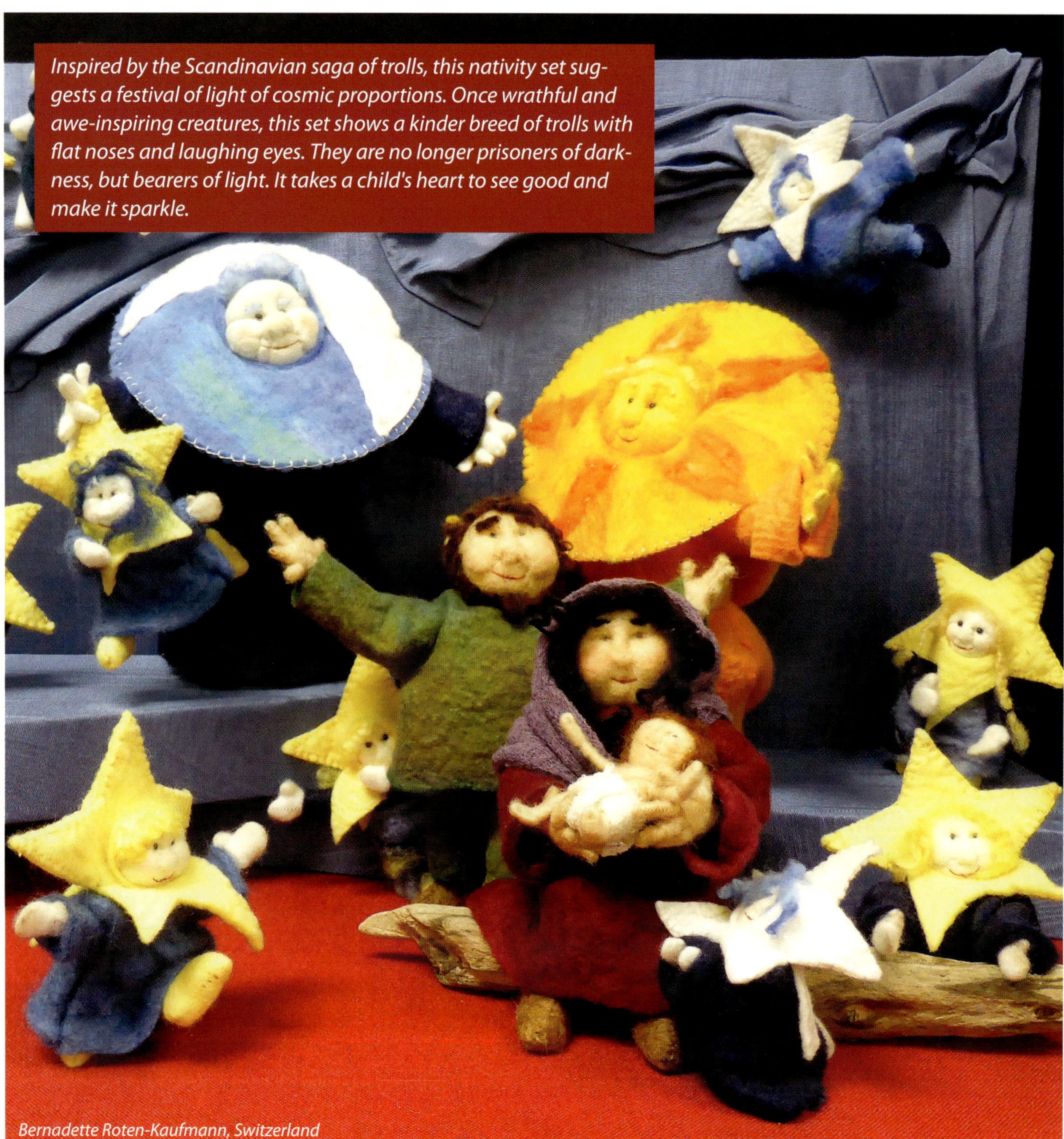

Inspired by the Scandinavian saga of trolls, this nativity set suggests a festival of light of cosmic proportions. Once wrathful and awe-inspiring creatures, this set shows a kinder breed of trolls with flat noses and laughing eyes. They are no longer prisoners of darkness, but bearers of light. It takes a child's heart to see good and make it sparkle.

Bernadette Roten-Kaufmann, Switzerland

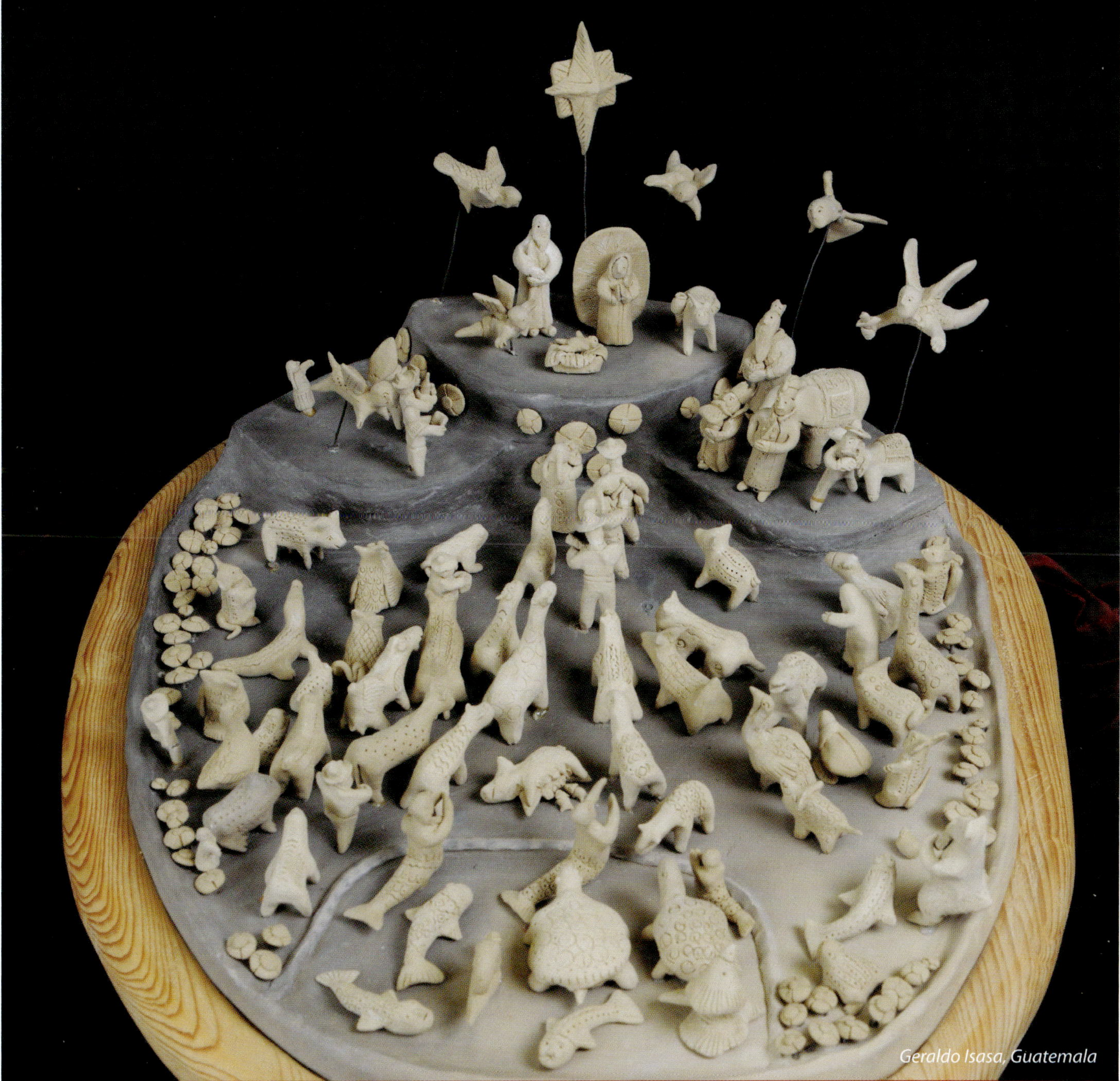

This tableau is brimming over with the life of creation gathering a great many of its representatives: animals of the deep and inhabitants of the air, creatures of past and present; those who sleep and those who make music. Whether noble or ordinary, man or beast, all are part of the same assembly gathered around the Lord of Creation. Uniform in color and execution, these little clay figures are offering their humble praise of the Incarnation.

Faithful Companions

Faithful Companions – this designation applies to ox and ass at the manger but can be extended to other animals for, indeed, some animals are always present at the birth of Christ. There is a great variety of them, mostly a consequence of inculturation, sometimes with a touch of humor, sometimes to convey some symbolic meaning but always with the intention to include all orders of creation in the event of Incarnation. There is the frightening kind of animals like hippo, warthog, and rhino. There are the typical animals of Africa, giraffe and elephant, the lion pictured in Mexican nativity sets, the rooster as reminder of Saint Peter's treason of Christ, or a brood of hens feeding on domestic bliss.

However, there are three groupings of animals which have a privileged station at the manger. First and foremost among them are ox and ass, the original and ever present companions of the

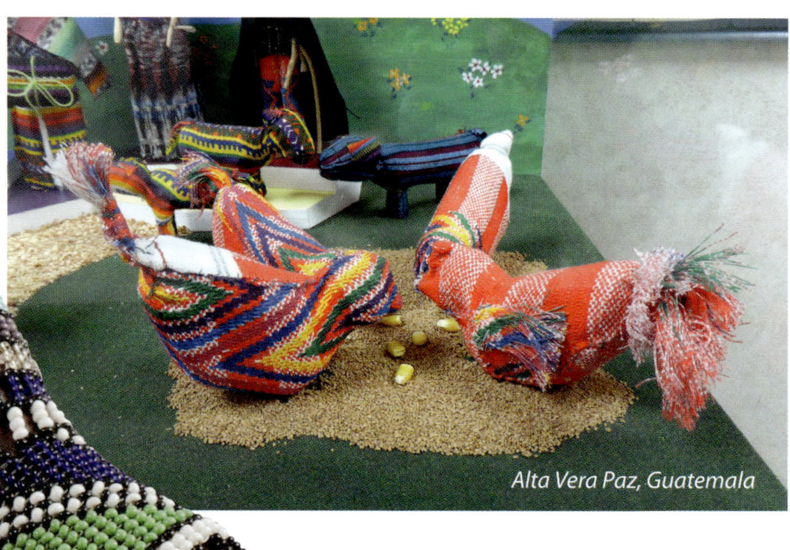

Alta Vera Paz, Guatemala

Ndebele Artisans, South Africa

Christchild. Their role is to symbolize commitment, dedication, and perseverance in the service of the Christchild.

Almost as frequently present at the manger as ox and ass are sheep and lambs. Aside from picturing the scriptural (shepherds' field) and geographic situation of the Nativity, sheep are not only the most frequently mentioned animal of the Bible, they are also the most loved and cared for creatures of God, after woman and man. In fact, sheep serve as symbols of human beings: unruly and recalcitrant at times, they are instinctively vying for the loving attention of God.

The third group of animals comprises horse, camel and elephant. Traveling companions of Magi or Kings, the three animals point to the universal outreach of Christianity. Representing the symbolic origin of the noble visitors to the manger, horse (Europe), camel (Africa), and elephant (Asia) are also the silent and dutiful servants of the God-seeking Magi bringing them safely to the longed for goal of their voyage.

Brazil

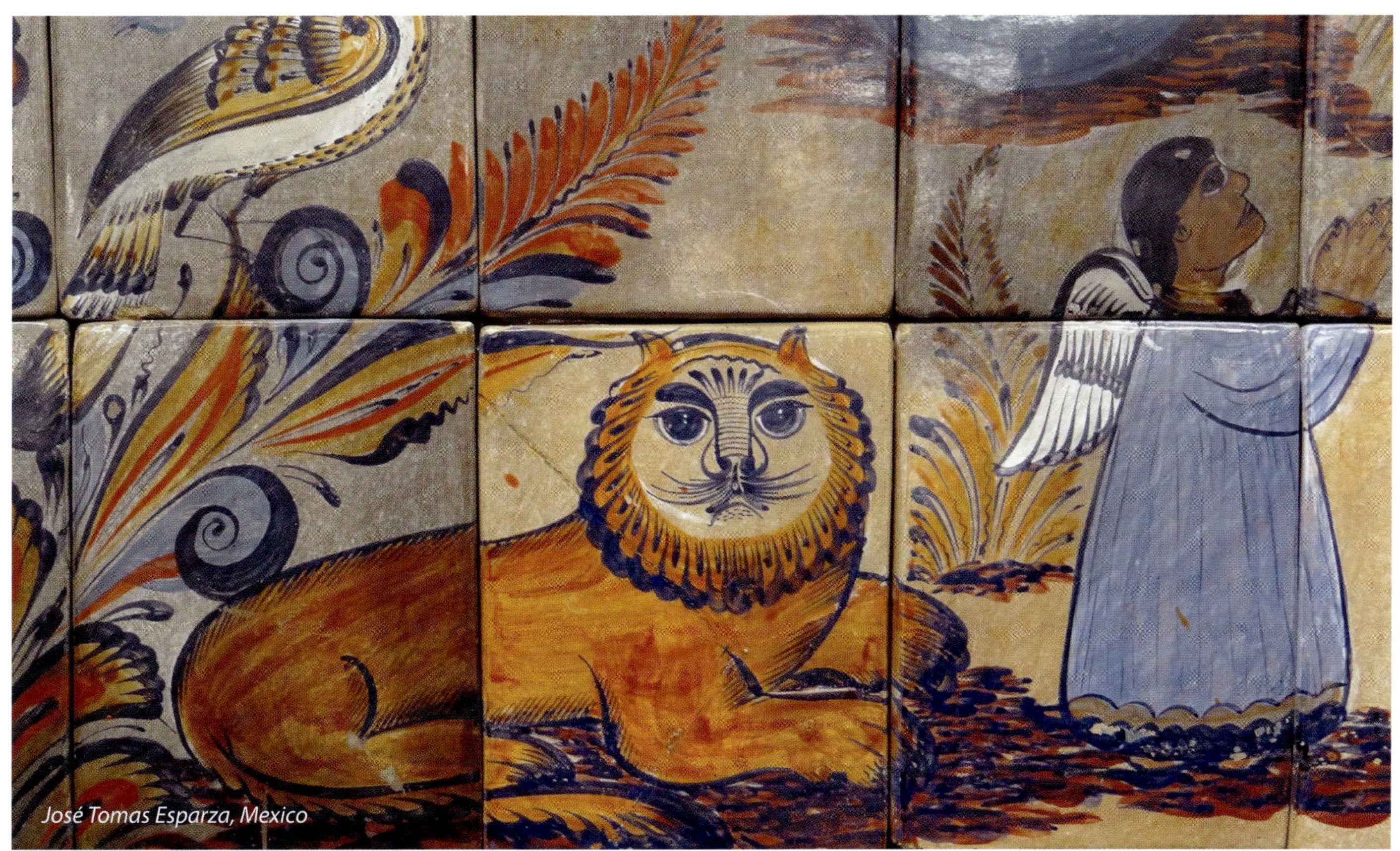

José Tomas Esparza, Mexico

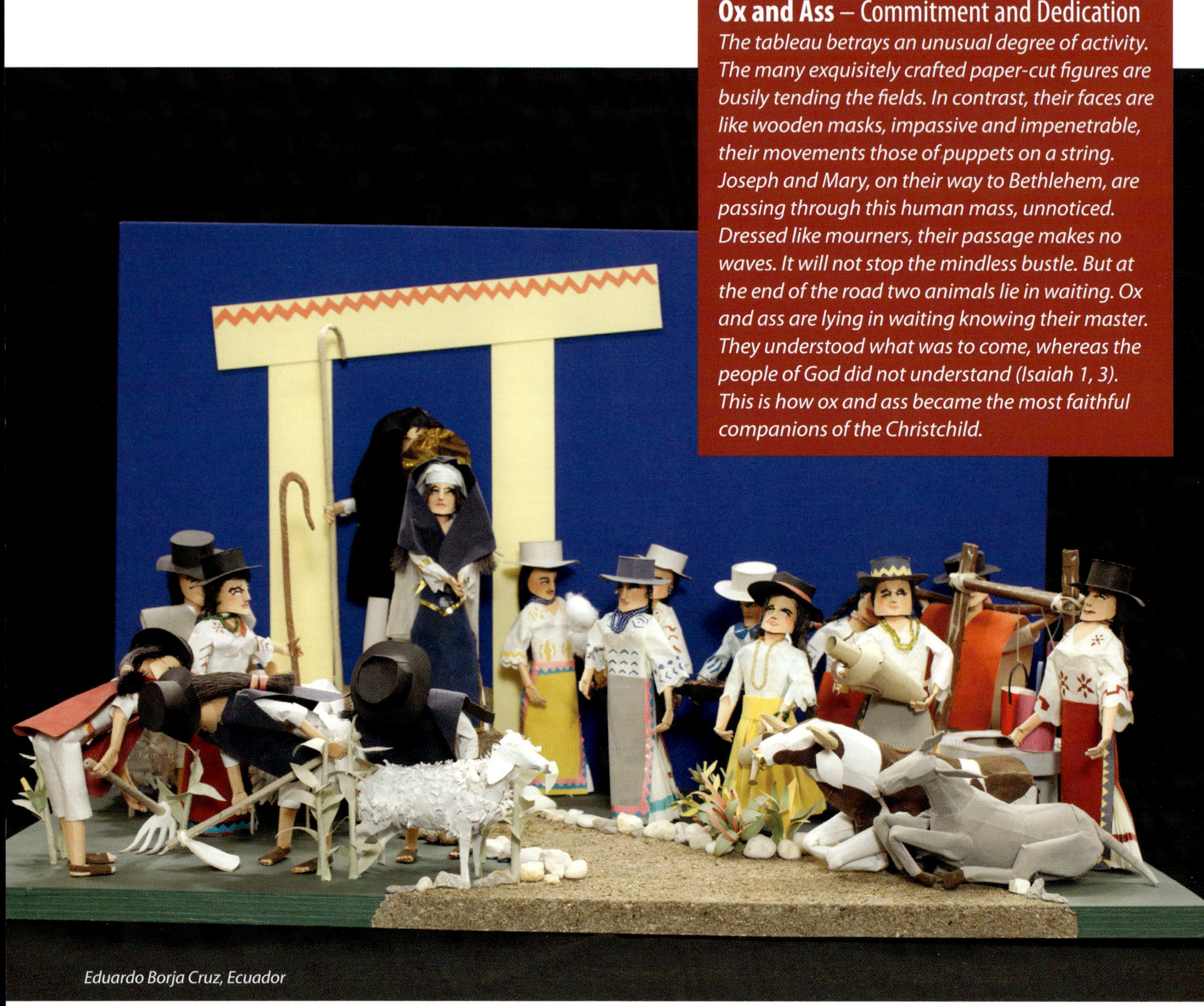

Ox and Ass – Commitment and Dedication

The tableau betrays an unusual degree of activity. The many exquisitely crafted paper-cut figures are busily tending the fields. In contrast, their faces are like wooden masks, impassive and impenetrable, their movements those of puppets on a string. Joseph and Mary, on their way to Bethlehem, are passing through this human mass, unnoticed. Dressed like mourners, their passage makes no waves. It will not stop the mindless bustle. But at the end of the road two animals lie in waiting. Ox and ass are lying in waiting knowing their master. They understood what was to come, whereas the people of God did not understand (Isaiah 1, 3). This is how ox and ass became the most faithful companions of the Christchild.

Eduardo Borja Cruz, Ecuador

Sheep – Care and Attention

The attention is captured by the somewhat unruly but eager flock of sheep in the center of the nativity scene. Stretching and tending necks and legs, they are pressing forward to get a glimpse of the one announced by the angel Gabriel. Sheep are mentioned more than 500 times in Scripture. Sheep are the favorite analogy to describe our relation to God. Sheep are clearly God's favorite animal. In a world filled with majestic animals like lions, horses, and eagles, the Lord chose sheep for his teaching and care. No wonder the flock of sheep in this set is pressing forward to have a glimpse of its future shepherd and redeemer.

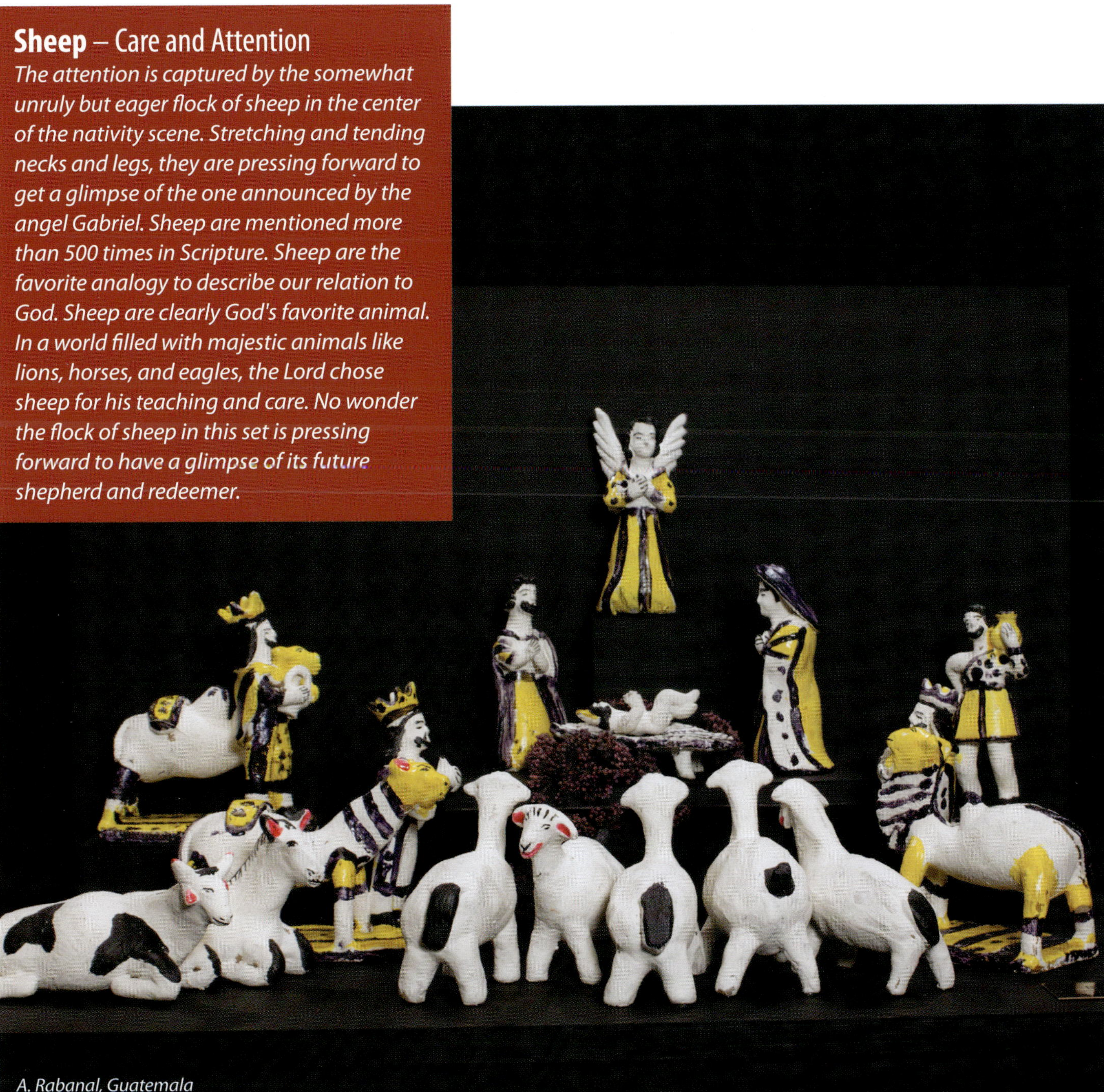

A. Rabanal, Guatemala

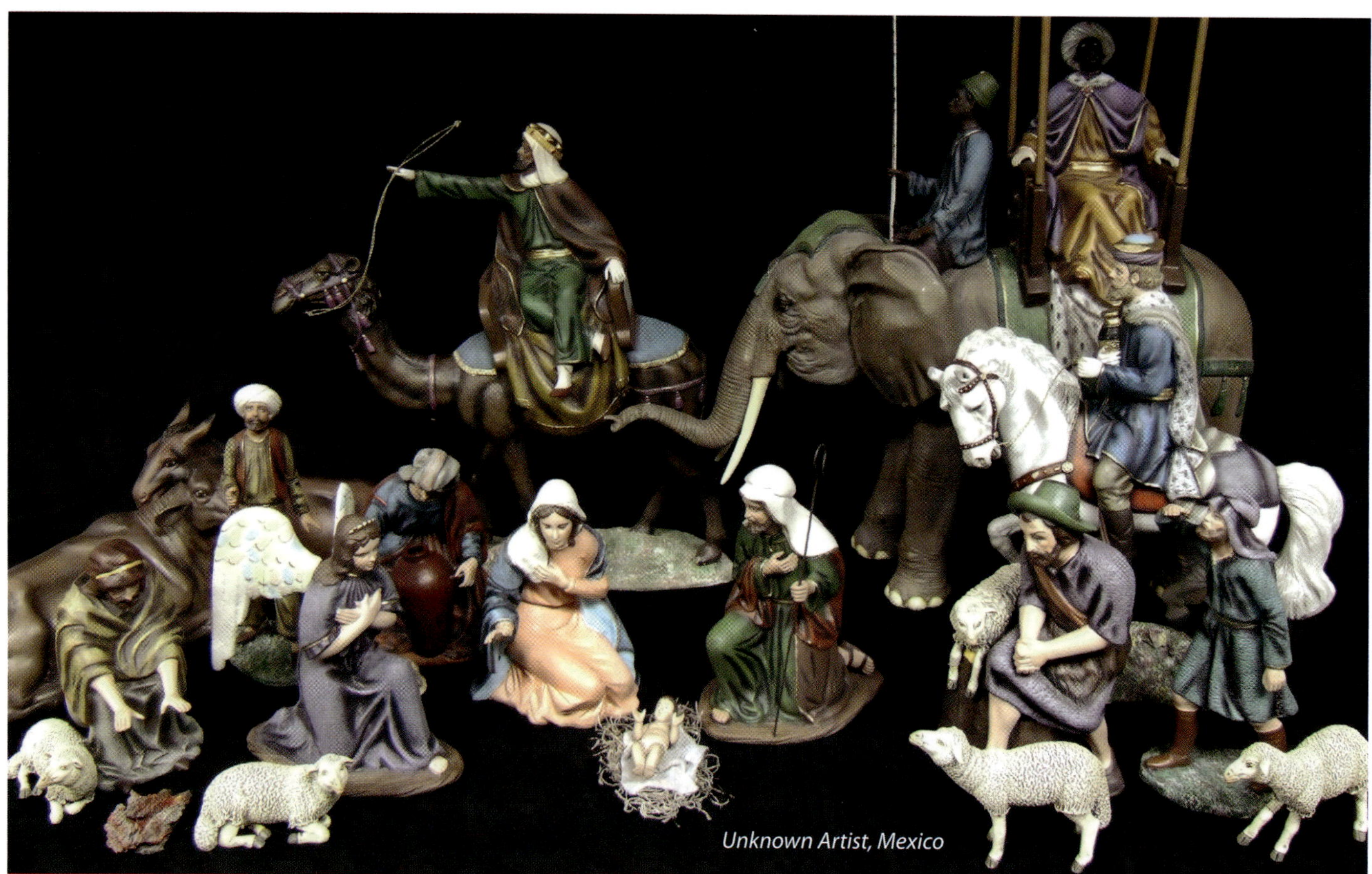
Unknown Artist, Mexico

Horse, Camel and Elephant – Journey and Goal

The classical beauty of these figures suggest an Italian or German origin... In fact, they are Mexican. There exists in Mexico, where Christmas lore is abundant and varied, a modest crèche tradition which goes back to the middle of the 19th century and the ephemeral reign of the luckless emperor Maximilian I. He brought to the new world samples of Austrian craftsmanship: a mixture of peasant style, gothic revival, and orientalism.

The most prominent feature in this tradition are the three kings. Dominant, they command attention. Dwarfing all other figures on their way, including the heavenly messenger, they do not look like weary God-seekers. They no longer seek, they have found. The three beautiful animals stand for the inner dispositions or human qualities which made this relentless search possible. The impatiently snorting white horse which carries Melchior, the King of Europe, is symbol of fearless enthusiasm without which no adventure was ever begun. But enthusiasm needs to be sustained by sheer bottomless energy as symbolized in the monumental elephant who shoulders effortlessly not only Balthasar, the Asian king, but also his throne, canopy and driver. The camel is a symbol of endurance and unerring direction. The desert represents no threat and holds no secret for this animal. It leads King Gaspar of Africa, and his companions, patiently and securely to the even greater King's manger.

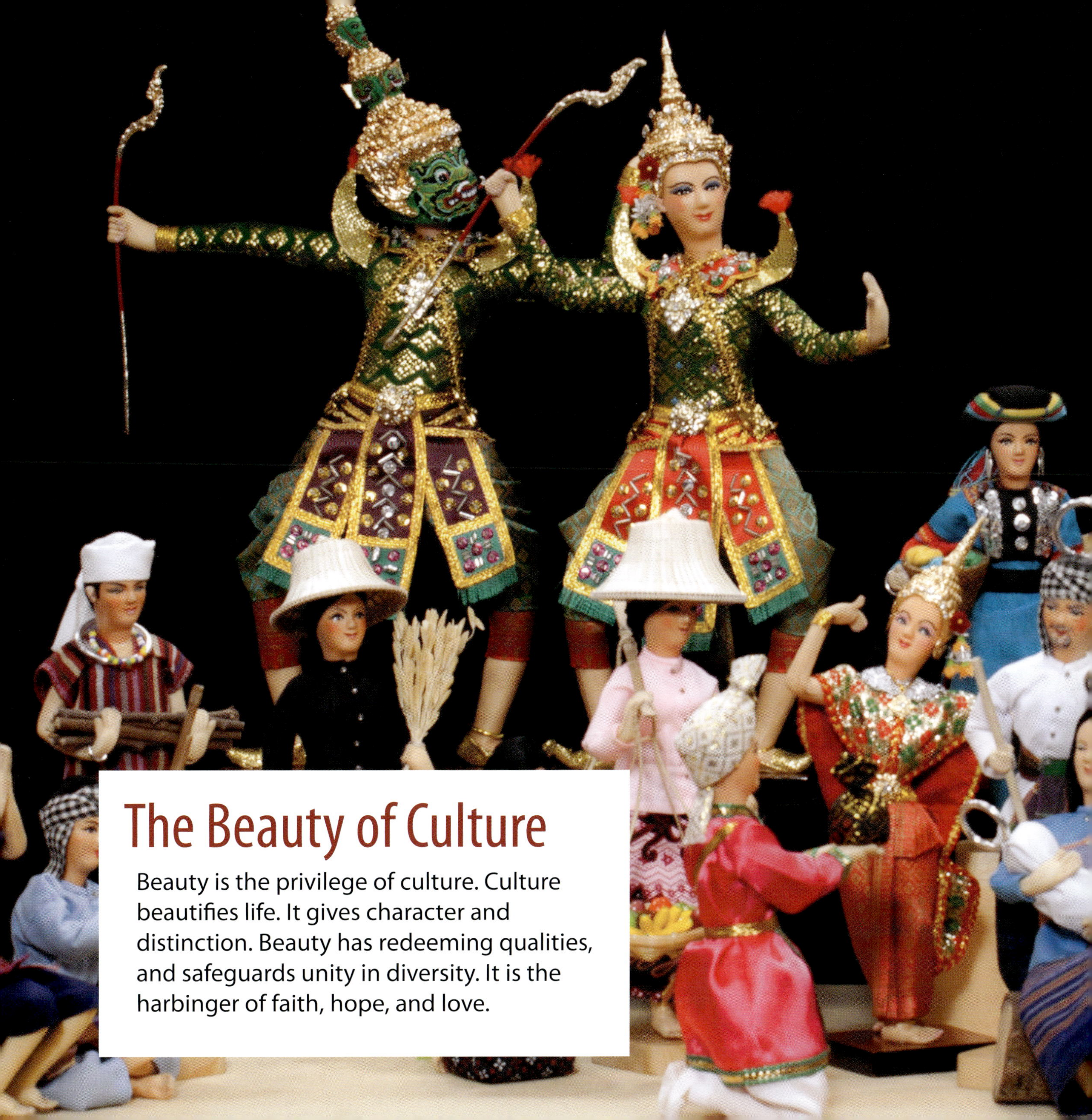

The Beauty of Culture

Beauty is the privilege of culture. Culture beautifies life. It gives character and distinction. Beauty has redeeming qualities, and safeguards unity in diversity. It is the harbinger of faith, hope, and love.

An Air of Nobility
The Challenge of Harmony
A Message Made Culture
Culture Made Spirit
Joy of the Moment

The Beauty of Culture

We are musing about the difference between cultures, about their variety and originality. However different they may be there is one thing that creates unity and commonality, and that is beauty. The beauty of culture lies in something that is more than culture, something universal, a spirit common to most people. We find that spirit in the dignity and nobility of individual figures of the nativity set. It is found in the harmony or unity of a set and its personages. Successful inculturation speaks a similar language when the message of Christmas and local culture combine in a perfect fit. And there is always beauty where the spirit of the event is made visible. Last but not least, beauty triumphs if the joy of the moment prevails against hardship or evil.

An Air of Nobility

The simple and unaffected grace of a posture or movement creates nobility. Nobility is human dignity lived in trial and hardship and transfigured by beauty.

The Challenge of Harmony

Harmony avoids uniformity and welcomes a touch of originality. Color and form reinforce the impression of unity in diversity which is the mark of true harmony. Harmony generates beauty.

A Message Made Culture

Successful inculturation is a challenge. It occurs when the cultural form translates the whole message of the Nativity in truth and beauty.

Culture Made Spirit

The visible form of whatever culture remains soulless, if it does not suggest the deeper meaning and spirit of the Christmas event.

Joy of the Moment

Christmas is a reminder of joy amid poverty, of hope inspite of despondency, and of love amid violence.

An Air of Nobility

In the "Land of the Thousand Hills" nature is frugal and cattle is king. At one time, Rwanda was owned by shepherds and farmers. This nativity set was made in praise of shepherding. Tall and slim, the figures are people on the move, some carrying long staffs, one of them with the little shepherd's hut on his left shoulder. Proud nomads and marchers, these shepherds are never servile, and their respectful pose is a gesture of noble devotion. The gesture of noble devotion is common to all of the figures, wise men and Holy Family alike. Movement is suspended for a moment only, the time of the shepherds' feast. In no time they will be on the move again, carrying in their hearts the joy of a moment.

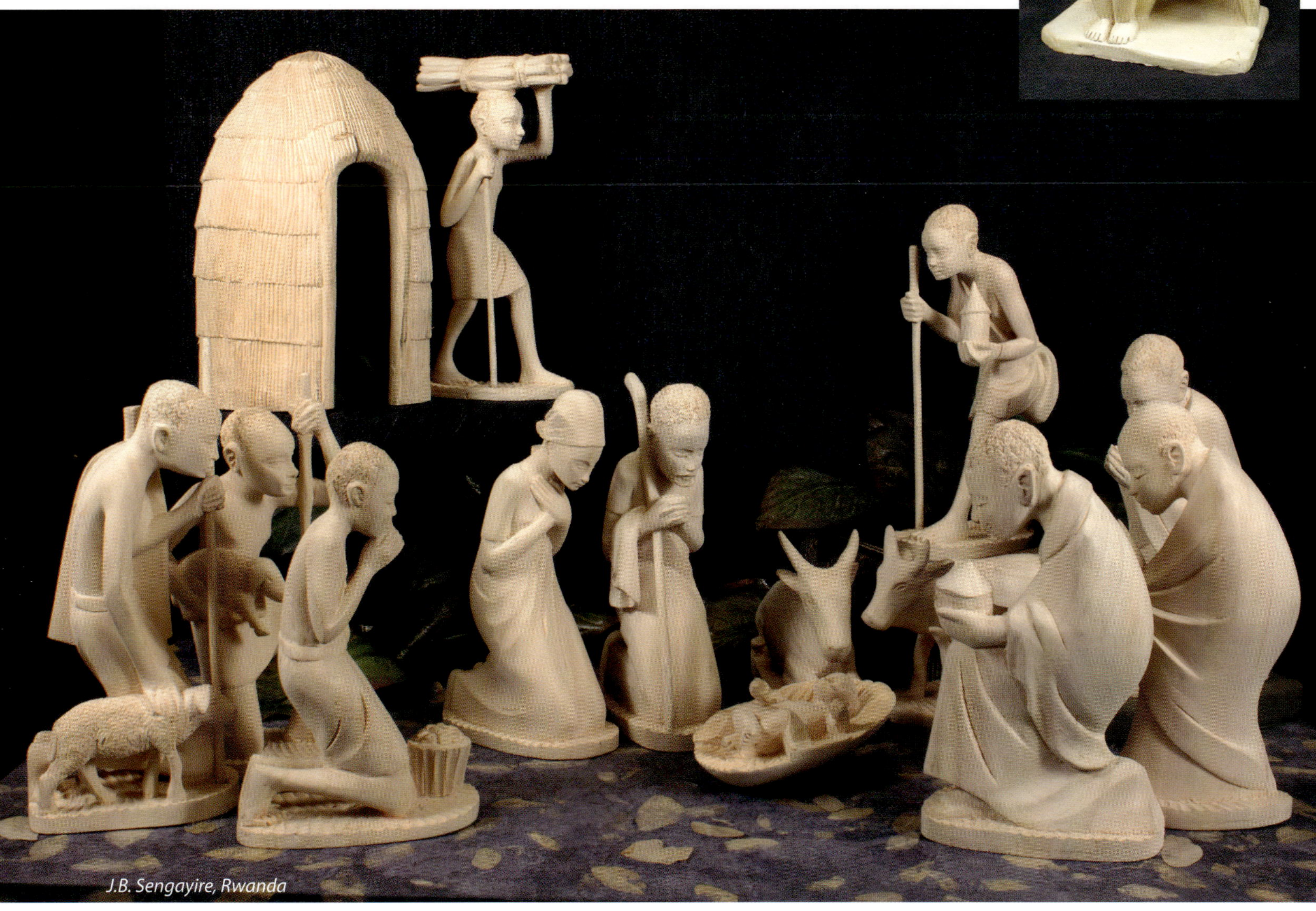

J.B. Sengayire, Rwanda

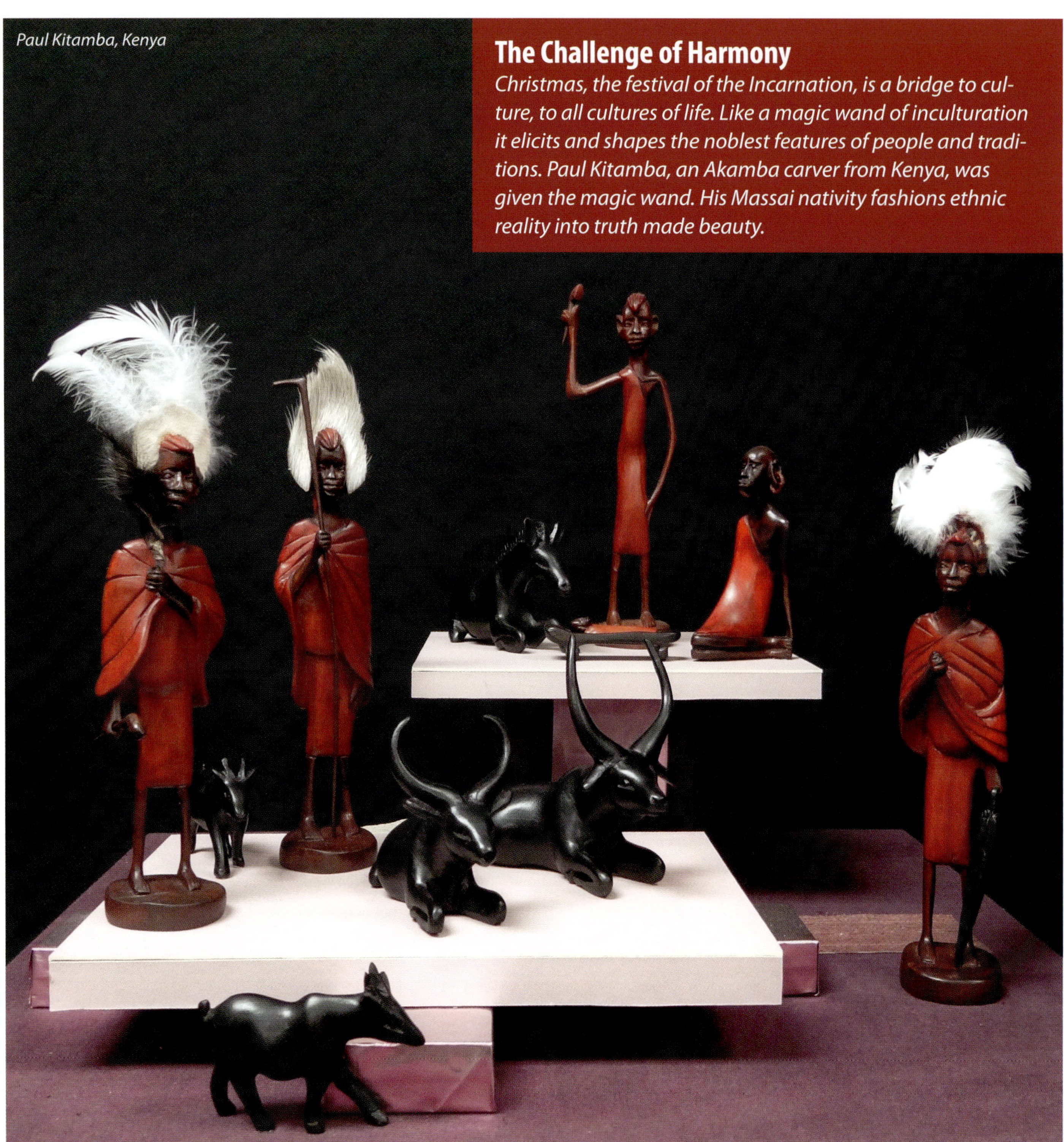
Paul Kitamba, Kenya

The Challenge of Harmony

Christmas, the festival of the Incarnation, is a bridge to culture, to all cultures of life. Like a magic wand of inculturation it elicits and shapes the noblest features of people and traditions. Paul Kitamba, an Akamba carver from Kenya, was given the magic wand. His Massai nativity fashions ethnic reality into truth made beauty.

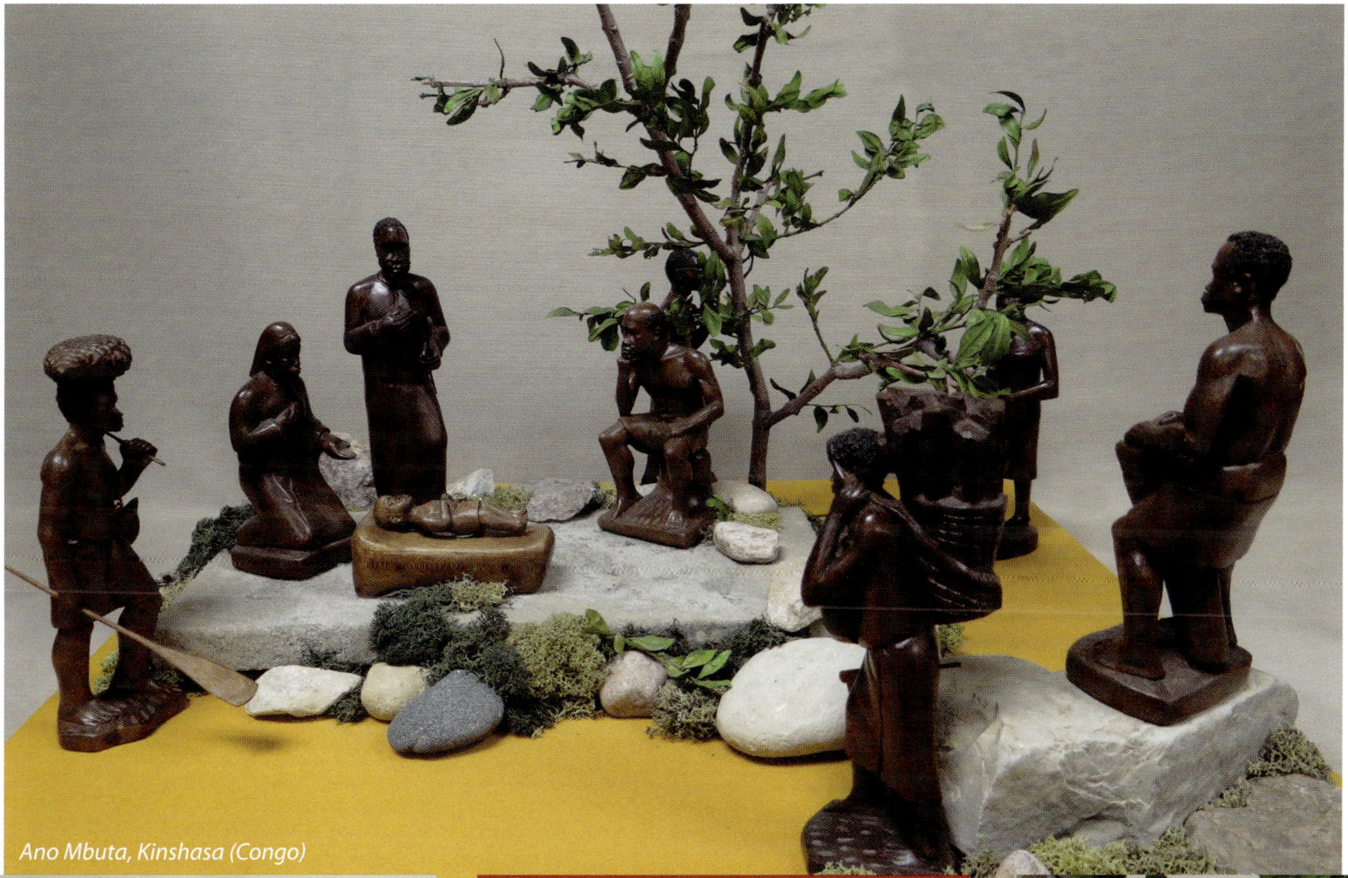

Ano Mbuta, Kinshasa (Congo)

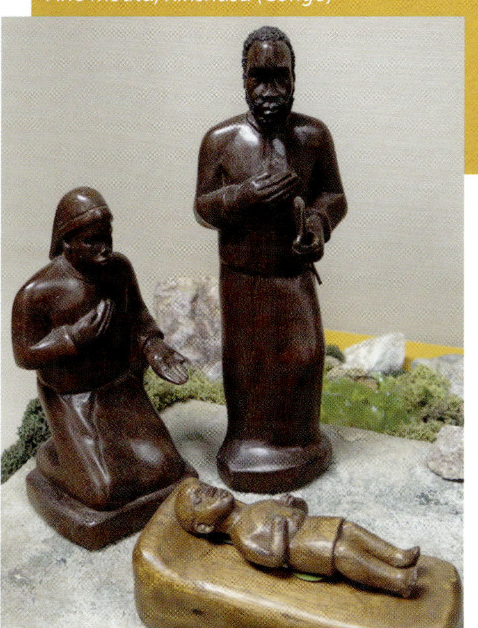

A Message Made Culture

The figures of this set, made of Lifaki wood, are of exquisite beauty not least because of the physical beauty of African men and women. The polished smoothness of the wood and the careful attention given to detail lend these figures a heightened expression of physical presence and realism. This set is an example of successful inculturation where the physical type meets sociological reality (various occupations) without diminishing the spiritual meaning of the Nativity scene.

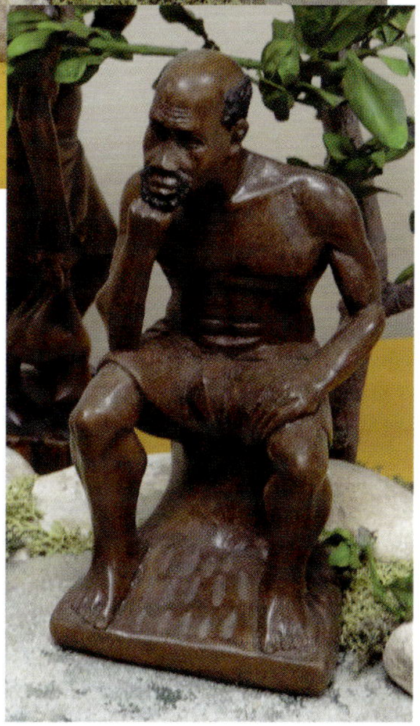

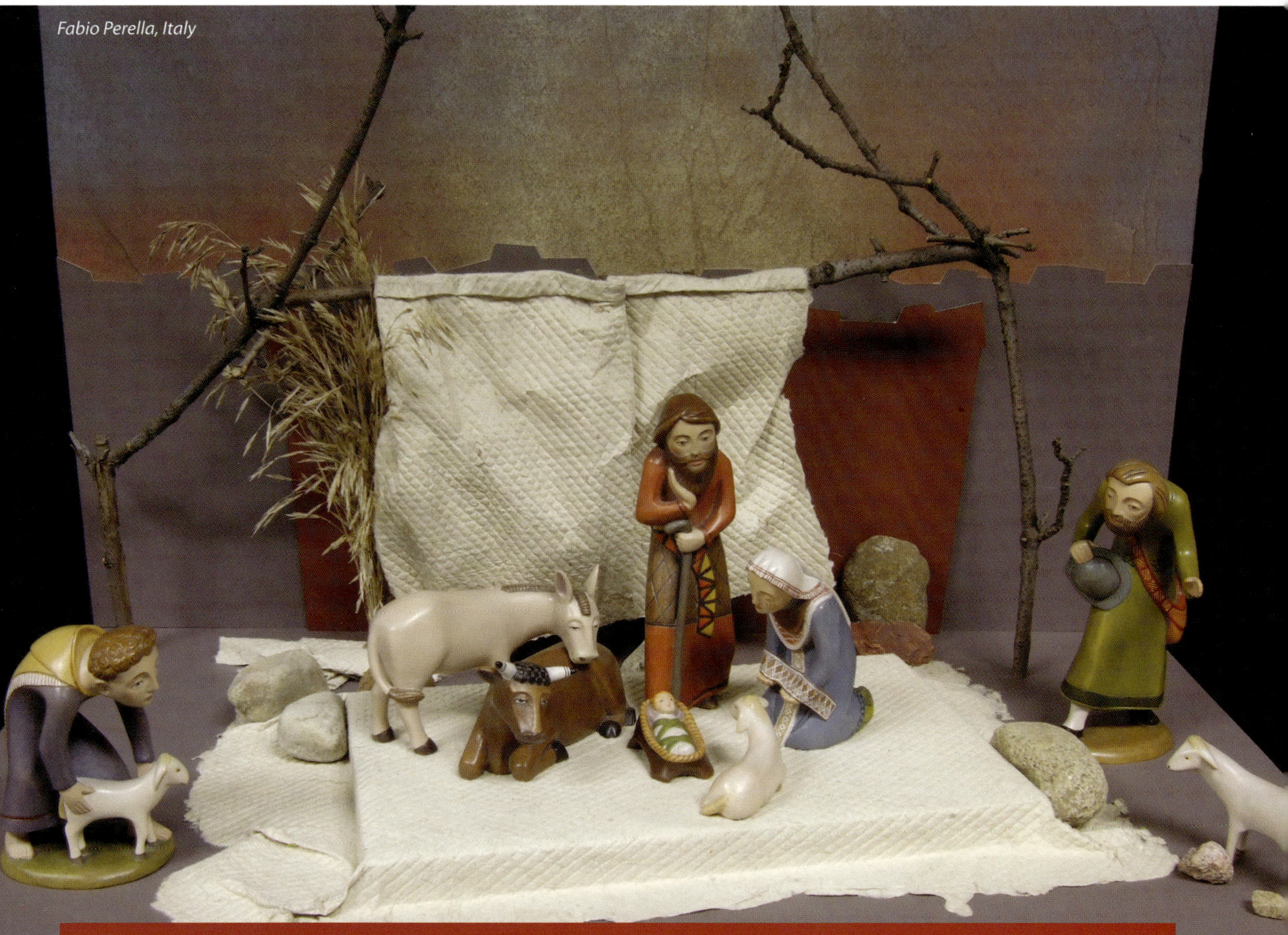

Fabio Perella, Italy

Culture Made Spirit

Each one of these figures is a little masterpiece in its own right. They all have a similar posture and express a common attitude or disposition. Their heads and necks are bent, and their backs are rounded. Superficial perception suggests stooped with age. But take another look at the unlined faces and bodies full of vigor. Their expression and posture is graceful, full of tender awe and loving admiration. Upright or kneeling, these figures stand mesmerized and entranced before the miracle of God become man. The finely carved silhouettes and delicately colored surfaces emphasize the spiritual quality which pervades the whole scene. Their expressions reflect faith. It invigorates the soul and transforms the body. Faith gives human existence a new lightness and spiritual sensitivity.

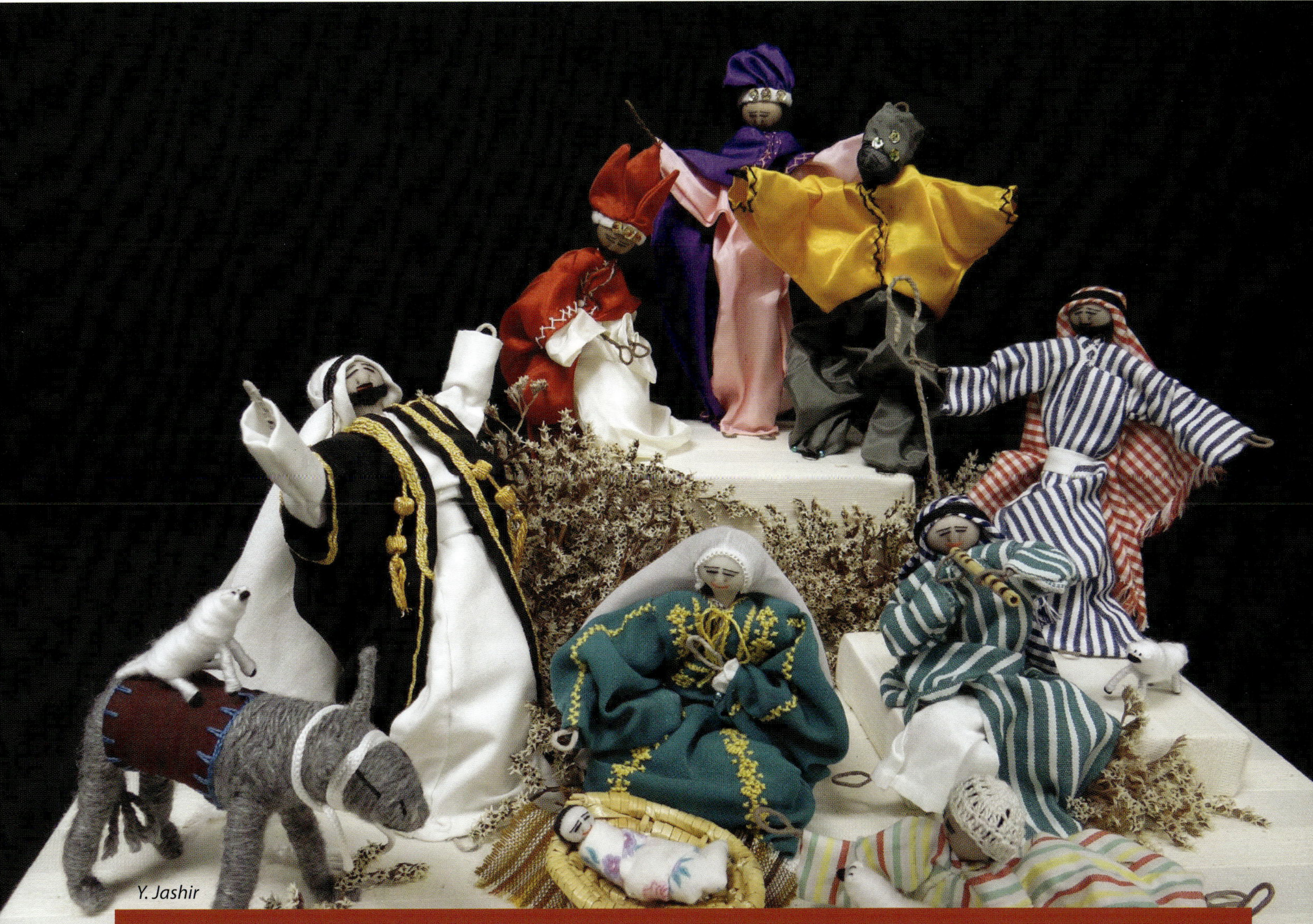

Joy of the Moment

Nativity sets made of olive wood are widely known. They represent one of two crèche traditions originating in Christian Palestine. The other tradition adopts fabric for its Nativity creations. If the wooden figures reflect the solemn character of Orientalist art, we discover a more genuinely oriental aura among the Nativity actors and actresses made of fabric. Colorful yet unpretentious, they suggest joy of life amid simplicity and hardship. This nativity set brings to life memories of sun and dust, the fragrances of the marketplace and the excited shouts of merchants. Most important, this Christmas scene wants to be a festive hymn of welcome to the Newborn. But somehow the impression lingers that joy is but for a moment, and that the bright intensity of this scene mercifully hides the long haul ahead, a trying journey for Palistine Christians.

Costumes in nativity sets are a welcome device to identify people, and their provenance and socio-cultural belonging.

"Clothes Maketh Man"

Is there a special meaning to costumes in the nativity tradition? The proverb "Clothes maketh man" is tinted with sarcasm about human vanity and hypocrisy. Erasmus' expression "The man is his clothing" (vestis virum facit) is indeed a call for honesty and personal authenticity. What counts is the real person, character and personality. However, costumes in nativity sets are a welcome device to identify people, their provenance, and socio-cultural belonging.

Michael Ayala's nativity set represents the different native groups of Ecuador. Their costumes are simple. There is no ostentation, only a difference in color and minor decorative elements on dresses.

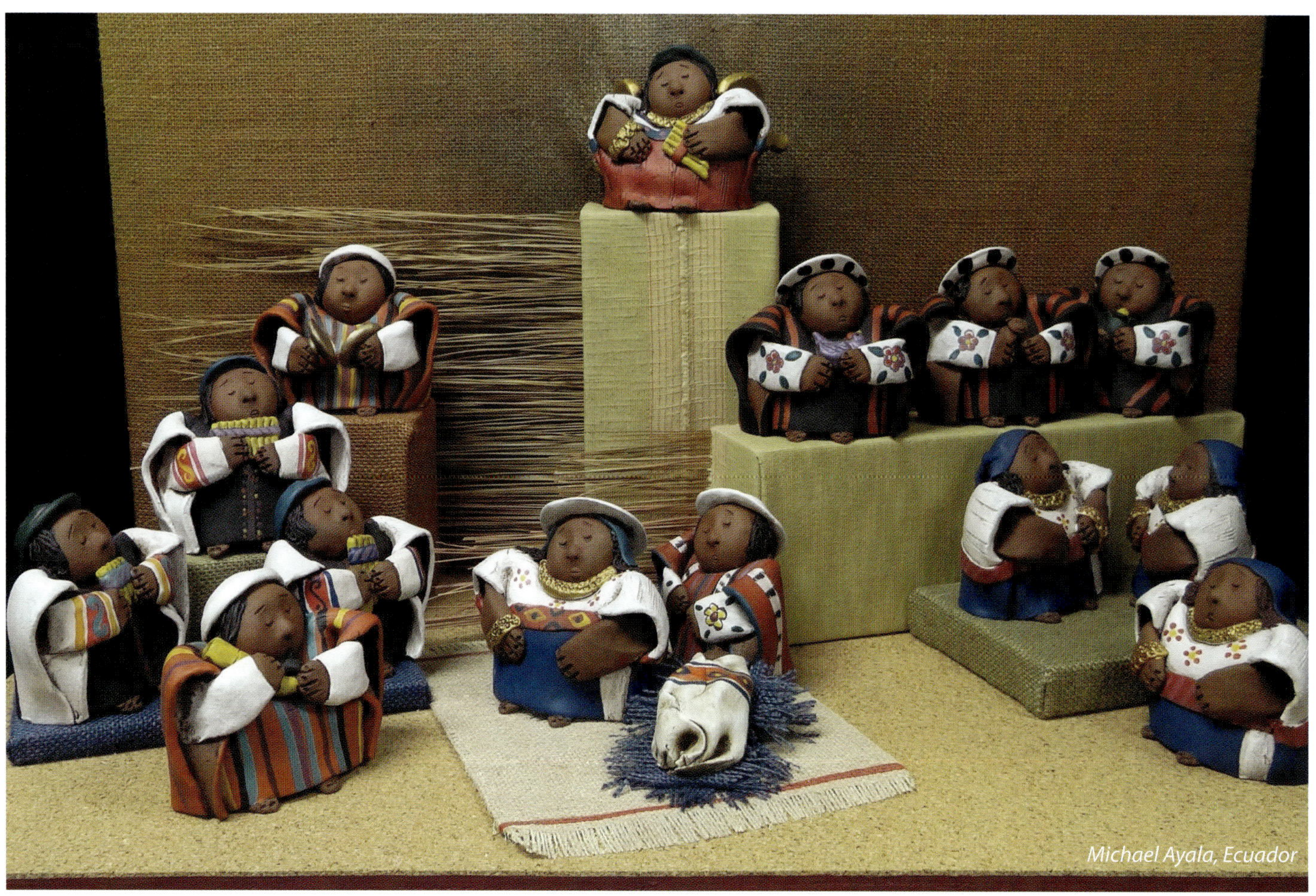

Michael Ayala, Ecuador

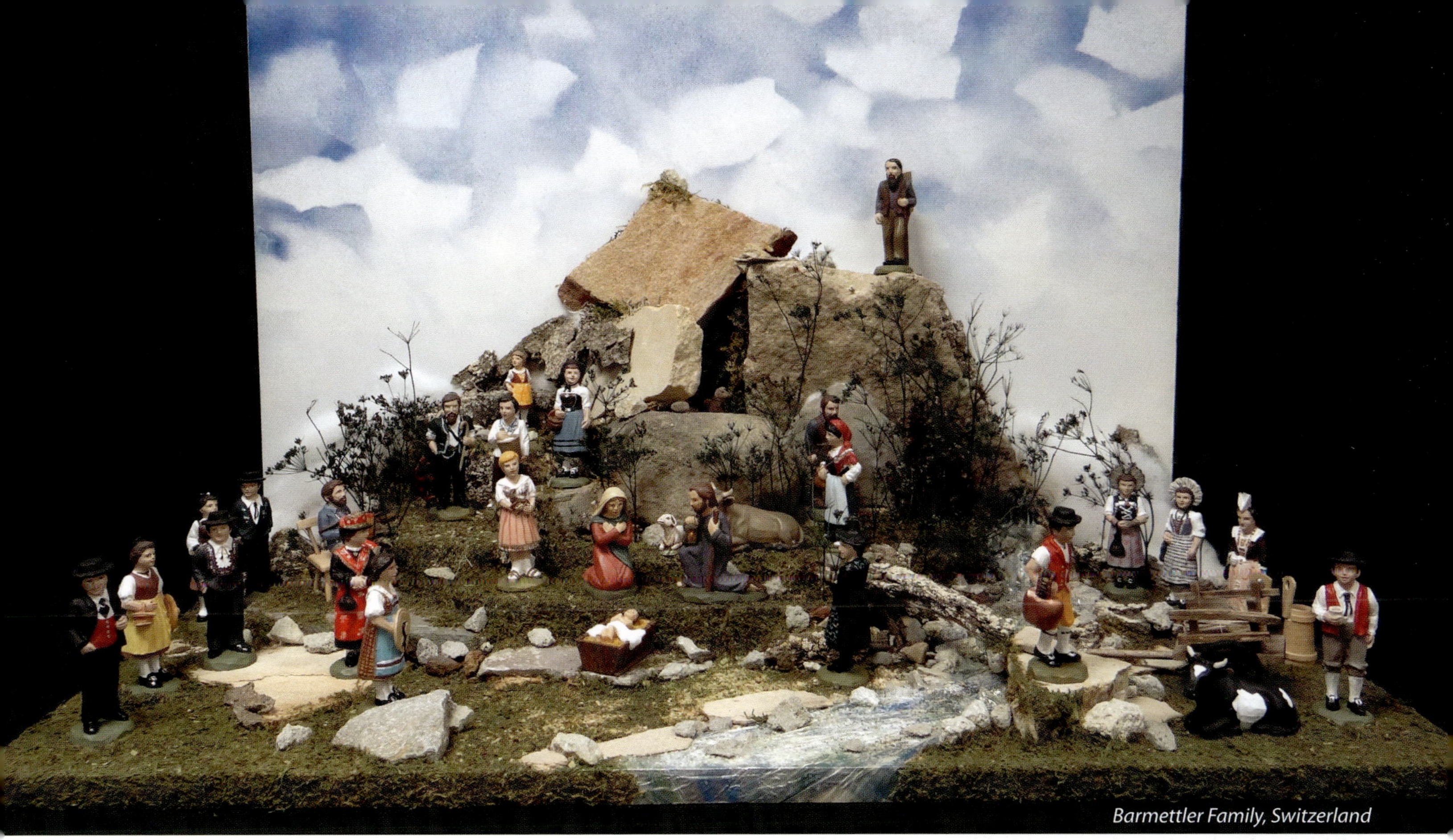

Barmettler Family, Switzerland

Swiss folklore is varied and rich. It represents four linguistic cultures and the twenty-four regions of Switzerland. Costumes are simple and colorful in the French and Italian speaking regions; they are more elaborate but subdued in the German part of the country. There was a time when the typical costumes were the daily and ordinary dress for men and women, replaced by more elaborate and decorative ones on Sundays.

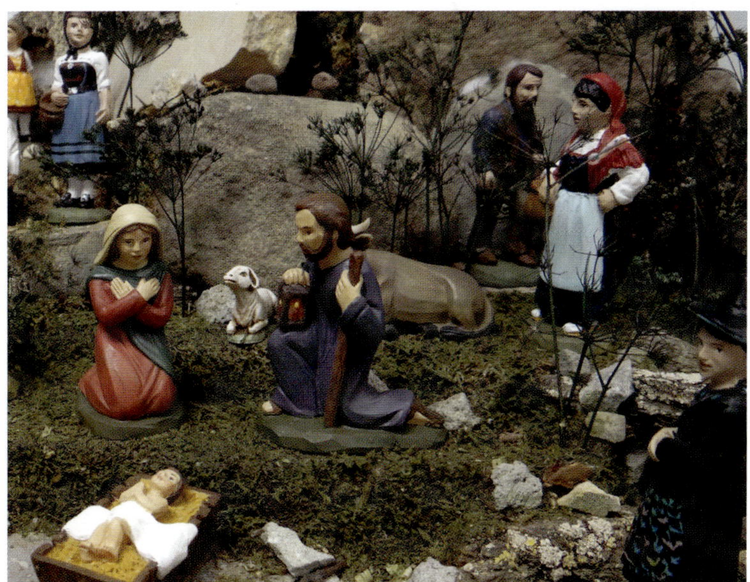

The costume can be more than only a socio-cultural label. It enhances the overall beauty of a nativity set, and is part of a colorful and joyful hymn to life as this is found in the nativity set from Ivory Coast made at the Katiola art studios outside of Abidjan.

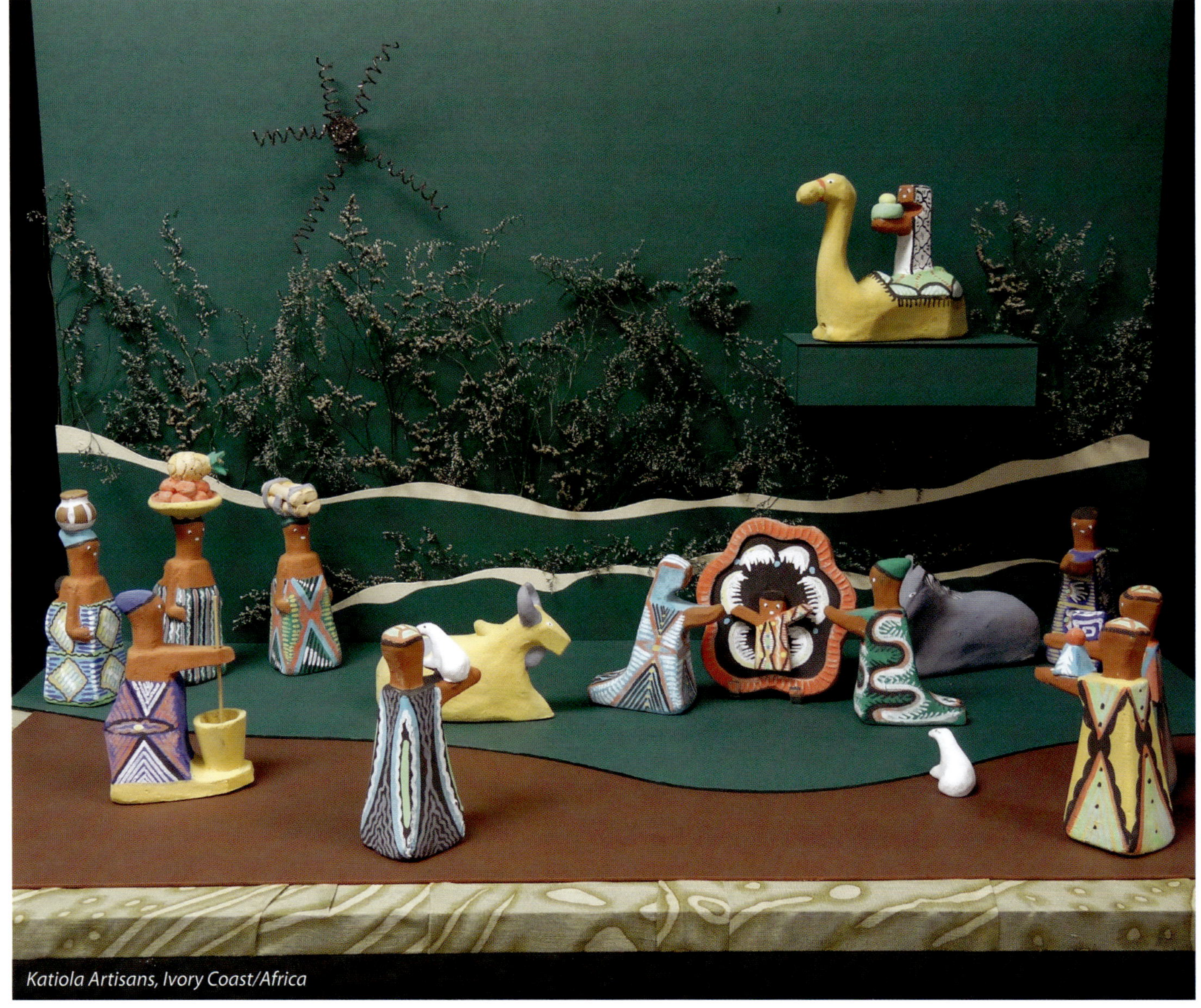

Katiola Artisans, Ivory Coast/Africa

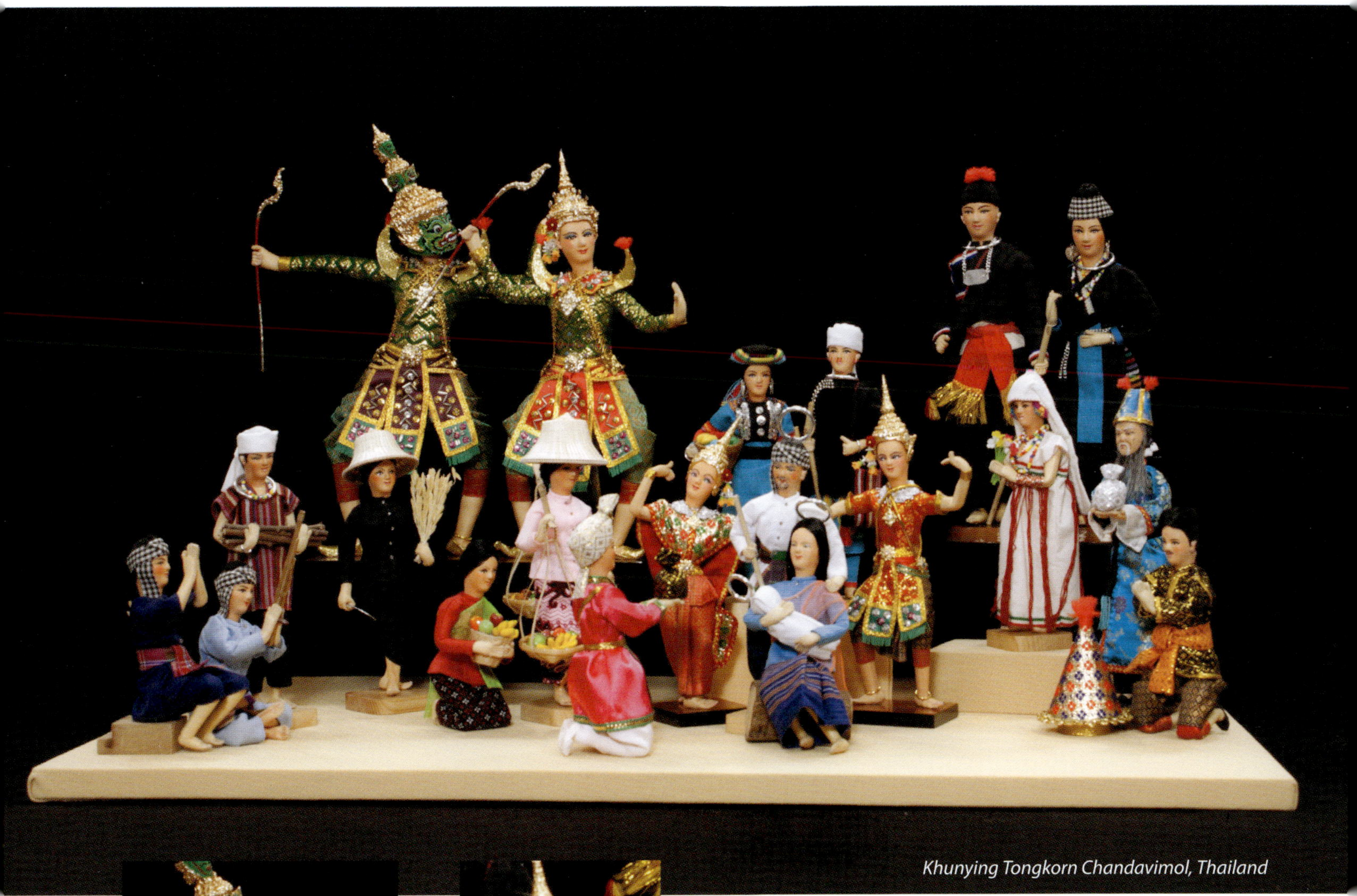

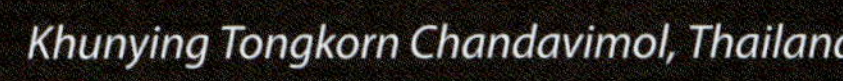

Khunying Tongkorn Chandavimol, Thailand

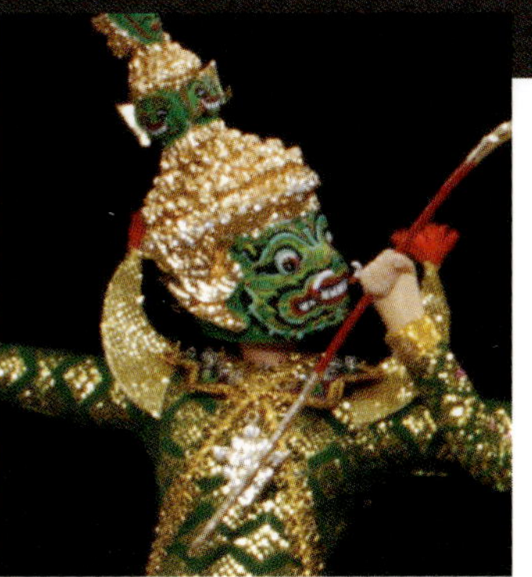

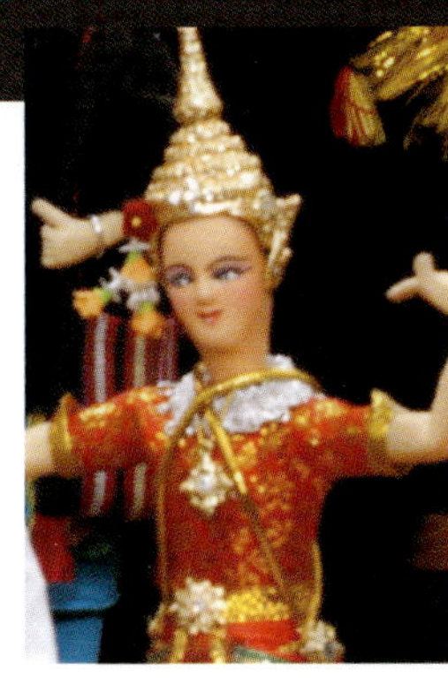

The nativity from Thailand, made of Bangkok dolls, is a true feast for the eye. In this set, costumes not only highlight the difference between the characters of the classical dance drama of Thailand, of Thosaganth and Rama, representatives of the hill tribes and prince and princess, but also the wise men dressed as Chinese Mandarin, Thai nobleman, and Indian prince.

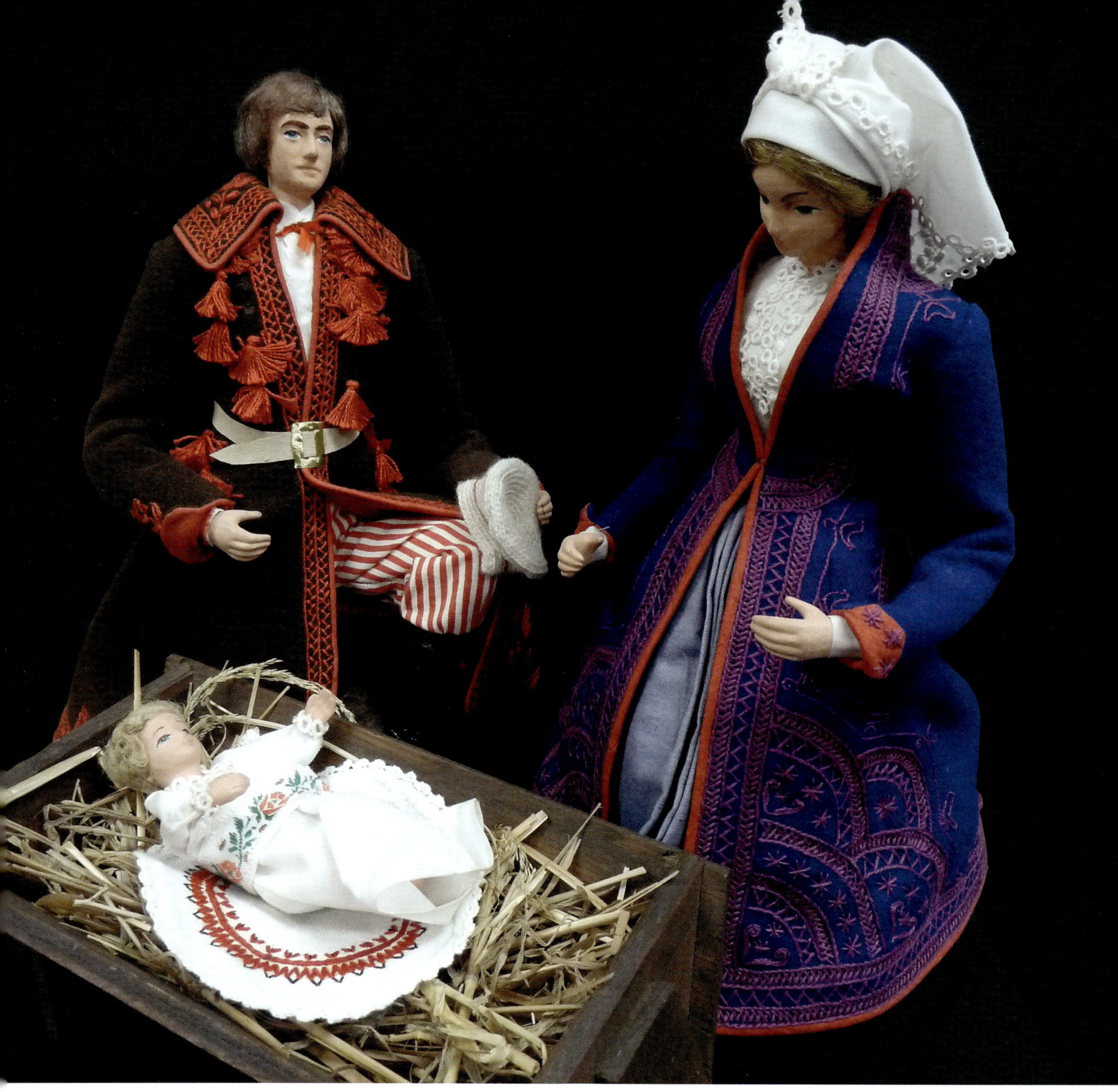

The distinctive costume beautifies not only the figure which wears it but also the surroundings. Take the figures of a nativity set representing the Kracow tradition and its dominant blue color. Following the "blue line" of local fashion, Mary is attired in a blue coat covered with intricate red stitchery (blue for Kracow; red for Poland). As a married woman she wears a headscarf, called babushba. Saint Joseph's costume matches the rich nobility of Mary's apparel. He is dressed in the typical Sukmana, the rider's jacket, and red and blue striped pants.

The history of this nativity set with the beautiful costumes helps to understand the deeper meaning of Christmas. The set was smuggled out of Poland during the Cold War period. Mrs. Danuta Romanowski, a great Polish lady, friend and helper of the Marian Library commissioned members of the Cepelia Folk Artists Collective of Krakow to create a nativity set which would be a witness of Polish art and faith. The luxury of texture and design of these noble costumes speak the language of Polish history. They are the voice of pride and praise of Polish culture. They are also the constant reminder of suffering overcome with indomitable faith.

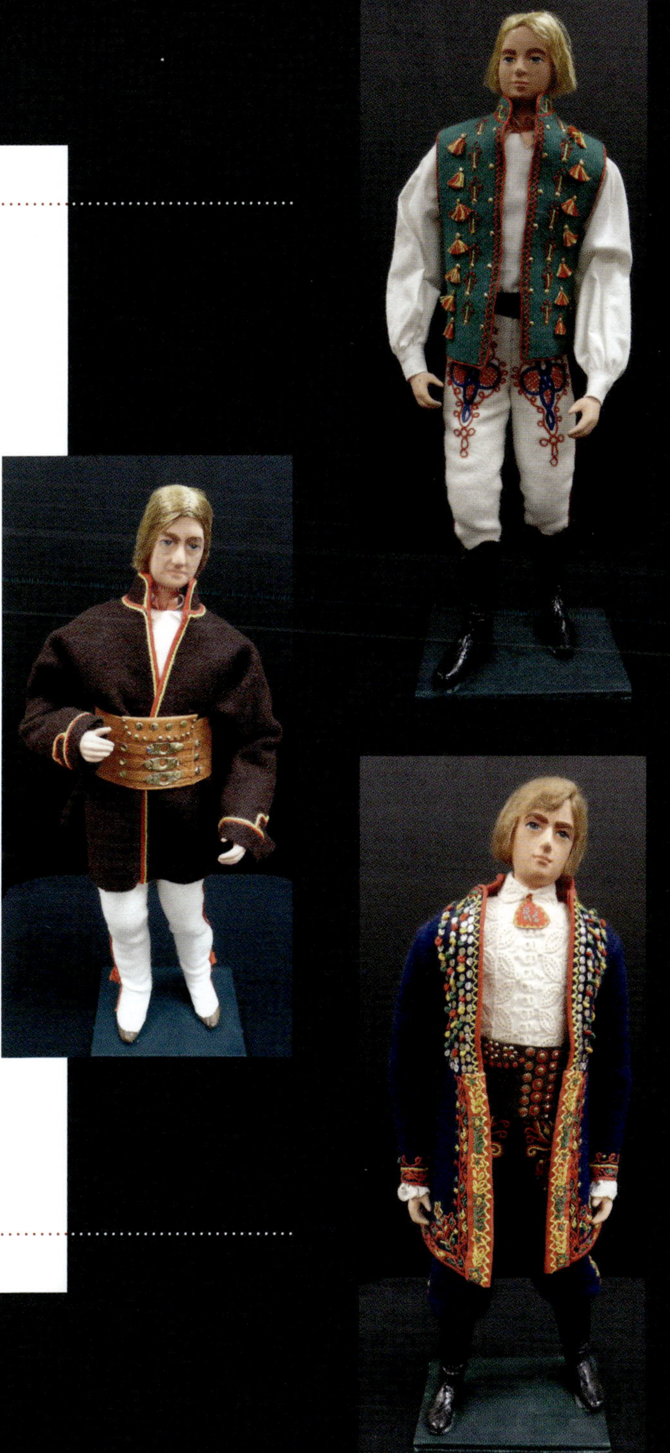

It is the same Incarnation commemorated, the same Christchild hailed and adored

For Regions and Seasons

The message for the whole world is also the message for all regions and for all seasons. It is a message for Egypt and for China, a message for Nepal and for Australia.

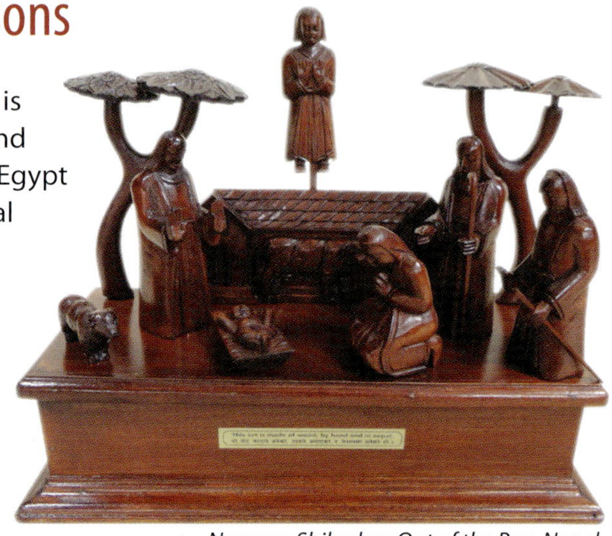

Narayan Shilpakar, Out of the Box, Nepal

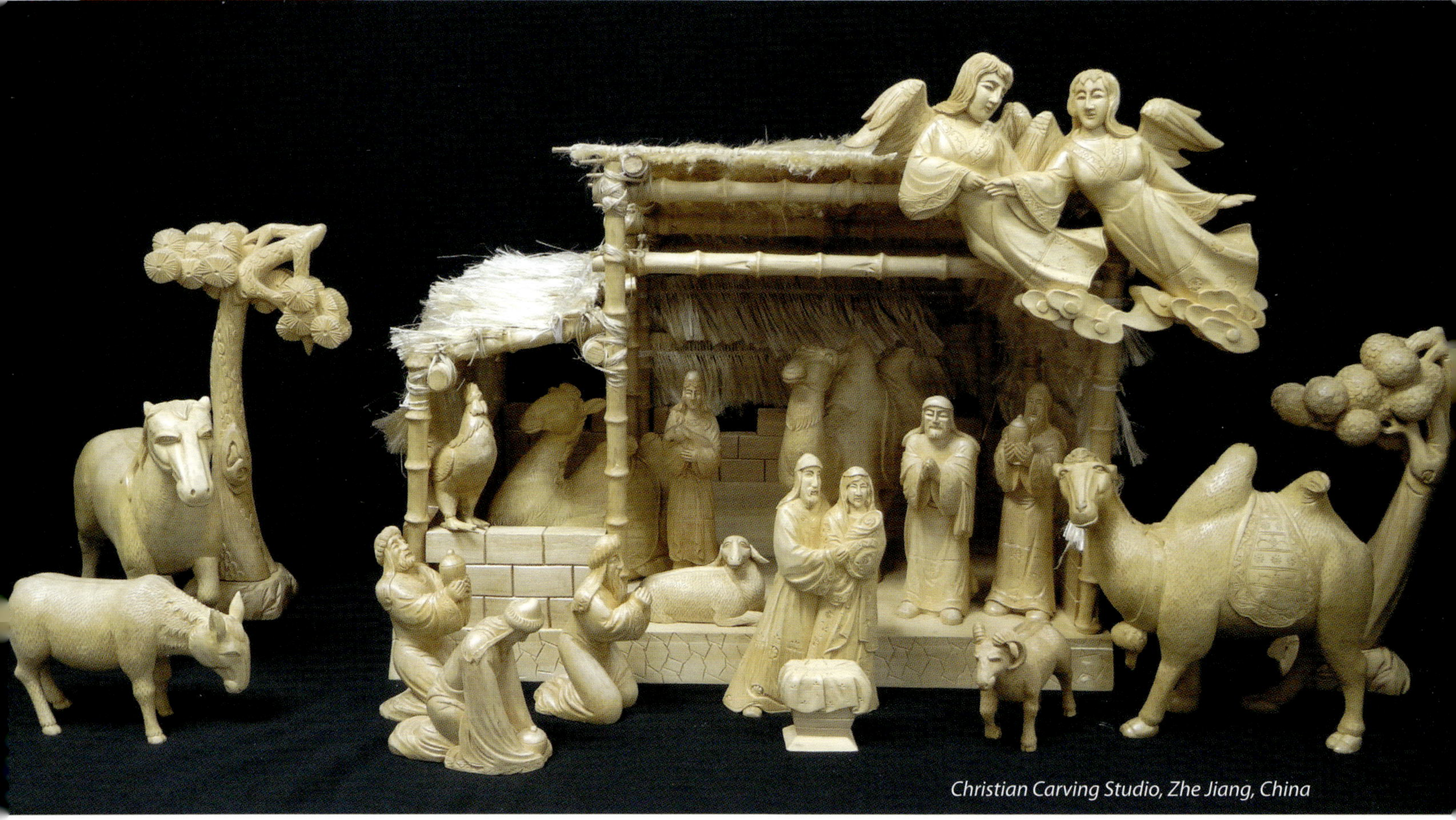

Christian Carving Studio, Zhe Jiang, China

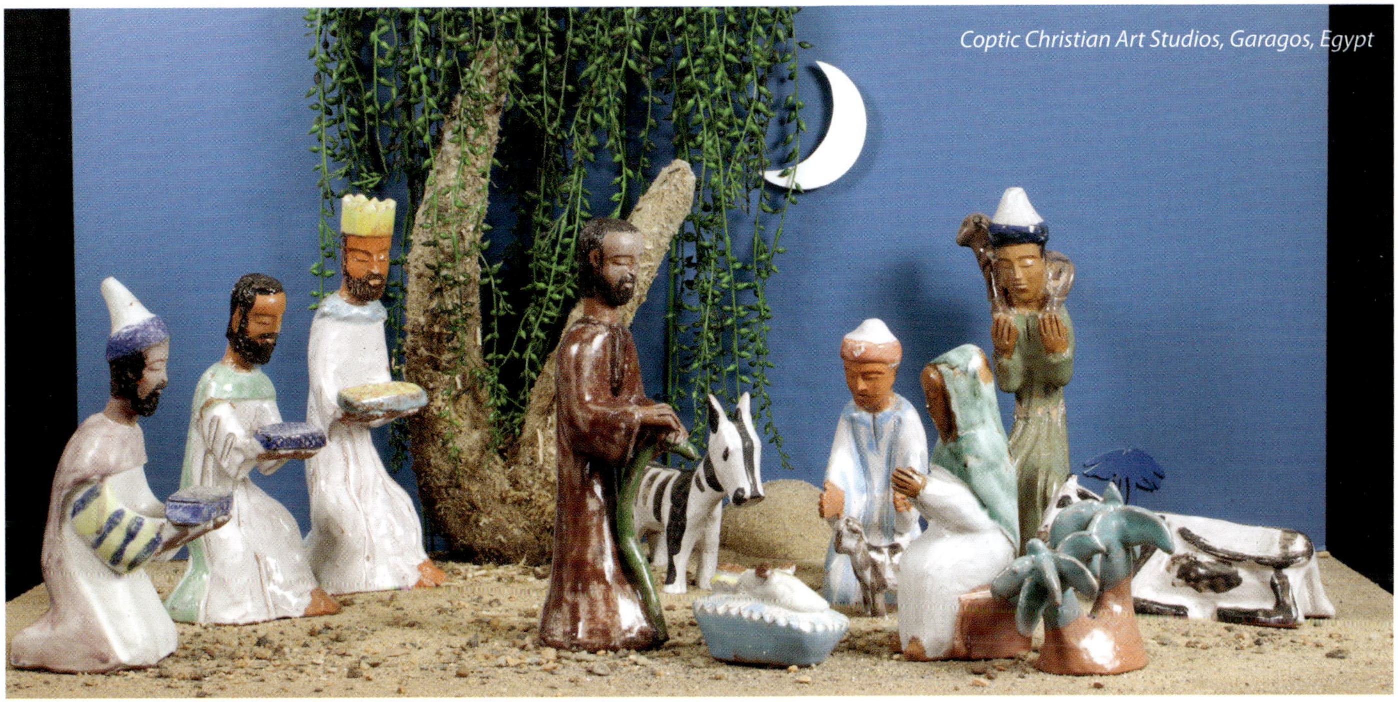

Coptic Christian Art Studios, Garagos, Egypt

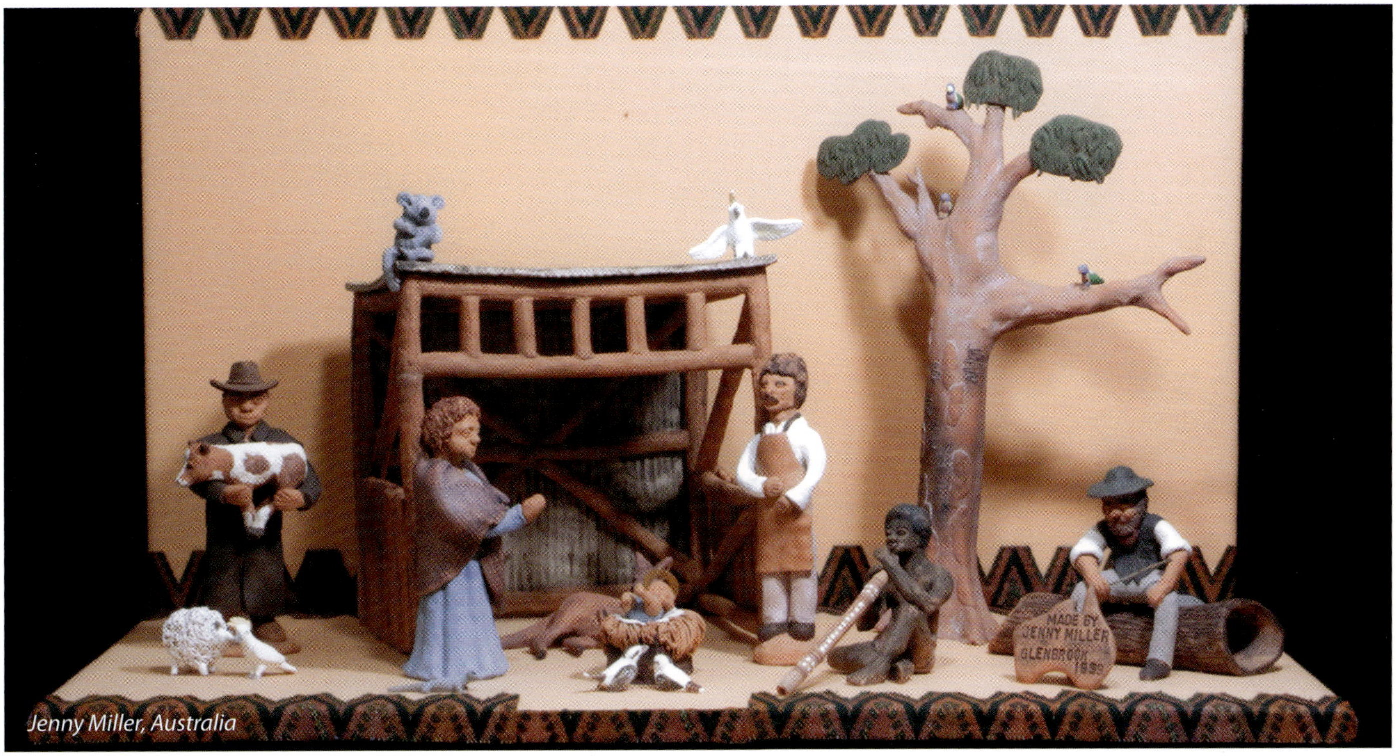

Jenny Miller, Australia

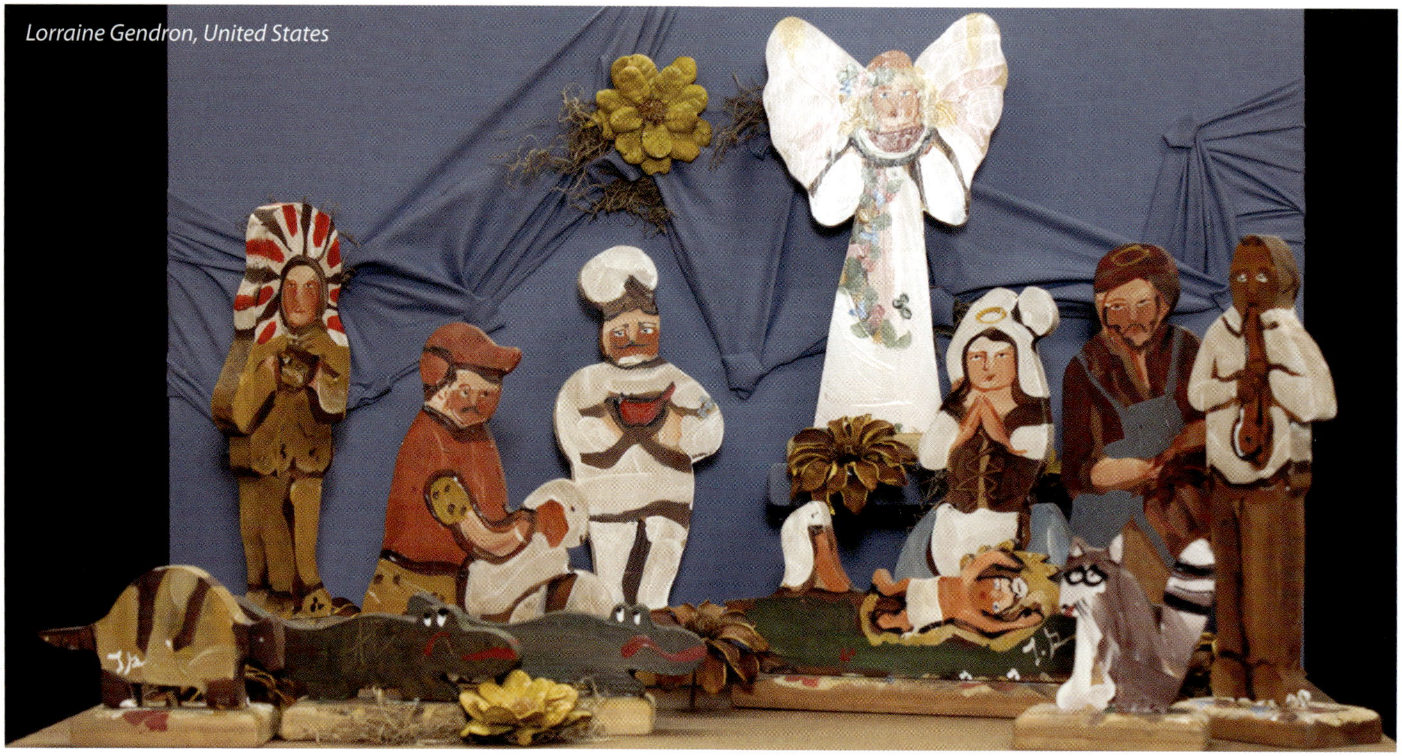

Lorraine Gendron, United States

North and South have different seasons but the same Christmas. A Cajun nativity features crocodiles, the Alaskan polar bears, but there is one manger.

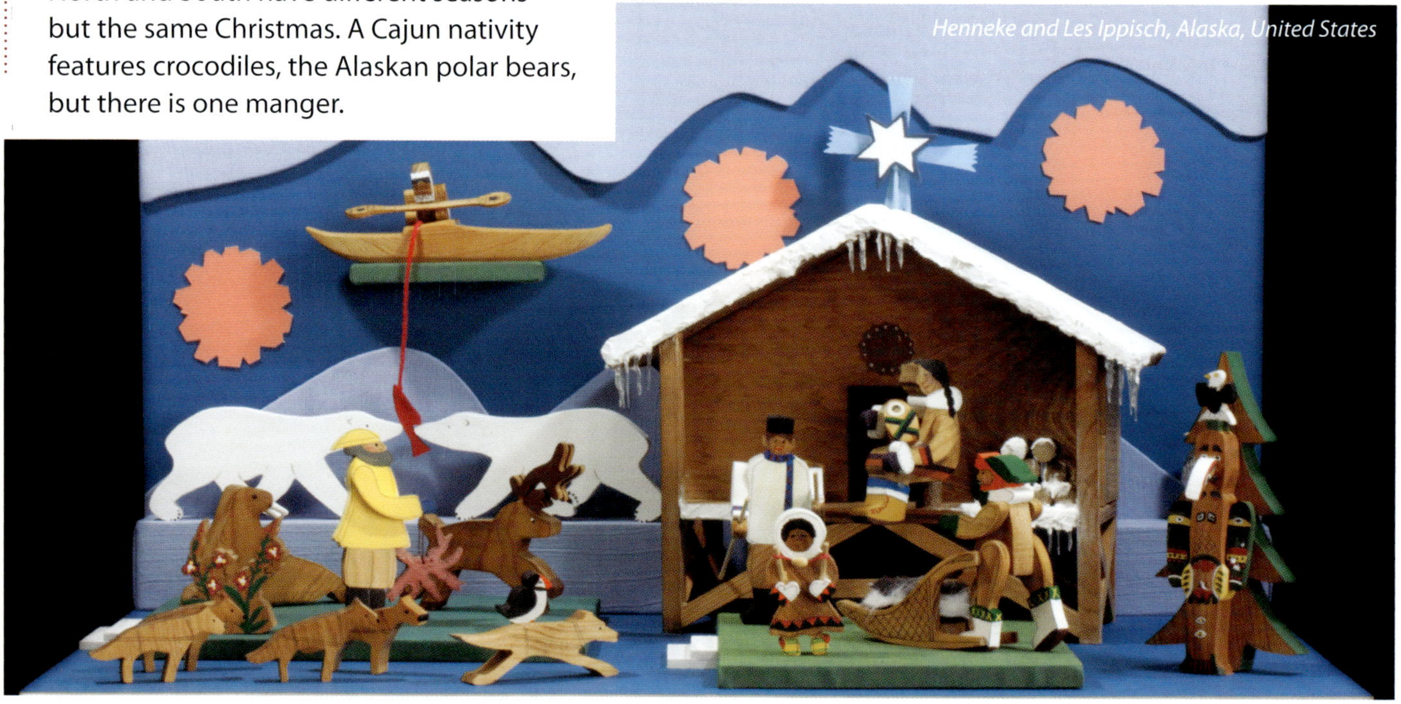

Henneke and Les Ippisch, Alaska, United States

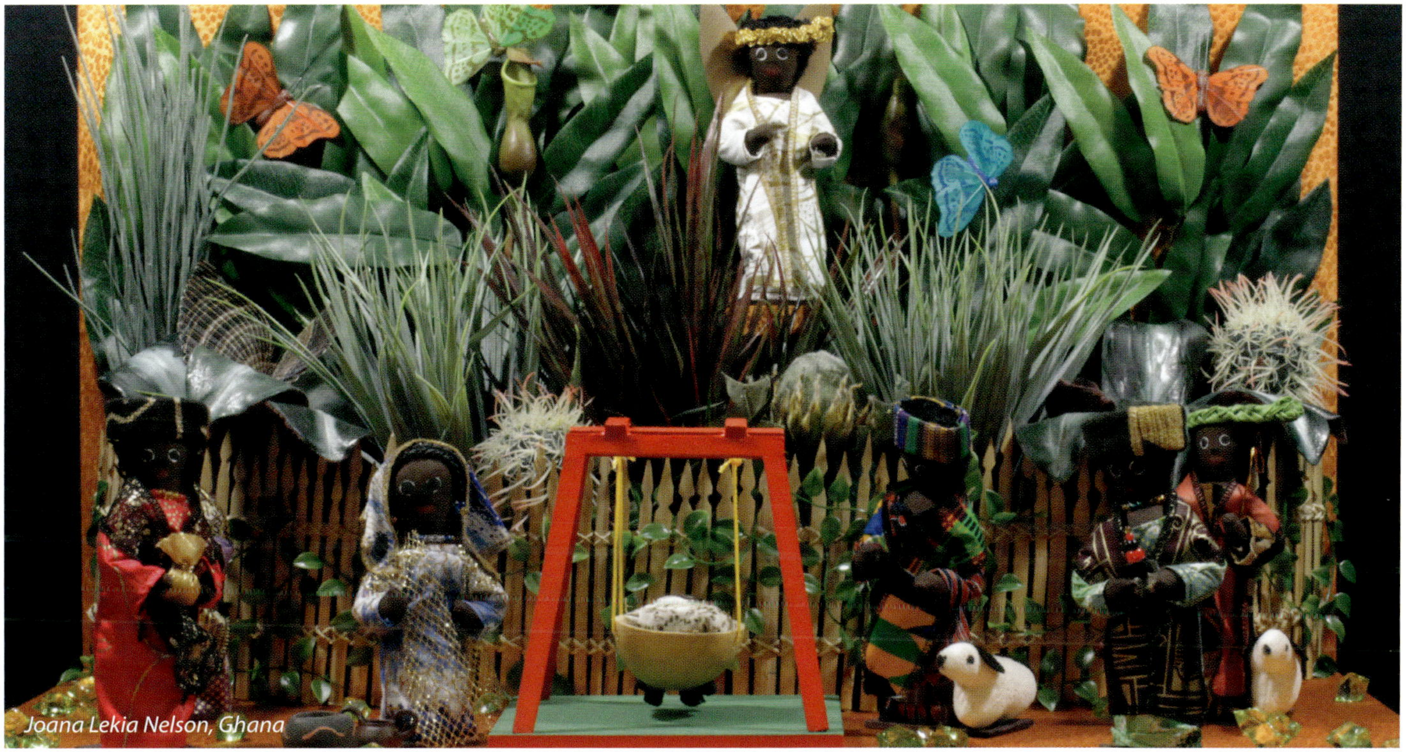

Joana Lekia Nelson, Ghana

The birth of Christ in the jungle conveys a different feel from that of the deep winter in Canada. Again, it is the same Incarnation commemorated, the same Christchild hailed and adored.

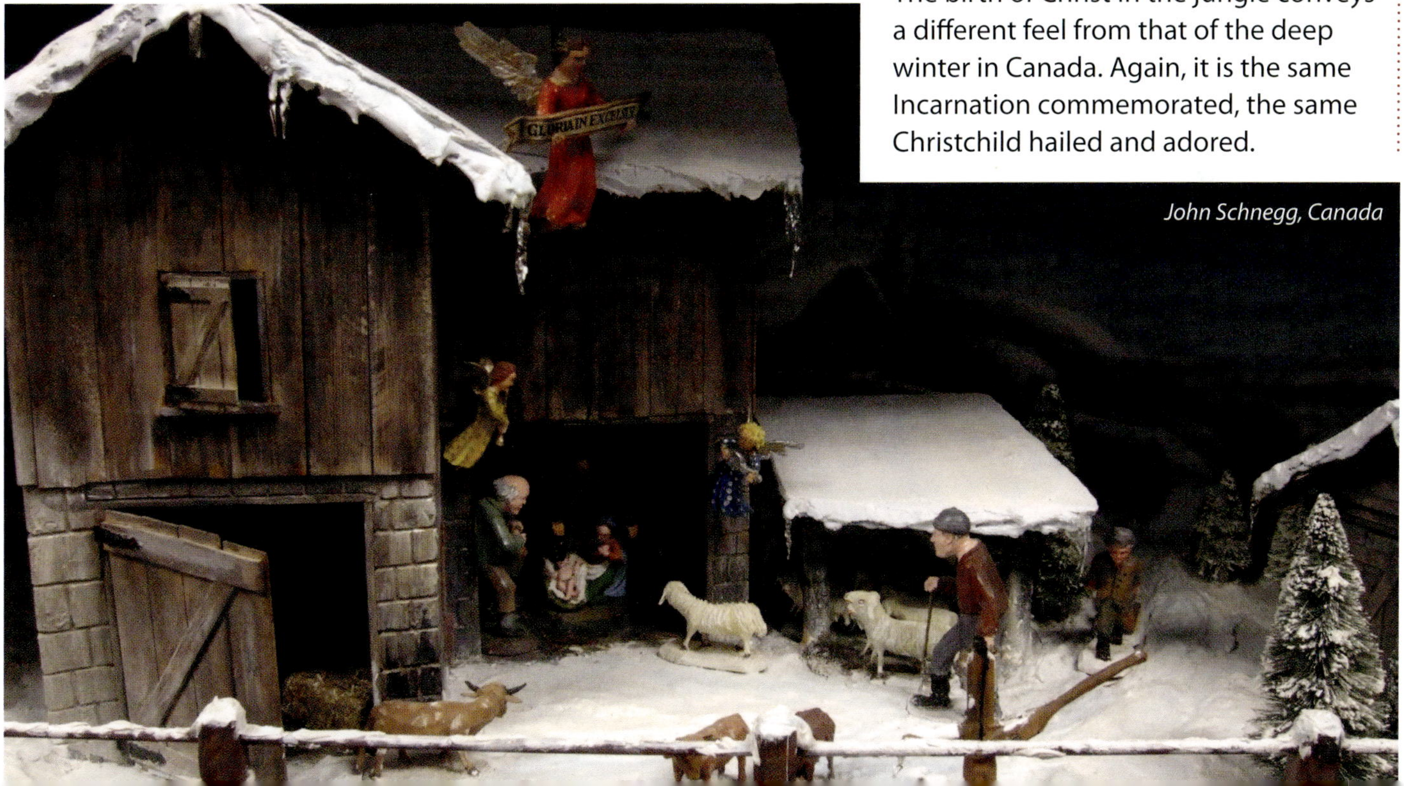

John Schnegg, Canada

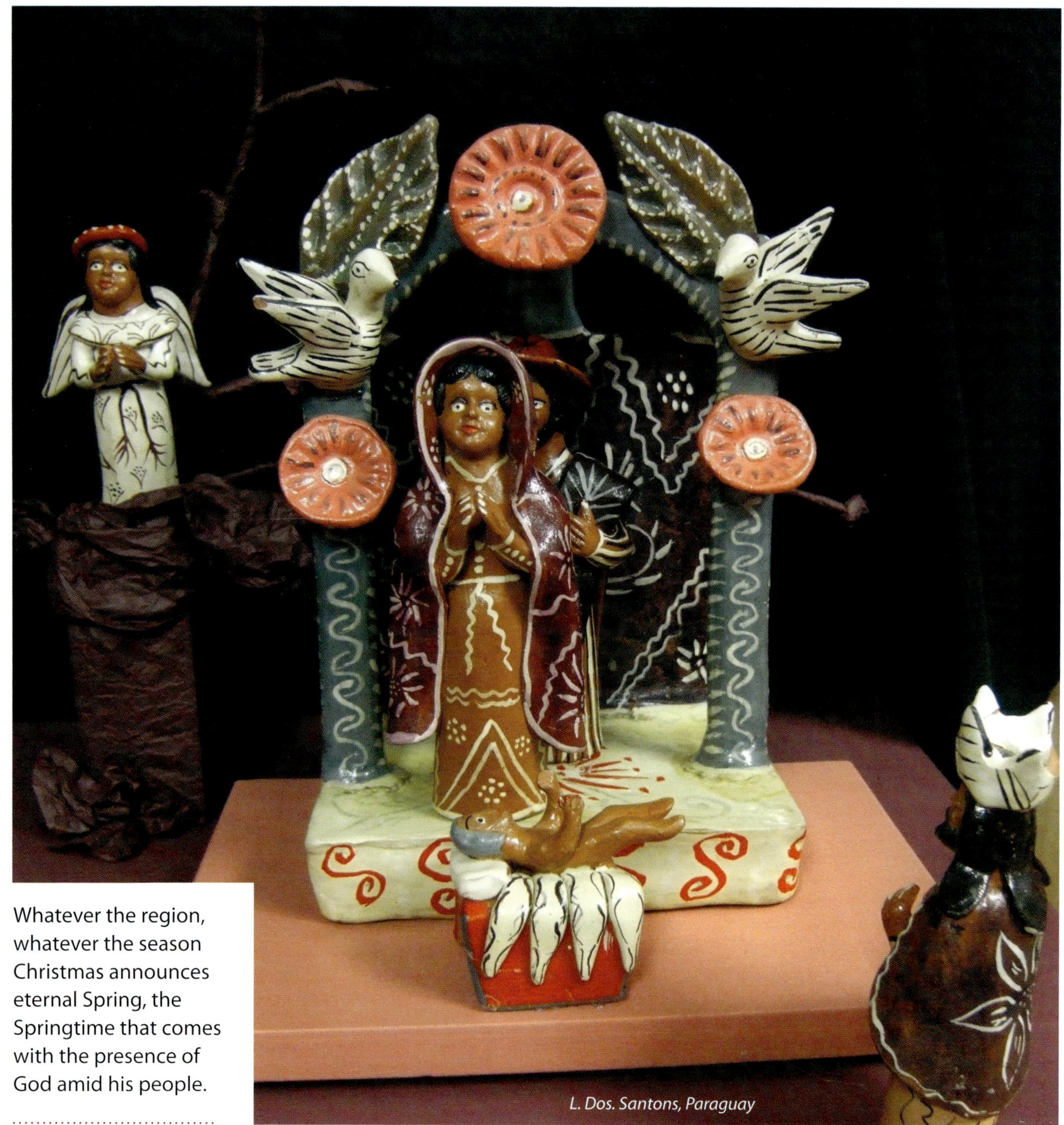

L. Dos. Santons, Paraguay

Whatever the region, whatever the season Christmas announces eternal Spring, the Springtime that comes with the presence of God amid his people.

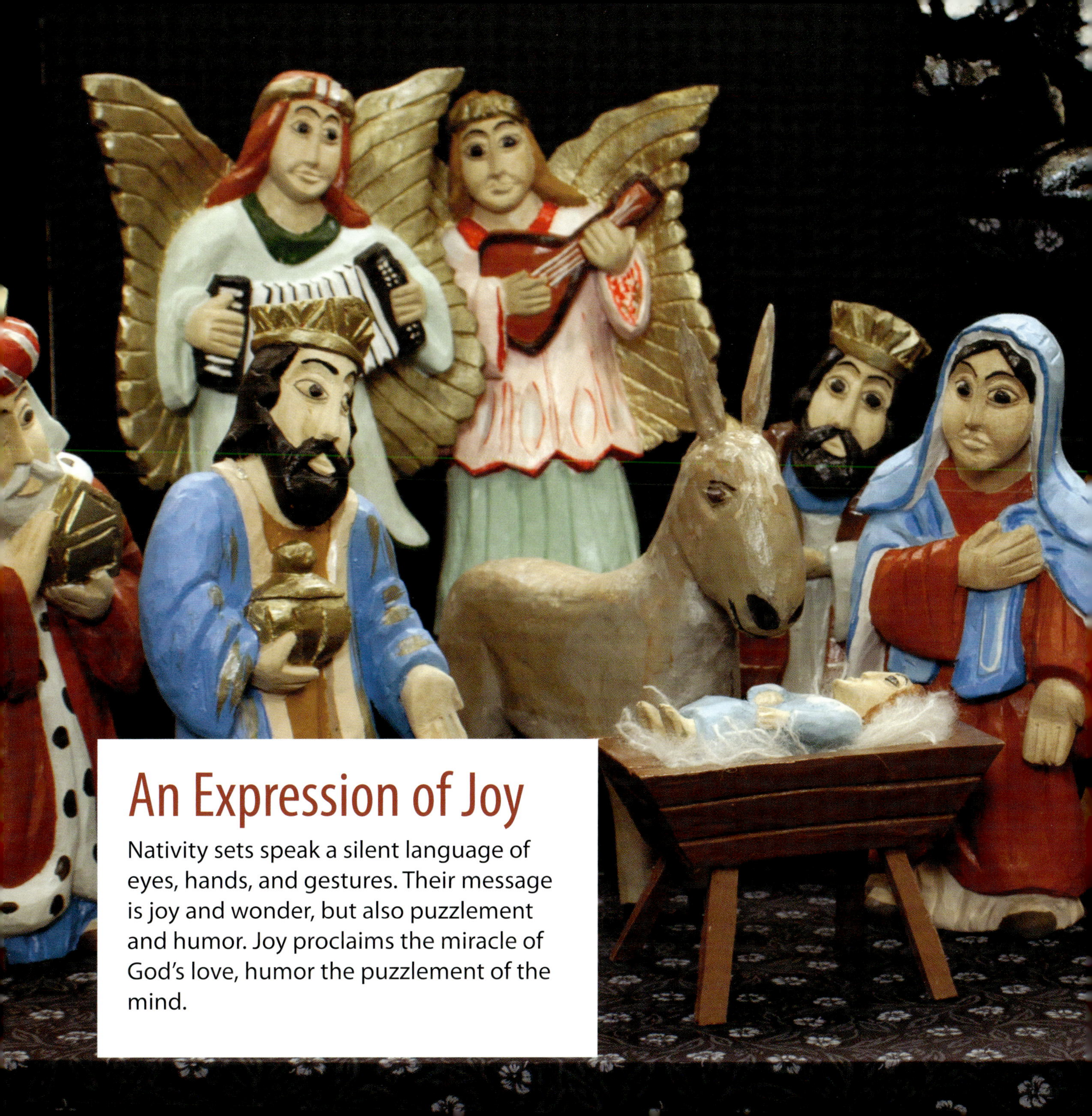

An Expression of Joy

Nativity sets speak a silent language of eyes, hands, and gestures. Their message is joy and wonder, but also puzzlement and humor. Joy proclaims the miracle of God's love, humor the puzzlement of the mind.

An Expression of Joy

One of the foremost expressions of joy is music and dancing. Many nativity traditions have added one or several musician angels to the set. Their role is to sing Gloria, the hymn that hails the marriage of heaven and earth in the birth of Jesus Christ. At a more popular level we find musicians among the shepherds playing a variety of instruments, the flute in particular. And there is the choir and the band. Music fills a variety of needs.

The Welcome

The Newborn is welcomed and announced at the same time. The coming of the Christchild opens a new and joyful era, leaving behind eons of yearning and darkness.

The Story

The music plays the role of a ballad and tells the story of Christmas, the event and its meaning. Carolers may take the place of the crèche figures – music replacing the image as is custom in Anglo-Saxon countries of the Reformation.

The Concert

Bringing together welcome and story, the concert hails the newborn king in the name of the people. Orchestra or band, angels or Mariachi musicians, melody and rhythm celebrate the joyful reunion of Redeemer and faithful.

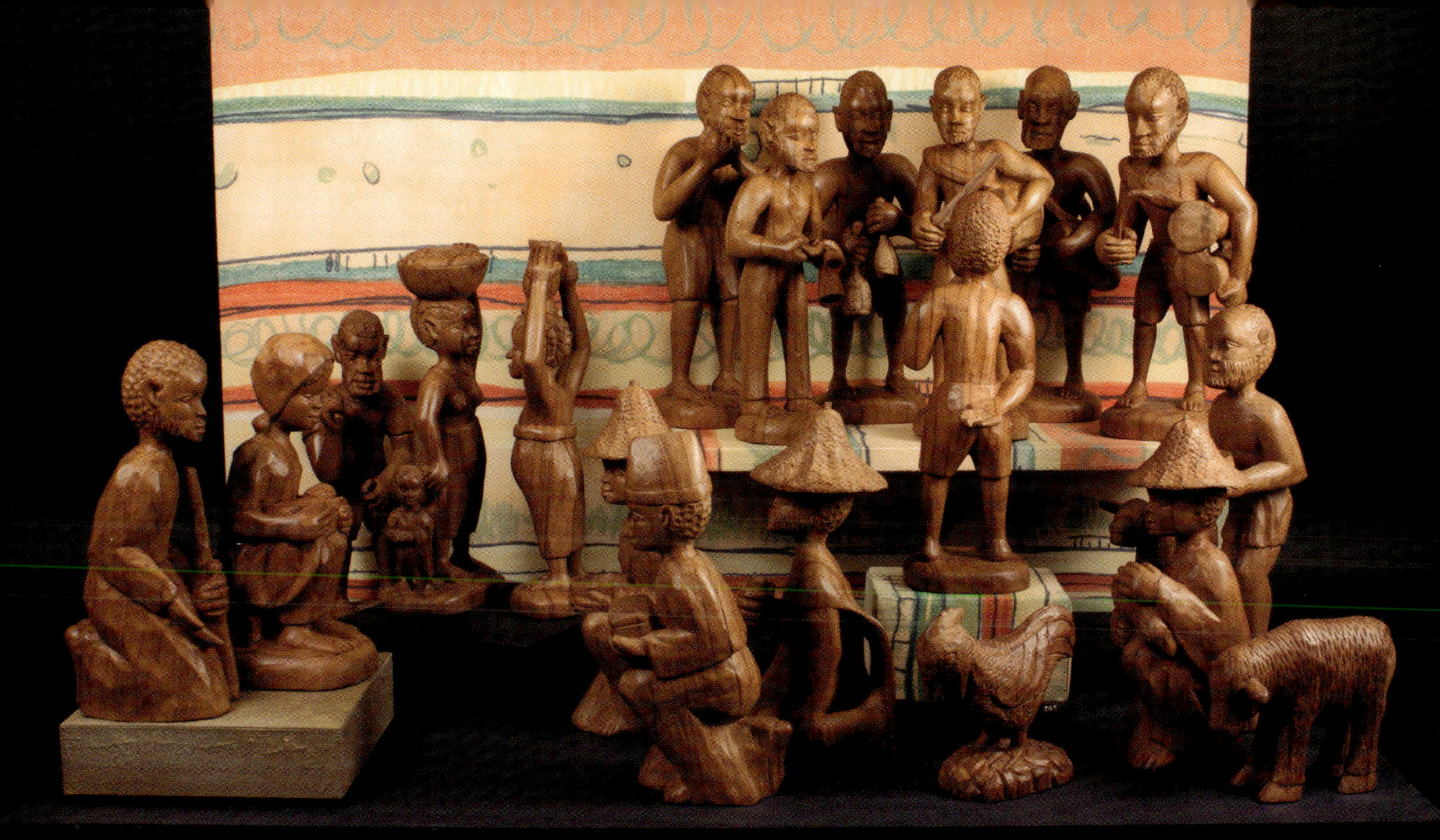

Roger J. Bawi, Togo/Africa

The Welcome

This nativity was carved by Roger J. Bawi, one of the most renowned artists of Togo. It was his aim to give the nativity scene some of the special flavor of the Kabiyè culture in the Northern region of Togo. At birth, the newborn is welcomed by the whole village. Among the many representatives of the population, there is, in particular, the so-called "traditional orchestra." It has a prominent place in this nativity set. The orchestra is composed of musicians playing the drum, the horn, the flute, a kind of rattle, and the gong. The drums, covered with animal hides, are the most important instruments. They create a festive atmosphere and harmony. The horn announces the happy event of Christ's birth, whereas the flute lends voice to the jubilant mood of the population. The musician who rhythmically shakes the rattle has a special name. He is called the "griot," a traveling poet and musician, and a herald of oral popular tradition. It is his role to welcome the baby in the name of its ancestors, and of the community with its tradition and customs. The gong player rounds off the musical welcome. He punctuates the rhythm of the drums, and adds a lighter touch to their deep voices. African culture is known for its zest for life. Thus, this Togolese nativity is a celebration of life with its many meanings.

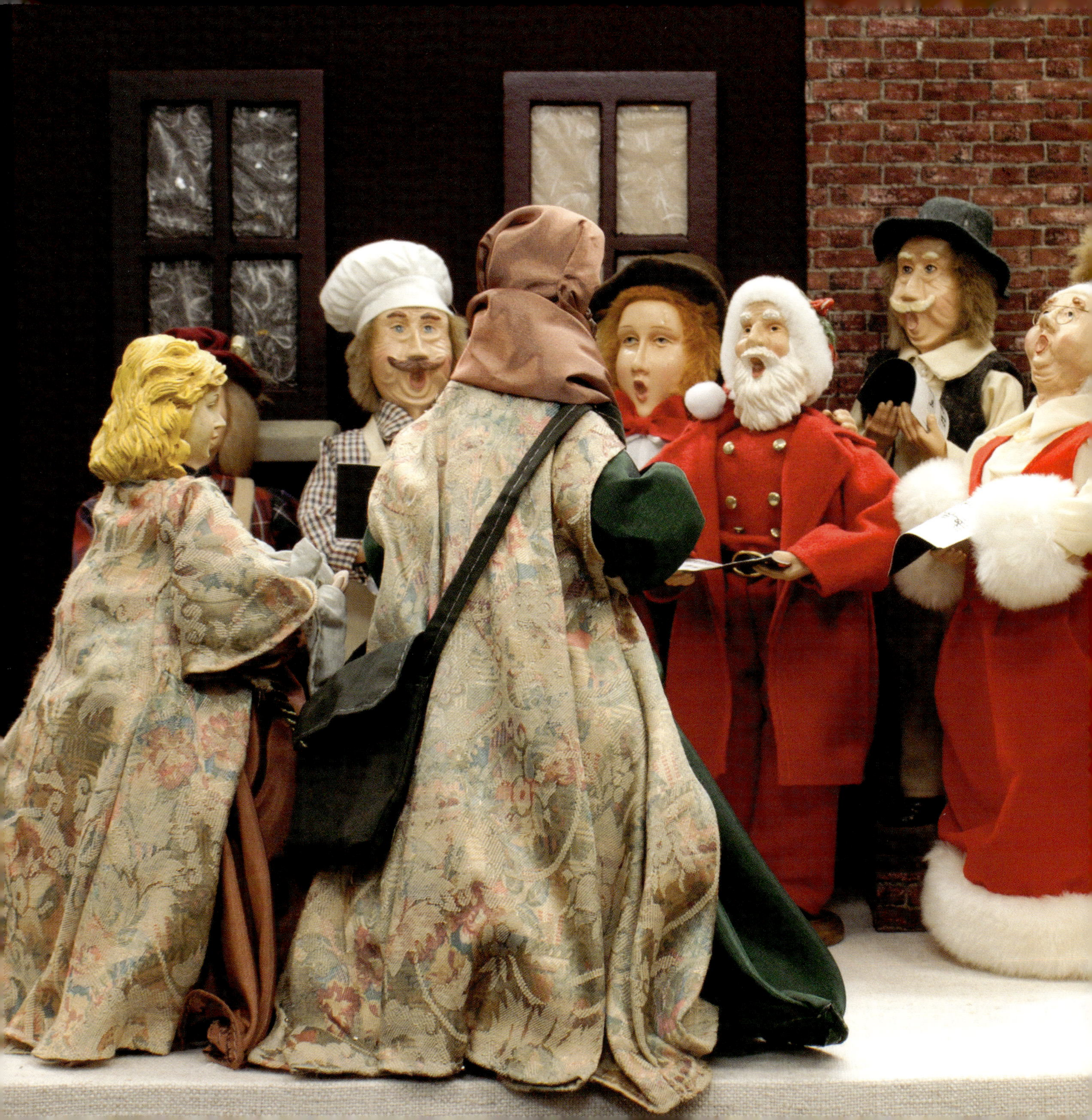

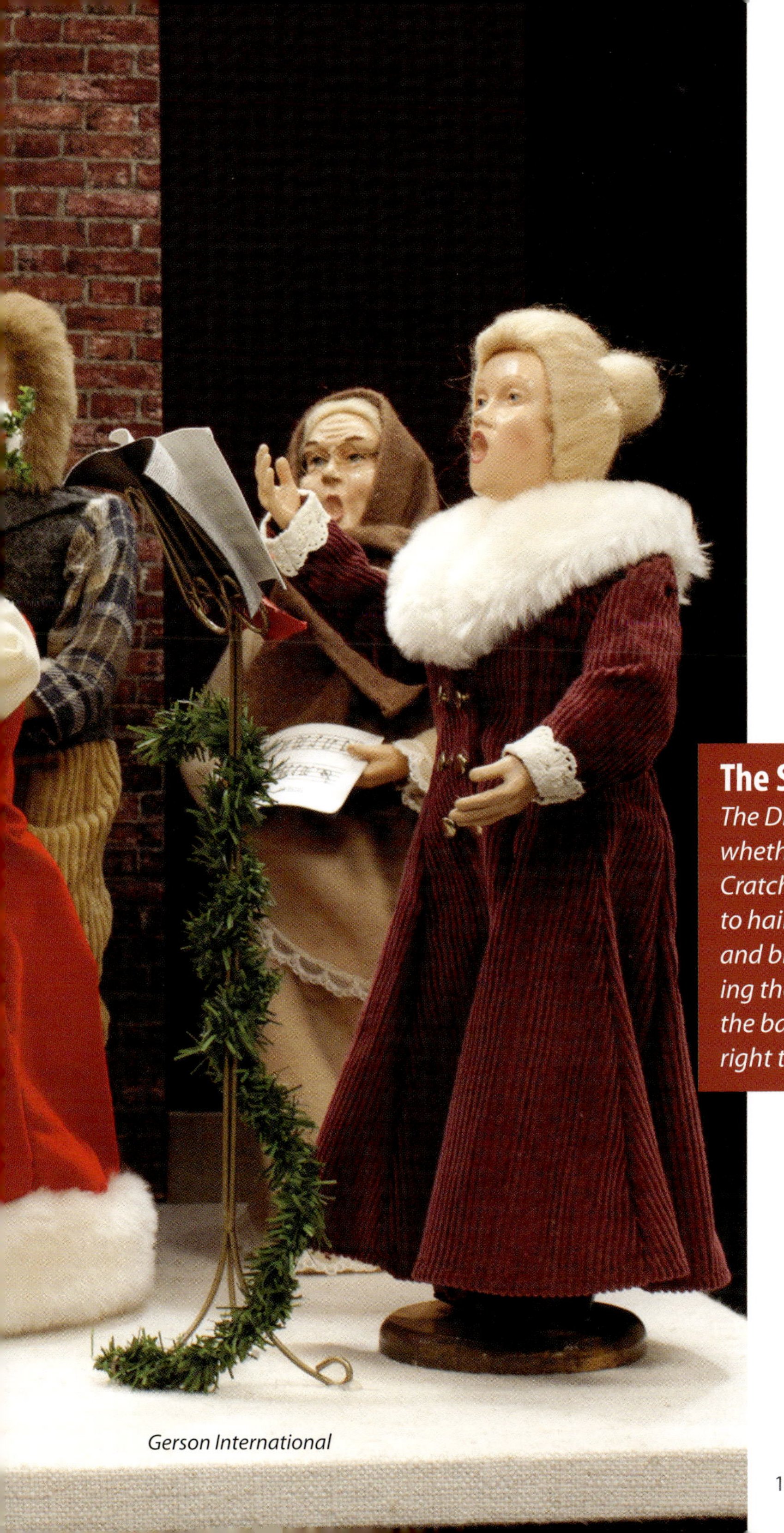

Gerson International

The Story

The Dickens Carolers have mutated many times over. But, whether Salvation Army or seafarer, Mr. Fezziwig and Mrs. Cratchit or Primadonna and Dandy, they all have but one voice to hail the newborn king … who remains invisible. In this set, and breaking with tradition, the infatigable chanters are receiving their just reward. The carolers no longer have to search for the babe Emmanuel in their songbooks. The Holy Family stands right there in front of them: a true carolers' reward.

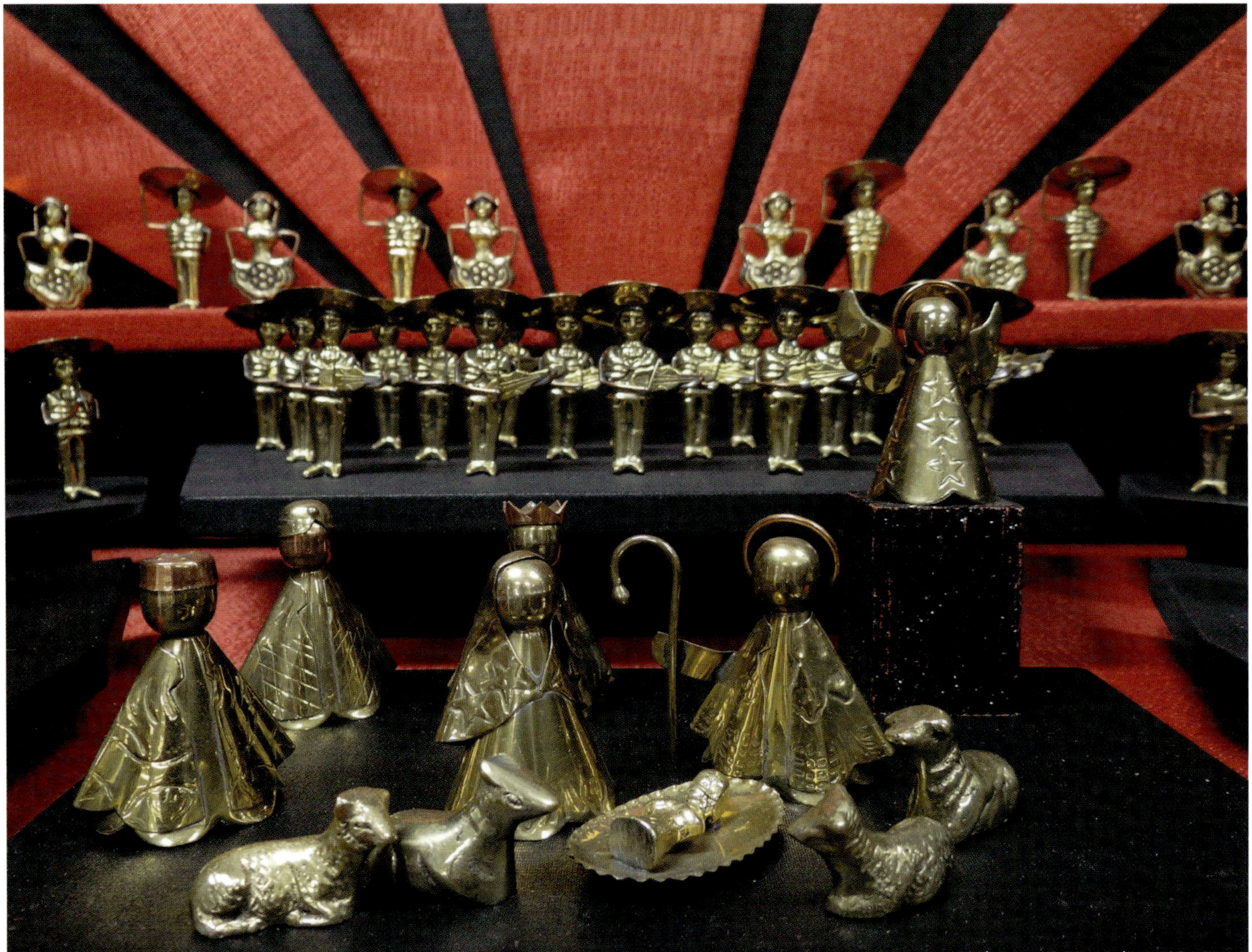

Unknown Artist, Jalisco, Mexico

The Concert

This nativity set is like an island in a sea of brass. But the brass is not just brass. This is a reunion of typical Mexican brass bands, called the Mariachis. You can intuit the festive and happy, but also the romantic and sentimental tunes of the Mariachi musicians. Only one of them made the tribune of honor reserved for the the traditional nativity actors. He represents the many trumpets, violins, guitars, vihuelas (small five-stringed guitar with rounded back) and guitarrons (six-stringed large vihuelas) artfully grouped behind him. The Mariachi tradition originated in the western Mexican state of Jalisco. It has become a symbol of Mexican music and culture. In this set, the Christchild's advent is hailed with the sound of Mariachi bands incorporated.

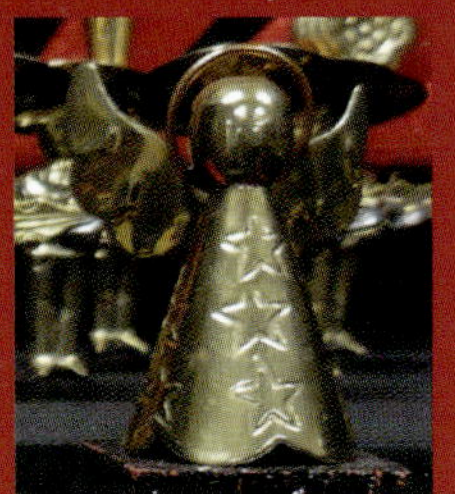

A Sense of Humor

Humor at the manger turns out to be a mostly kind and gentle defense mechanism put in place and operated to lighten and brighten the weight and darkness of the mystery. Whose mind is valiant enough to bear the weight of a God-man? Who will suffer to be smothered in mystery? There comes a point when our sensitivity reacts and tries to give names to what is nameless, faces to what seems faceless. The mystery of the Nativity, sublime and awesome as may be, has a deeply human side. Humor occurs when this human side is claimed and for a moment, stands on its own feet, sometimes human, even all too human feet. The methods to achieve humor are varied.

Relief

There is great relief, and thus humor, in showing the Christchild in all his ordinariness of a normal human baby, accidents not excluded.

Superiority

Playful humor indulges in a trace of superiority by changing the script of the play, putting a big nose on a slim face, or giving new names to venerable acquaintances. This happens when the holy family and their visitors find themselves changed into candle snuffers.

Defense

Making the impossible possible, letting pigs fly, is a humorous way of taking matters in our hands and building a solid defense against the crushing weight of what is intangible and imponderable.

Fun

Fun is a somewhat heavy-handed and sometimes raucous form of humor. Popular in tone and expression, fun insists on equality for everybody, and puts an accordion in the hands of the angel.

Delight

There is a finer form of humor which seeks joy before pleasure, and gives enchantment rather than simple thrill. When crèche figures perform a tree ballet instead of dancing Polka humor becomes true delight.

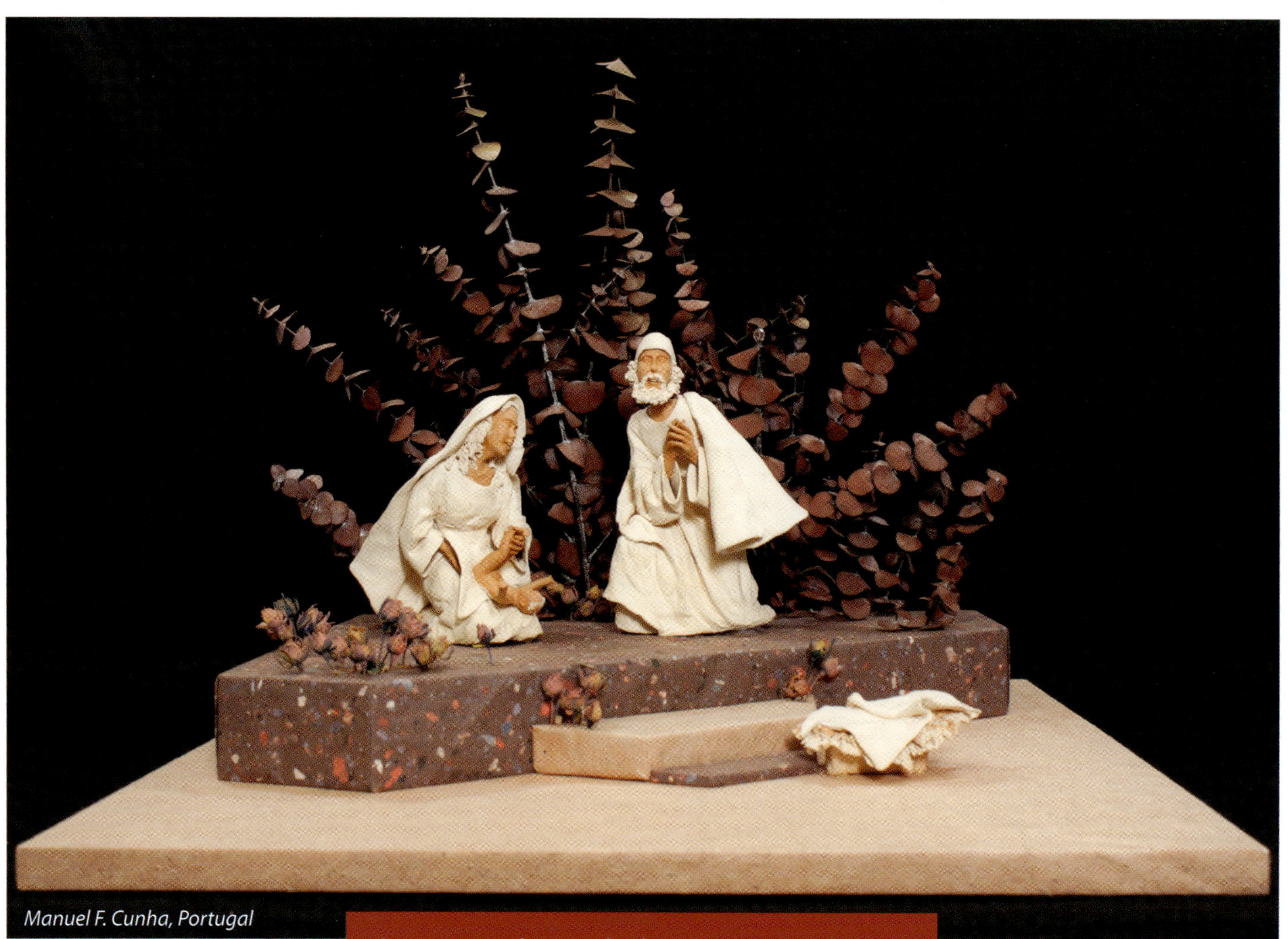

Manuel F. Cunha, Portugal

Sometimes, obsessively, the adult mind seeks to appropriate the Christchild. We want him to be like us, to be one of us. What better example than to show him in a truly human situation. Accidents happen. Lofty sentiments come tumbling down as the inquisitive eye discovers the "accident." Shocking? Not so for the mother. With practiced hands, and a smile on her lips, she remedies the situation.

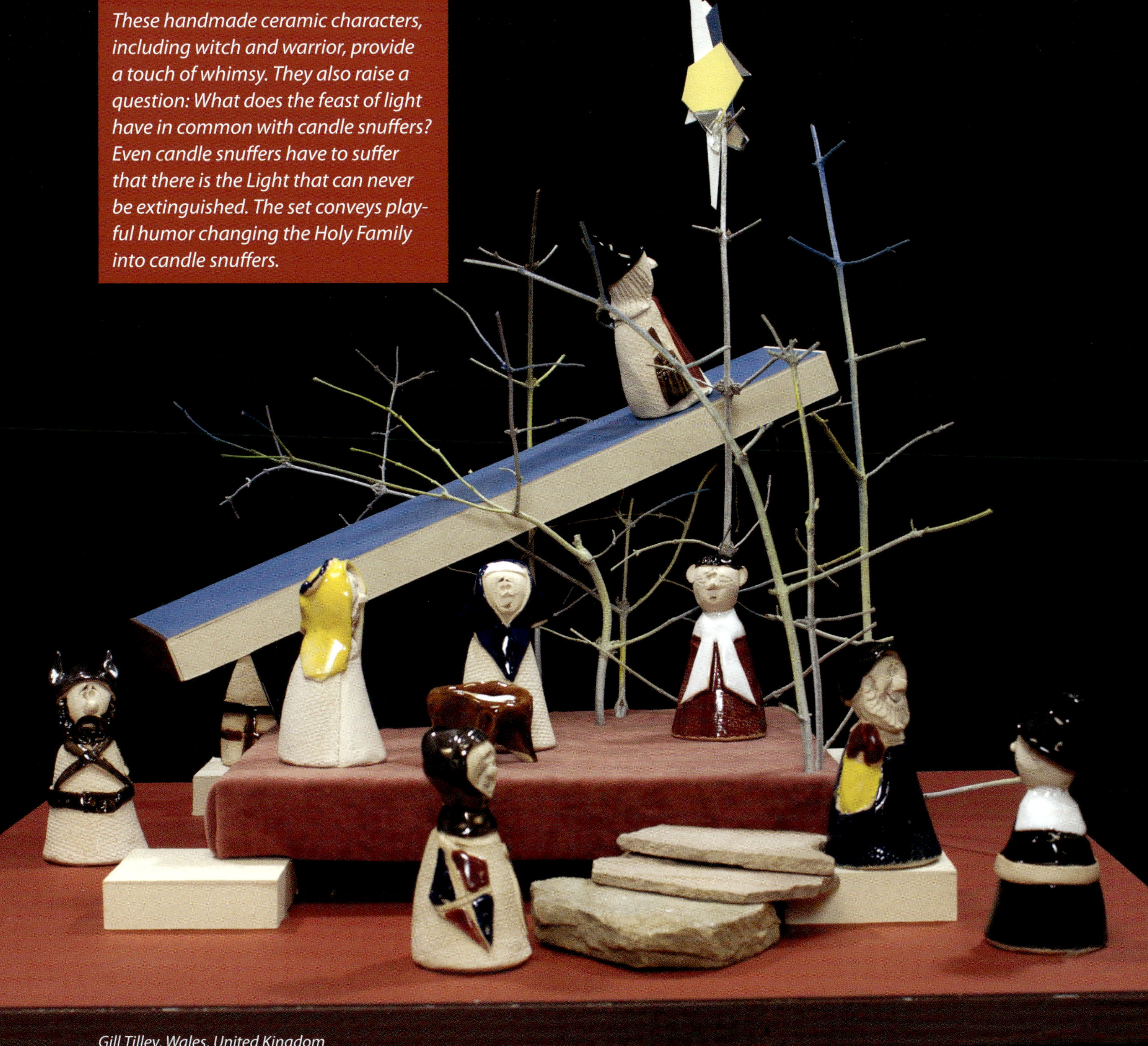

These handmade ceramic characters, including witch and warrior, provide a touch of whimsy. They also raise a question: What does the feast of light have in common with candle snuffers? Even candle snuffers have to suffer that there is the Light that can never be extinguished. The set conveys playful humor changing the Holy Family into candle snuffers.

Gill Tilley, Wales, United Kingdom

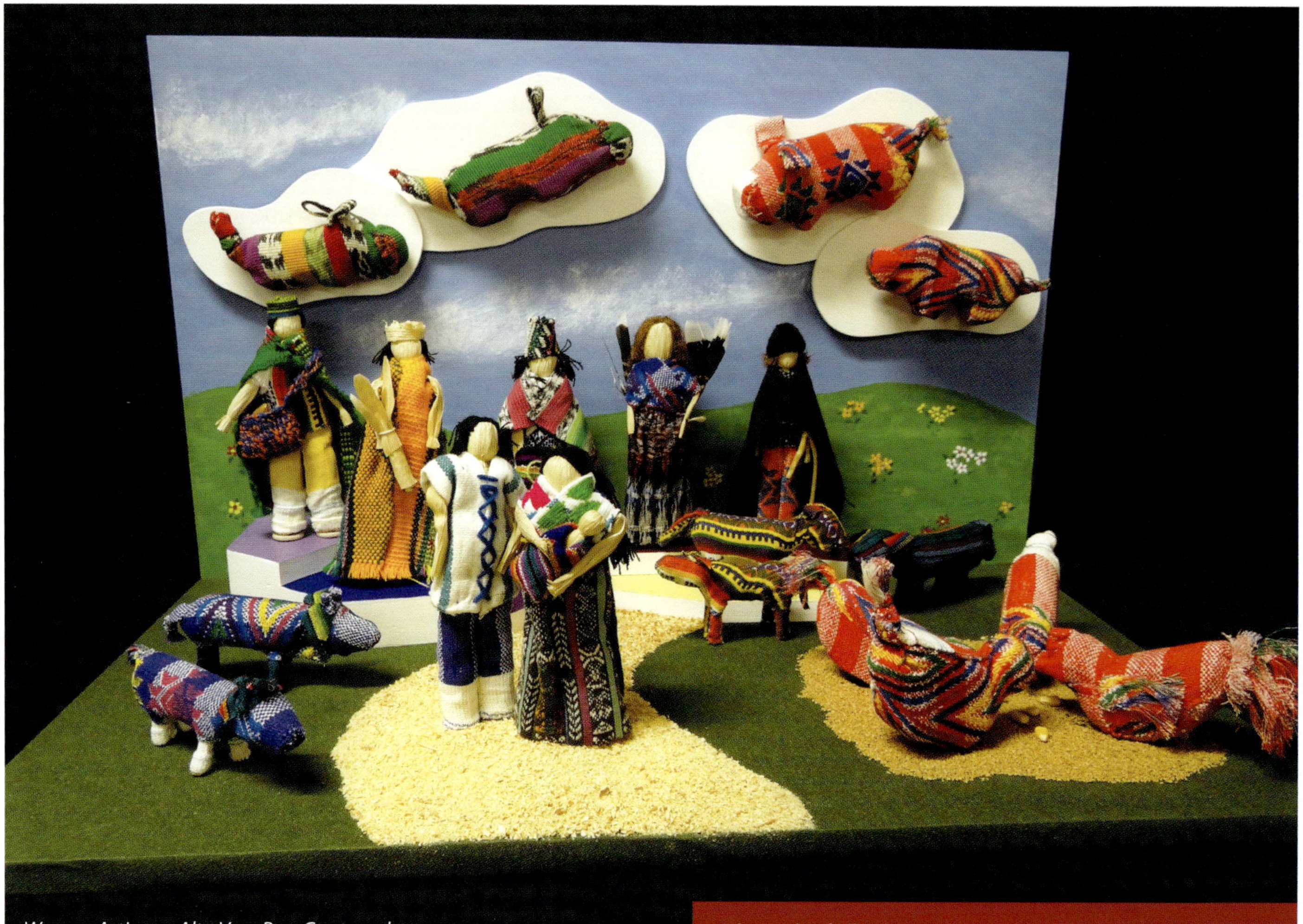

Women Artisans, Alta Vera Paz, Guatemala

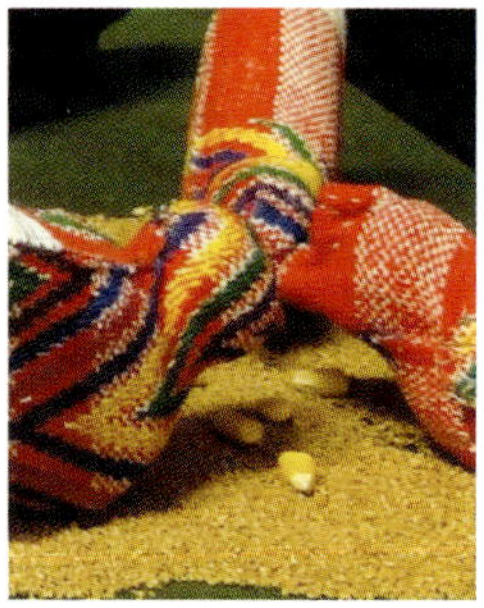

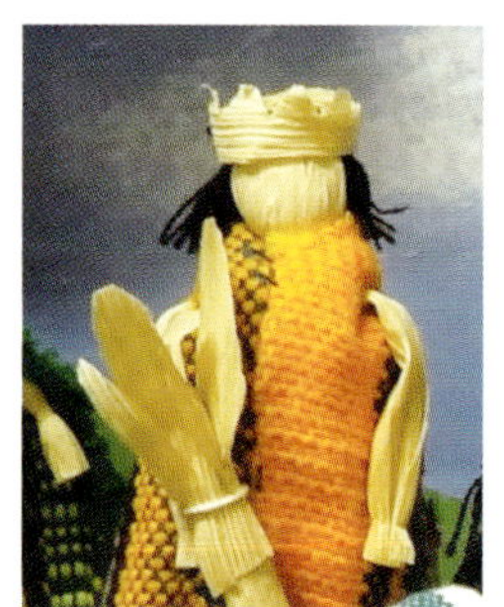

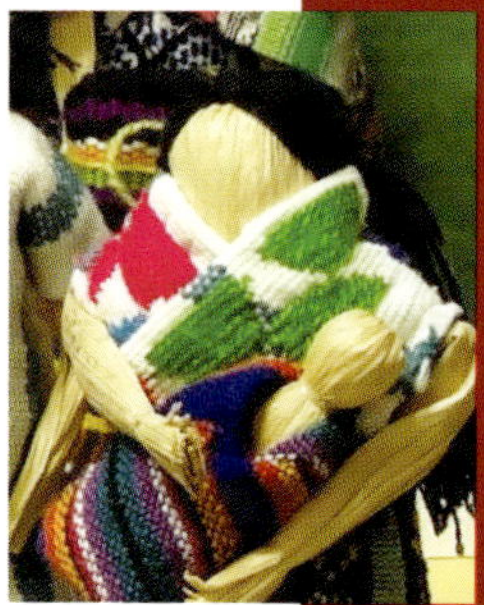

The colorfully dressed pigs sailing along with the white cumulus clouds bring to memory the well-known adage "When Pigs Fly." The saying is used to indicate that something will never happen, or when it happens it must be truly miraculous. For those who ponder the meaning of the Incarnation, the expression "When Pigs Fly" may readily come to mind. But the miracle happened! The flying pigs are no longer a sign of the impossible but an invitation to grateful wonderment.

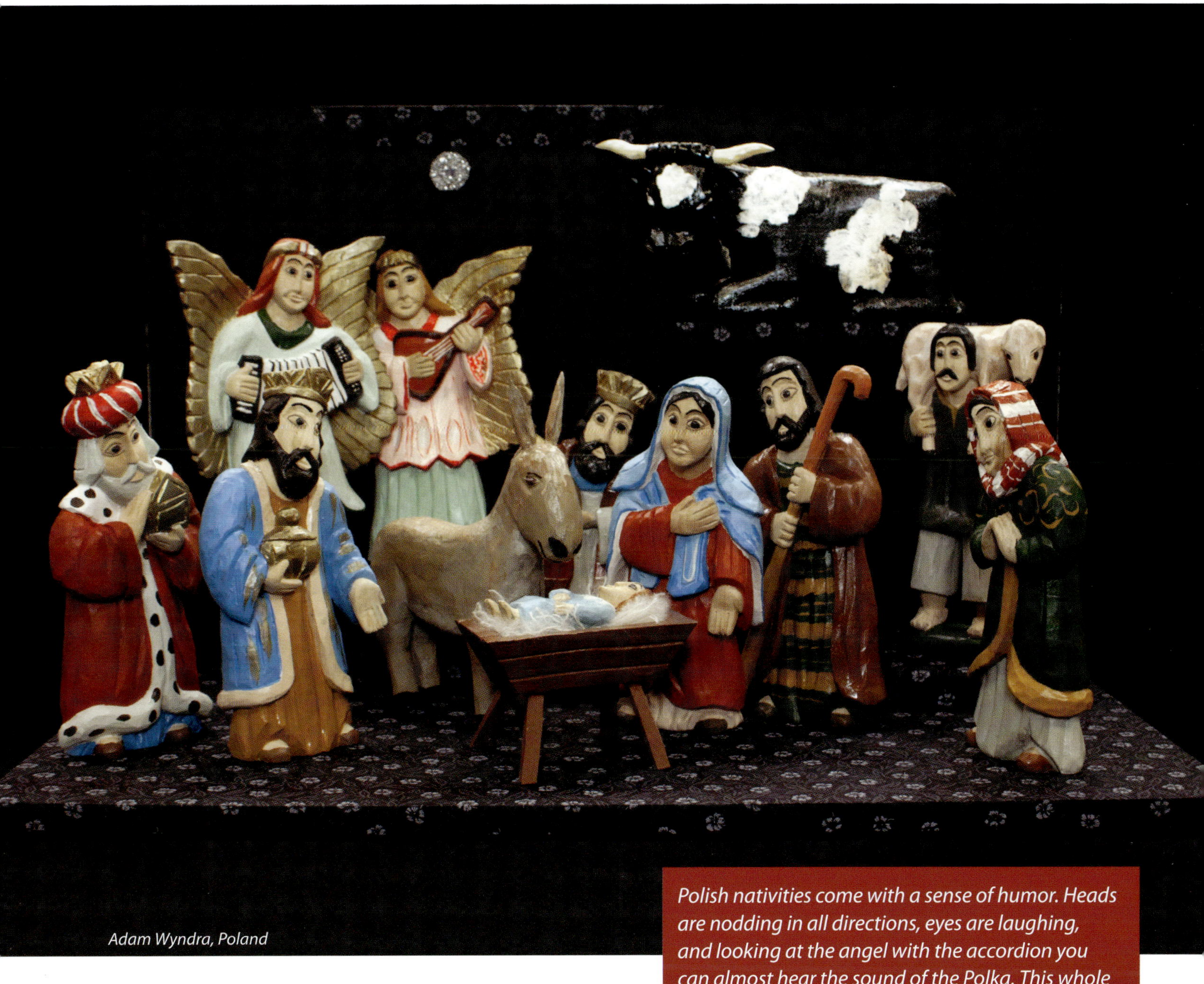

Adam Wyndra, Poland

Polish nativities come with a sense of humor. Heads are nodding in all directions, eyes are laughing, and looking at the angel with the accordion you can almost hear the sound of the Polka. This whole scene is dancing for joy and good humor. Even the ox seems to enjoy his lofty position.

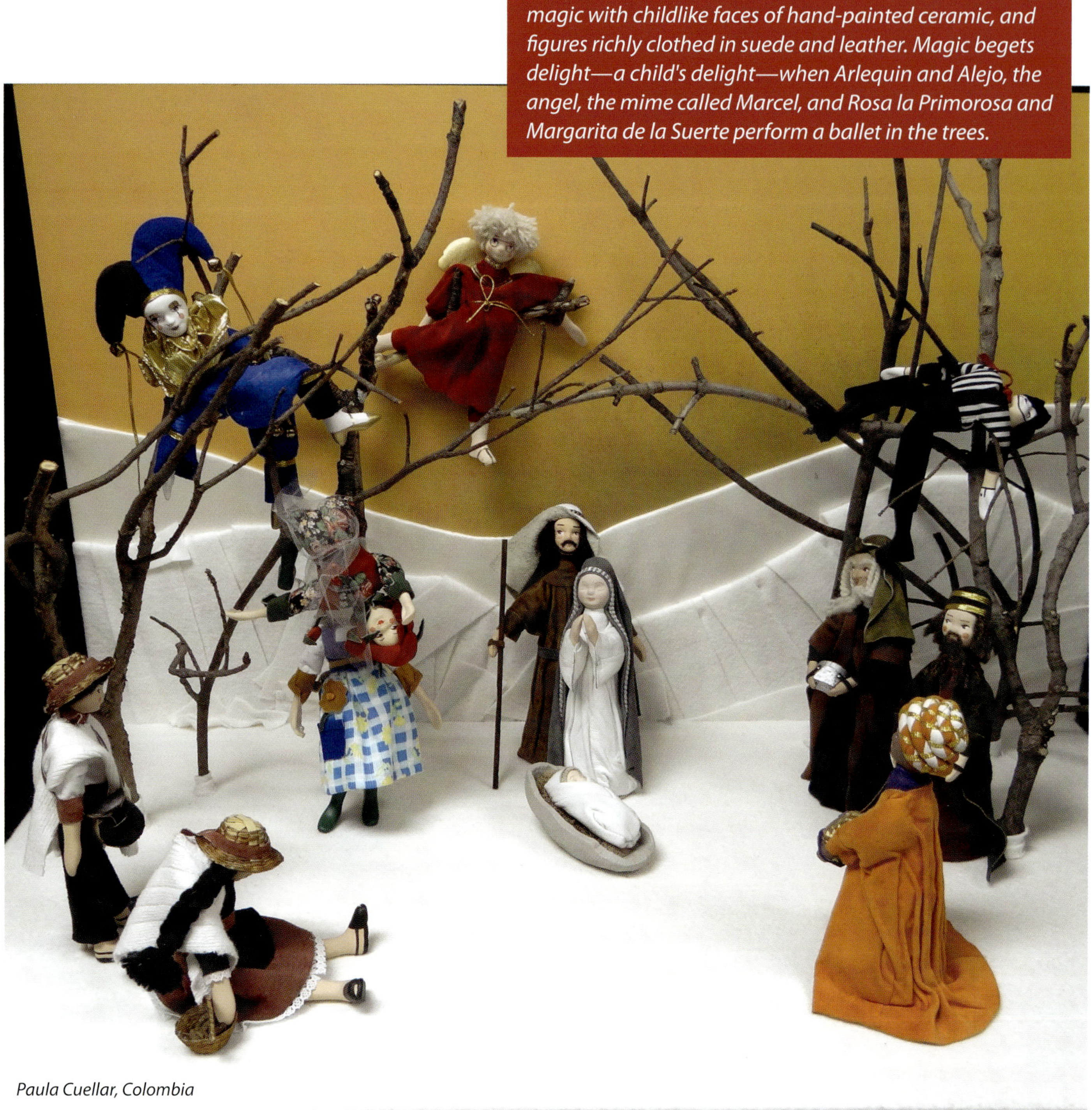

Paula Cuellar of Personitas de Colección (Bogotá) creates magic with childlike faces of hand-painted ceramic, and figures richly clothed in suede and leather. Magic begets delight—a child's delight—when Arlequin and Alejo, the angel, the mime called Marcel, and Rosa la Primorosa and Margarita de la Suerte perform a ballet in the trees.

Paula Cuellar, Colombia

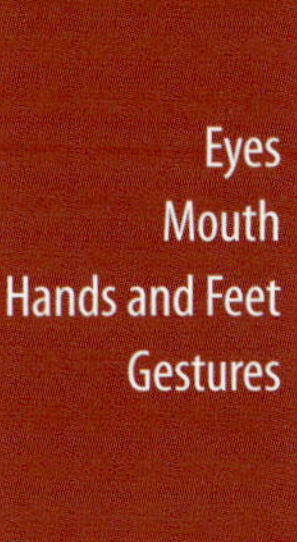

The Language of the Body

The body speaks. Postures and gestures speak their own and special language. They frequently translate cultural values, or lend a silent but expressive voice to emotions, and the habits of the heart. Eyes, mouth, hands and feet, and gestures can be most talkative.

Eyes

They belong to a visual culture. Wonderment lies in the wide open eyes. The sharpened eye tries to pierce a mystery. Eyes may be the language of the heart.

Mouth

The wide open and rounded mouth can be a sign of life, of breathing, of animated clay. In such case, the mouth is the most distinctive part of the face, sometimes the only visible part. The open mouth in some traditions announces an oral culture familiar with storytelling.

Hands and Feet

Hands and feet, big and strong hands and feet, speak the language of the earth. Riveted to the soil, dependent on the earth, but also receiving from it the fruit of their labor, hands and feet have a message of steadfast rootedness and not seldom of dignified poverty.

Gestures

The gesture, any gesture, frequently extends and expresses an inner disposition. It gives unity to the whole body, and often life and harmony to the whole scene and all its crèche figures.

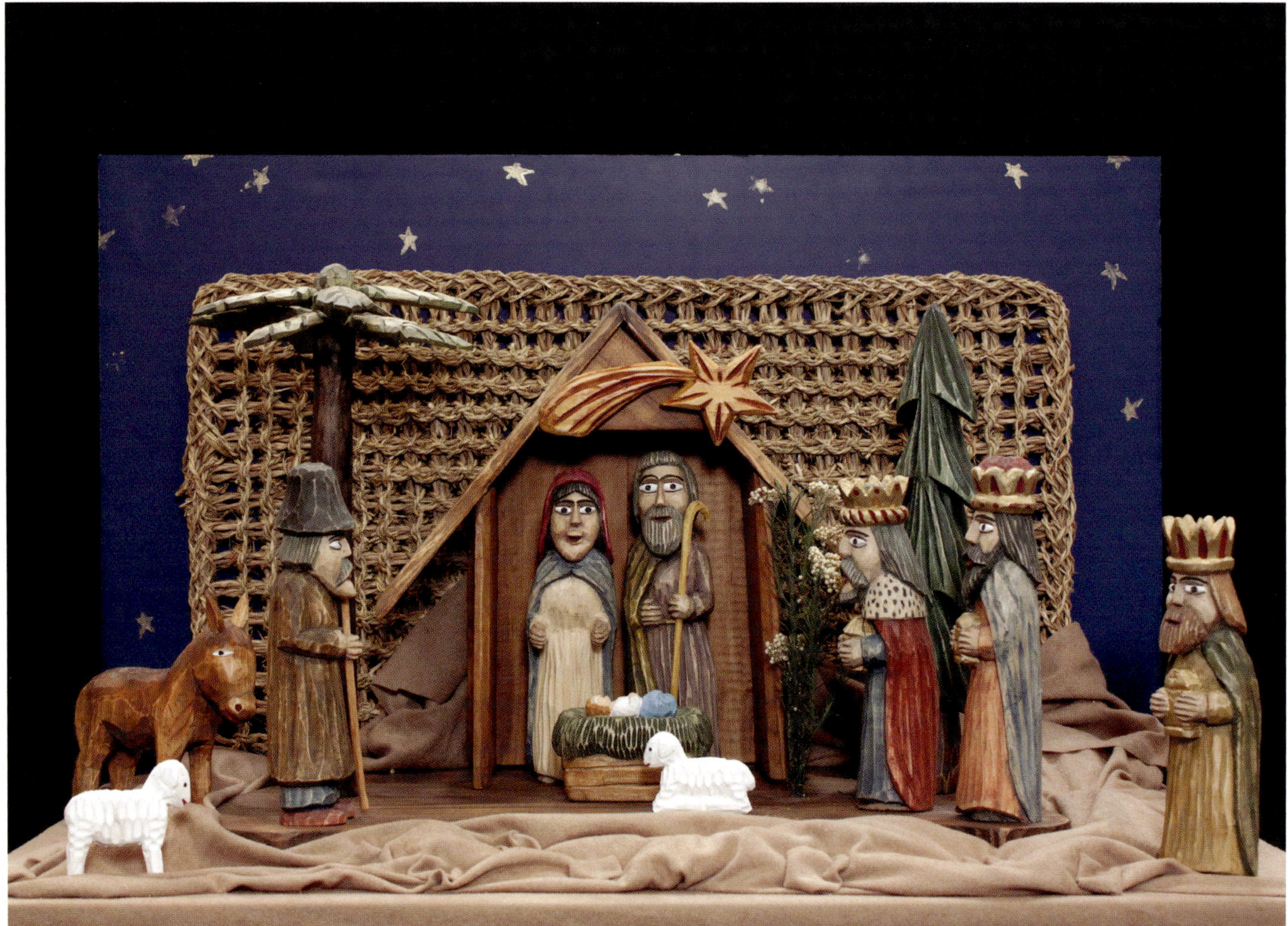

Unknown Artist, Poland

Eyes

Although of unknown artist, this nativity set owes its existence to a famous woodcarver tradition of the southern region of Poland where the woods are dense and the winters are long. During this period of forced immobility, many a farmer took up carving and became a master of the penknife. A thriving folk art developed.

But look at the faces in this set. The faces have bulging eyes, worse, they seem like piercing eyes x- raying the onlooker. In fact, these big eyes are a symbol of fixed and undisguised rapture. In the language of popular art, they are bulging in wonderment and eager to pierce the mystery before them.

Mouth

This Christmas scene by Mary Lucero of Jemez Pueblo is one of the most sophisticated of our collection of Pueblo nativities. The artist painted her little figures with an abundance of detail: eyes and hands are carefully drawn; even the turquoise necklaces are not forgotten. Structure and color give this set a feathery lightness. The set suggests a choir of singing angels. All the little actors have the typically wide open mouth of Pueblo nativities. The open mouth is a symbol of people alive and well. They are telling a wondrous tale. Telling is important in Indian culture with its mainly oral tradition.

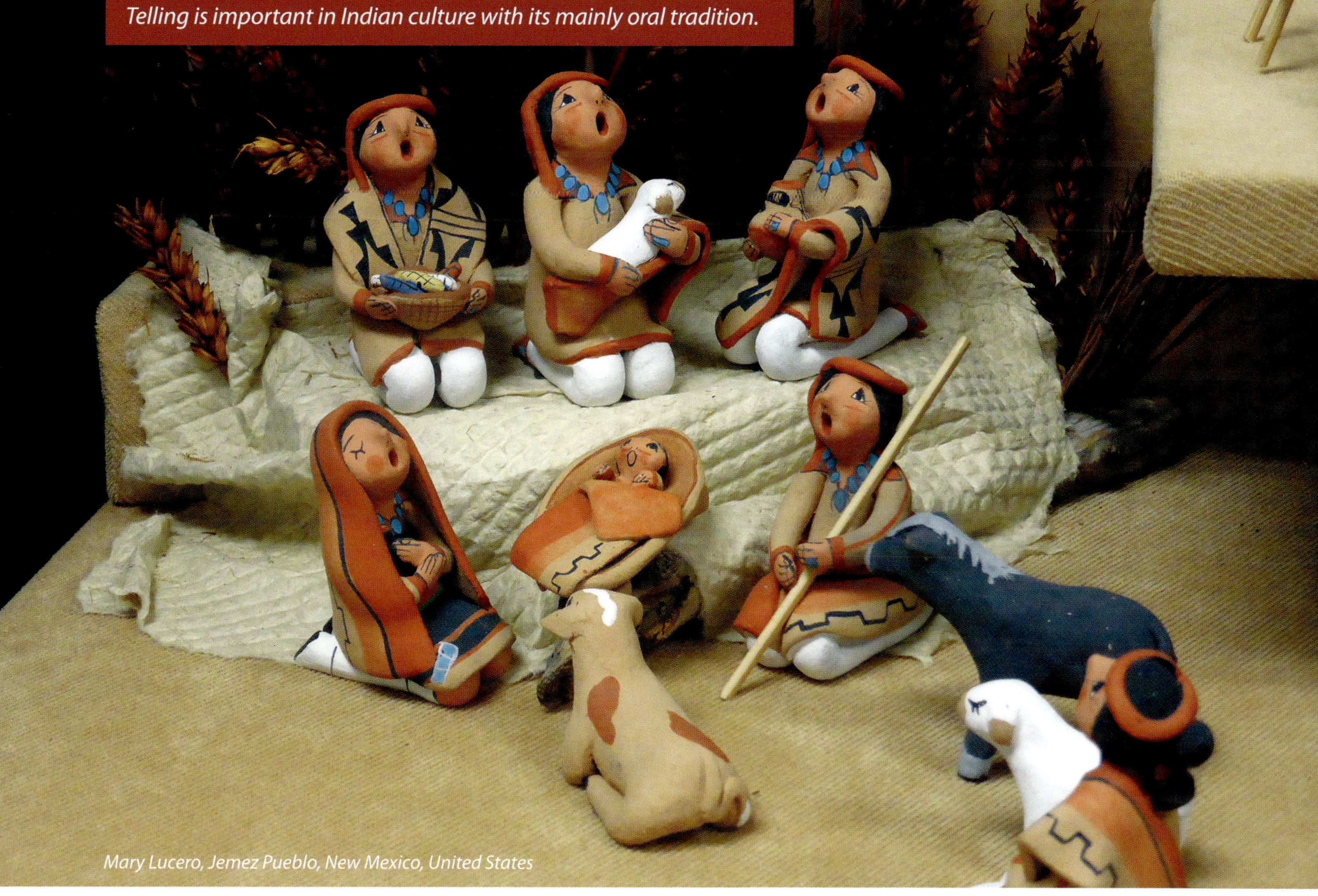

Mary Lucero, Jemez Pueblo, New Mexico, United States

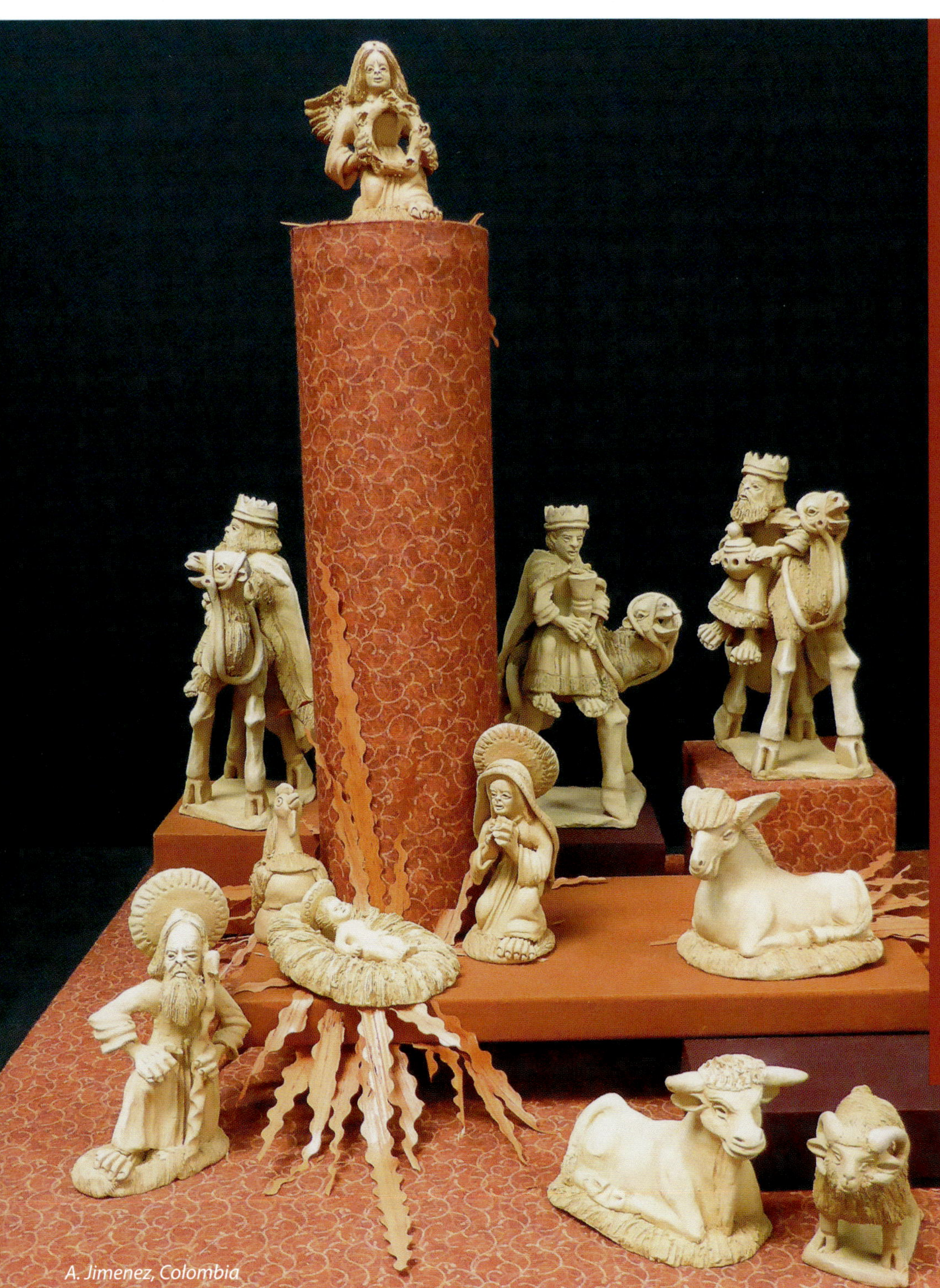

Hands and Feet

This sturdy and earth-bound Nativity offers an overall impression of solid foundation and stability. The figures are little masterpieces escaping an amorphous and formless world of clay. But there is more. Take a closer look at their hands and feet. They are of disproportioned size and shape. They are huge and bony. They are impressive, and the true actors of the story played out in this set. See the intensity of Mary's prayer expressed in the huge folded hands; Saint Joseph, a giant hand on his hip, is positioned like the guardian angel of paradise; the Magi-Kings sitting on sturdy, long-legged and broad-hooved camels, are reigning in the animals with strong and massive fists. Hands and feet have their own language. In this set, it is a language of intense concentration and disciplined strength directed to the one who calls himself "Prince of Peace."

Gestures

Crafted by Sukodono Mennonite Woodcarvers of Japara, Indonesia, the decorative and geometric motifs of their carvings are derived from Asmal tribal culture. Similar designs are found on houses, canoes, and totem poles. Message and expression of these figures are not in the detail or volume of their bodies, but in the intensity of their gestures.

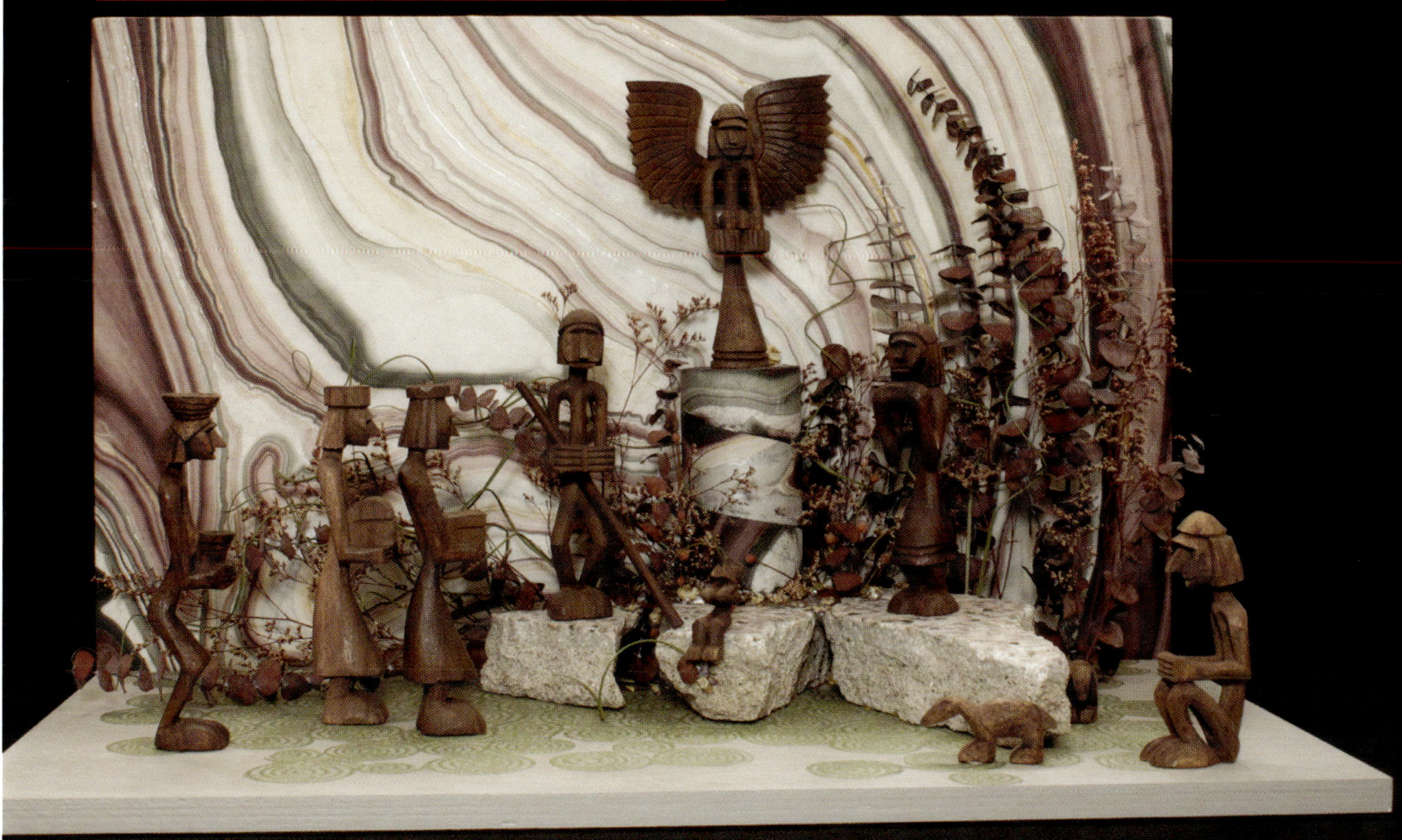

Taman Petra, Indonesia

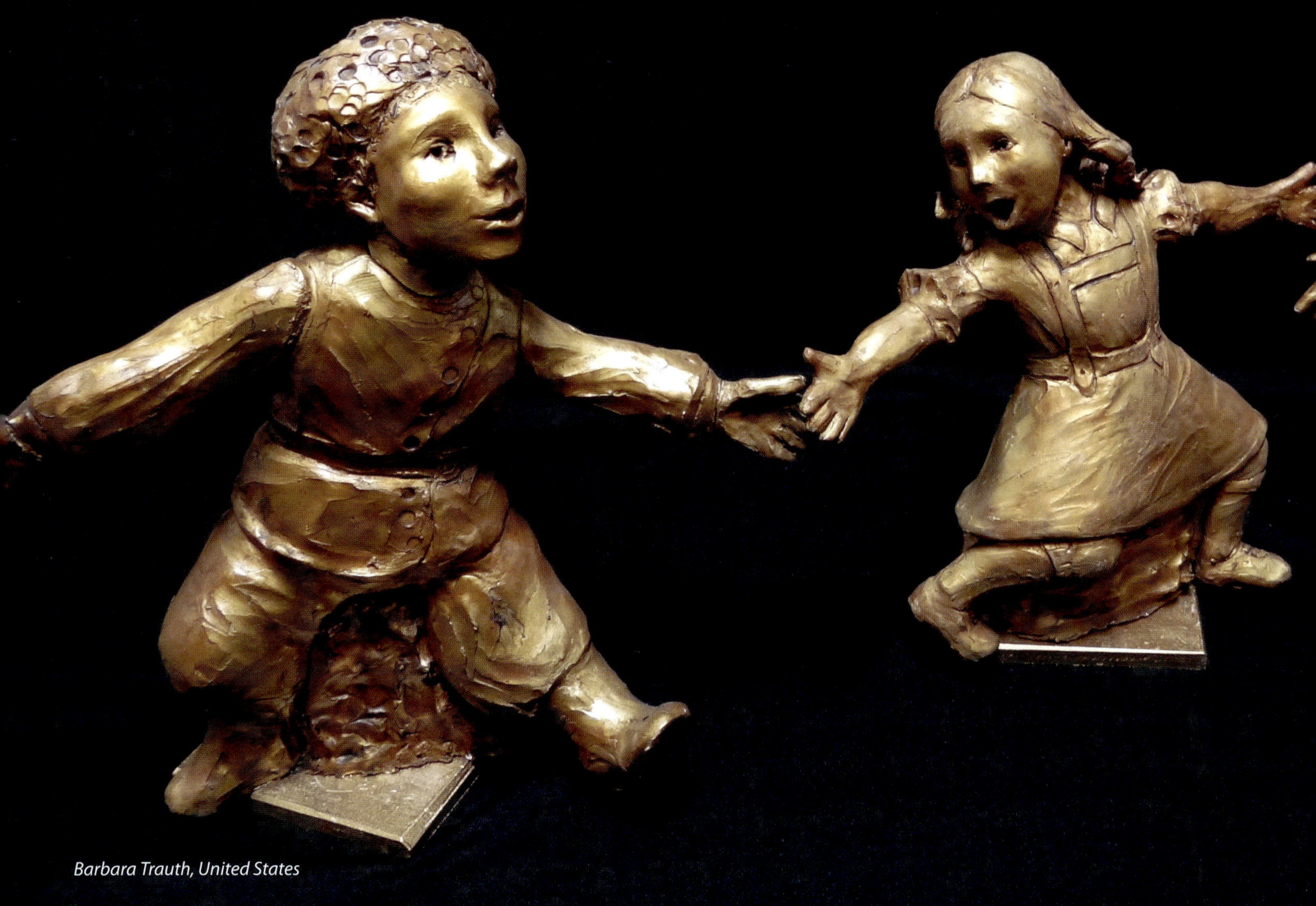

Barbara Trauth, United States

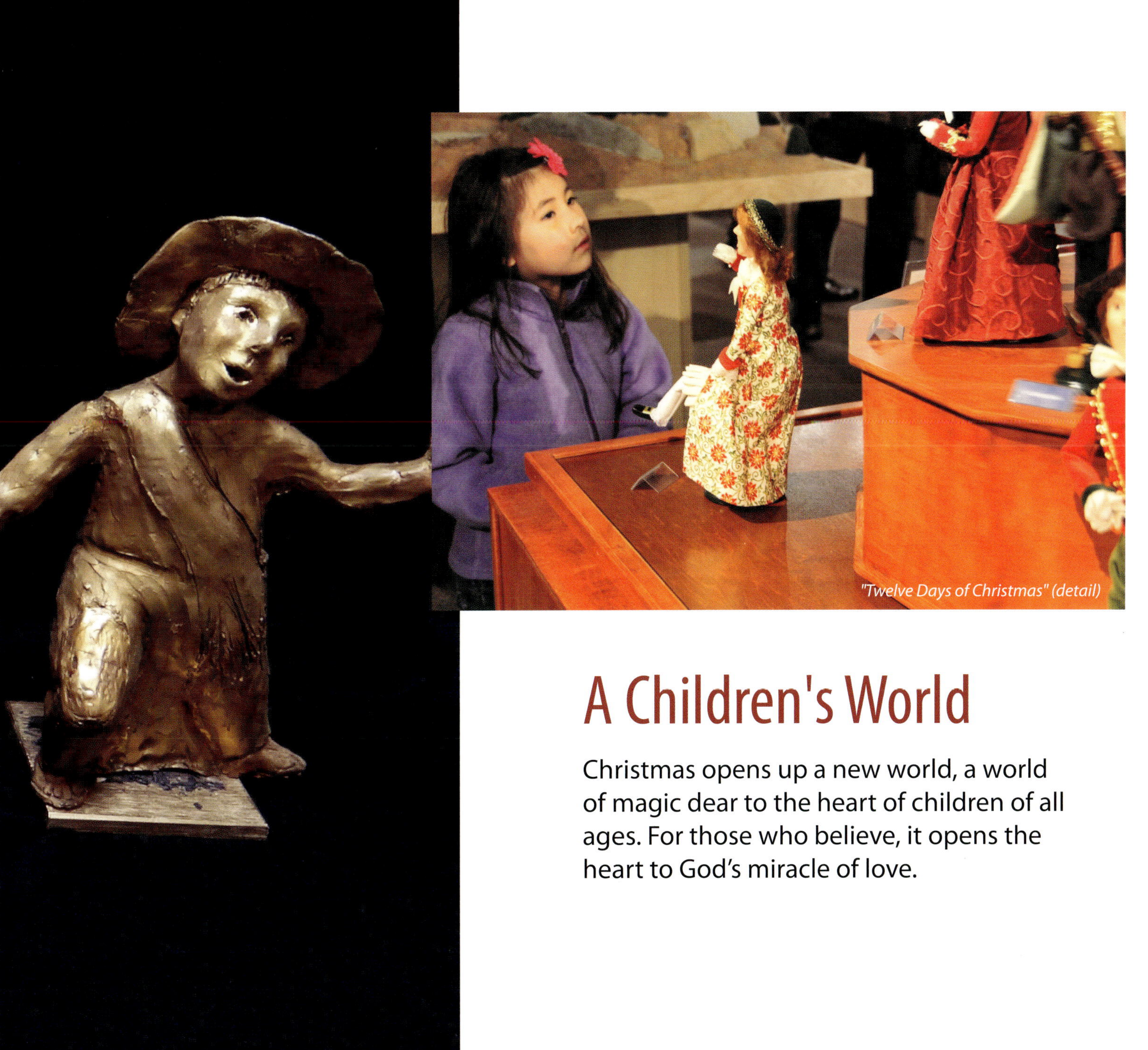
"Twelve Days of Christmas" (detail)

A Children's World

Christmas opens up a new world, a world of magic dear to the heart of children of all ages. For those who believe, it opens the heart to God's miracle of love.

A Children's World

For many adults a feast for children, Christmas invites everybody to meet the Christchild. Shepherds and Magi were no children, and it takes an adult mind to ponder the enormity of the mystery of mysteries. Does it? Christmas became a children's feast in post-Enlightenment times, in the latter part of the 19th Century, and in the first half of the 20th Century. The appeal to childlikeness in front of the mystery of the Incarnation was an attempt to counter and avoid the rationalism of the time. This reaction may have lost sight, in part, of the need for unity of faith and reason in all things religious.

However, this is not to object the spirit of childlikeness. Nativity sets create a children's world and offer it to all of good will. It is hoped that adults will learn from children how to look at the Nativity with children's eyes. There are many ways adults can learn from children.

Style or Statement?

A number of contemporary Nativity traditions have adopted a childlike style. Figures and faces have a decidedly childlike look. Quaint and sweet, these nativity sets have an endearing quality at first sight. The question they raise is about authenticity. Are they too mushy and whimsical? Do they make a statement of sentimental callowness?

Rediscovering Simplicity

A second look may discover an important quality of the child's world. The ability to see what is, the simple truth behind what is appearance, and the spontaneous grasp of what is right.

Awe and Admiration

There is endless curiosity in a child, but also a graced and bottomless ability for wonderment. Reality is always new. The child's ability to discover it never fails.

Recreating the World

A children's world is a laboratory of creation and recreation, the ability to give new names to old things, and the joy to create new worlds.

Another Christchild

Children are the representatives of the Christchild, his little prophets. The childlike soul is a joyful soul, ready to speak out for the Christchild in truth and constant wonder.

A Festive World

A world of spontaneity and wonder, of simple truth and joyful transformation, the world of children is led into a celebratory gathering to hail the Christchild and his mother.

Eddie Walker, United States

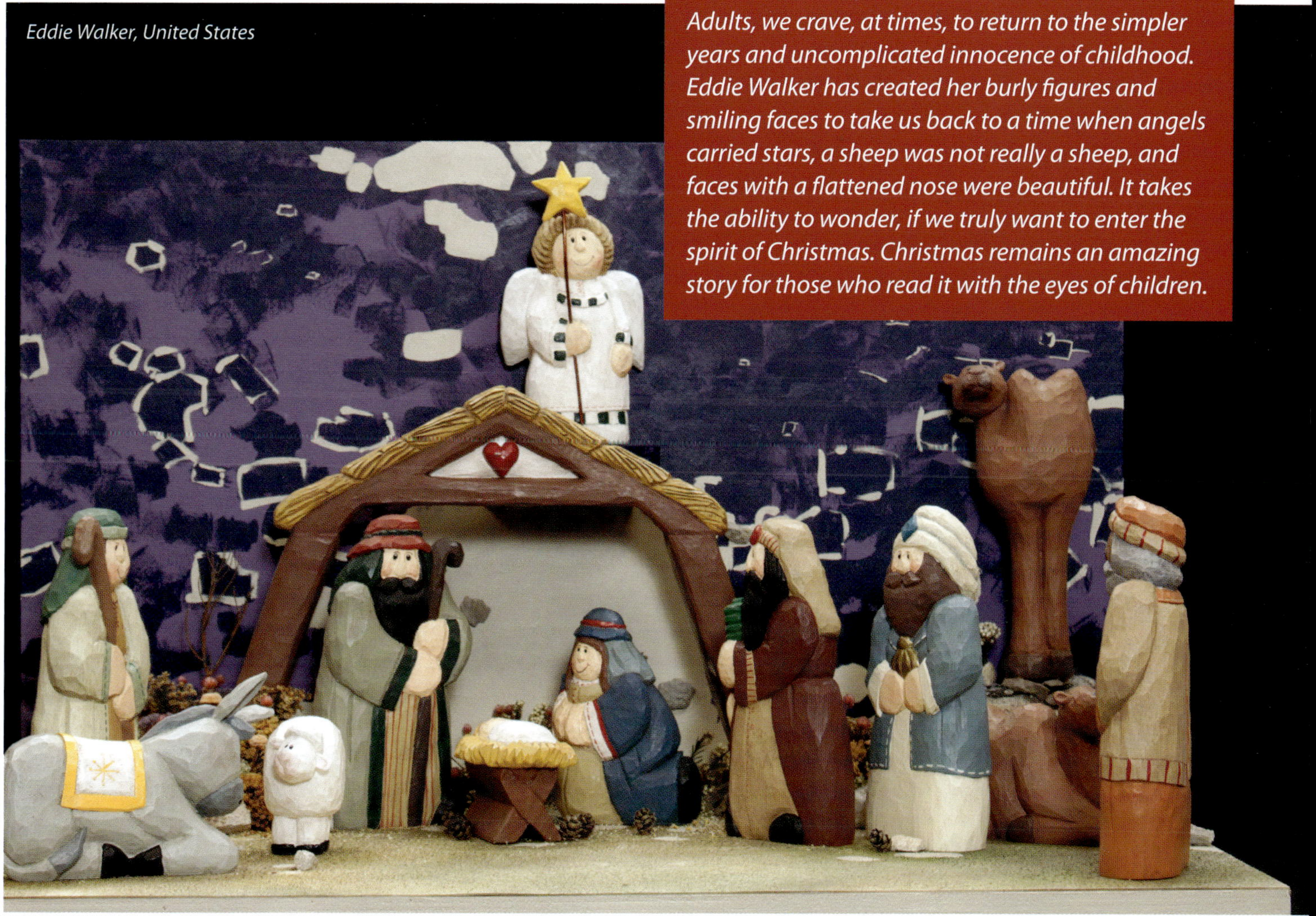

Style or Statement?

There is the child, and there is a child in the adult. Adults, we crave, at times, to return to the simpler years and uncomplicated innocence of childhood. Eddie Walker has created her burly figures and smiling faces to take us back to a time when angels carried stars, a sheep was not really a sheep, and faces with a flattened nose were beautiful. It takes the ability to wonder, if we truly want to enter the spirit of Christmas. Christmas remains an amazing story for those who read it with the eyes of children.

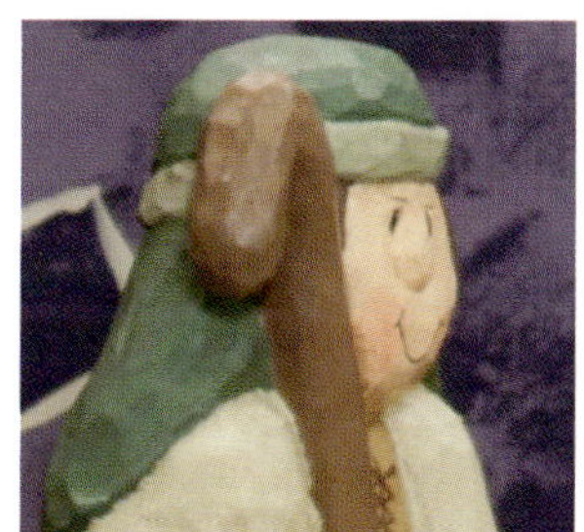

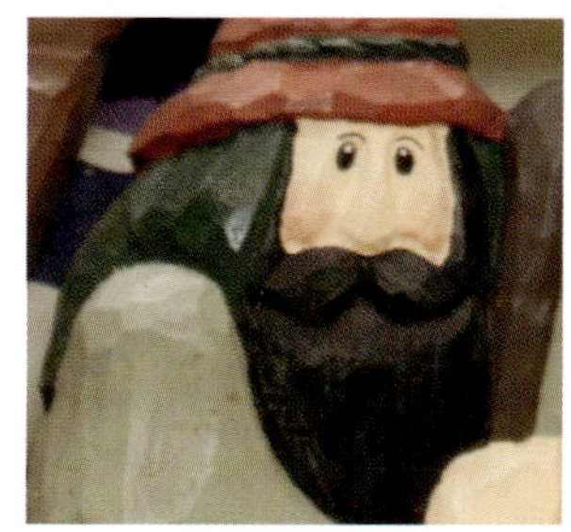

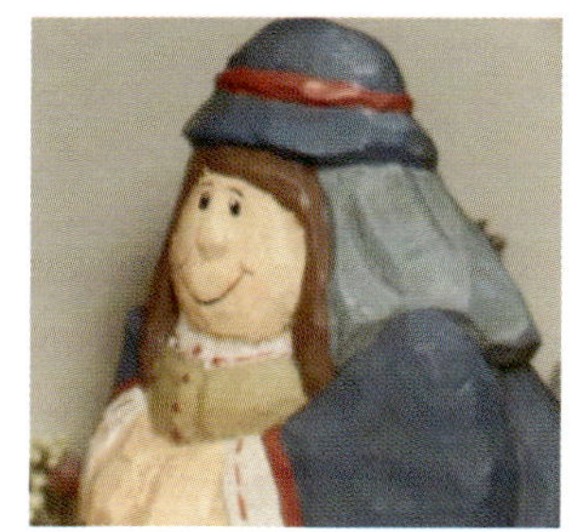

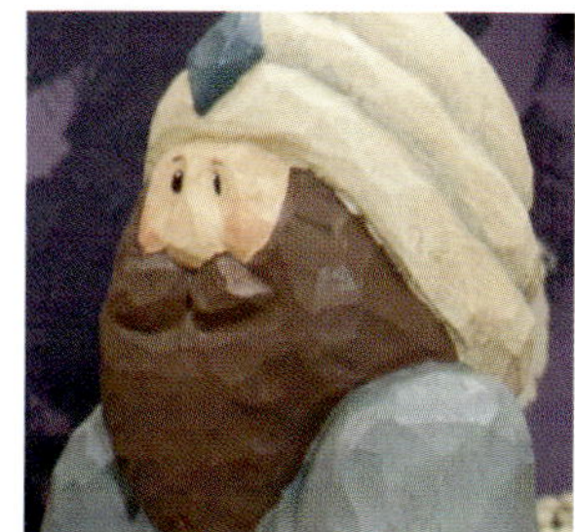

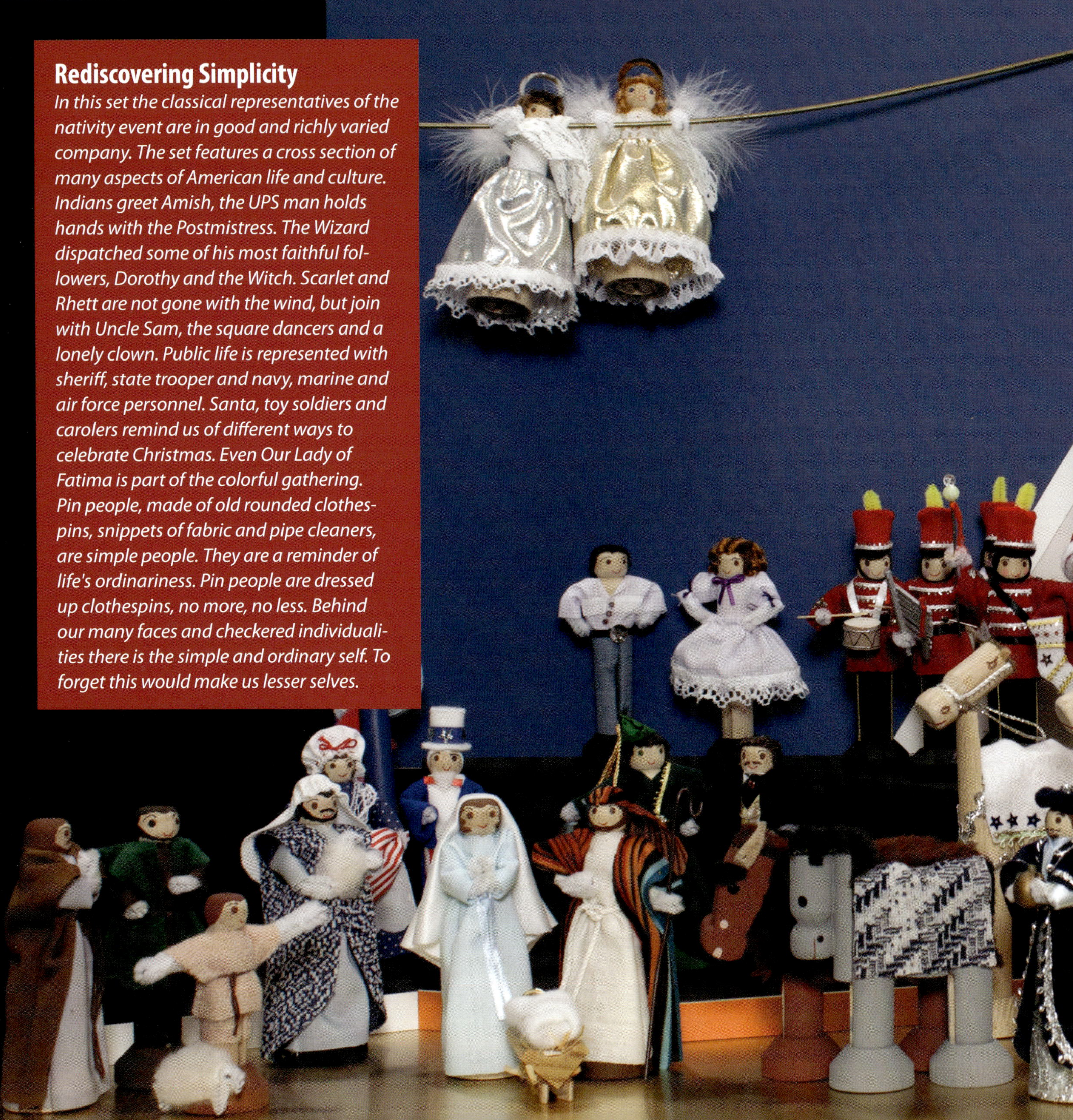

Rediscovering Simplicity

In this set the classical representatives of the nativity event are in good and richly varied company. The set features a cross section of many aspects of American life and culture. Indians greet Amish, the UPS man holds hands with the Postmistress. The Wizard dispatched some of his most faithful followers, Dorothy and the Witch. Scarlet and Rhett are not gone with the wind, but join with Uncle Sam, the square dancers and a lonely clown. Public life is represented with sheriff, state trooper and navy, marine and air force personnel. Santa, toy soldiers and carolers remind us of different ways to celebrate Christmas. Even Our Lady of Fatima is part of the colorful gathering. Pin people, made of old rounded clothespins, snippets of fabric and pipe cleaners, are simple people. They are a reminder of life's ordinariness. Pin people are dressed up clothespins, no more, no less. Behind our many faces and checkered individualities there is the simple and ordinary self. To forget this would make us lesser selves.

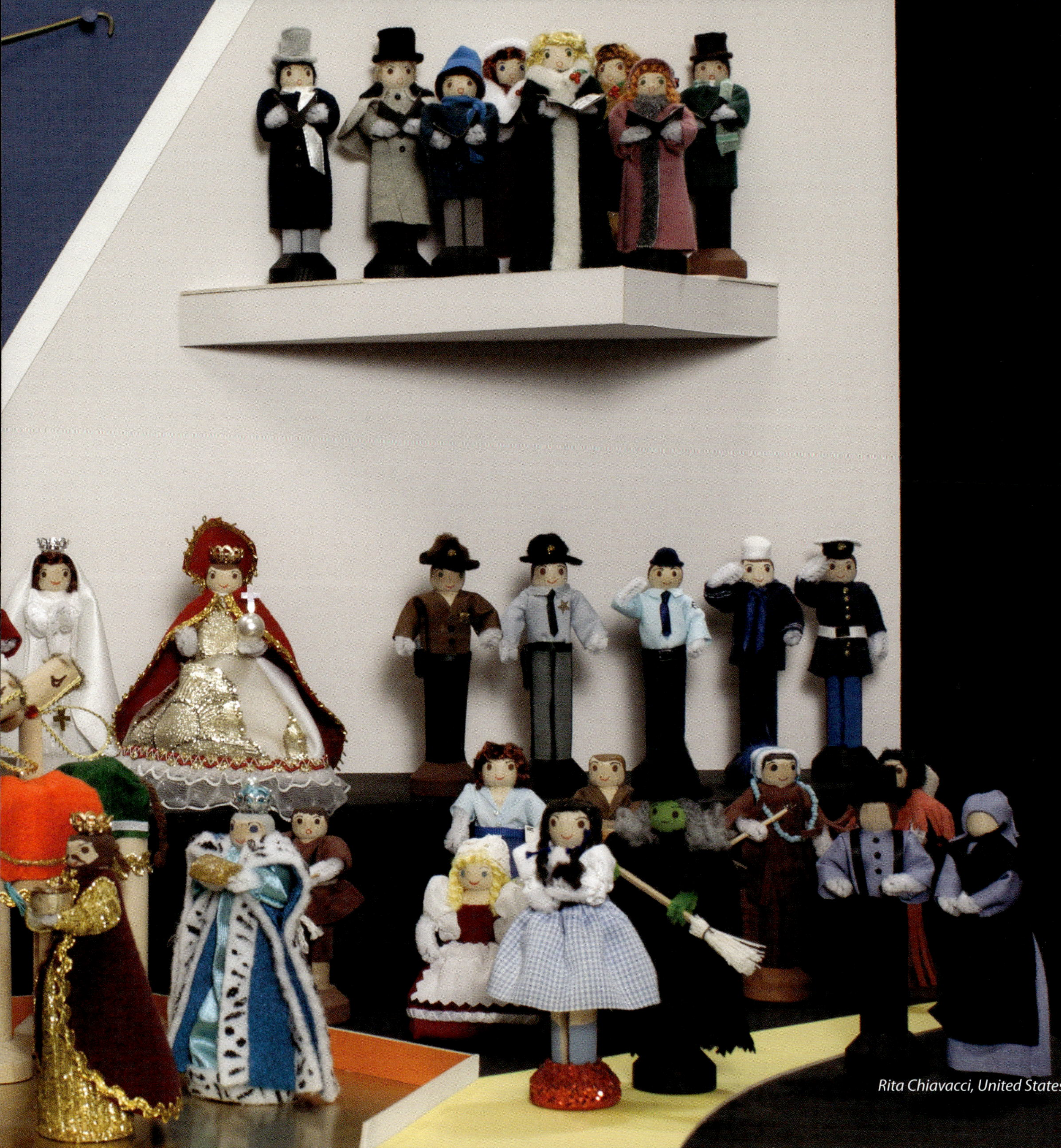

Rita Chiavacci, United States

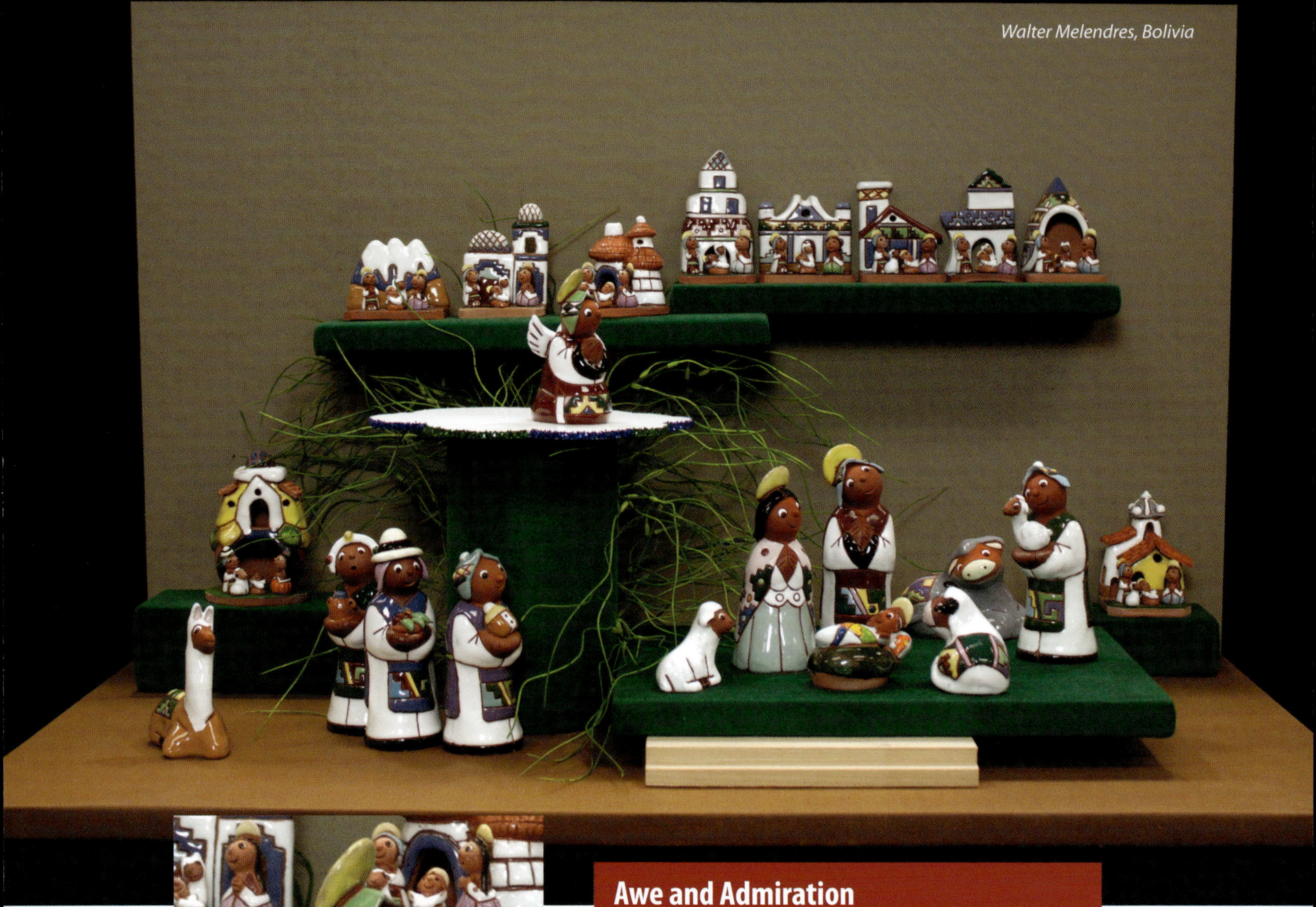

Walter Melendres, Bolivia

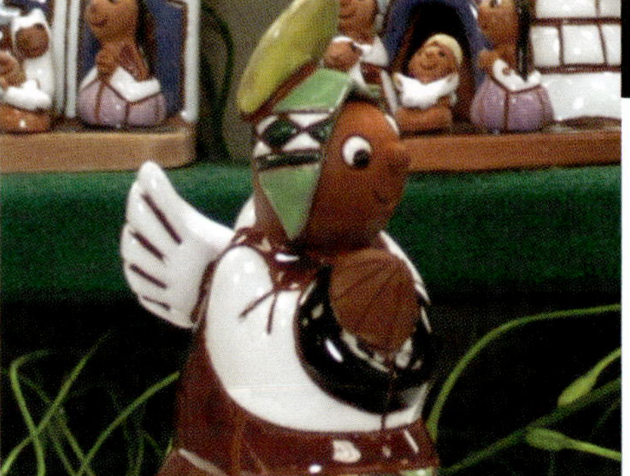

Awe and Admiration

These figures from Jesús de Machaca (Bolivia) are affectionately called "Tilinchos," meaning "small" in Aymara, the local language. Though dressed in the colorful costumes of the Aymara culture, their one characteristic feature is their eyes. Wider than heaven and darker than amber, they are an ever-moving kaleidoscope of frank curiosity and bottomless wonder. A true child's delight of conquering the world.

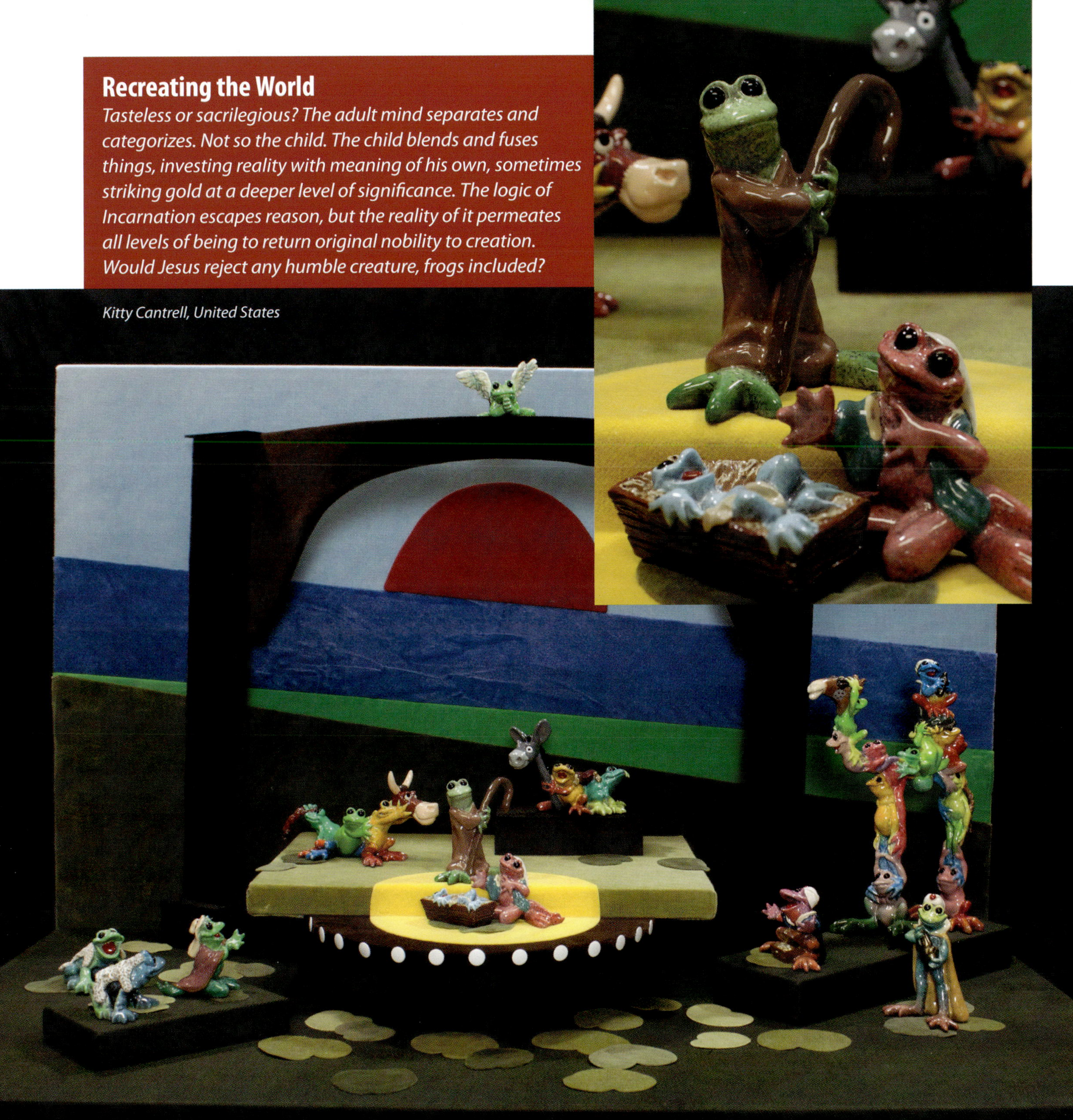

Recreating the World

Tasteless or sacrilegious? The adult mind separates and categorizes. Not so the child. The child blends and fuses things, investing reality with meaning of his own, sometimes striking gold at a deeper level of significance. The logic of Incarnation escapes reason, but the reality of it permeates all levels of being to return original nobility to creation. Would Jesus reject any humble creature, frogs included?

Kitty Cantrell, United States

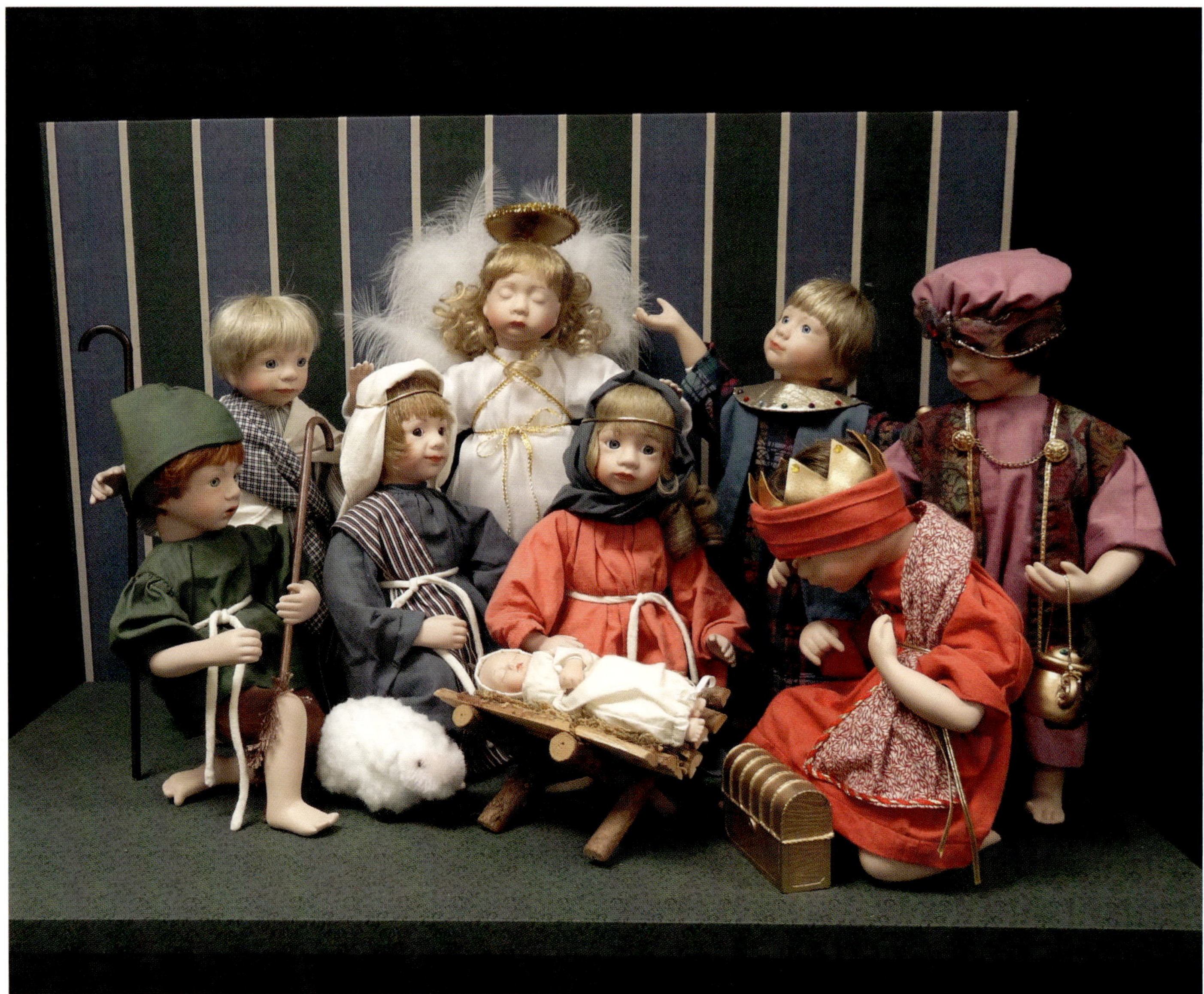

Julie Good-Kruger, United States

Another Christchild

Dolls can be handled, dolls are look-alikes, dolls are fetishes of children and childlike souls! They represent an echo of paradise lost, and a promise of paradise retrieved. In sum, these beautiful Good-Krüger collectibles are like little prophets of the Christchild.

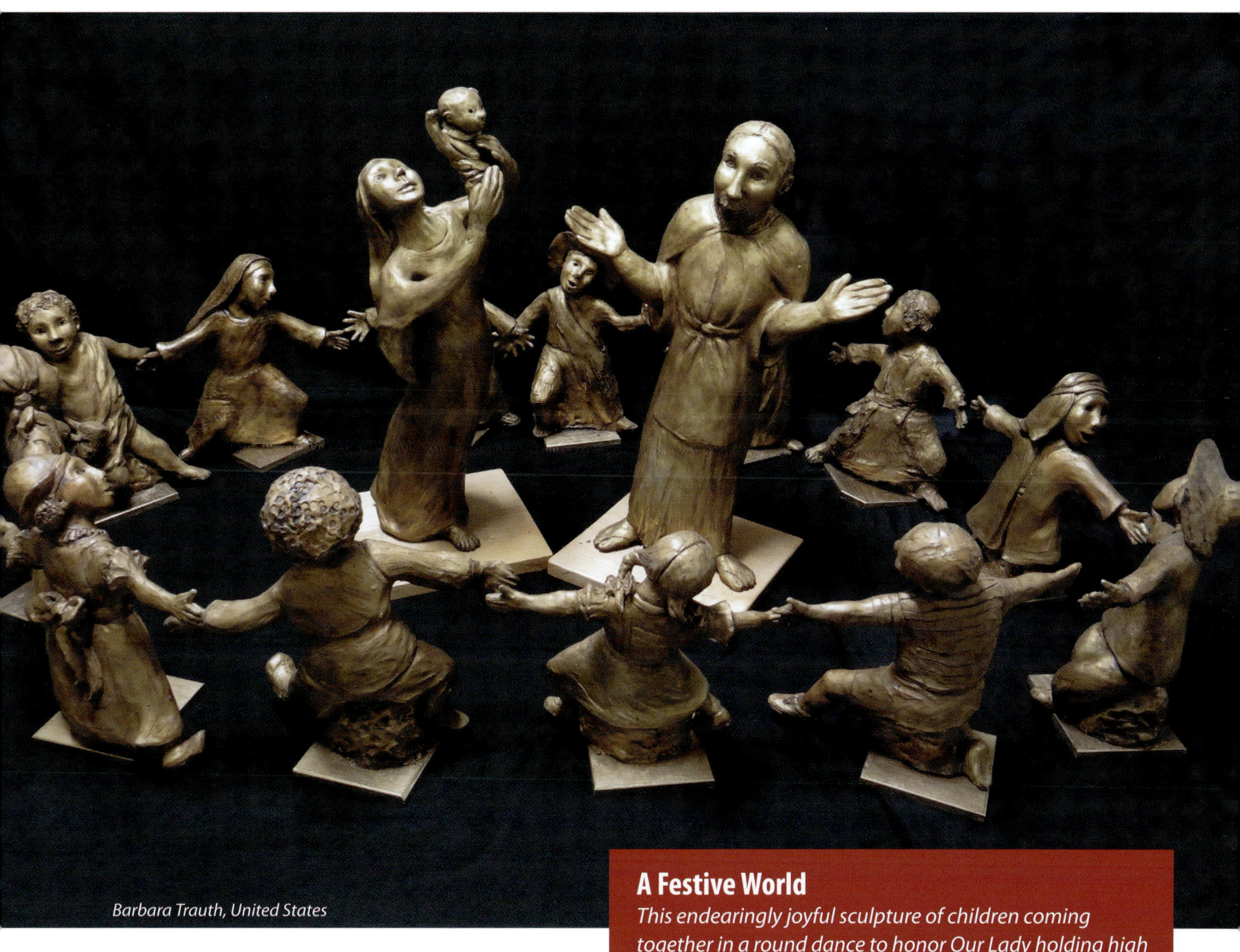
Barbara Trauth, United States

A Festive World

This endearingly joyful sculpture of children coming together in a round dance to honor Our Lady holding high the Christchild illustrates one of the many facets of Barbara Trauth's art. Representing many cultures and customs, the merry-go-round of the thirteen children reflects the new world, a world initiated by the Incarnation and still in the making. The children's dance is a dance of hope, the joyful celebration of better things to come.

A Need for Magic
A Language of Enchantment
Moving but Incongruous
A New Wisdom

A Touch of Magic

Magic is one of the spontaneous and mandatory ingredients of the Nativity tradition. Magic is the consequence, in popular fashion and expression, of the deeper meaning of the Incarnation. The fact that God becomes man changes the understanding of what is, and what is not, of what was, and what will be. All at once, a sheep is no longer a sheep, a polar bear kneels at the manger, and animals speak in human tongue. Pious imagination to convey a touch of magic is like a bottomless well. To give a sense of the depth, magic transforms the order of reality: animals behave like human beings; seasons are changed, and winter is now summer, the barren landscape a paradise of bloom and ready harvest.

A Need for Magic

Evading reality carries a hefty price tag, but the need for magic is omnipresent. The magic of Christmas is only one form of seeking the possible impossible. The mystery of the Incarnation is like a magic carpet lifting us up to where we have a different, and hopefully more objective vision of the reality we left behind.

A Language of Enchantment

Who can understand magic? What is its language? The name of magic is enchantment, made up of part surprise and part humor. However, the secret of enchantment is revealed when the spirit follows the heart in meditating the message of Christmas.

Moving but Incongruous

There is magic when moose and polar bear meet at the manger. As incongruous as may appear to reason, what moves heart and senses holds sway over narrow logic.

A New Wisdom

True wisdom has the power to change and transform. Wisdom put in the mouth of a frog has the power of magic; of magic that enchants, moves, and transforms.

A Need for Magic

Casual, colorful and coquet: the cotton backdrop has all the ingredients of the magic carpet it would like to be. A carpet that sweeps you off your feet and takes you to the wonderland of Christmas magic, which is located, as this set suggests, on the ramp to heaven. It is densely populated with the white armies of the heavenly hosts hailing the Holy Family. Shepherds and sheep follow suit, only the magi are still at some distance. Like the Christchild, you have to be unafraid to ride the magic carpet, and a friend of the angels. Take a look at the pieces of doubled yarn. Build your own magic carpet, it says, you need it to reach the heavenly ramp.

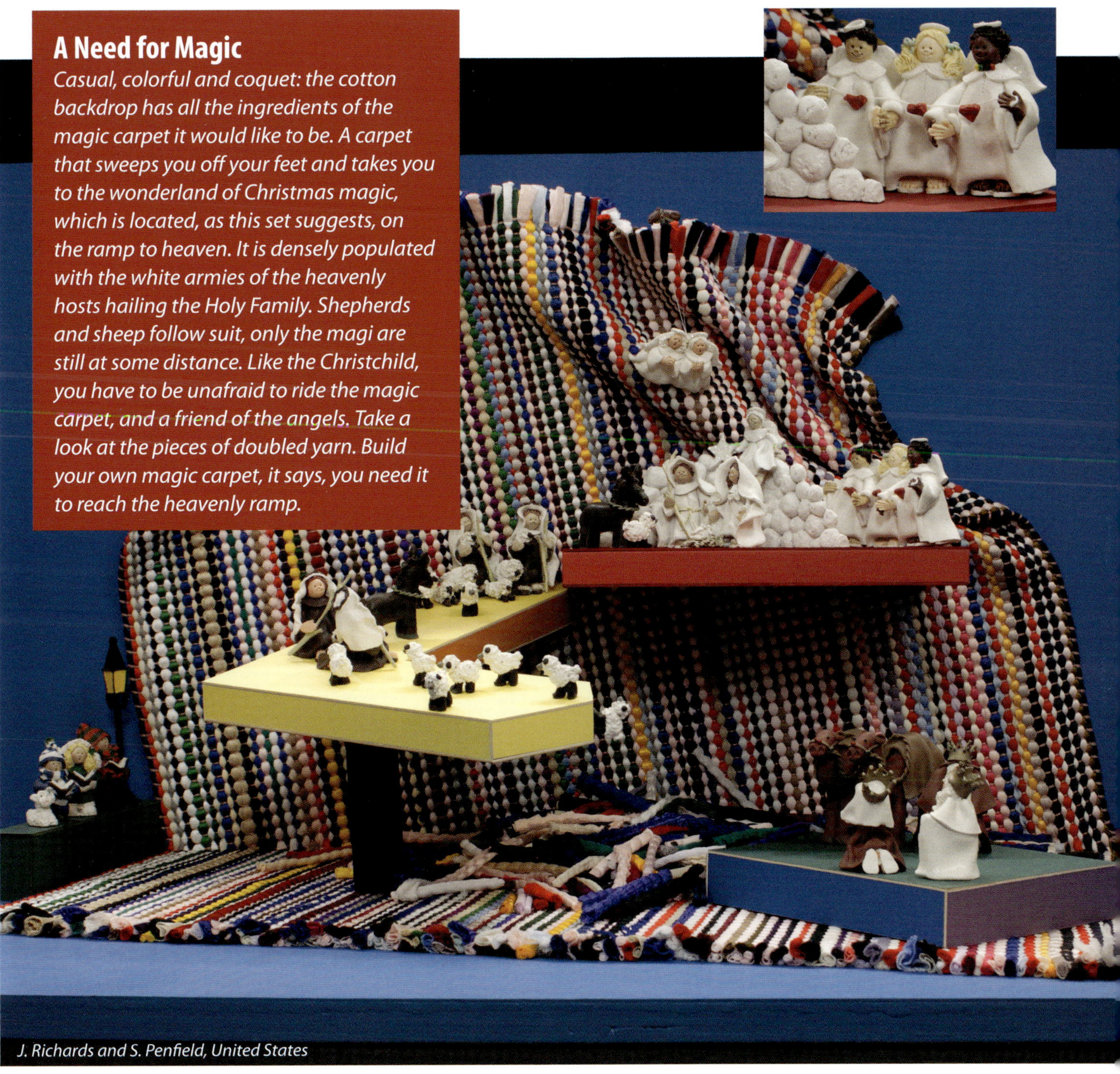

J. Richards and S. Penfield, United States

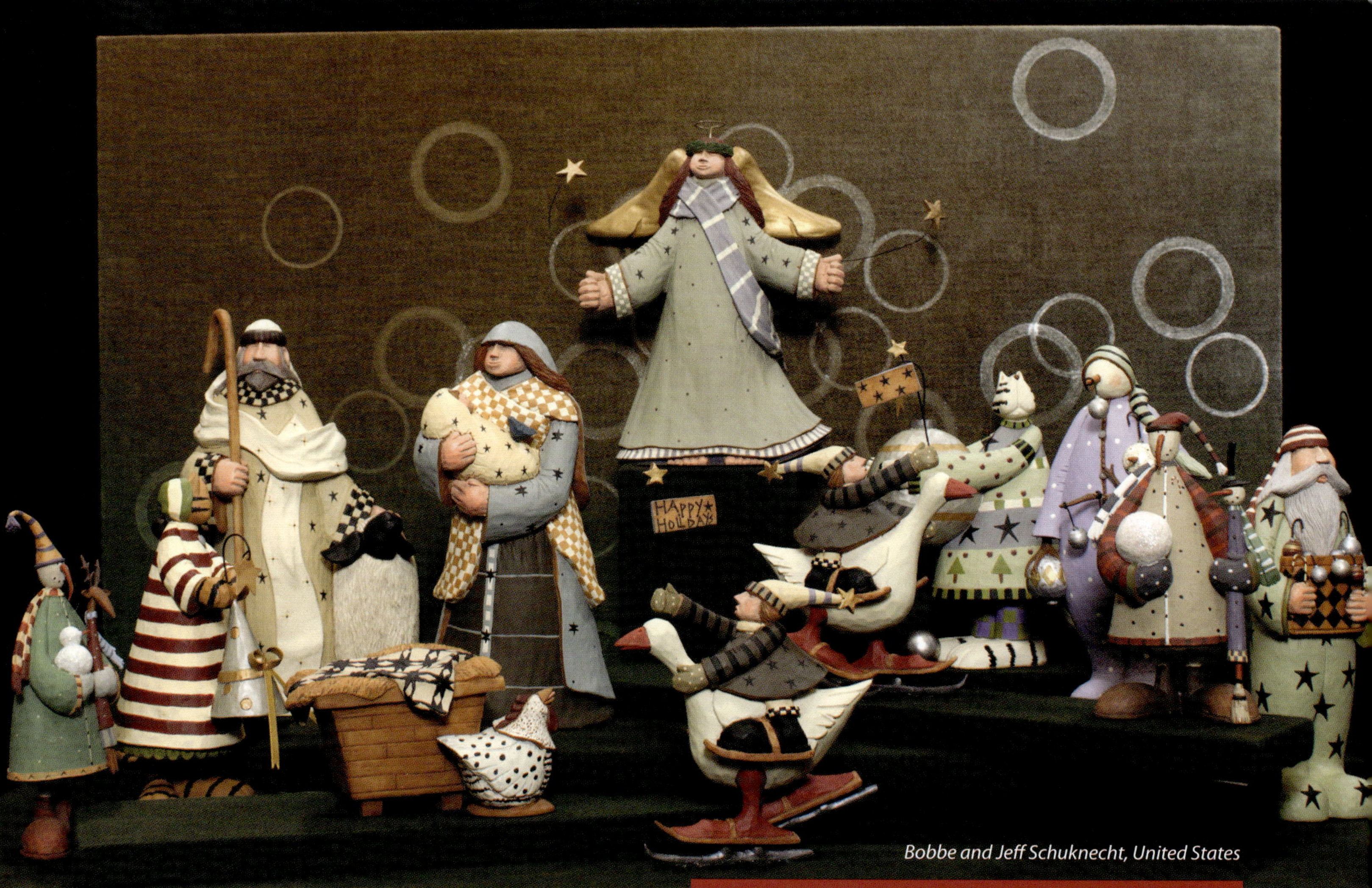

Bobbe and Jeff Schuknecht, United States

A Language of Enchantment

Jeff and Bobbe Schuknecht have a Tolkien mindset tempered and lightened by a Midwestern practical sense of humor. A "Final Touch," "Last Minute Detail," and "Night Before Christmas," are gathered around the Holy Family. "Flake and Friends," and "Snow Buds" drop by together with "Christmas Slumber Party." And here is fly-by-night "Holiday Goose" on skates. Will she stop and stay? Ask your child. Who else can understand the enchanting and bewitching world of the Schuknechts?

Moving but Incongruous

This nativity set locates the Christ event among the Native Americans of the Northern Pacific coast. It shows the outline of the typical Big House decorated with totem designs. The baby is surrounded by a checkered but colorful company of people and real and mythical animals. The most prominent among the animals are moose and polar bear, pointing out that the Northwestern natives were both hunters and fishermen. Their food was deer and moose, salmon, seal, and whale.The Northwestern Indians performed sacred dances donning costumes representing mythical animals such as the thunder bird, or like in this Nativity scene, disguised themselves as frog and beaver, both of them belonging to the "sacred center" of the land. This Nativity brings together in peaceful harmony many and disparate worlds: land and sea, humans and animals, hunters and hunted, myth and reality, indigenous religion and Christianity.

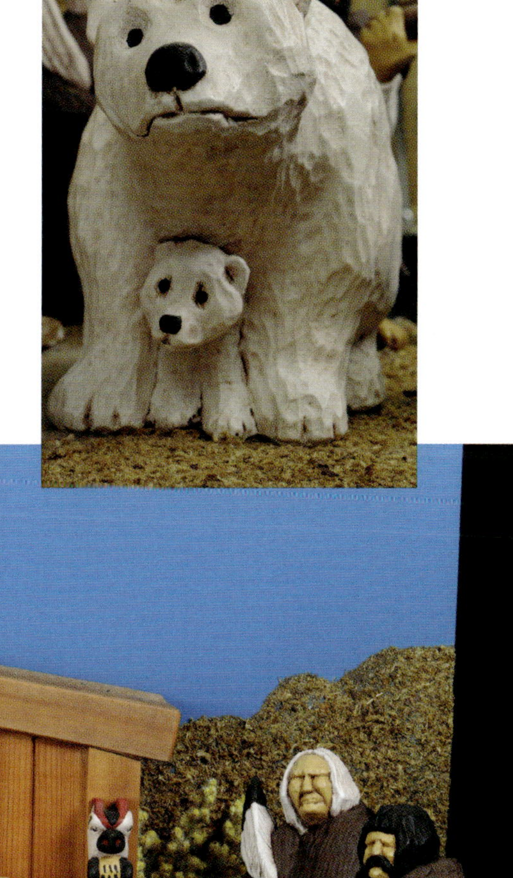

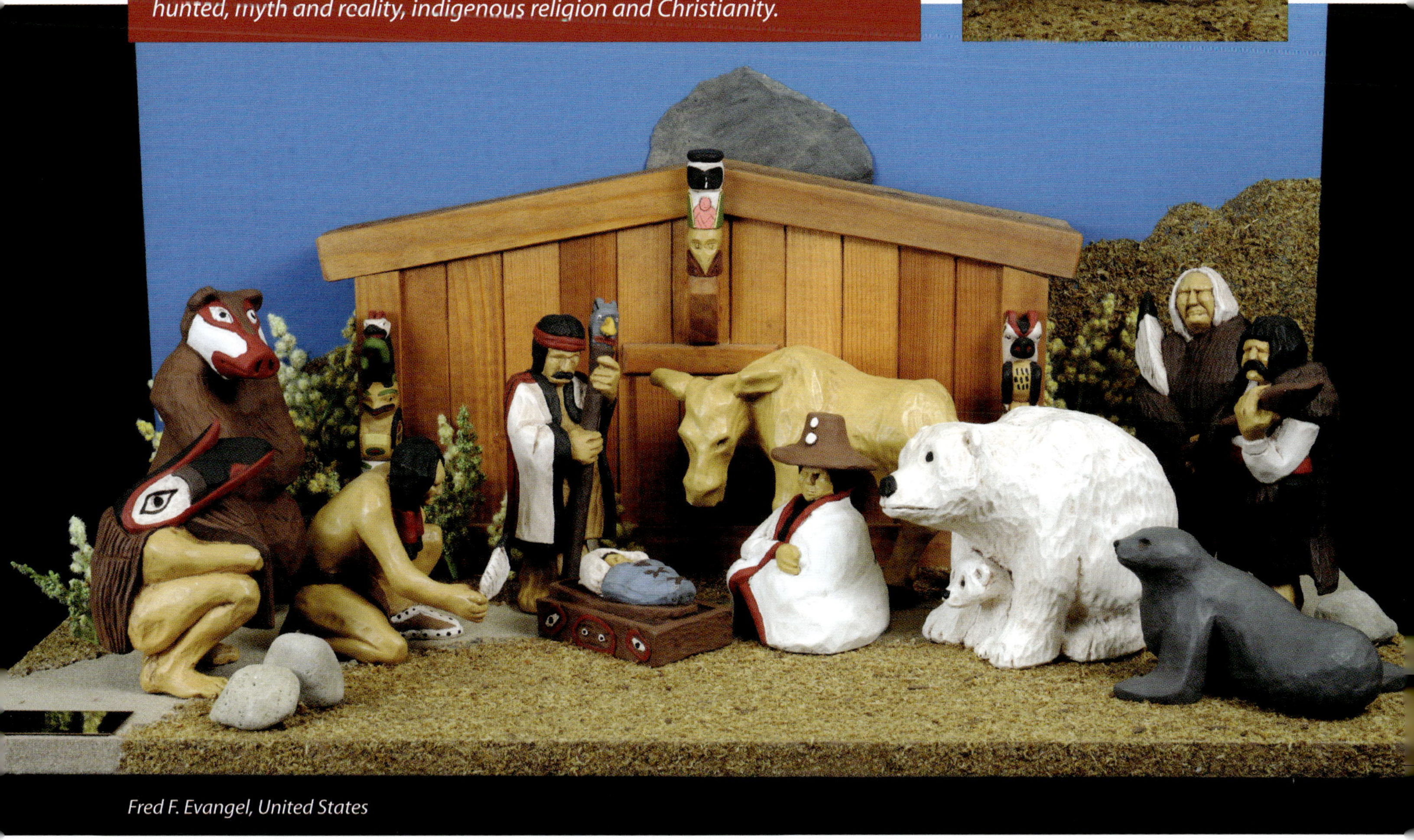

Fred F. Evangel, United States

A New Wisdom

Reycita Garcia of San Juan Pueblo relishes the soft hues of earthen colors, but her figures are "westernized." Saint Joseph is dressed cowboy style, the child wears Doctor Denton's baby pajamas, and Mary proudly shows off the many buttons on her dress. However, the special feature of this set is the frog. He is a storyteller. Frogs are figures of wisdom and symbols of transformation. He tells the story of life from its simplest expression in water and mud to the coming of Jesus, the life-giver himself.

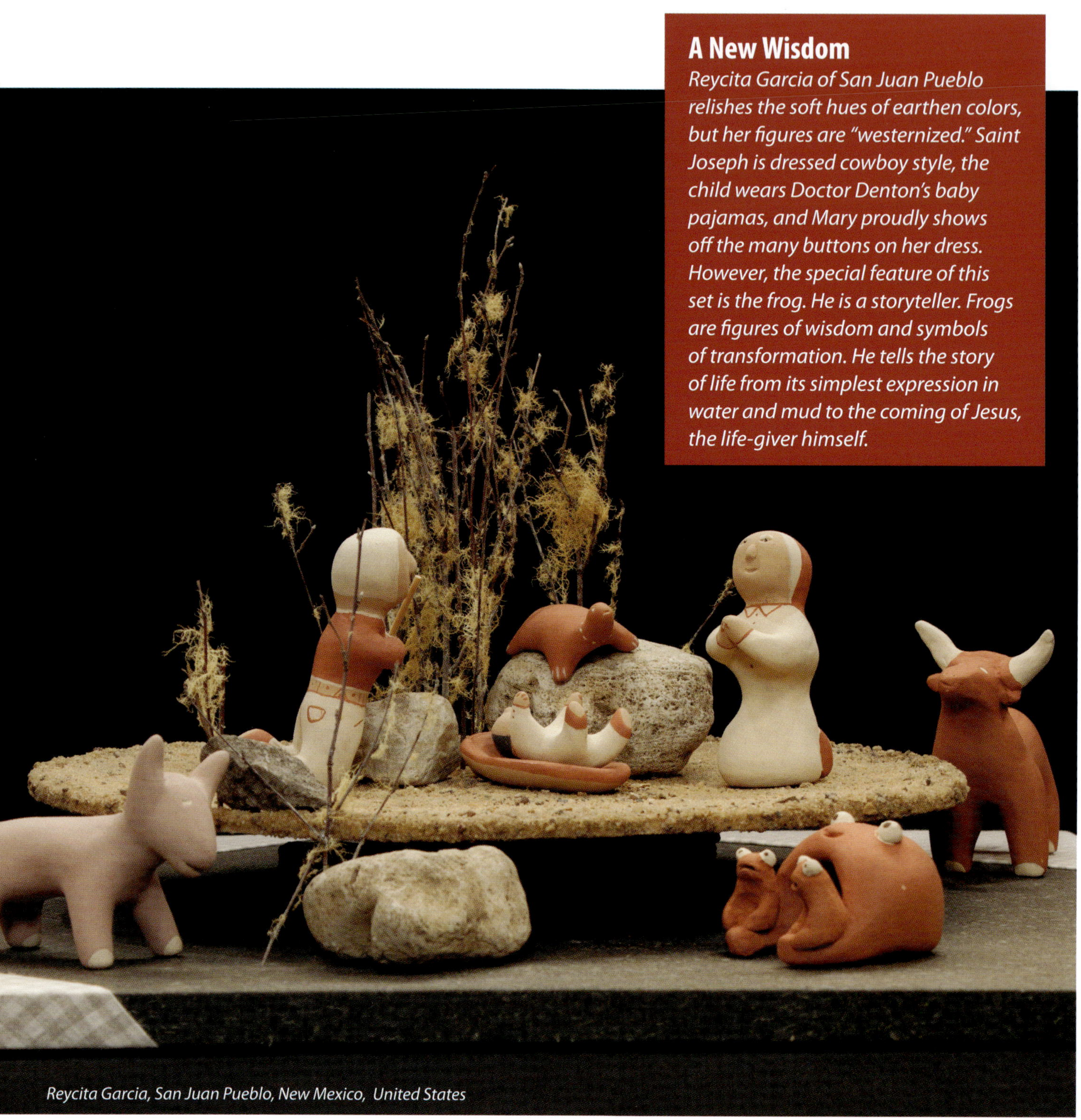

Reycita Garcia, San Juan Pueblo, New Mexico, United States

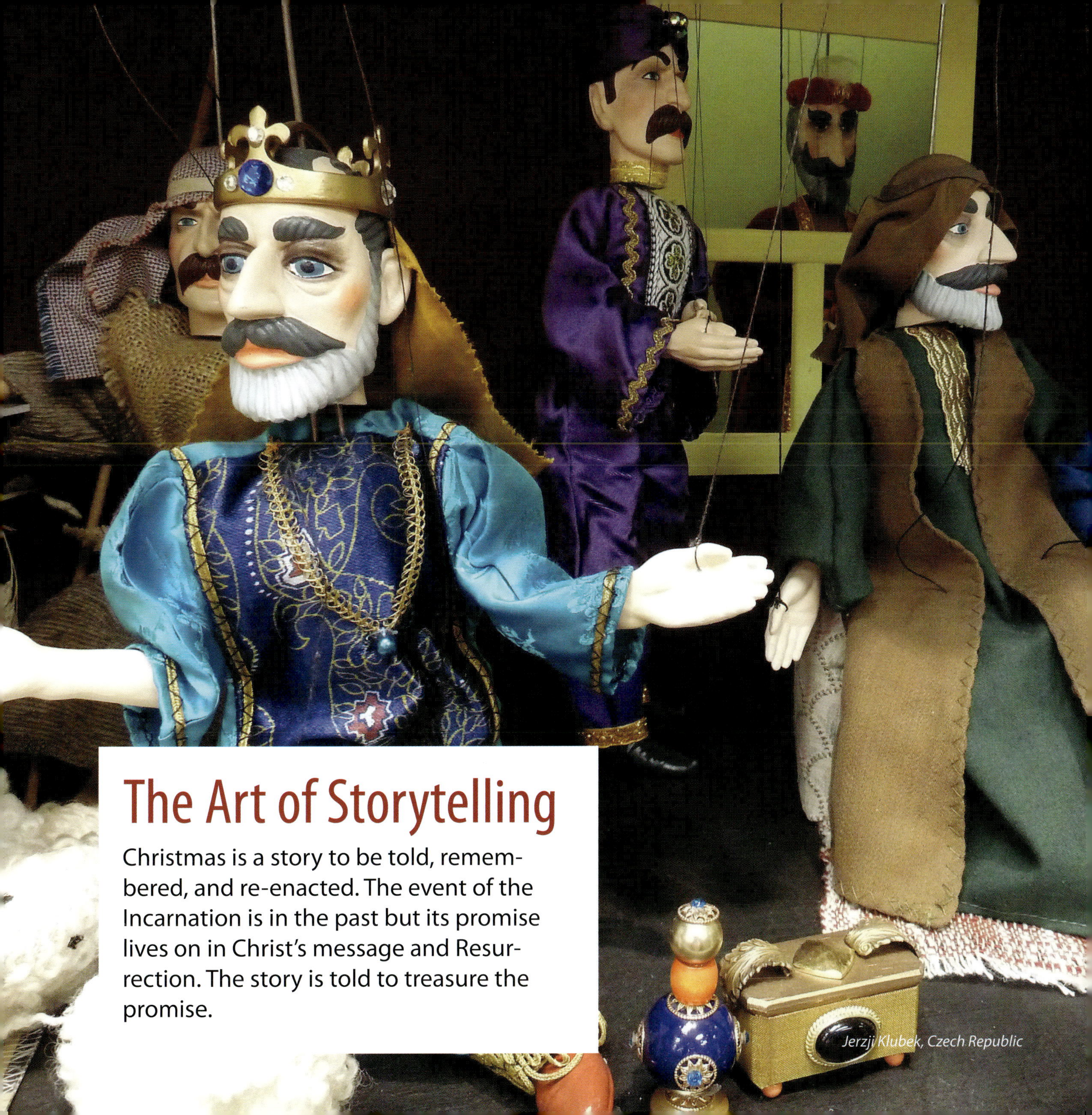

The Art of Storytelling

Christmas is a story to be told, remembered, and re-enacted. The event of the Incarnation is in the past but its promise lives on in Christ's message and Resurrection. The story is told to treasure the promise.

Jerzji Klubek, Czech Republic

The Art of Storytelling

Christmas is one of the most popular and most frequently told stories of world literature. Traveling from one culture to another the story never lost its endearing voice, or the cutting edge of its message. But there are a variety of ways of telling the story. Culture again brings out the special nuance, a new tone, and the hidden meaning. Storytelling in the Nativity tradition is a silent art because it is a visual art. It is a painted message, mainly.

Painted Figures

Painted figures and tattoos are an integral part of tribal art. The painting, ornamental figures, designates membership, rank or station in life. At a higher level of artistic creation, painted figures may express the joy and praise of life.

A Coded Message

Painted houses may convey a secret message, and express in coded ornaments the values, prayers, and emotions typical of a particular culture.

A Special Story

Some cultures develop their own method of storytelling. Maconde art from Tanzania is by definition a form of storytelling. Each work of art has a narrative value, and as such is unique. It should not be copied.

The Story as Life Line

Oral culture is a predominantly story culture where traditions are passed on, assimilated and cherished. The wide open mouth of the storyteller, and the ornamental design on vestments, frequently combine to tell the story of life, its challenge and rewards.

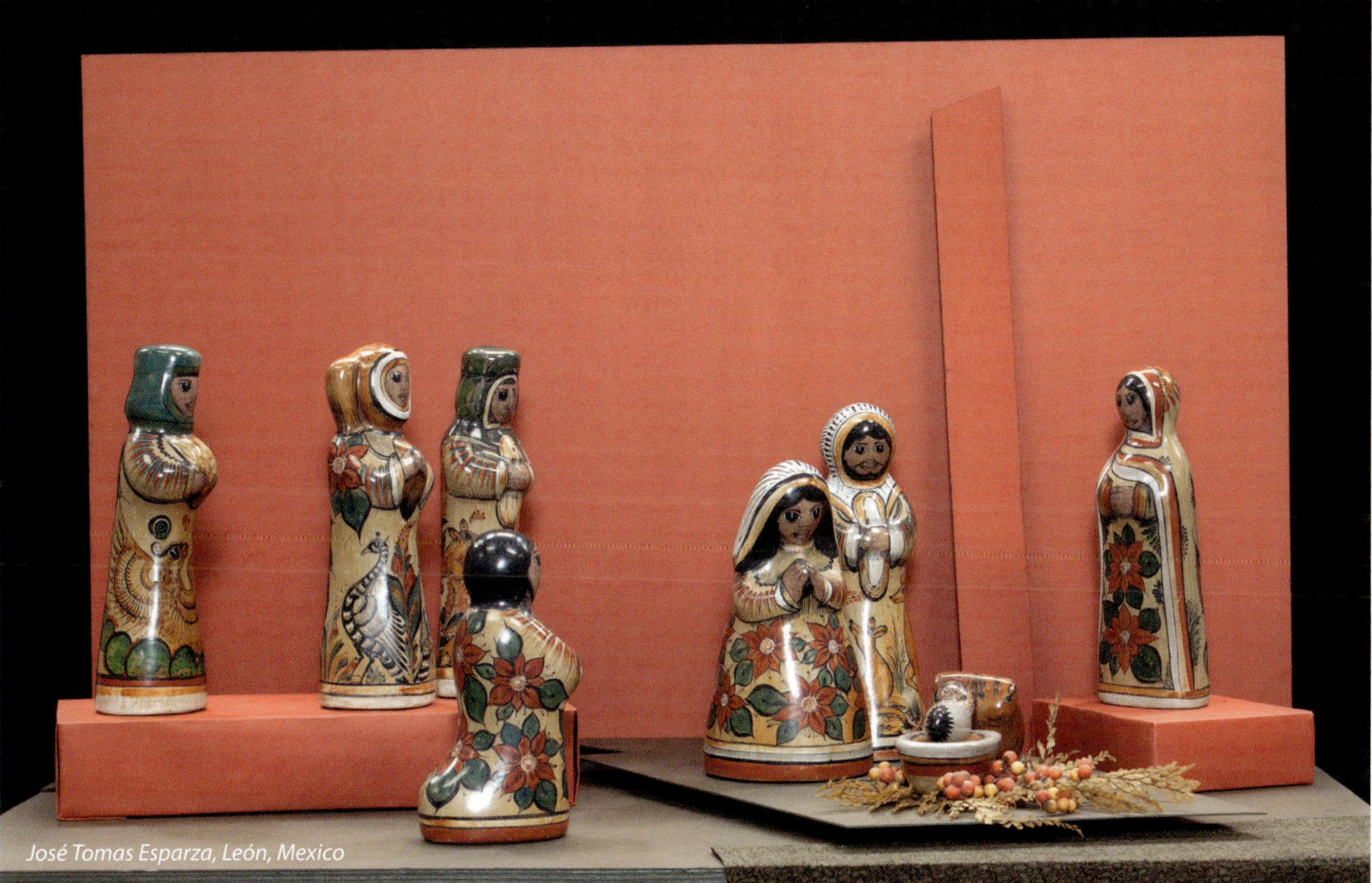

José Tomas Esparza, León, Mexico

Painted Figures

The artist of this set is from Tonala in the state of Jalisco (Mexico). He has won Mexico's presidential award for his art. Esparza creates his nativity sets using pre-Columbian techniques inherited from his ancestors. The clay is dug from the hillsides near his town, and the dyes are all natural materials. The distinctive features of this set are the lively and varied decorative elements, mainly floral and animal figures interspersed with geometric ornaments. The ornamental design of the figure is the real reason for this nativity set. Christmas rose, peacock or rabbit: they all tell and proclaim, in so many voices, the wonders of life.

A Coded Message

The colorful animals and the painted house illustrate Ndebele (Nguni people of South Africa) culture and design. The strong and vivid geometric patterns of the painted house have symbolic meaning. They are used as code to express values, prayers, and emotions typical to the Ndebele people. The origin of this secret symbolic language lies in the conflict between Ndebele and Boer farmers in the late 19th century. Harsh life and suffering, as well as horrible punishment led to this form of secret communication among tribal groups. The two midwives in this setting (upper right) emphasize the role of Ndebele women. They watch over tradition. Women are the artisans of Ndebele design of painted houses and complex beadwork. Christmas is a coded message to be opened with loving faith.

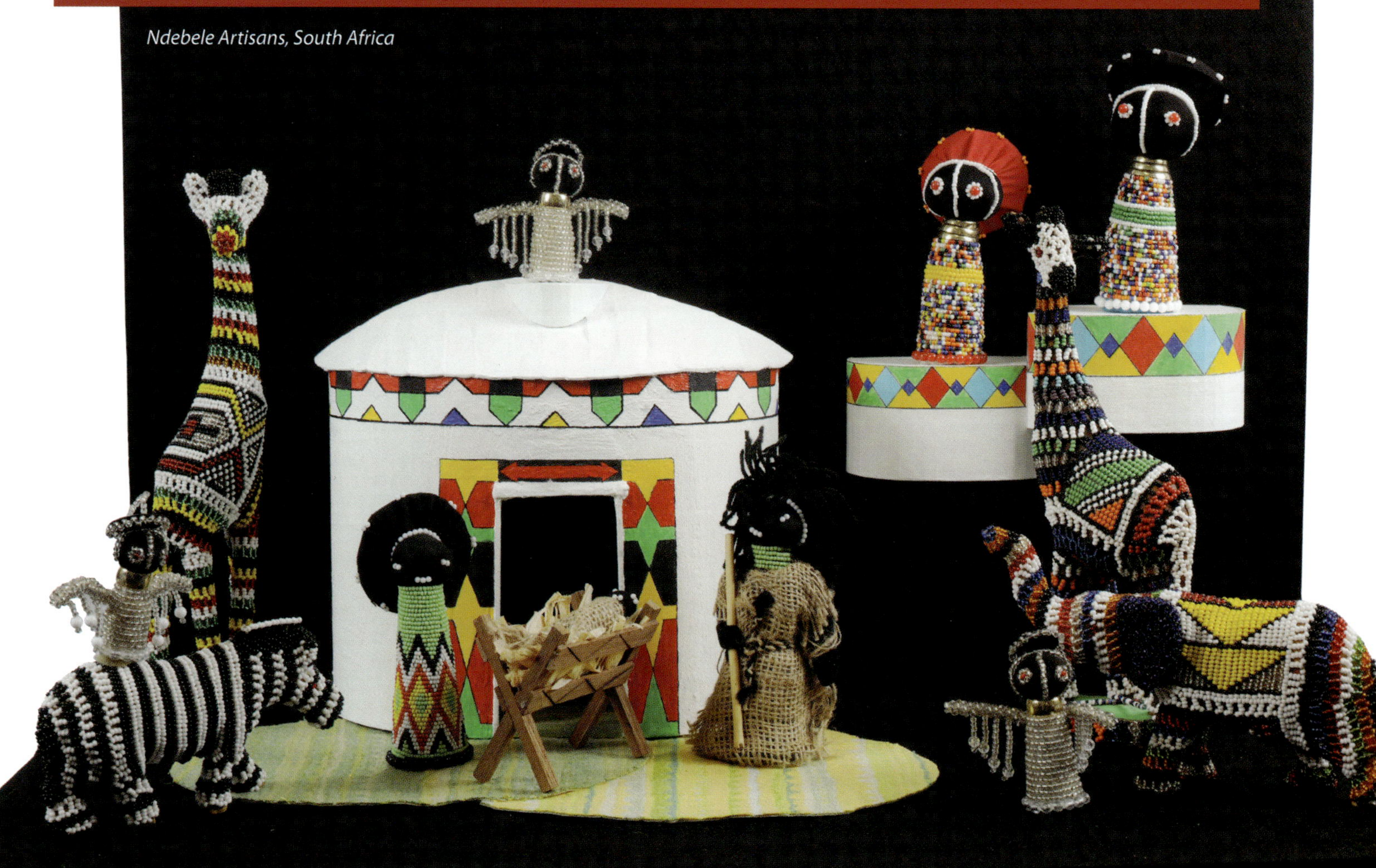

Ndebele Artisans, South Africa

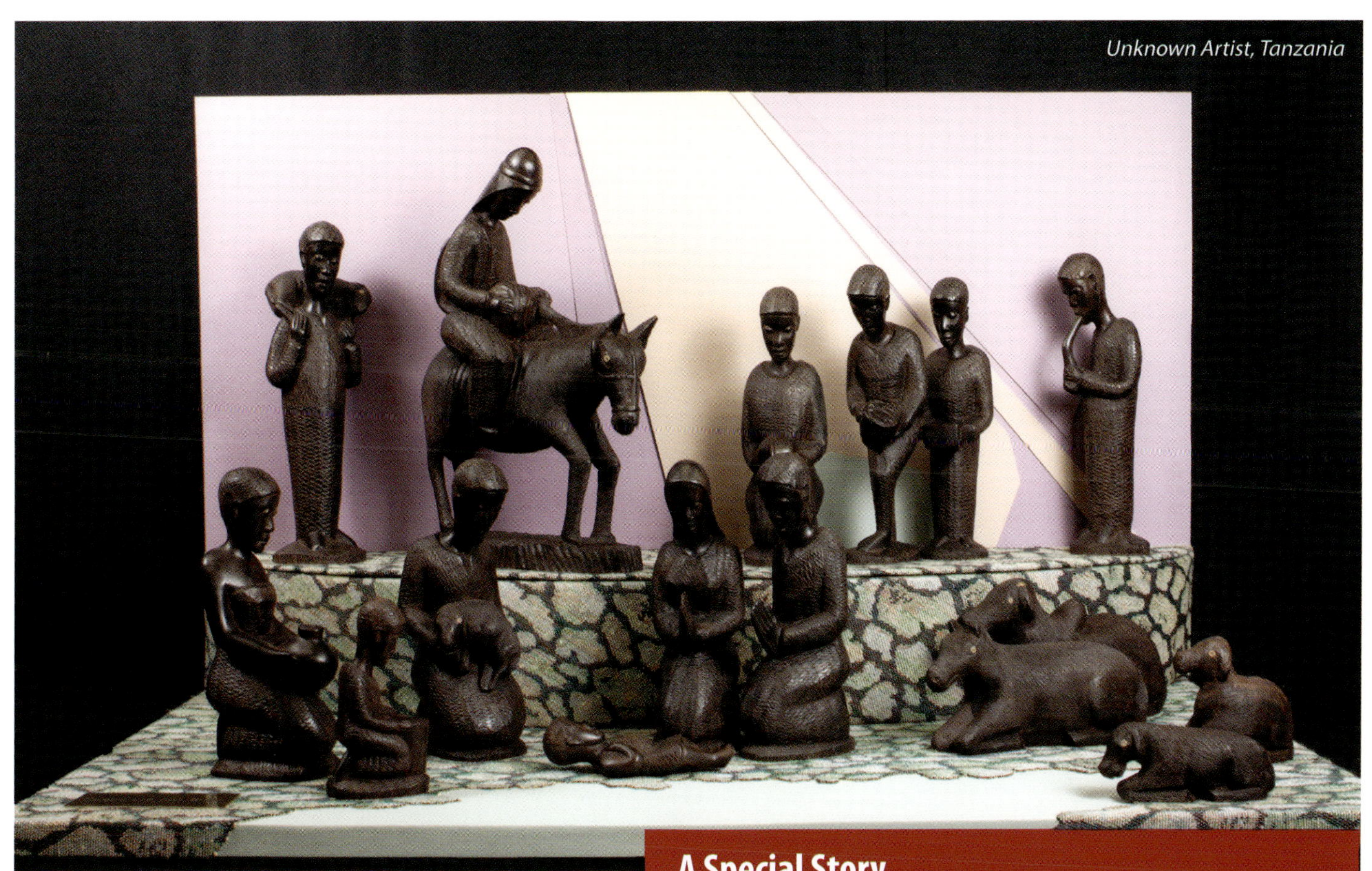

Unknown Artist, Tanzania

A Special Story

Carved from black wood or Mpingo, this Makonde (Tanzania) nativity set is a gift of Daniel E. Pilarczyk, Archbishop of Cincinnati, to the Marian Library. The peaceful glowing figures are a worthy tribute to the art of the Makonde. Its style has evolved from simple and rustic patterns to highly decorative elements and sophisticated symbolism. The art of the Makonde follows two important criteria: A piece of art is, by definition, an original that cannot be copied. Second, art is a form of storytelling. Each work of art has a unique narrative value. These characteristics are the perfect criteria to recreate the uniqueness of the greatest story ever told.

The Story as Life Line

These figures by Mary Toya of Jemez Pueblo are a modernized version of the traditional Pueblo crèche figures. They are heavy with clay, rudimentary in execution for face and hands, but of exquisite coloring and ornamental design. The two principal ornaments used here are symbols of corn and rain, the lifeline of people threatened by drought and desert. The open mouths of Mary and Joseph symbolize the voice of experience and tradition, the age-old wisdom of survival.

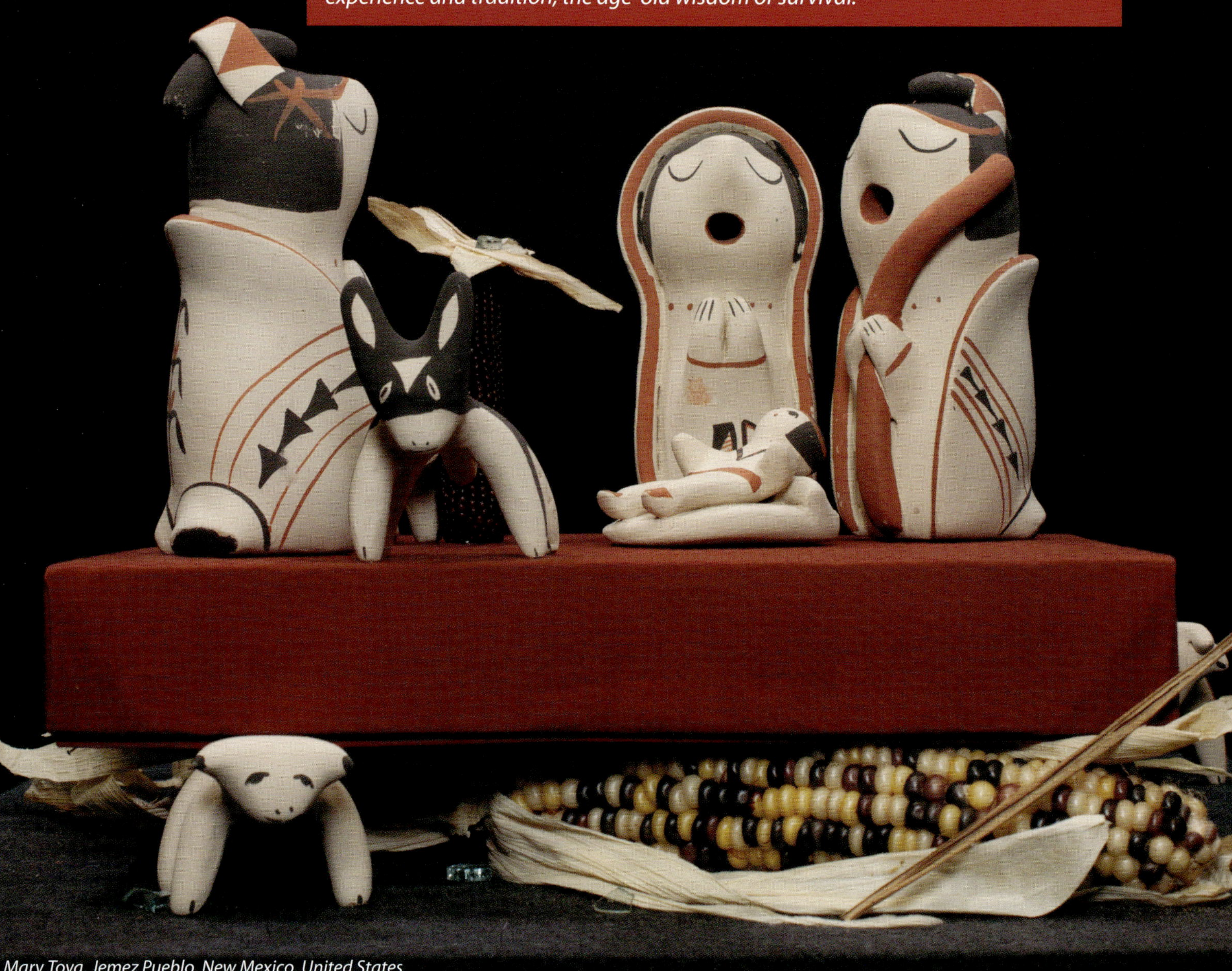

Mary Toya, Jemez Pueblo, New Mexico, United States

A Story within the Story

The Nativity story is filled with drama. The bucolic scene of the Christchild in the manger is surrounded by events of trial and hardship, by acts of violence and destruction, not least the massacre of the innocents. Most prominent among these dramatic scenes are the *Shelter Seeking* and the *Flight to Egypt*. In some Nativity representations they are part of a sequence of events, but in others they are given separate attention.

Shelter Seeking

Highlighting the rejection of the holy couple by those who could have afforded hospitality, this scene received special attention in the German crèche culture.

Flight to Egypt

A pendant to the Nativity scene, the Flight to Egypt again highlights rejection and persecution of the Holy Family.

"Los Reyes" – the Kings

Part of the Latin American tradition, for example, Puerto Rico, this custom centers on the episode of the magi, and follows the early Christmas tradition of the Epiphany, of Jesus Christ revealed to the World. Nativity sets of this tradition may limit themselves to the presentation of the three kings.

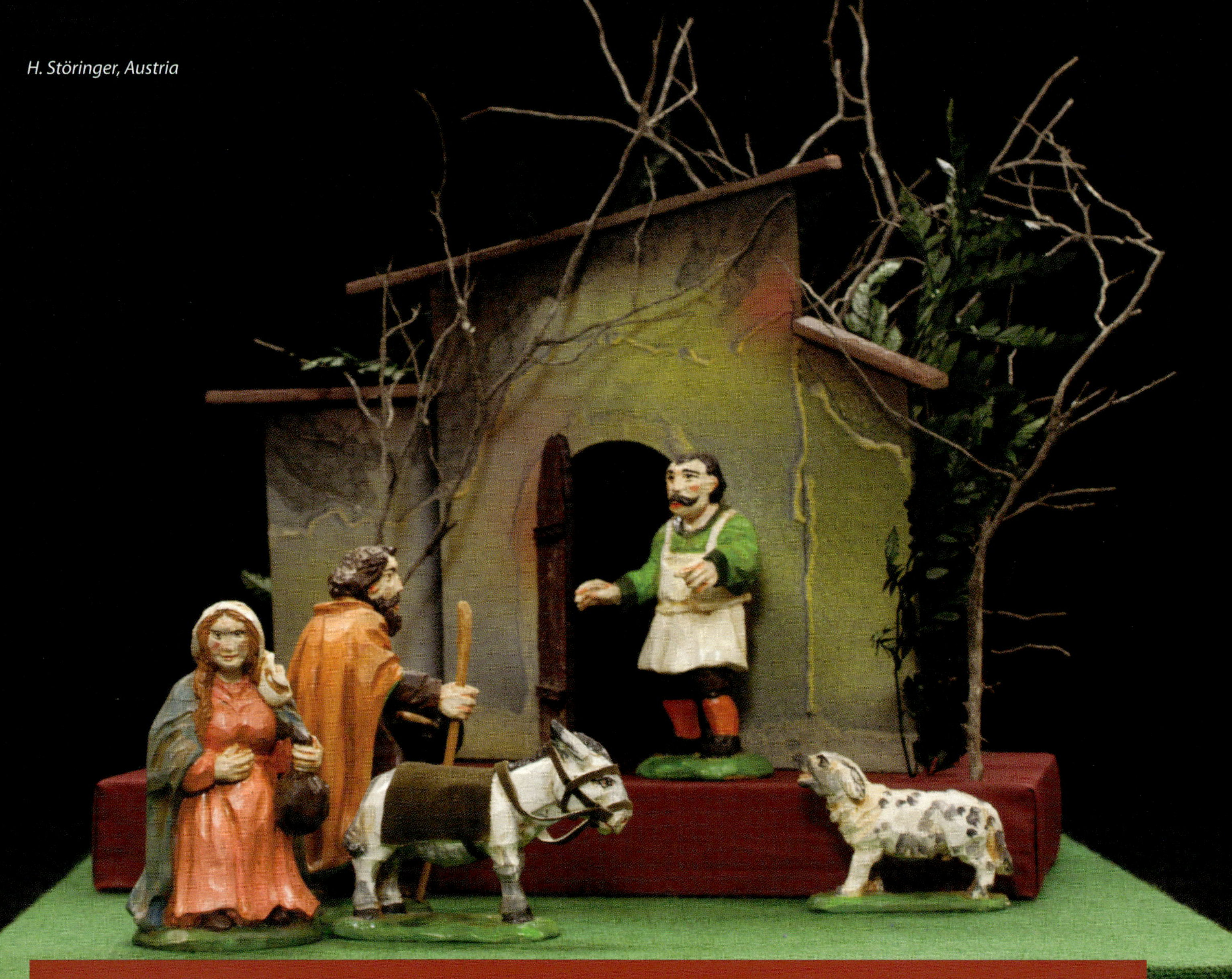

H. Störinger, Austria

Shelter Seeking

Horst Störinger's shelter-seeking group ties in with the extended Christmas tradition. This includes not only the Nativity but also the events immediately preceding and following it, for example, the holy couple's search for accommodation in Bethlehem and the Flight into Egypt. The shelter-seeking scene usually shows Mary sitting on a donkey; Joseph is leading the animal. The couple is threatened by the innkeeper and his dog. In this scene all figures are on foot. The wood carving is rough and imitates the style developed by amateur woodcarvers, mostly farmers. Shelter-seeking is not limited to figures. It is frequently reenacted in Hispanic culture as Posada. Families visit each other to share in the joy of the impending event of the Nativity. Where the holy couple found only locked doors, people now open their doors and extend hospitality in the name of Jesus Christ, the rejected one.

Flight to Egypt

Jil Gurule's Flight to Egypt is not devoid of humor and a touch of class. Humor is often the only viable answer to trial and hardship, and it takes class to brave the inevitable. The flight into Egypt is a symbol of rejection and persecution. It projects and seals the Christian condition to come. Walking after Christ leads to the manger, but also into Egypt. Ultimately, the road of Christmas leads to the Resurrection.

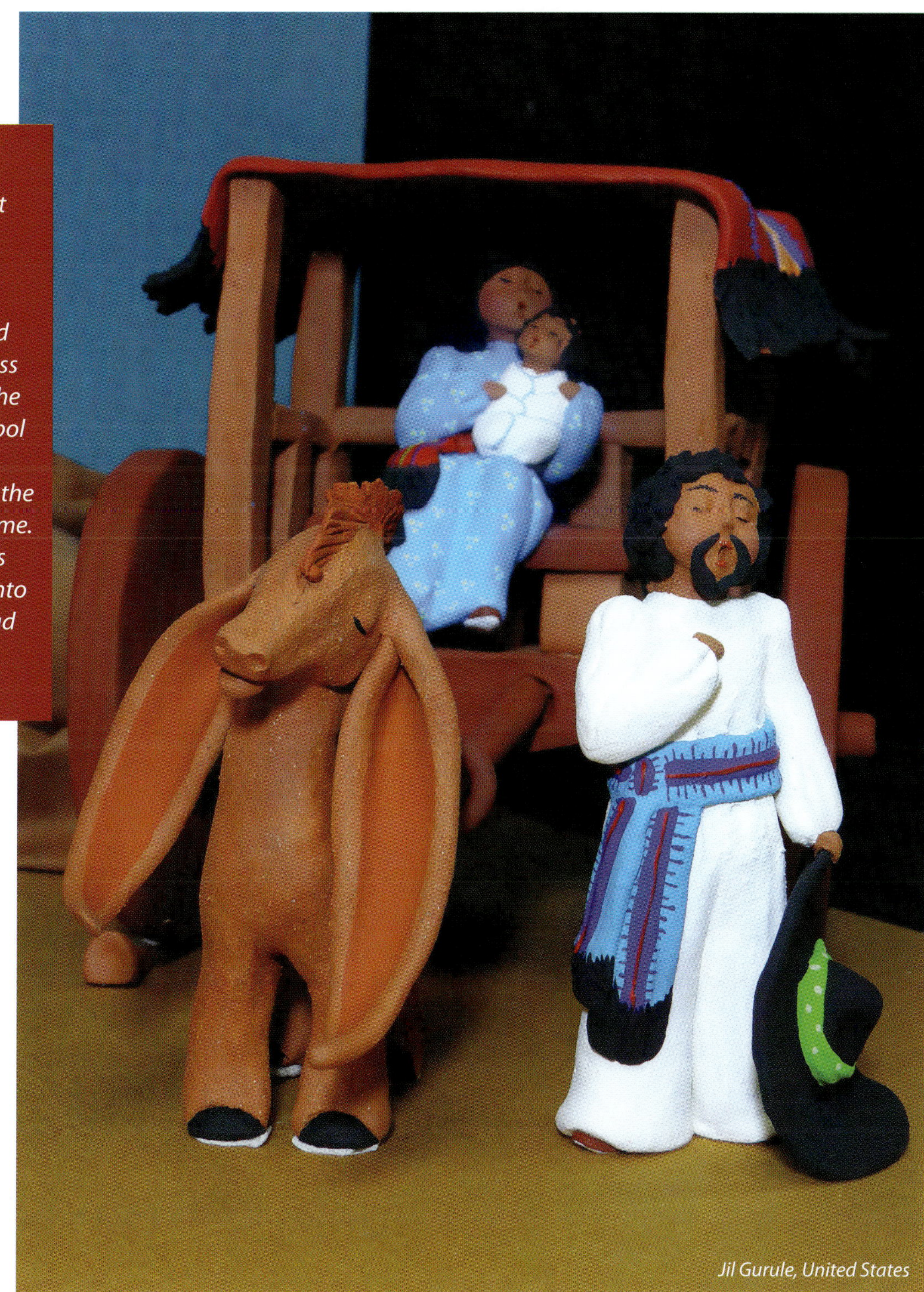

Jil Gurule, United States

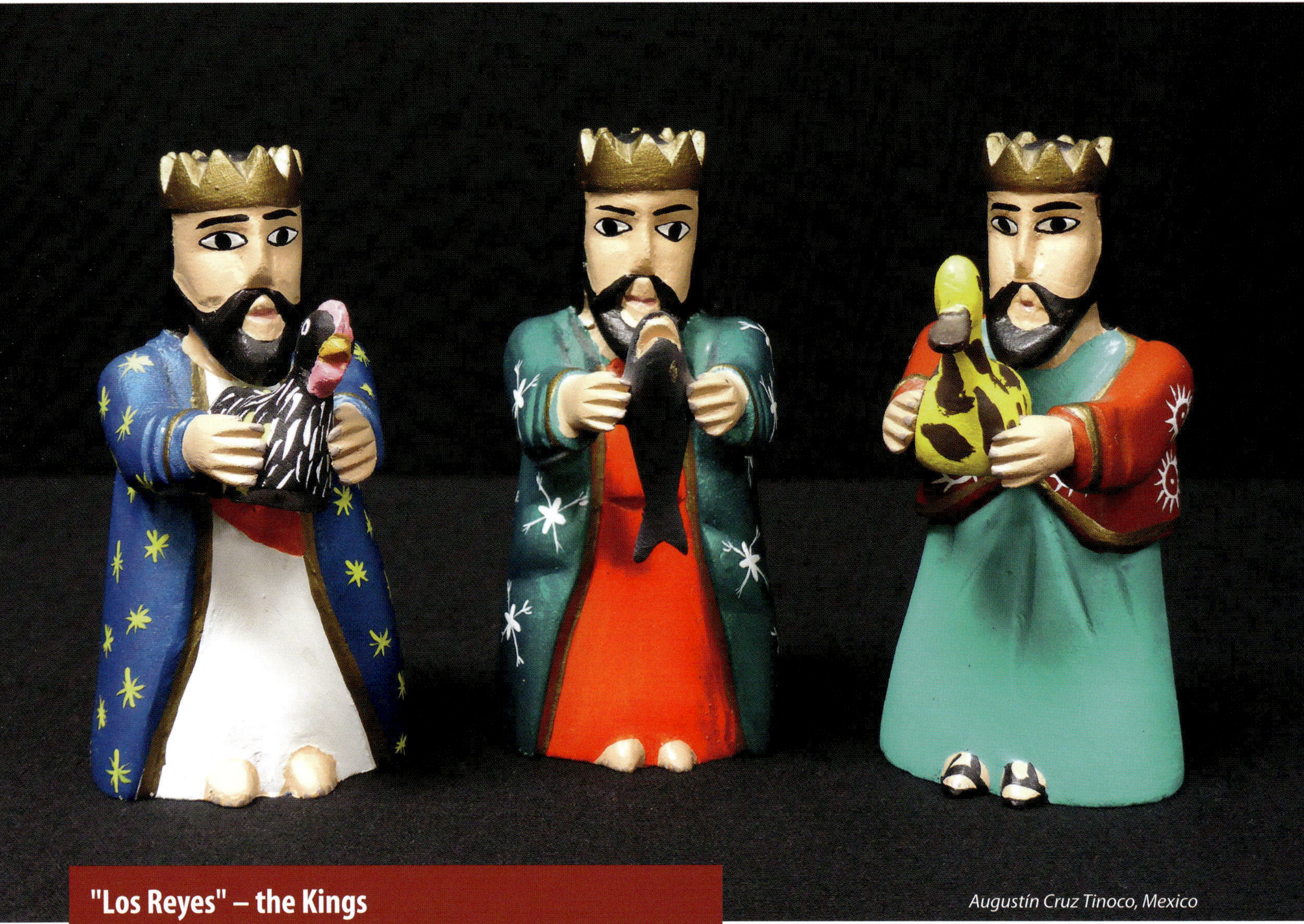

Augustín Cruz Tinoco, Mexico

"Los Reyes" – the Kings

Christmas on January 6? Epiphany is the great celebration of God's revelation in his Son. Jesus Christ is for the whole world represented in the magi or kings. A number of Latin countries (for example, Italy and Spain) maintain the original date of the Nativity and celebrate Christmas on January 6. Special prominence is given to the kings. They are the gift-bringers. They are the origin of many customs involving caroling and plays. Who will be the king/queen of the day? The one who finds the charm (bean or tiny figure of the Nativity) hidden in the cake of the kings.

Games People Play

The expression 'Games people play' ought not to be taken lightly. Modern Pedagogy has heavily invested in all forms of play, mindful of the Latin proverb that by playing, much can be learned *(ludens discere)*. We find among our nativity sets examples which come with a pedagogical agenda. Figures invite handling and playing; a whole set contains a message composed of many parts. The games are many, the purpose seems simple … but not always.

The Sound of Music

Combining sound and movement, the music box became the ideal lullaby for the Christmas story.

In the Limelight

Telling the story while playing the parts creates a world of wonder where the marionettes are kings and queens, the puppeteer a humble servant, and the spectator master of the game.

Playing for Life

Is there a play which is sacred conveying the promise of new life and regeneration? As popular as Nine Men's Morris may be, the Morabaraba board carries an equally rich history and culture.

A Mnemonic Device

Games can be deadly serious when a simple song about Christmas (Twelve Days of Christmas) teaches about faith and protects life, and a mnemonic device harbors a coded message on how to avoid death.

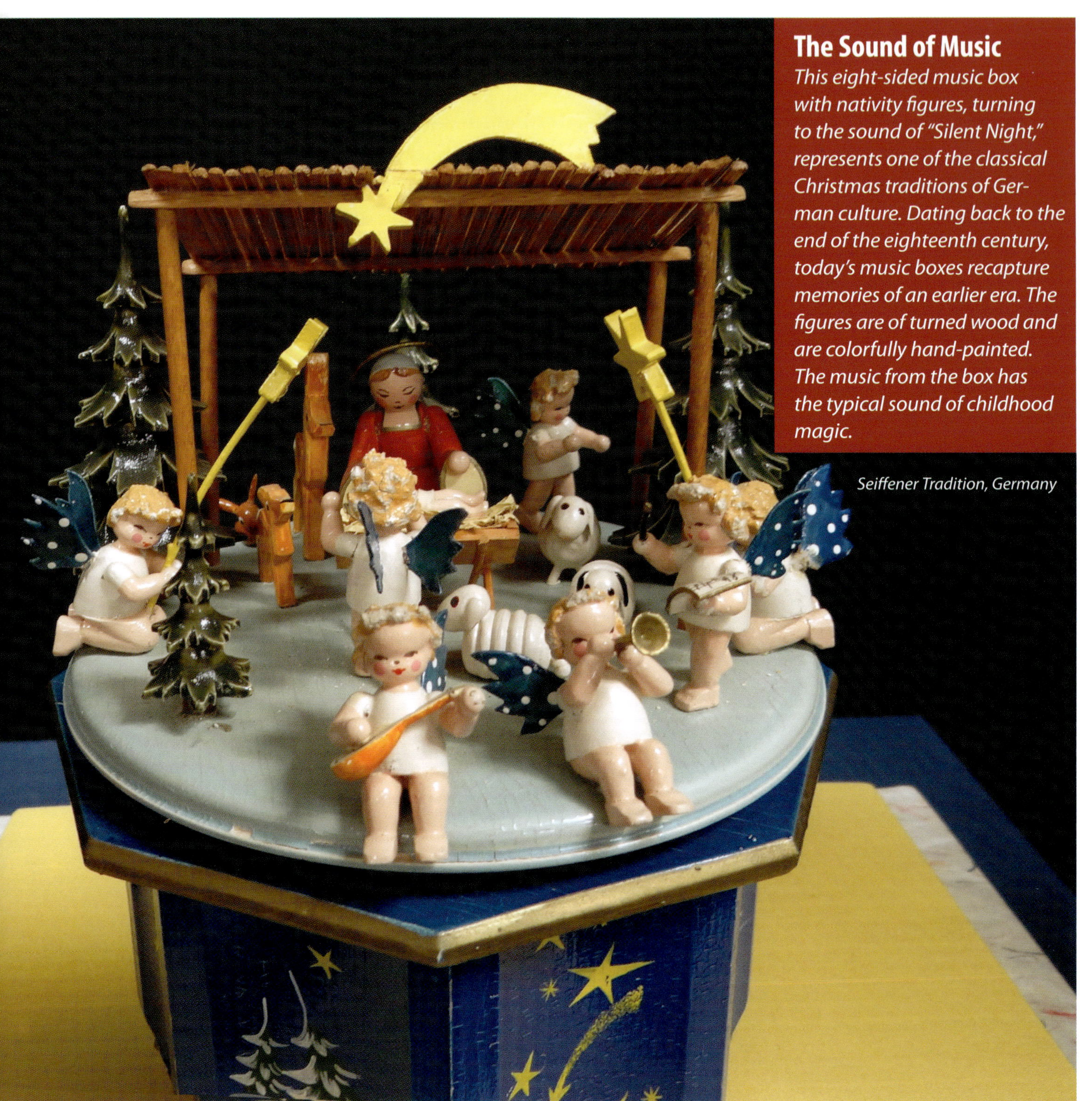

The Sound of Music

This eight-sided music box with nativity figures, turning to the sound of "Silent Night," represents one of the classical Christmas traditions of German culture. Dating back to the end of the eighteenth century, today's music boxes recapture memories of an earlier era. The figures are of turned wood and are colorfully hand-painted. The music from the box has the typical sound of childhood magic.

Seiffener Tradition, Germany

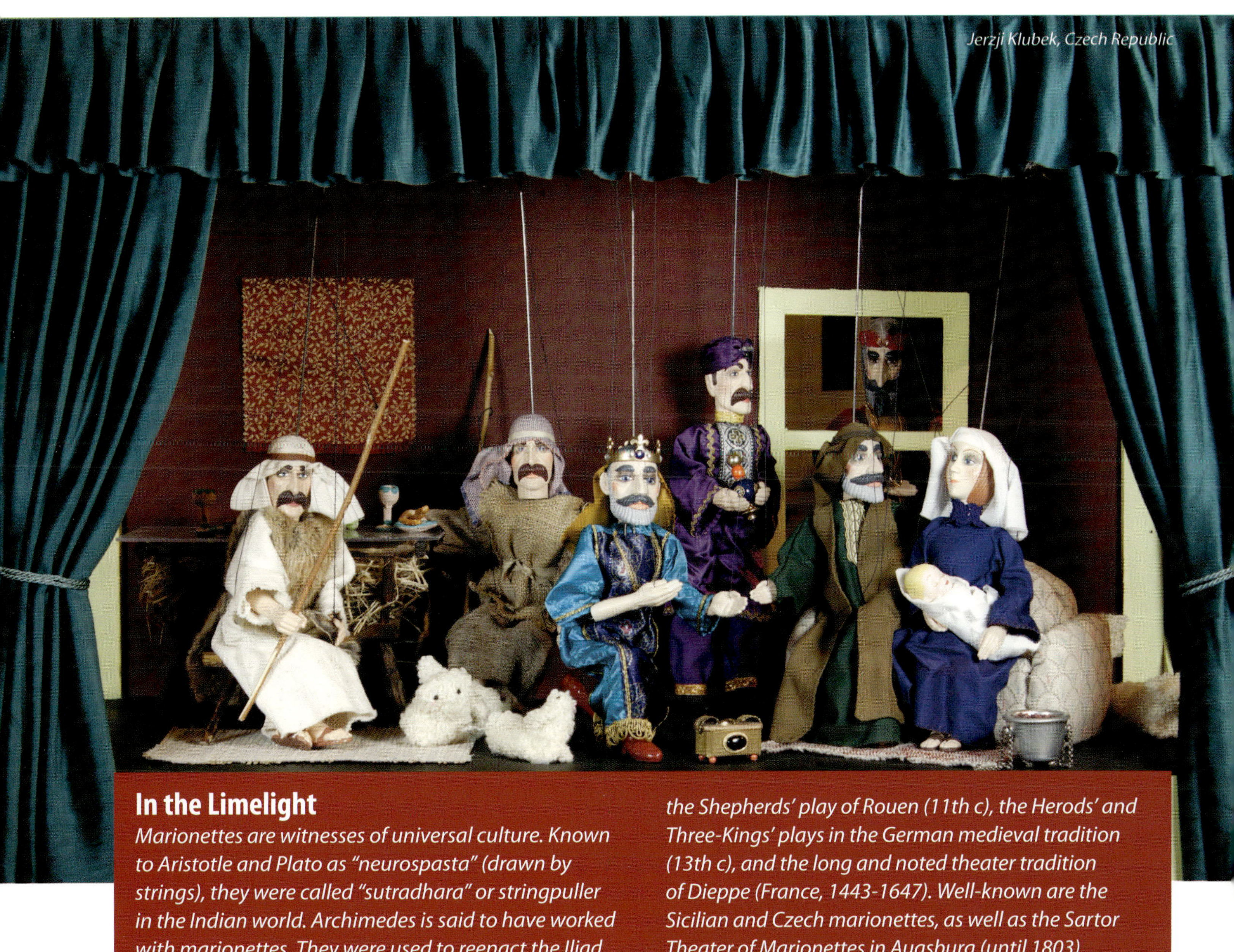
Jerzji Klubek, Czech Republic

In the Limelight

Marionettes are witnesses of universal culture. Known to Aristotle and Plato as "neurospasta" (drawn by strings), they were called "sutradhara" or stringpuller in the Indian world. Archimedes is said to have worked with marionettes. They were used to reenact the Iliad and Odyssey. The Christian world inherited puppetry from Roman theater tradition and medieval Italy. It is believed that the word marionette originated from little figures of the Virgin Mary or "Marydolls." Marionettes are precursors of the nativity set or crèche. They were used in morality plays and mysteries, for example, in the Shepherds' play of Rouen (11th c), the Herods' and Three-Kings' plays in the German medieval tradition (13th c), and the long and noted theater tradition of Dieppe (France, 1443-1647). Well-known are the Sicilian and Czech marionettes, as well as the Sartor Theater of Marionettes in Augsburg (until 1803).

This set is reminiscent of human playfulness. Grave concerns, high hopes, and difficult truths are frequently dealt with playfully -- not least because we are all children when faced with the hard facts of life such as human drama, death, and life to come.

Playing for Life

Morabaraba is a game and popular among youth in the southern regions of Africa. In our culture it is called Nine Men's Morris. The board consists of three concentric squares of increasing size. It is believed to be one of the oldest games in history and is found in many countries of the world. Found in Egyptian temples as well as Medieval cathedrals, the Morris square was sacred. The central square is known in some cultures as the square of regeneration and new life. We have set Mother and Child in the center of this imitation Morabaraba board. In Christian culture they are the very symbol of regeneration. Joseph Marufu is a Shona sculptor. His figures, meek and withdrawn, share in his personal tragedy. Joseph is referred to as an albino. His skin produces little melanin pigment. His condition means that he works indoors in a poorly lit environment.

Joseph Marufu, Zimbabwe

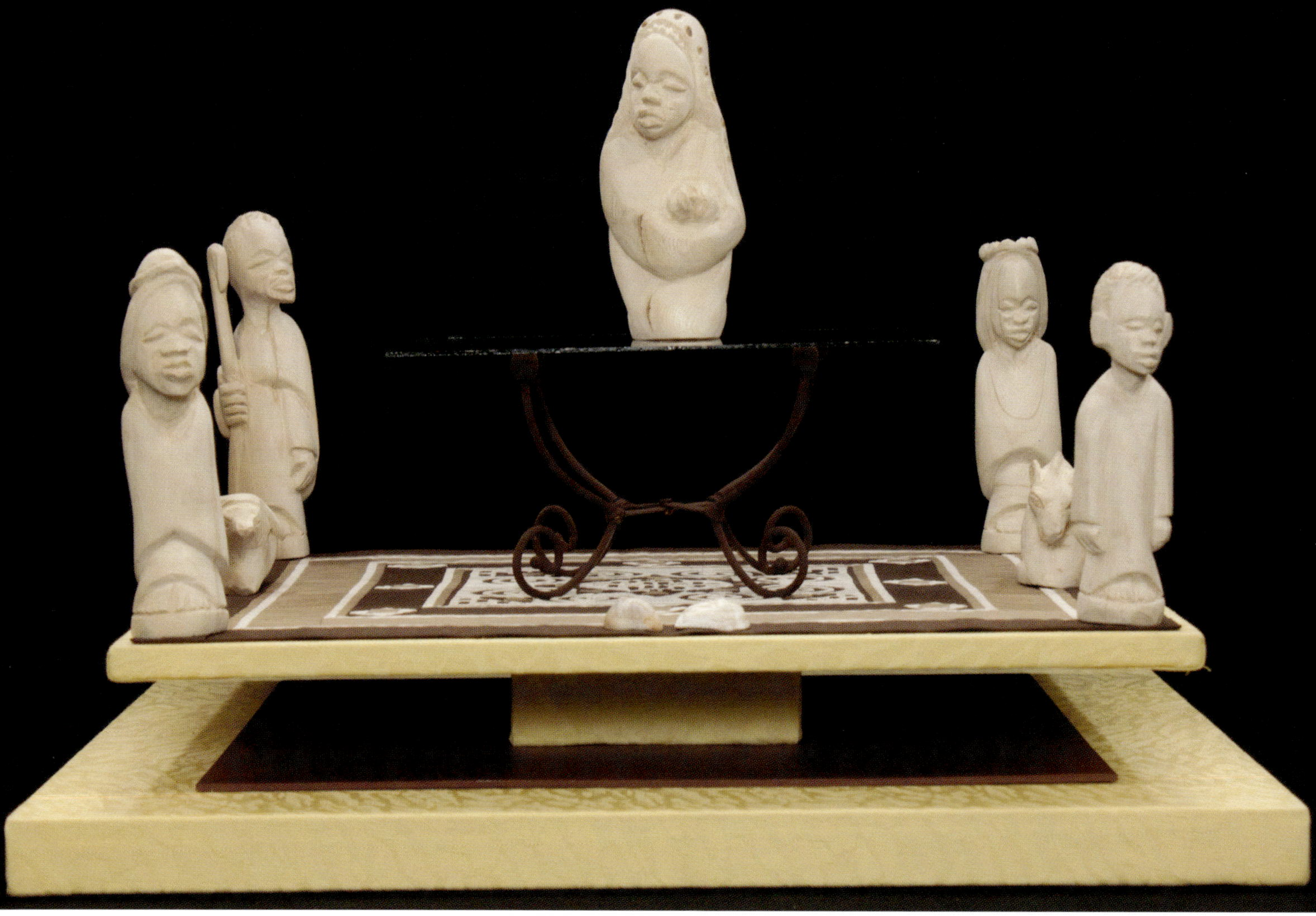

A Mnemonic Device

There was a time when "Twelve Days of Christmas" was an underground catechism. It was the catechism song of English Catholics during the time of persecution (1558-1829), when both private and public practice of the Catholic faith was prohibited by law.

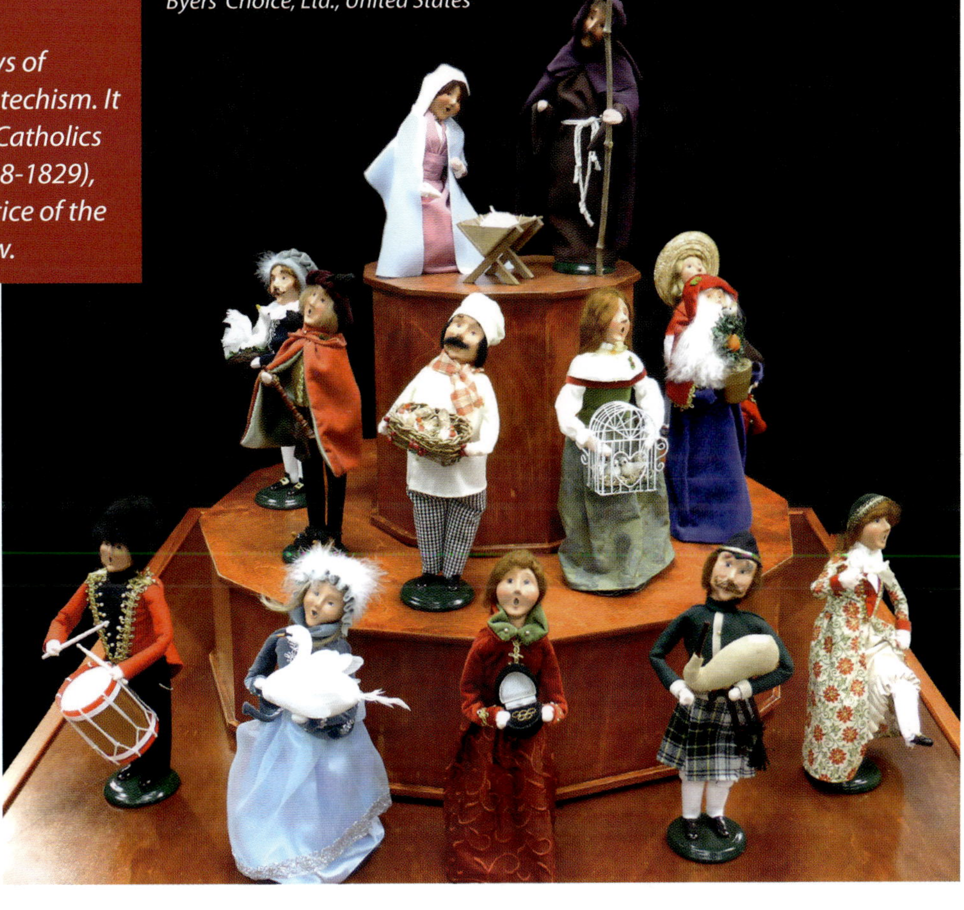
Byers' Choice, Ltd., United States

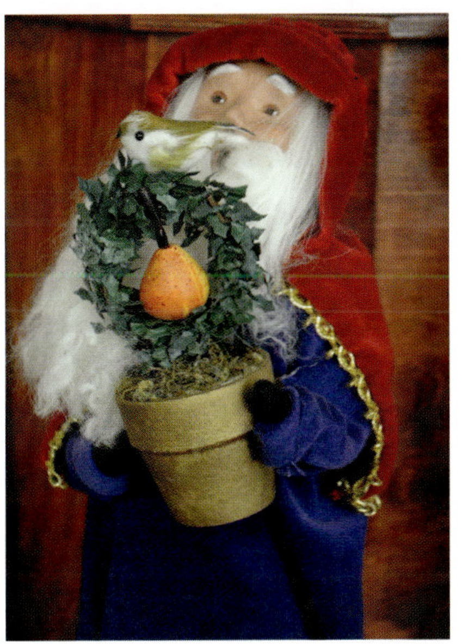

The strange gifts of the song were hidden teachings of the Catholic faith. The "true love" means God. The "partridge in a pear tree" refers to Jesus Christ who shelters the persecuted Catholics under his wings. He is number one. The following numbers and symbols are a mnemonic aid of essential truths of the Catholic faith.

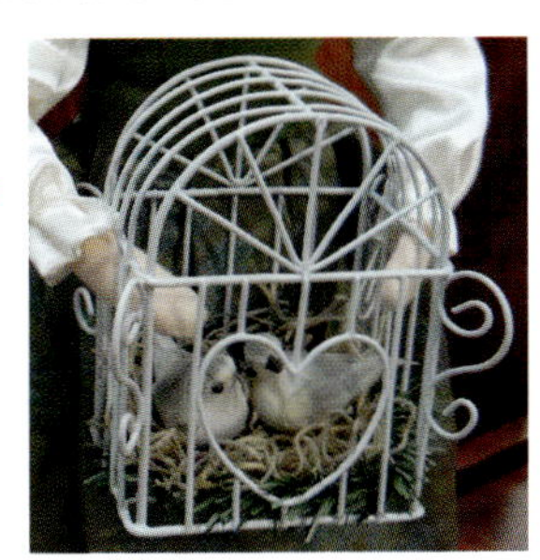

2 Turtle Doves = Old and New Testaments

3 French Hens = Faith, Hope, and Charity

4 Calling Birds = Four Gospels

5 Golden Rings = Pentateuch, the first five books of the Old Testament

6 Geese A-laying = Six Days of Creation

7 Swans A-swimming = Seven Gifts of the Holy Spirit

8 Maids A-milking = Eight Beatitudes

9 Ladies Dancing = Nine Fruits of the Holy Spirit

10 Lord A-leaping = Ten Commandments

11 Pipers Piping = Eleven Faithful Apostles

12 Drummers Drumming = Twelve Truths of the Apostles' Creed

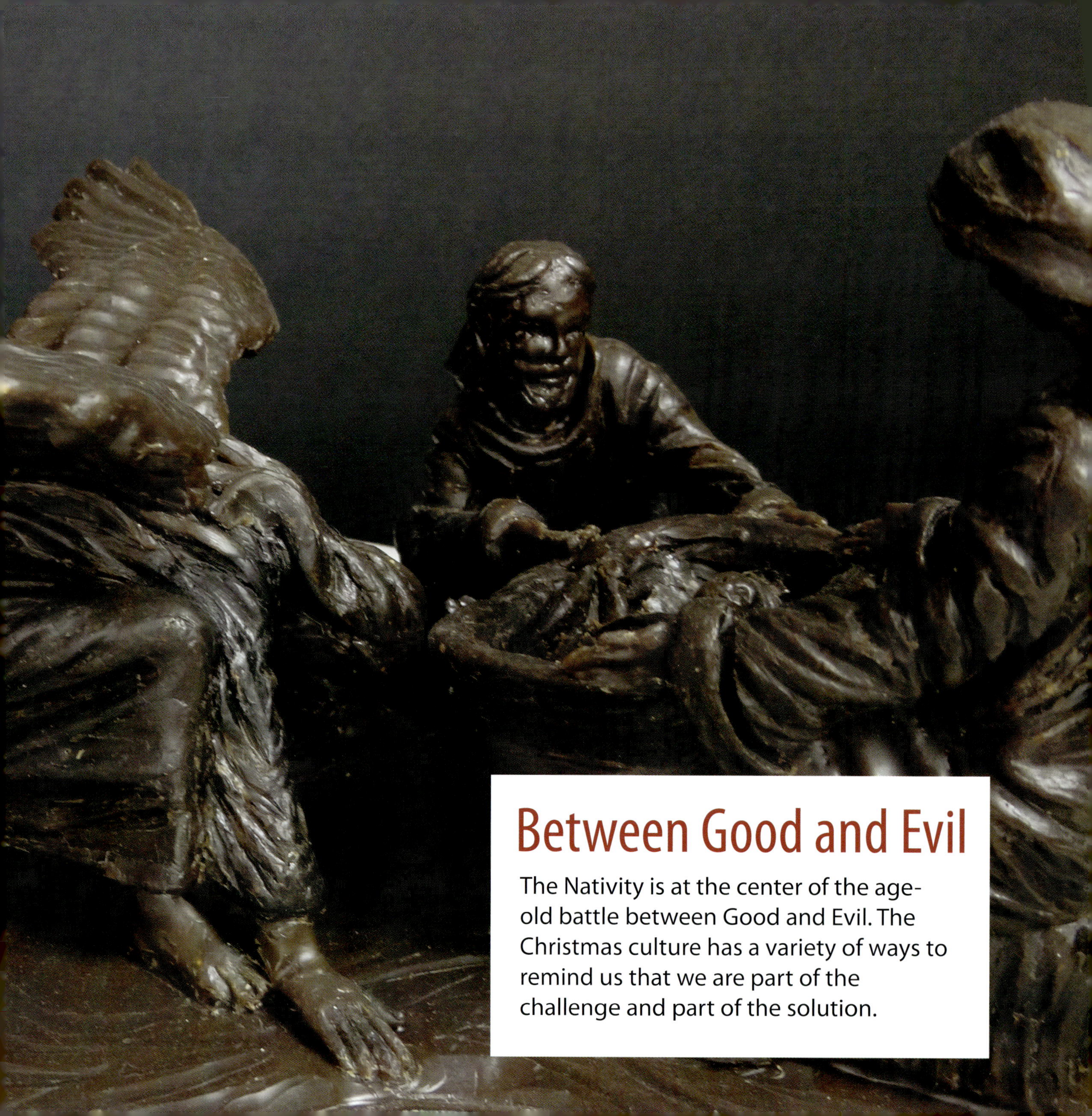

Between Good and Evil

The Nativity is at the center of the age-old battle between Good and Evil. The Christmas culture has a variety of ways to remind us that we are part of the challenge and part of the solution.

Life is Theater
Angel and Devil
Darkness and Light
Paradise Retrieved

Between Good and Evil

Christmas has very definite childlike and magic accents which suggest a world of innocence and facile bliss. There is a different side to the Nativity. The Incarnation of Jesus Christ raises the question of salvation, and therefore the question about the relationship between Good and Evil. The representation of evil in nativity sets is frequently one of resistance to, of menace and threat to the goodness of God in the newborn king. The Nativity can be seen as a stage where good and evil confront each other, sometimes understood as culture of death resisting the new culture of life in Jesus Christ. The personification of evil, the devil, has a place in some nativity sets, and so has the rooster, a symbol of treason. In some Nativity traditions of the Northern hemisphere, it is the symbolism of light and darkness which represents the primordial combat between the forces of good and evil. Sometimes the separation between good and evil is marked by a fence, to single out those who belong to the Christchild from those who are separated and excluded.

Life is Theater

The stage is a welcome prop to dramatize, but also to ease the struggle between good and evil.

Angel and Devil

The opposition between good and evil is personified in the figures of angel and devil.

Darkness and Light

The winter equinox in Northern countries is frequently used to symbolize the progressive transformation of darkness into light brought about by the event of Christmas.

Paradise Retrieved

The Fall, the temporary victory of evil, is overcome by the Incarnation, the beginning of paradise retrieved.

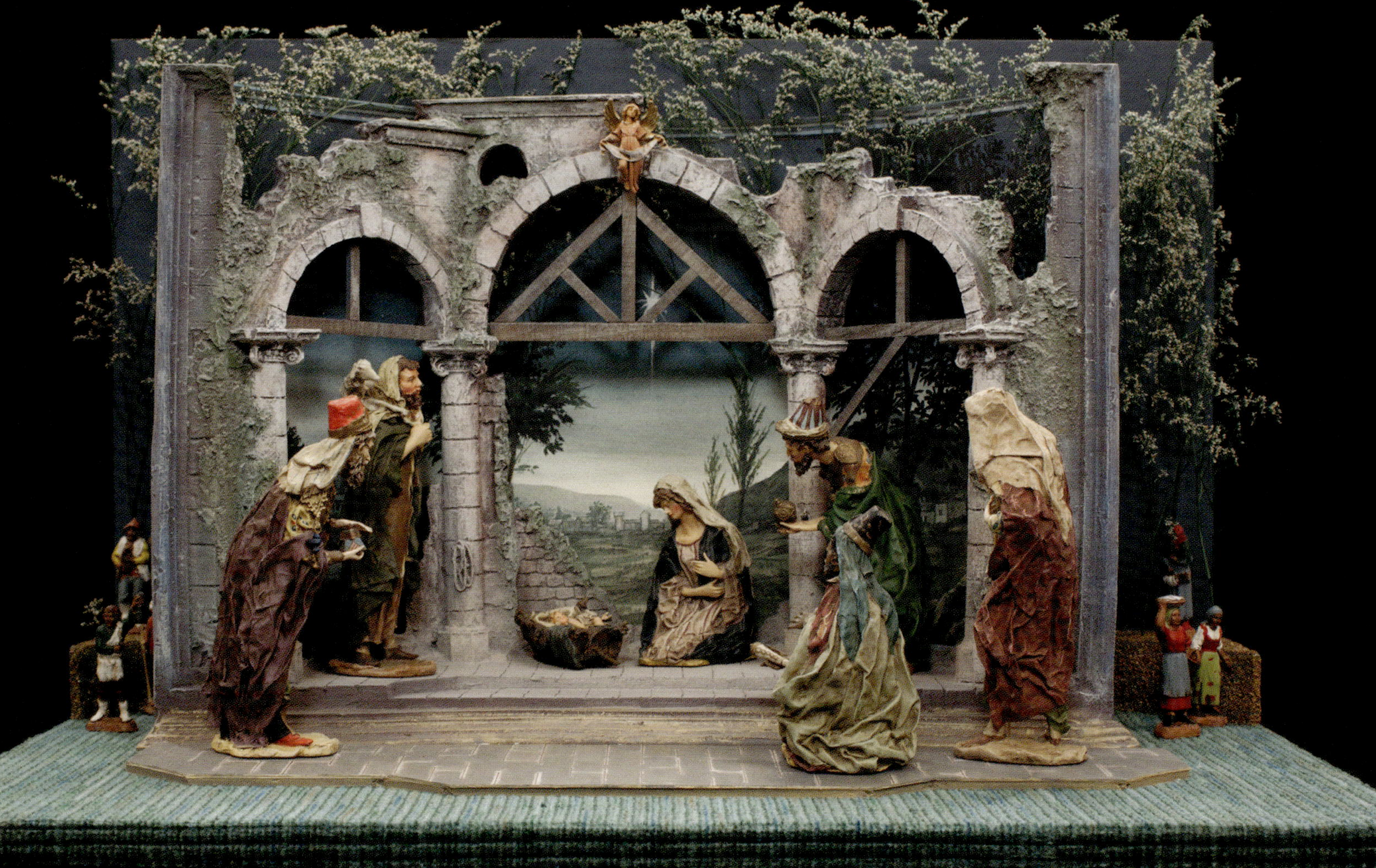

Angela Tripi and Peter Wolf, Italy

Life is Theater

This set wants to convey drama. Its setting is the stage and its scenery, the customary ruins of Italian crèches. The actors strike poses of reverence and submissiveness. They are clothed in flowing robes, indicating wealth and refinement for the magi, and decently covered shabbiness for the others, for the Holy Family and the lone shepherd. In the wings are standing more actors waiting to enter the scene. The backdrop reaches into a distant landscape painted in colors of chiaro-scuro, suggesting a battle between darkness and light. The main symbolism of the Christmas message are the ruins. The monuments and temples of pre-Christian cultures slowly disintegrate and collapse. Out of their ruins grows new life and a new culture. Growth and development are not easy. Light and darkness will clash frequently, but the Child in the manger is a constant measuring rod for goodness and evil.

Angel and Devil

Carved from the soft and worm-eaten wood of a cork tree, this set creates the impression of a ragged and rocky terrain. At its center, there is a cave built into the tree trunk which shelters the baby and his parents. The figure of Mary, standing upright and silhouetted as Our Lady of Lourdes, looms from the cave and dwarfs even the humble elephant who is begging to enter. Right and left of the cave are the minuscule streets and city blocks of "little town of Bethlehem." The most fascinating figures are the angel and the devil. The angel sits on one of the promontories surrounding the cave. He reverently watches over the Christchild. With his immense and streaming mane of hair and feathers he looks like one of the eerie and terrifying figures of William Blake's illustrations of the Apocalypse. Behind the Angel's back, crouching literally between a rock and a hard place, is the coarse figure of the devil. The earliest and permanent adversary of Christ-Redeemer, he is a popular figure in many nativity scenes. For a time, he is held in check by the angel, but for how long? The unknown artisans of this rustic and uncouth but moving creation are experiencing a most personal odyssey between heaven and hell: they are palsied people.

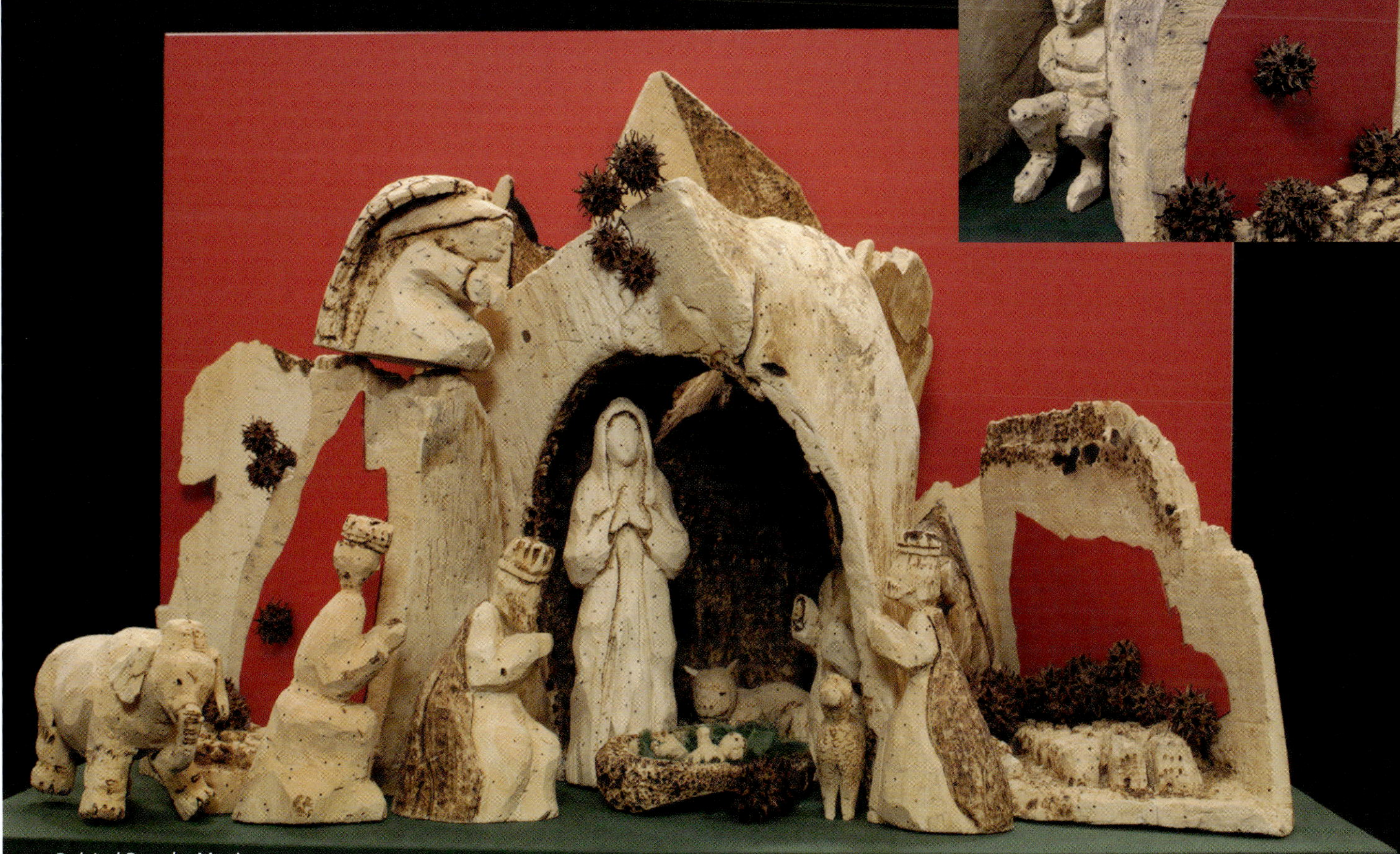

Palsied People, Mexico

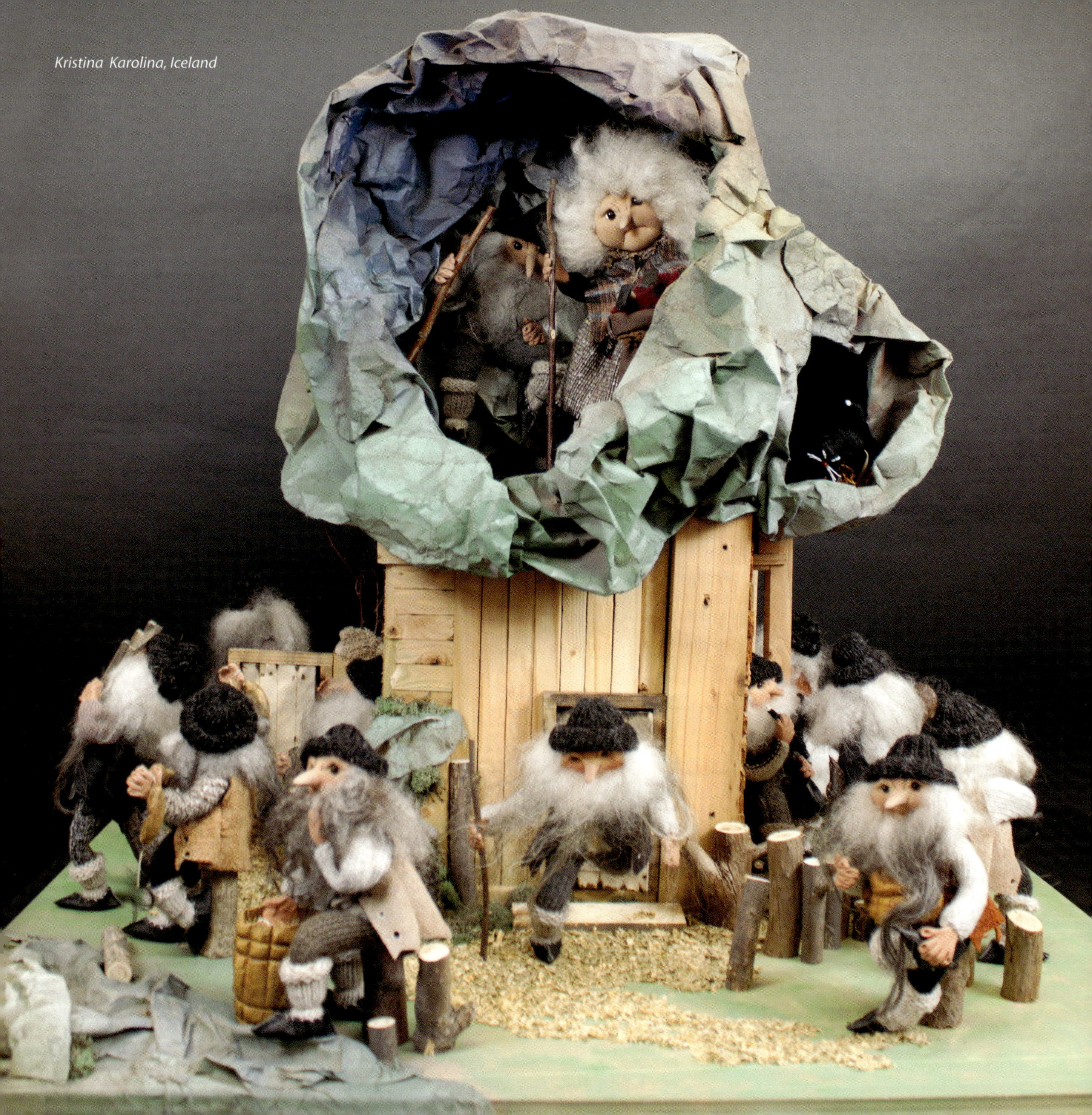

Kristina Karolina, Iceland

Darkness and Light

Kristin Karolina dressed her Yuletide lads in sheepskin and wool of her homeland. Mischief is written all over the bearded faces of the "bad boys," presented here in groups of three and four. Gryla, the witch, and Ragamuff, her lazy husband, are waiting in their cave on the mountain for the return of the thirteen lads. The Christmas scene, in style and materials identical with the other figures, is set apart, and highlights the deeper meaning of the Yuletide tradition. The Story of the Yulemen Yuletide of the North of Europe is not limited to Christmas. Long before the Christian era, it meant the joyful moment when the sun, after having been a prisoner of darkness for too long, slowly but surely reasserted its right over light and day. What better symbol to highlight the meaning of Christ's birth, frequently compared to the rising sun? The folktale of the Icelandic Yuletide lads links both these events. The ballad of the Giantess Gryla (18 c.) speaks of thirteen lads coming down from their snowy mountains, one each day. On Christmas day, they leave again, one at a time, the last one departing on Epiphany. Who are these Yuletide lads? They are "bad boys" who like to have fun at the expense of innocent people. The children better hide their toys, and kitchen maids cover their pots and pans for the Yuletide lads are a greedy lot. They are taking after their parents, Gryla and Ragamuff, "loathsome folks who played on humans many a hoax." Unbelievable but true! Gryla, the giant witch, collected children in her bottomless bag. No wonder the lads are pranksters with an evil streak. Fencepost Pat , the first to come, always scares the sheep. Gully empties the milkpail. Shorty, with the long white beard, steals the whole pan laden with meat. Ladle Licker likes to lick the porridge ladle. Pot Scraper adores what is crisp or burnt. Skirt Blower makes people sick blowing a breeze. Door Banger likes to make noise. Yoghurt Glutton as the tale says, empties "barrel, bowl, and plate," even before people awake. Sausage Snatcher is after the row of juicy sausages. Window Peeker has an evil eye, and Doorway Sniffer hides behind closed doors: both of them have sticky little fingers. Meat Hook steals the Christmas steak with rod and hook, right up through the chimney. The last to come on December 24 is called Candle Beggar. He sweeps the holiday candles wherever he can get them. Come December 25, the feast of new light, the spooky guys disappear, one a day. On January 6, the thirteenth day of Christmas, they are all gone, the hissing yuletide cat on their heels. The mischief is now over, light has triumphed over darkness. The days grow longer, and Jesus' birth is announced to the whole world.

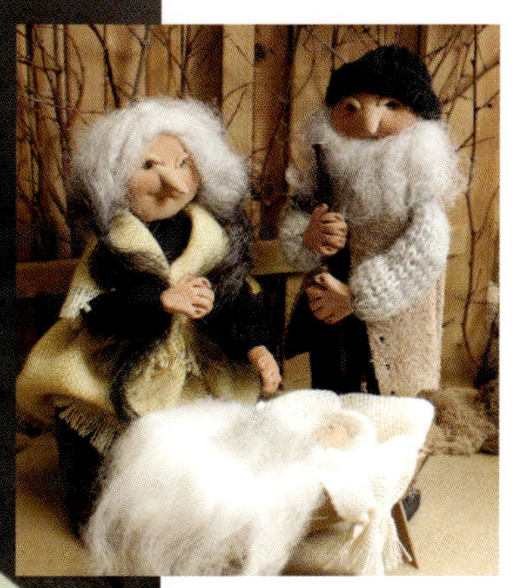

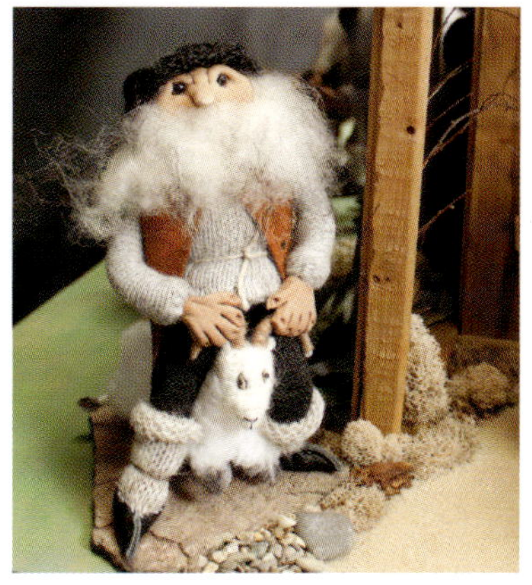

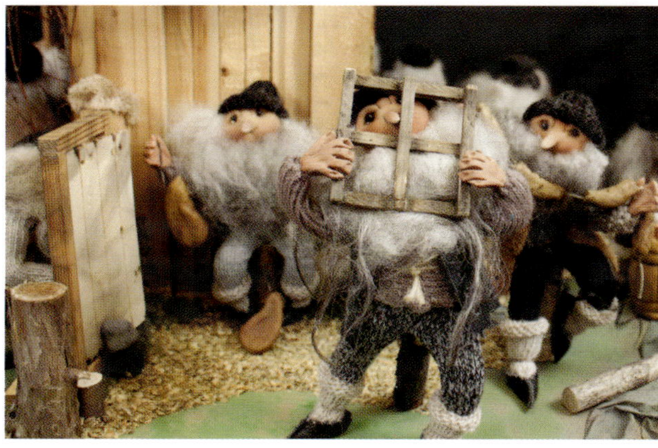

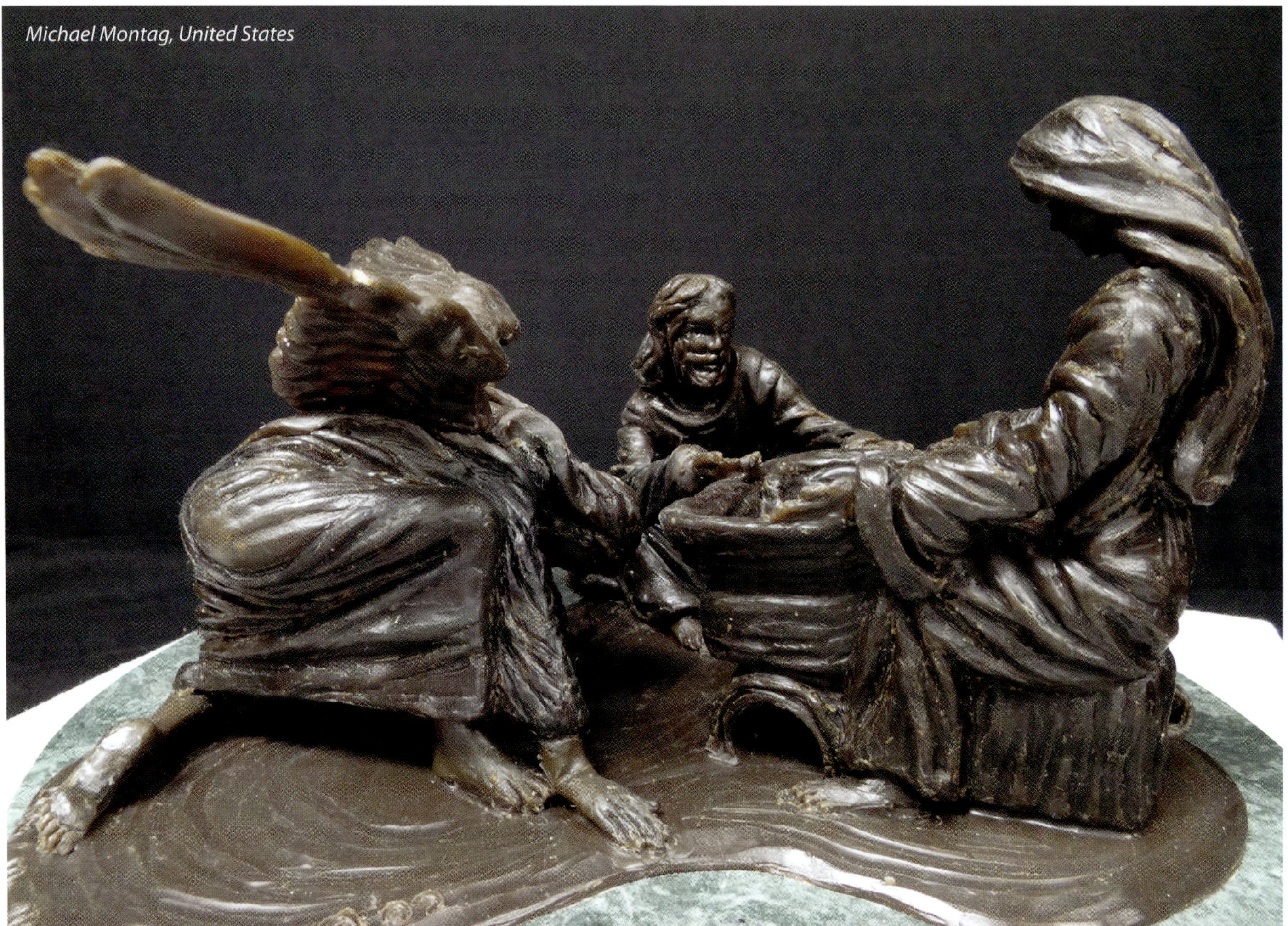
Michael Montag, United States

Paradise Retrieved

Michael Montag of Elkhorn, NE, works primarily with bronze and aluminum. His passion is the casting of the human person ranging from portraiture and relief panels to full-figure works of heroic scale. Seeing value in both traditional and contemporary modes of expression, Michael's art frequently attempts to combine realism and abstraction. Here, working with black wax, the artist offers a study in movement and static. The Holy Family embodies quiet and peaceful harmony. In contrast, the magnificent angel prostrates his powerful body in awkward worship before the cradle. His posture may resemble that of a fallen angel. His superior spirit humbly praises the hidden grandeur of the Christchild announcing paradise retrieved.

Similarities
Convergence
Complementarity
Unity

Where Culture and Religion Meet

Where heaven decides to mingle with earth and enters history – a way to describe the Incarnation! – there we have the beginning of an ongoing interaction between religion and culture. Different religions frequently clash and develop their own cultural values and visible identity. Closer inspection reveals there exists communality, even complementarity. Religion frequently stresses what a different creed, for whatever reason, overlooked or rejected. The magic of Christmas seeks unity. It abhors separation and opposition. The Christmas tradition shows that culture and religion can meet in a variety of ways. Some of the more common ones are to point out similarities, highlight convergence, reveal genuine complementarity, and unity.

Similarities

The study of world religions often attests similar origins, central values, and ultimate meaning of life. The Nativity culture compares, and makes visible what is kindred. Doing so, it builds bridges.

Convergence

Where Christianity entered the life of peoples, it frequently assimilated important patterns of their culture to point out convergence at some level. This happened when Christianity entered the Kiva.

Complementarity

Catholic Christianity is reputedly visual. The Christian denominations of the Reform hail the Word, and developed a great musical tradition. In many ways, these two traditions are complimentary, not only in theological matters but also in their cultural sensitivity. Ark and Manger complement each other.

Unity

Unity in space and time is never simple. Unity in human life is the result of give-and-take, effort and mutual recognition, of progressive harmony on the way to the best of two worlds.

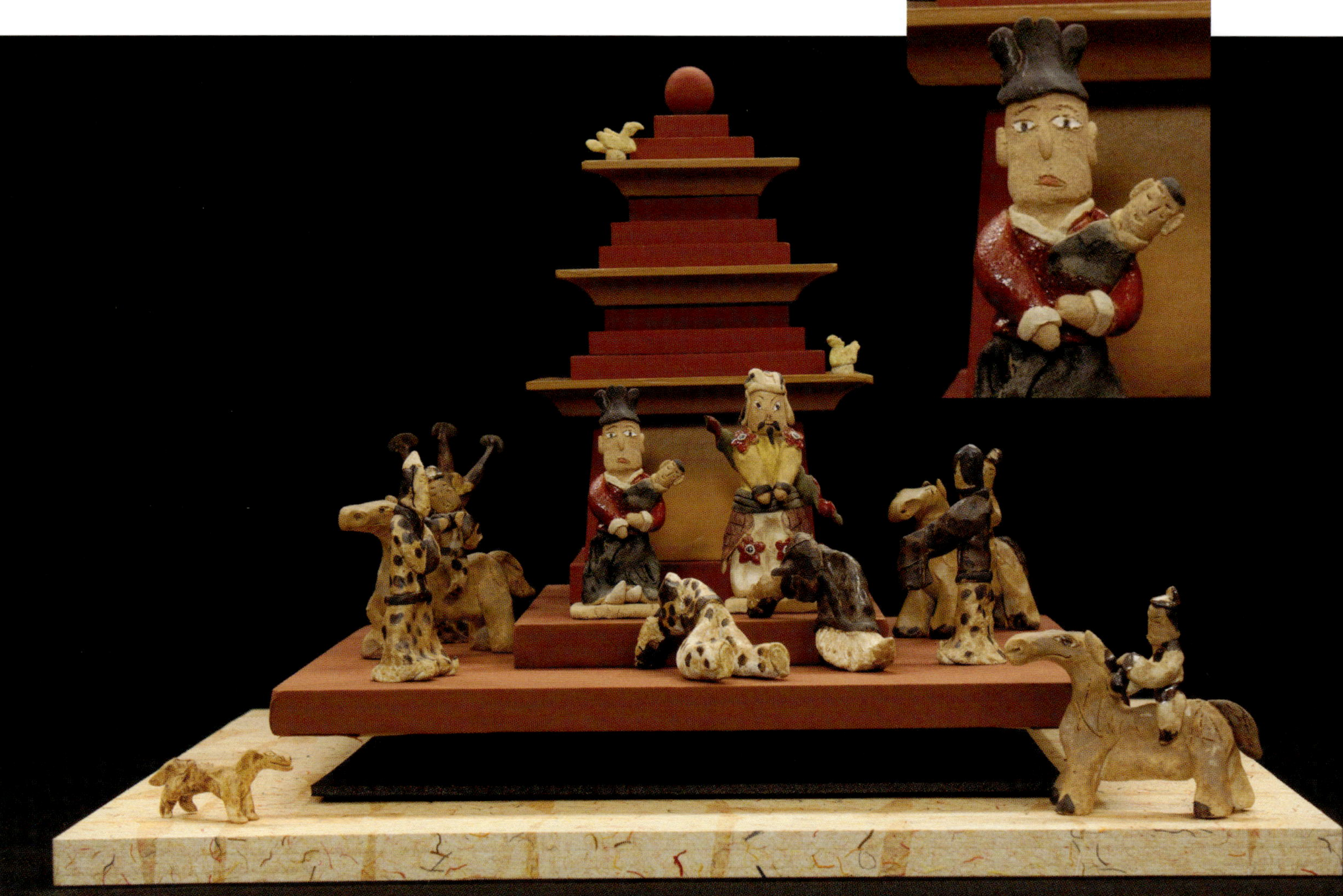

Sung June Yim, Korea

Similarities: Lady Mi and Mary

Sung June Yim is a ceramic artist from the Seoul region in South Korea. He frequently seeks artistic inspiration in early Korean history and Chinese literature. The central characters of this set are Lady Mi and warrior Jo Ja Ryong from the Chinese classic "The Three Dynasties." Lady Mi moves with her child through enemy territory. She is wounded. Jo Ja Ryong, the great warrior, rescues the baby but is forced to leave the mother behind. Shepherds and magi of this set are characters of the Koguryo Dynasty (37 B.C.-668 A.D.). They can be recognized by their dotted vestments. The bowed figures with long sleeves pay respect to the baby, and the three mounted musicians, with their woodwind and percussion instruments welcome him with a serenade. Originally not intended as nativity, these typically cultural figures are bridge builders between peoples, their history, and their religious beliefs.

Convergence: Kiva and Church

There are three sets in this setting. To the left is Mary Lucero's sophisticated Pueblo nativity. The artist painted her little figures with an uncustomary abundance of details; even the turquoise necklaces are not forgotten. Structure and choice of color give this set a delicate beauty contrasting with Edwina Tortalita's more statuesque and stately figures (right).

The central set is also from Jemez Pueblo. It features a Kiva, the house of prayer in the traditional Indian religion. Kivas are surrounded with mystery and great respect. A ladder leads into the Kiva. A second ladder stands out from the circular building and reaches into the sky. The vertical poles are of uneven length. They symbolize the two principal directions of human life: earth (the shorter pole) and sky (the longer pole), signs of material and spiritual values. Santana Seonia's nativity set of the Kiva suggests that Christmas has entered the Kiva. It points to a possible convergence between old and new religion.

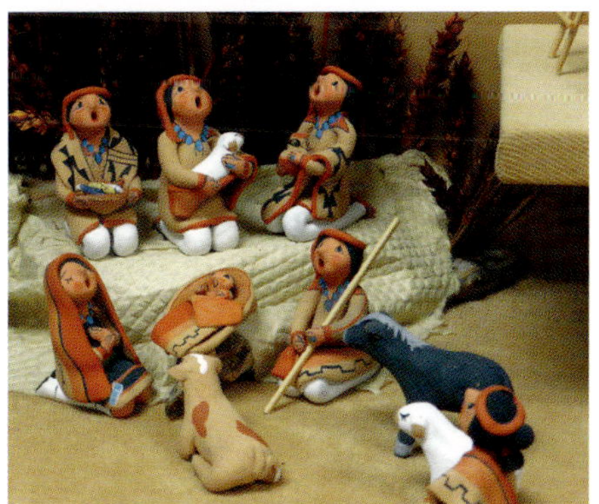

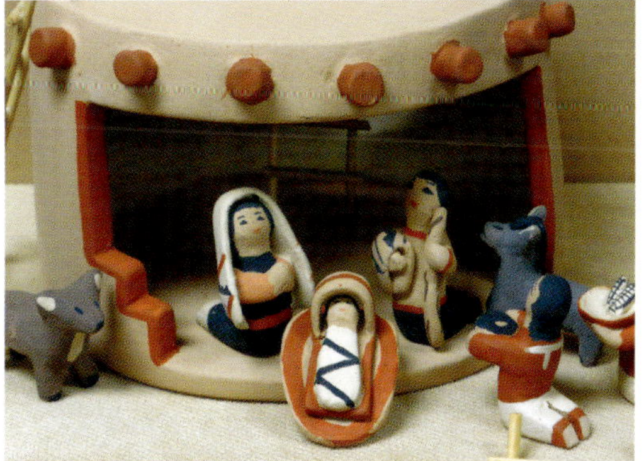

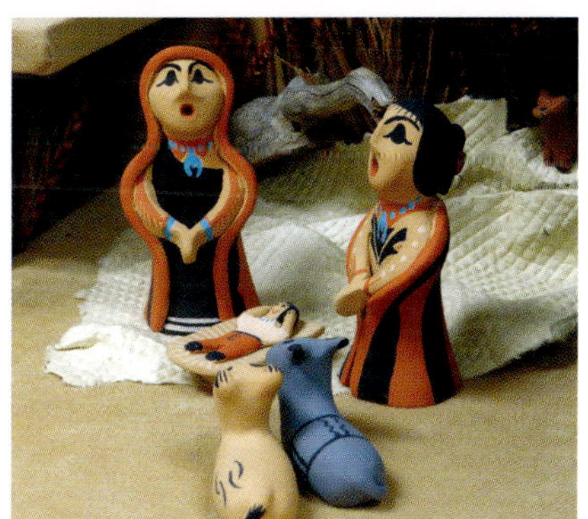

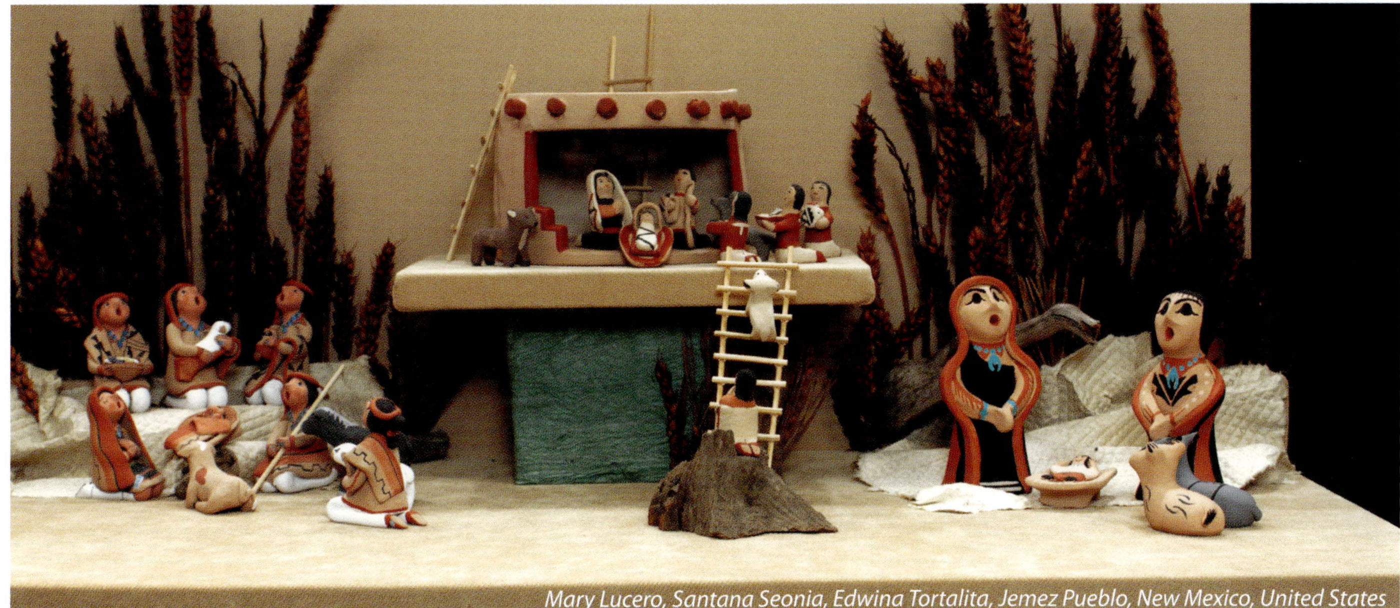

Mary Lucero, Santana Seonia, Edwina Tortalita, Jemez Pueblo, New Mexico, United States

Complementarity: Ark and Manger

Noah's Ark leads to the manger. Both ark and manger are symbols of salvation. Both are destined to hold and protect life. Both are eventually left behind. The big difference lies in the finality of the manger. It holds and protects the Son of God himself. No greater gift will ever be entrusted to human hands. Noah's Ark protects human life; the manger offers God's own life to the world. From Ark to Manger, God's love intensifies. It points out that true life is in God. We sometimes forget that the way of salvation led from Ark to Manger. The Suffering Servant (Ecce Homo) in this set represents sum and substance of truth amid distraction.

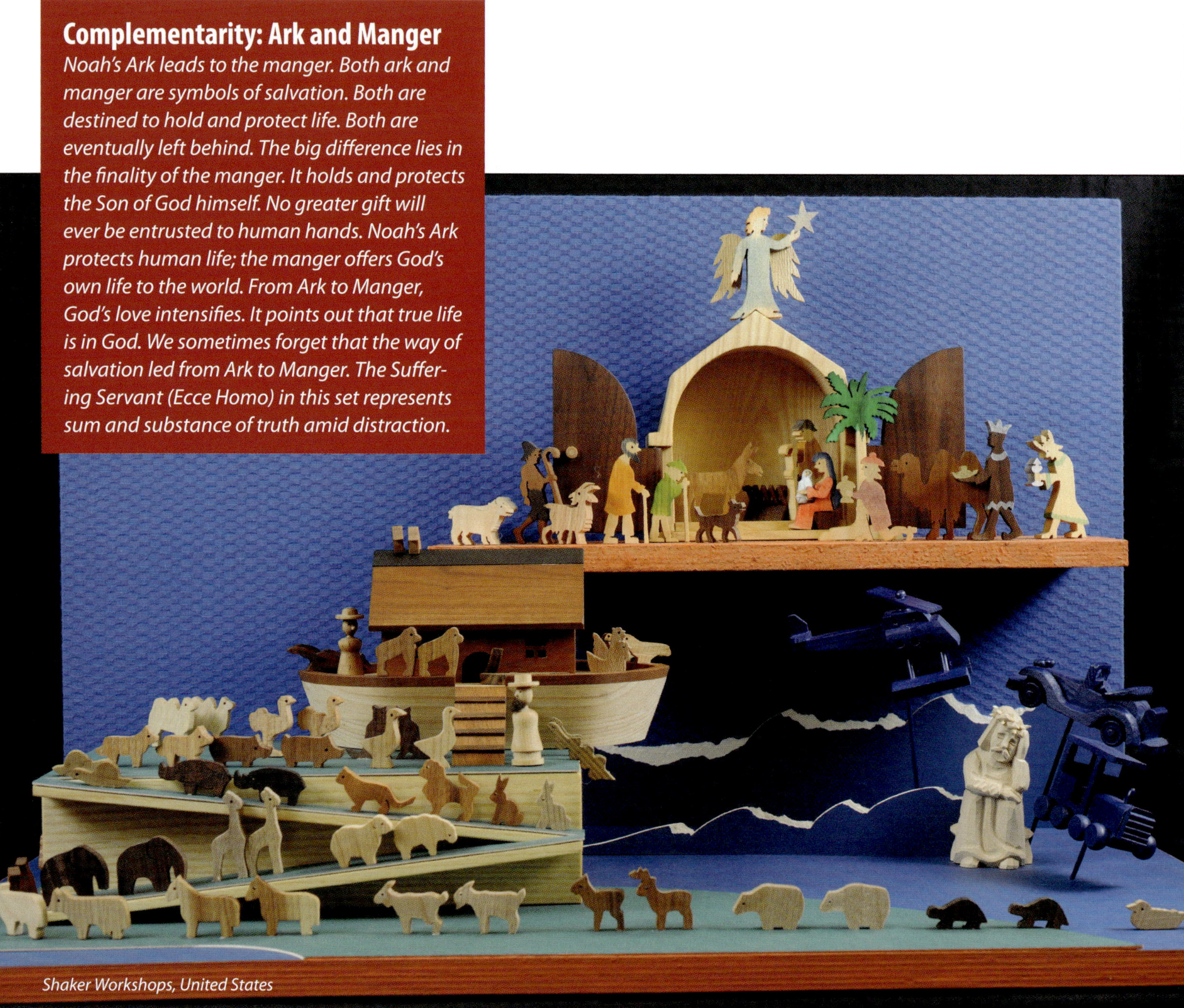

Shaker Workshops, United States

Unity: Two in One

Alsatia is a long and narrow strip of land in eastern France bordering Germany. Its culture is a happy combination of the proverbial "joy of life" of France, and the hard-working and efficient character of Germany. As in Provençal tradition, Alsatian Santons reflect various activities and model typical local costumes. Exquisitely painted, they are ambassadors of the Alsatian way of life. Among the thirty-two clay figurines, you will find the lady with the cabbage cart (highlighting sauerkraut, the national dish), the girl carrying a Gugelhopf (typical Alsatian pastry) for baby Jesus, and the proud Strasbourg Belle dressed in her Sunday costume. The holy couple in local attire looks much like the ordinary people they used to be in their time. Huddled together in loving respect, they contemplate with pride the Son of God in his Alsatian cradle.

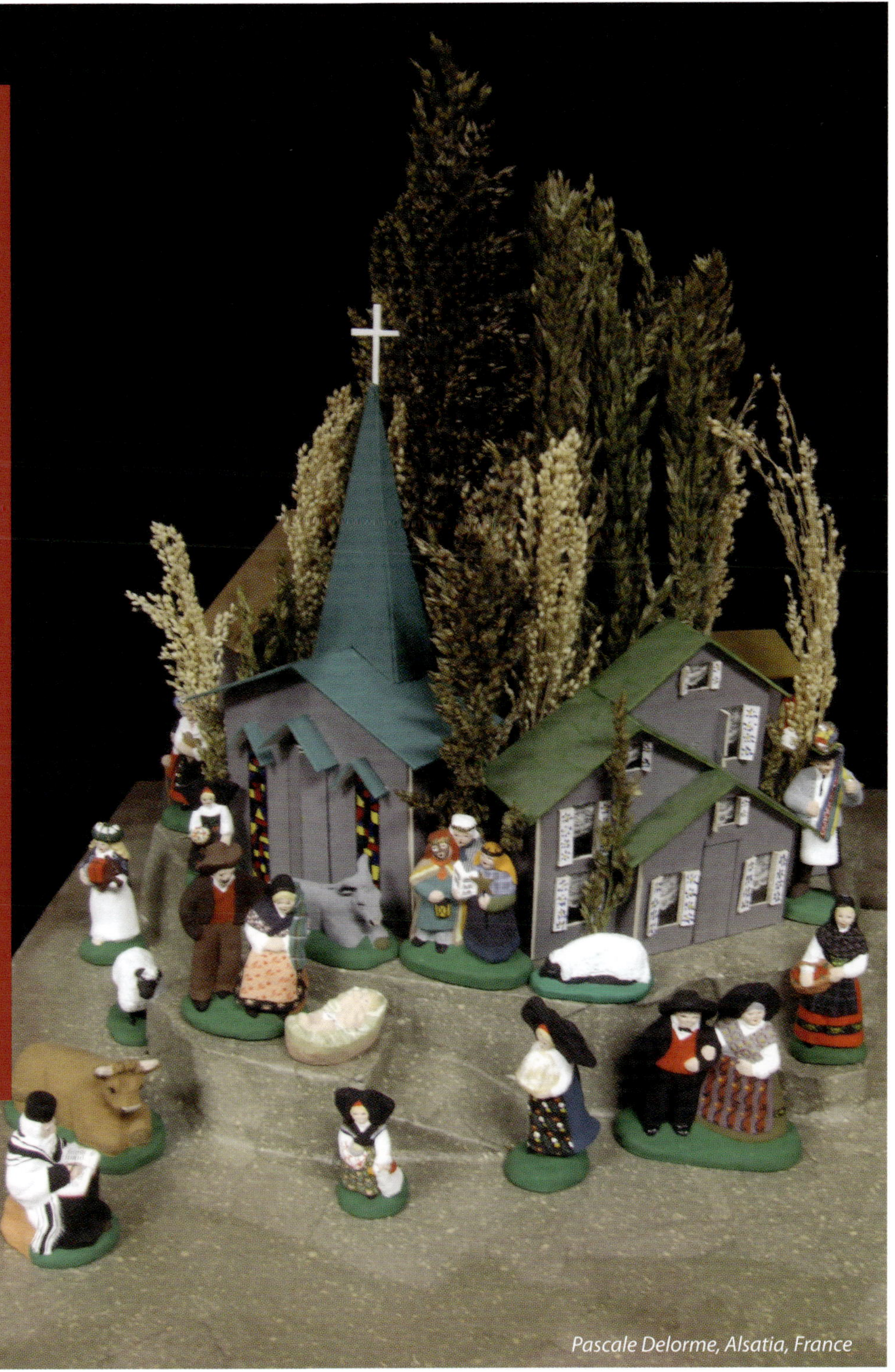

Pascale Delorme, Alsatia, France

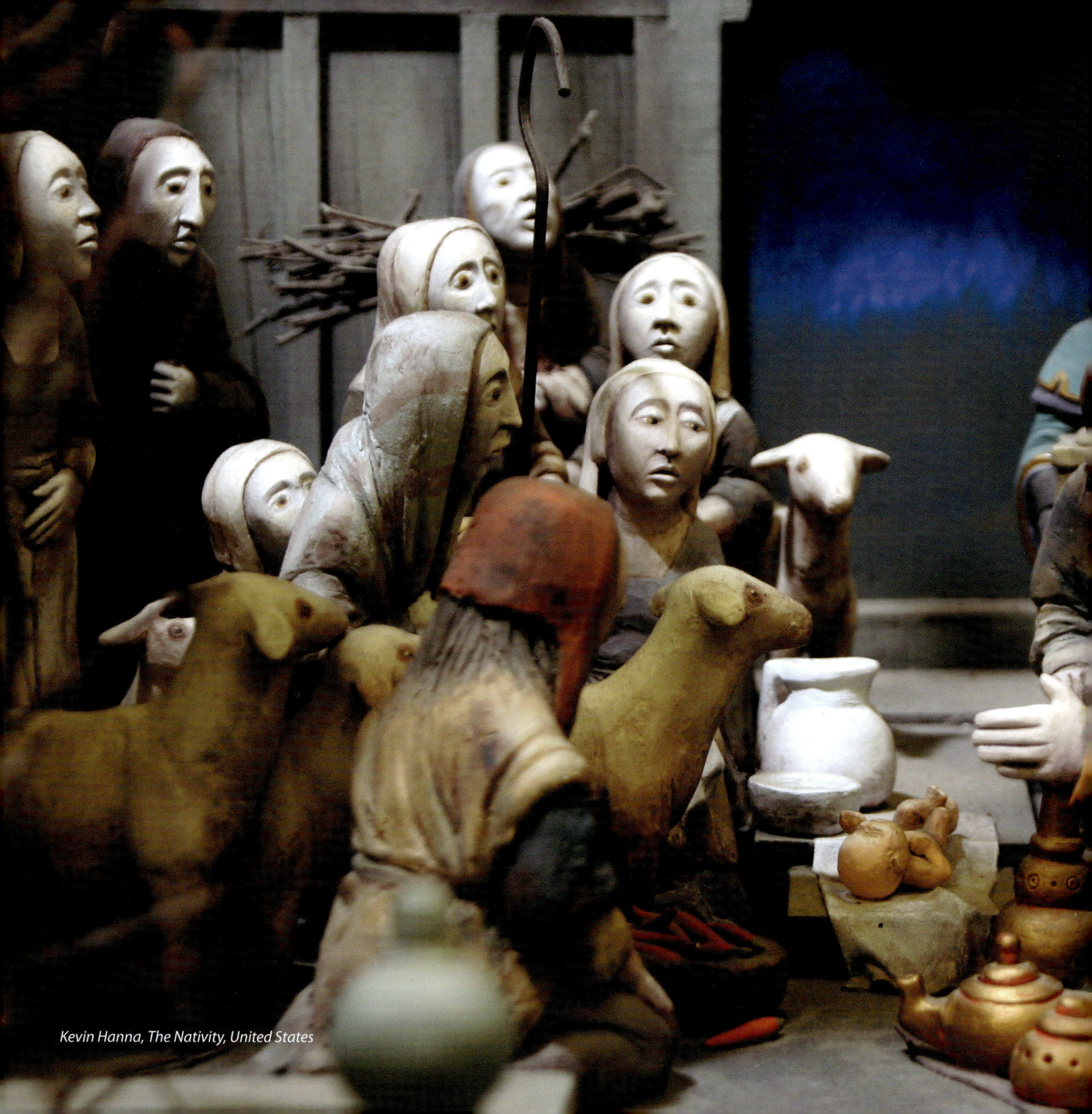

Kevin Hanna, The Nativity, United States

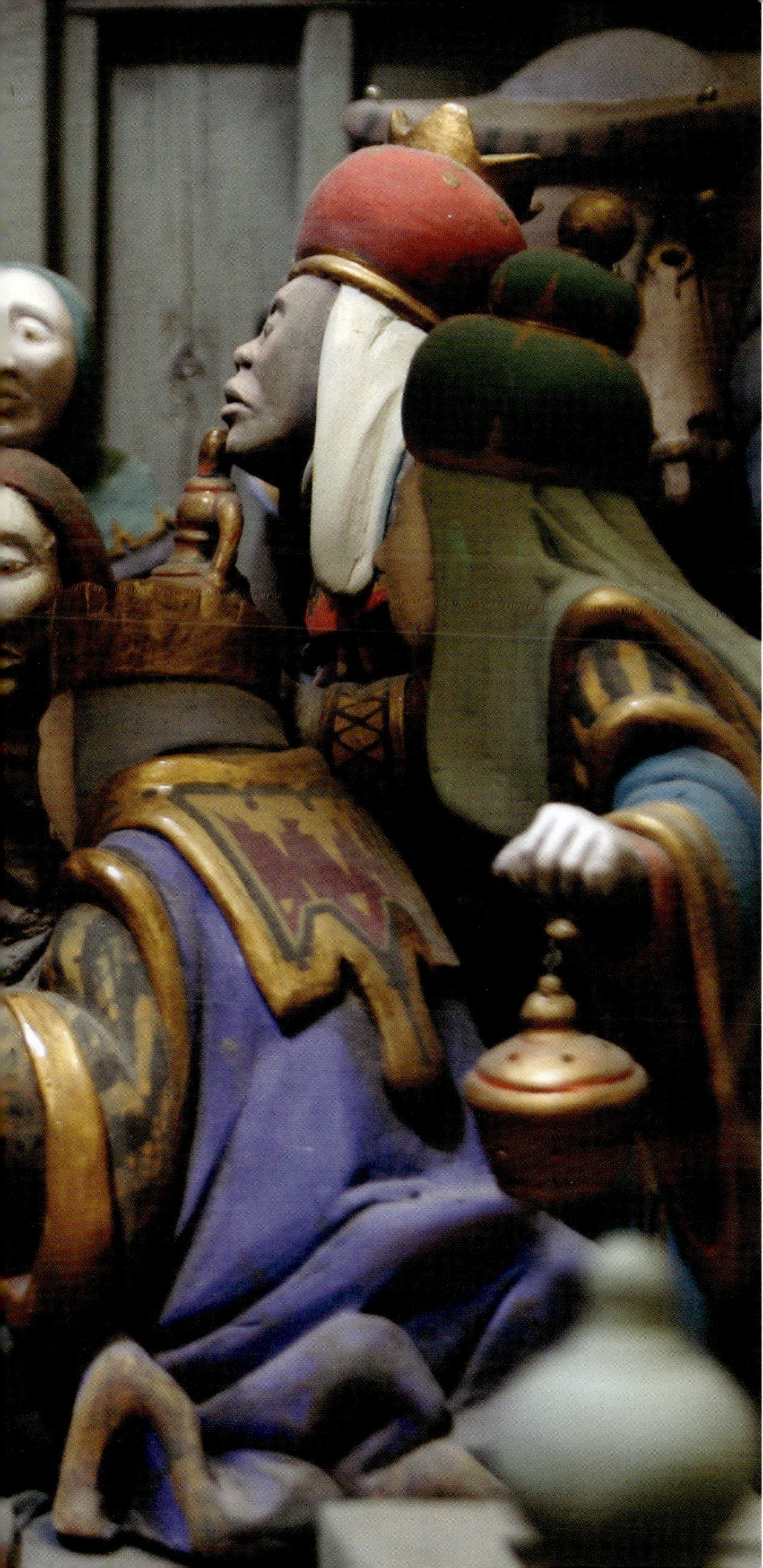

A Moral Compendium

The Crèche culture reveals the many concrete challenges of human existence, of problems dealing with psychology, morals, and politics. Pointing out issues, the message of Christmas would like to be part of the solution.

There is no difference between rich and poor at the manger

A Moral Compendium

Nativity sets are bearers of moral lessons and psychological observation about human life, about our deepest cravings and greatest joys. Some of these lessons are hidden in symbols, others read like an open book of accusations or challenges to our behavior. One of these lessons is the persistent reminder that there is no difference between rich and poor at the manger. Both are called, both are present.

A different lesson illustrates the age-old wisdom that only the simple of heart are open to the mystery of the Nativity: the pure of heart of this set.

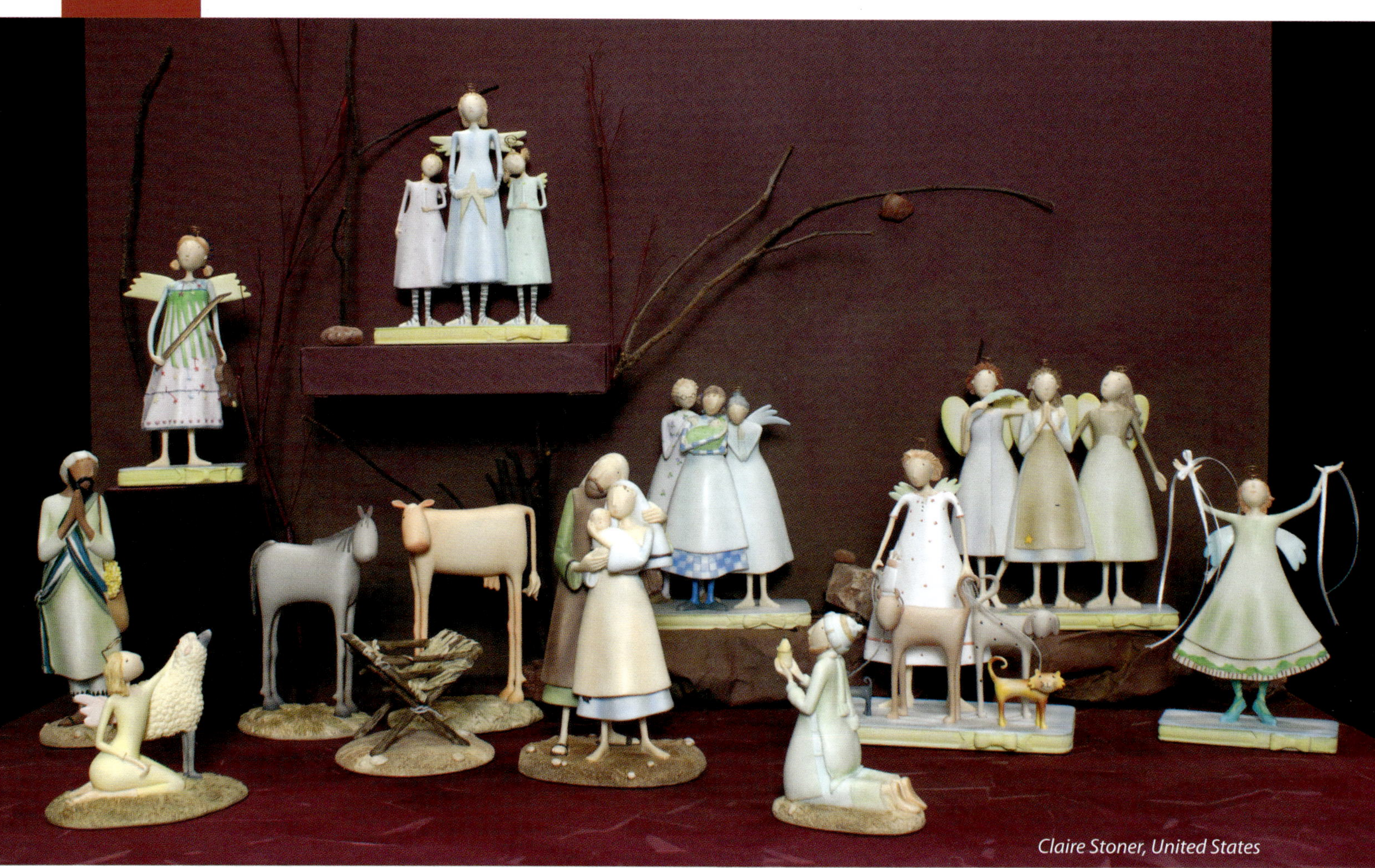

Claire Stoner, United States

Our life remains a mystery; it is in some ways like a sealed scroll we take to the manger in the hope that the Christchild will open and decipher it for us.

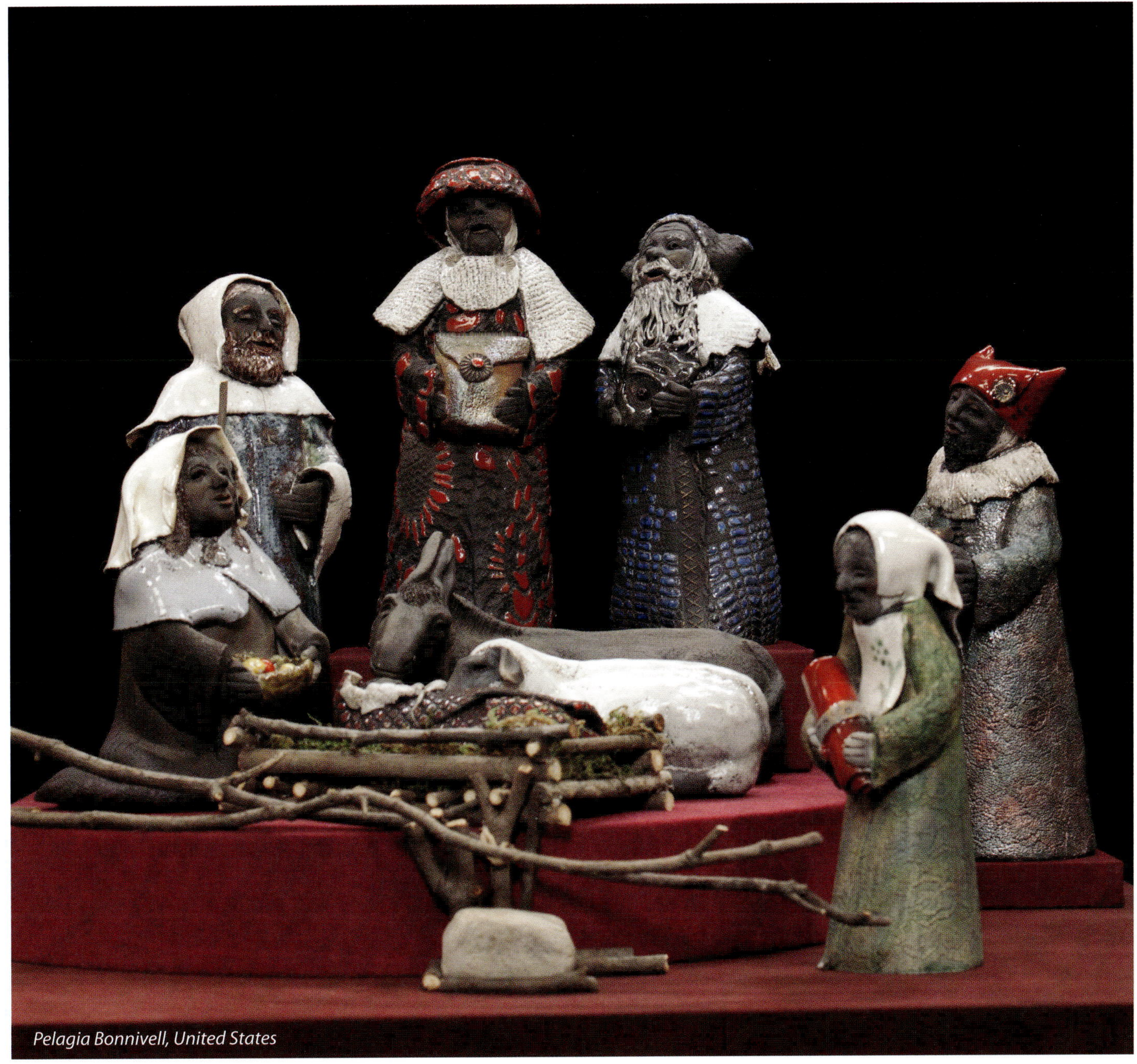

Pelagia Bonnivell, United States

We expect the encounter with the Christchild to give us new meaning, new purpose in life. There is, indeed, new life in old skins (our set) when we become a gift to others.

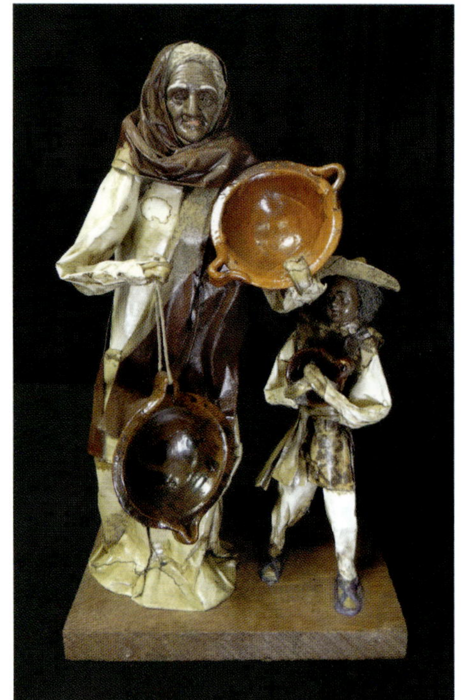

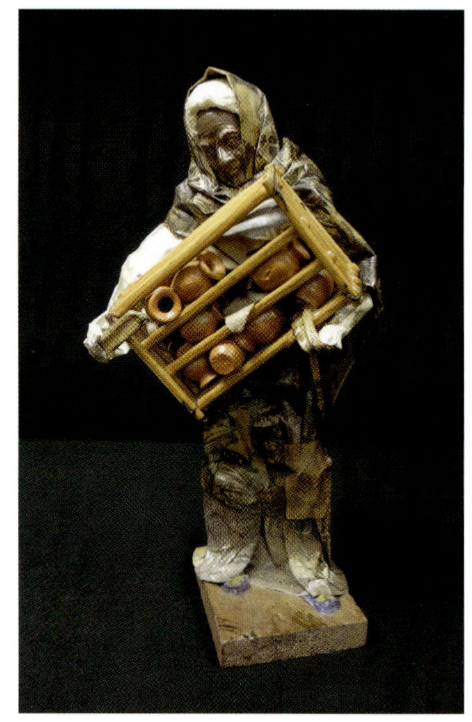

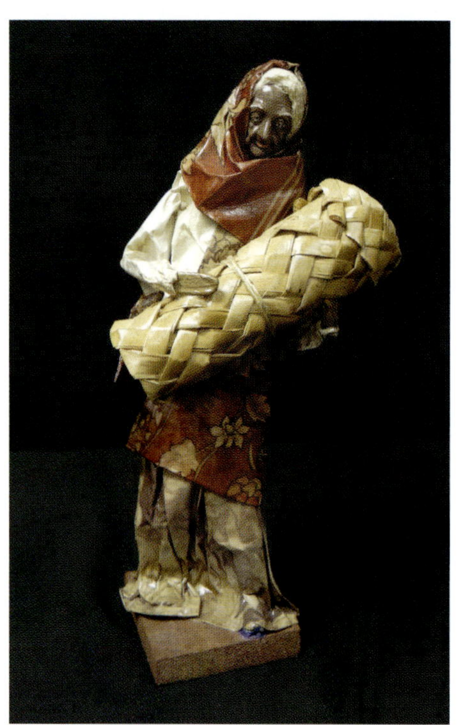

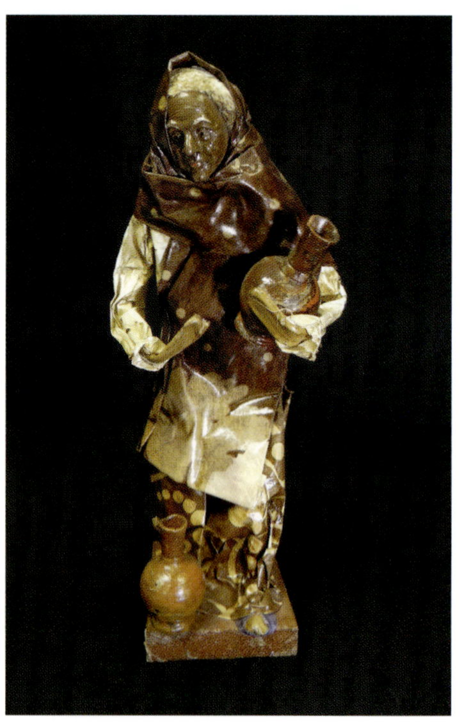

Raphael Arista, Mexico

The crèche language is frequently a symbolic language. It needs deciphering. There is the tradition of the twins, two identical figures representing our egocentric tendencies. How difficult is it to look beyond our personal concerns and interest. In most of what we do we see but ourselves (twin). The Christchild will free us from ourselves, from our alter ego, from our twin, represented in the two identical shepherds.

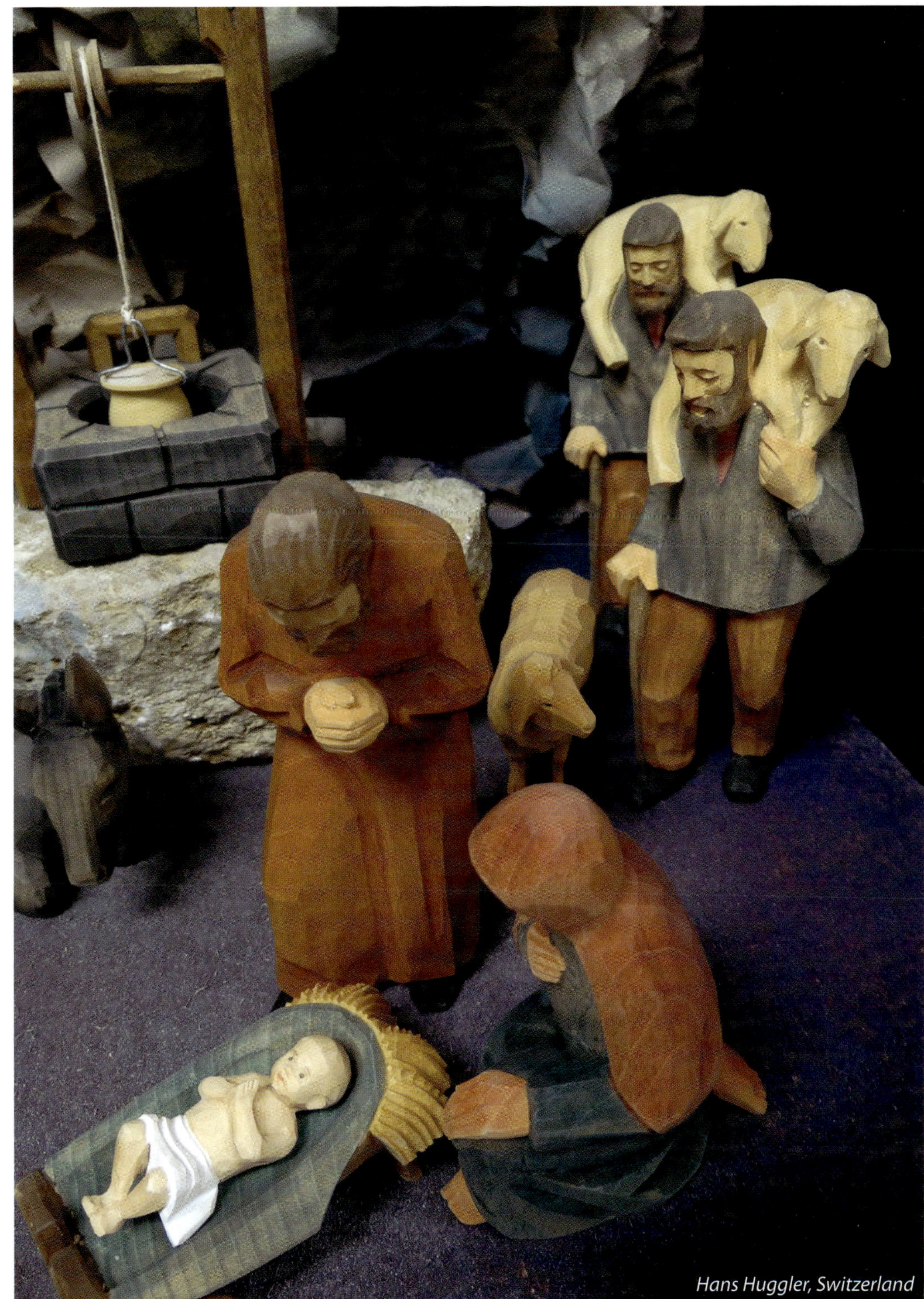

Hans Huggler, Switzerland

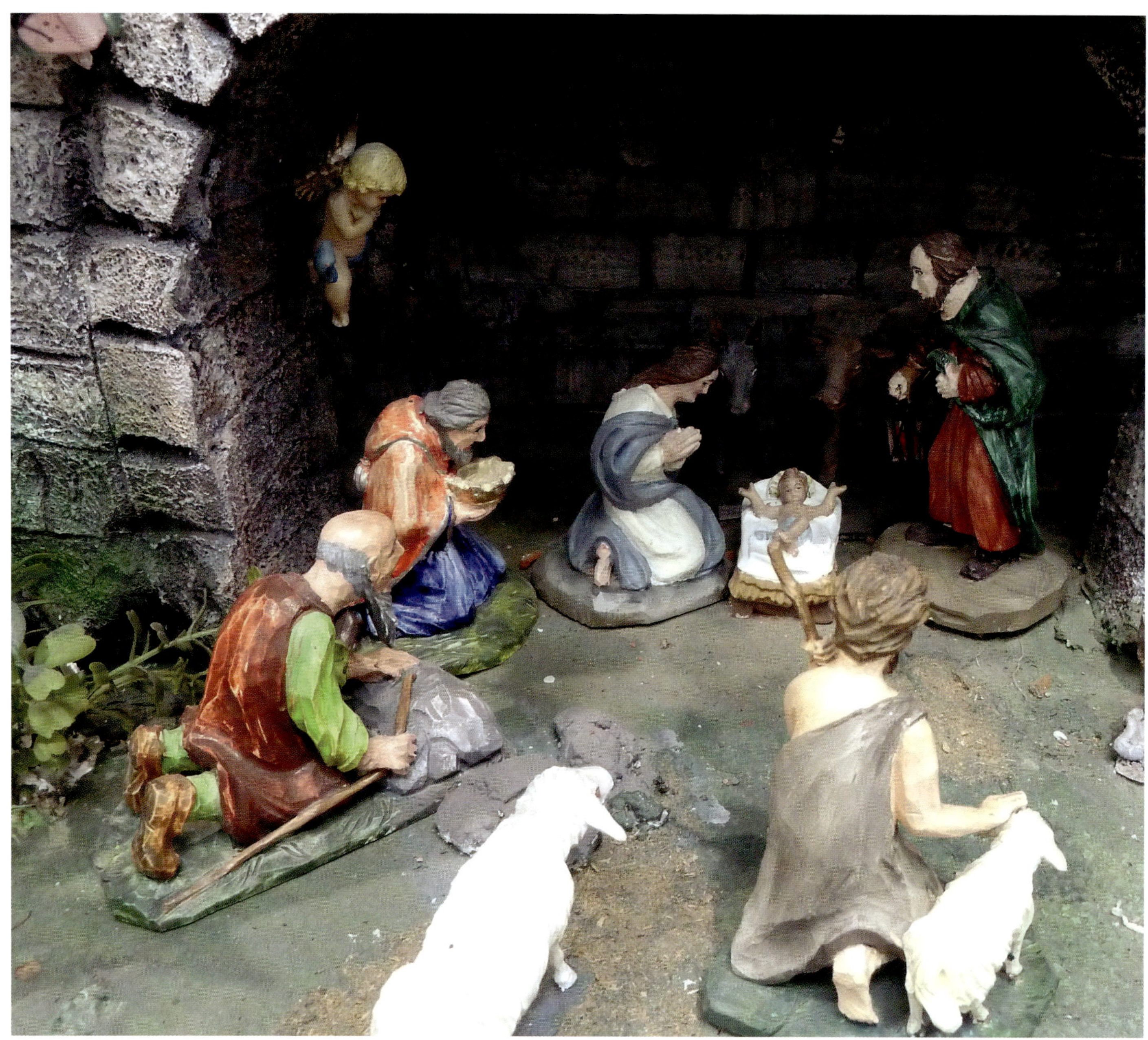

John Schnegg, Canada

Crèche culture pays attention to human development. Young shepherds (right, standing) can be playfully indifferent to the manger; older and wisened shepherds bring gifts to the child and kneel in adoration.

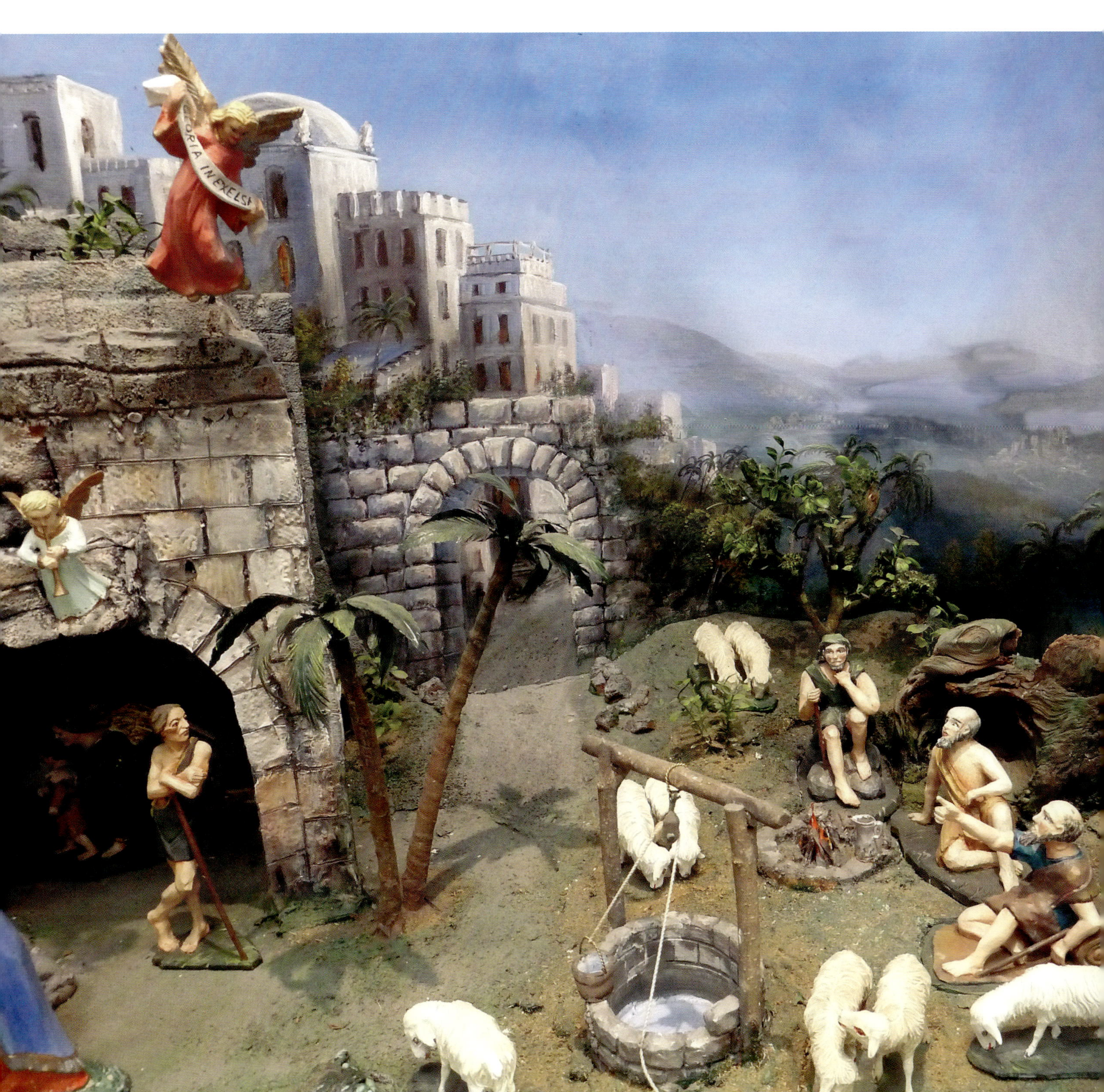
GLORIA IN EXELS

More and similar symbolizations were mentioned and shown in the first part of this book (see pages 29-53). In the end, everything in the Nativity representation is related to the Christchild, and how we relate to him. Will the journey to the manger end in silent praise and adoration?

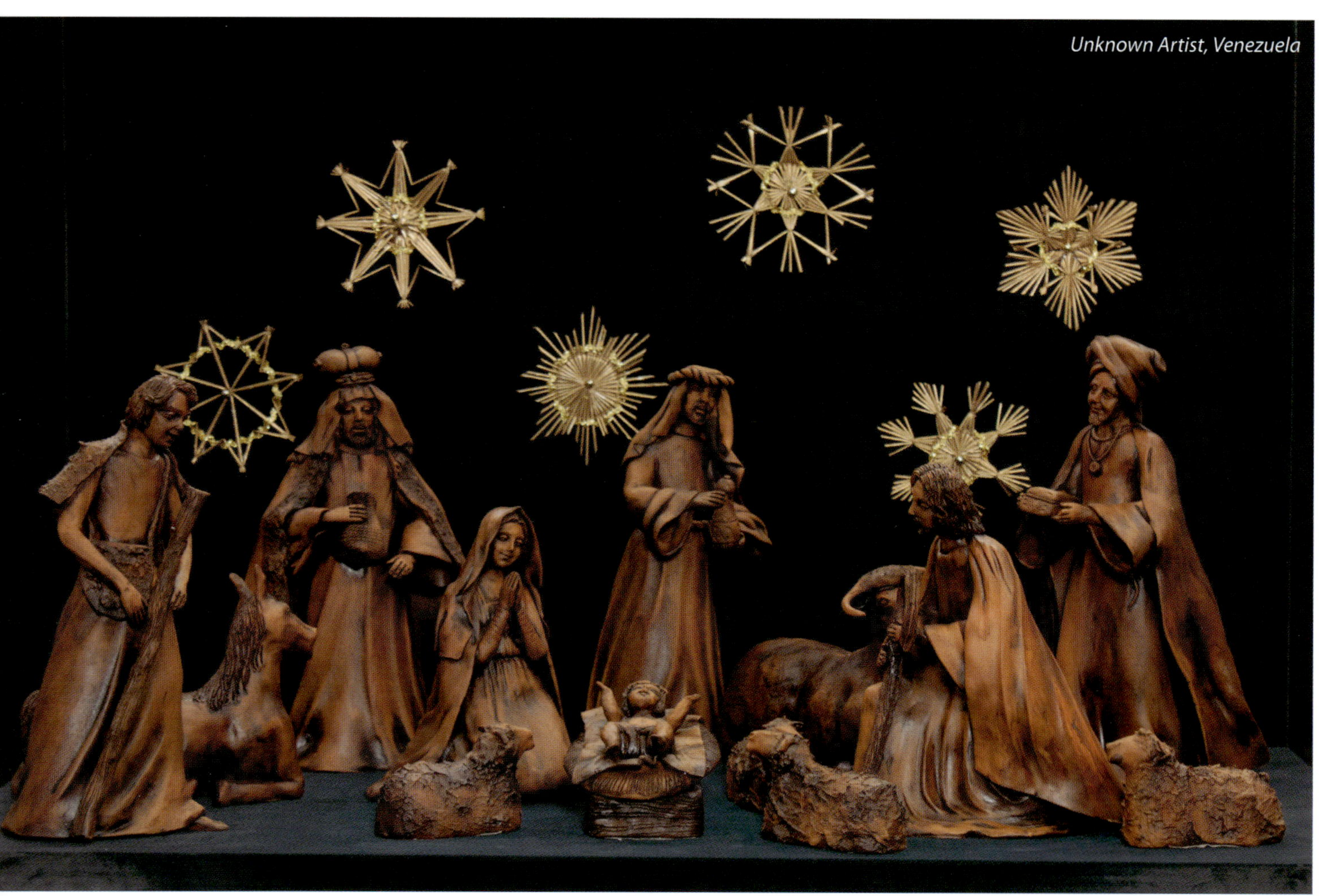
Unknown Artist, Venezuela

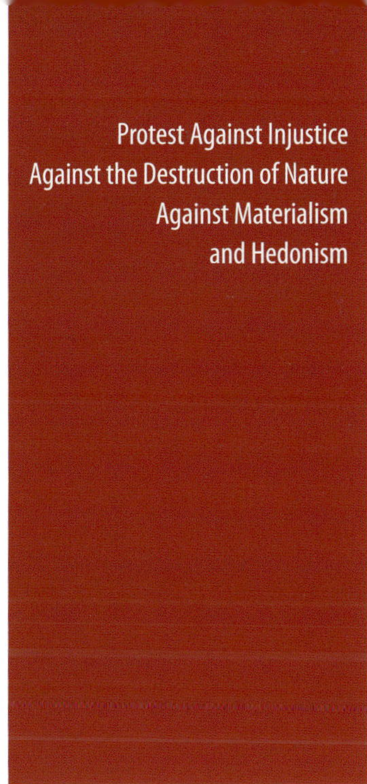

A Political Manifesto

Is there a political message in the Christmas story? Politics re-entered the crèche tradition in the second half of the 20th century. This is not a first. The birth of the God-man has always been both a challenge for all, and an accusation for the lukewarm and lazy. So it was for the medieval mysteries. They were a public examination of conscience on where the spectators stood: on the side of Christ, or on that of his adversary, the devil? The Counter-Reformation used the Nativity representation to highlight the visual and real presence of God among us – a way to "counter Reformation"! In the 18th century the first domestic nativity sets raised social issues: what will Jesus, the Redeemer, do for the poor miners languishing in the belly of the earth? Later still the question was: what answer does the Christchild offer to oppose the secularized ideologies of Nazism and Communism? Recent nativity sets speak a similarly pointed language.

Protest Against Injustice

How can the message of love be compatible with political hypocrisy and empty promises?

Against the Destruction of Nature

The pristine beauty of the Nativity is only one side, the fictitious or Potemkin side of reality. There is another side, the ugly side of reality. It has the face of exploitation, of greedy developers and investors.

Against Materialism and Hedonism

Does Christmas take us back to the poor and ignored King of kings? Or has the original message been swallowed up by materialism and its principal instigator: hedonism?

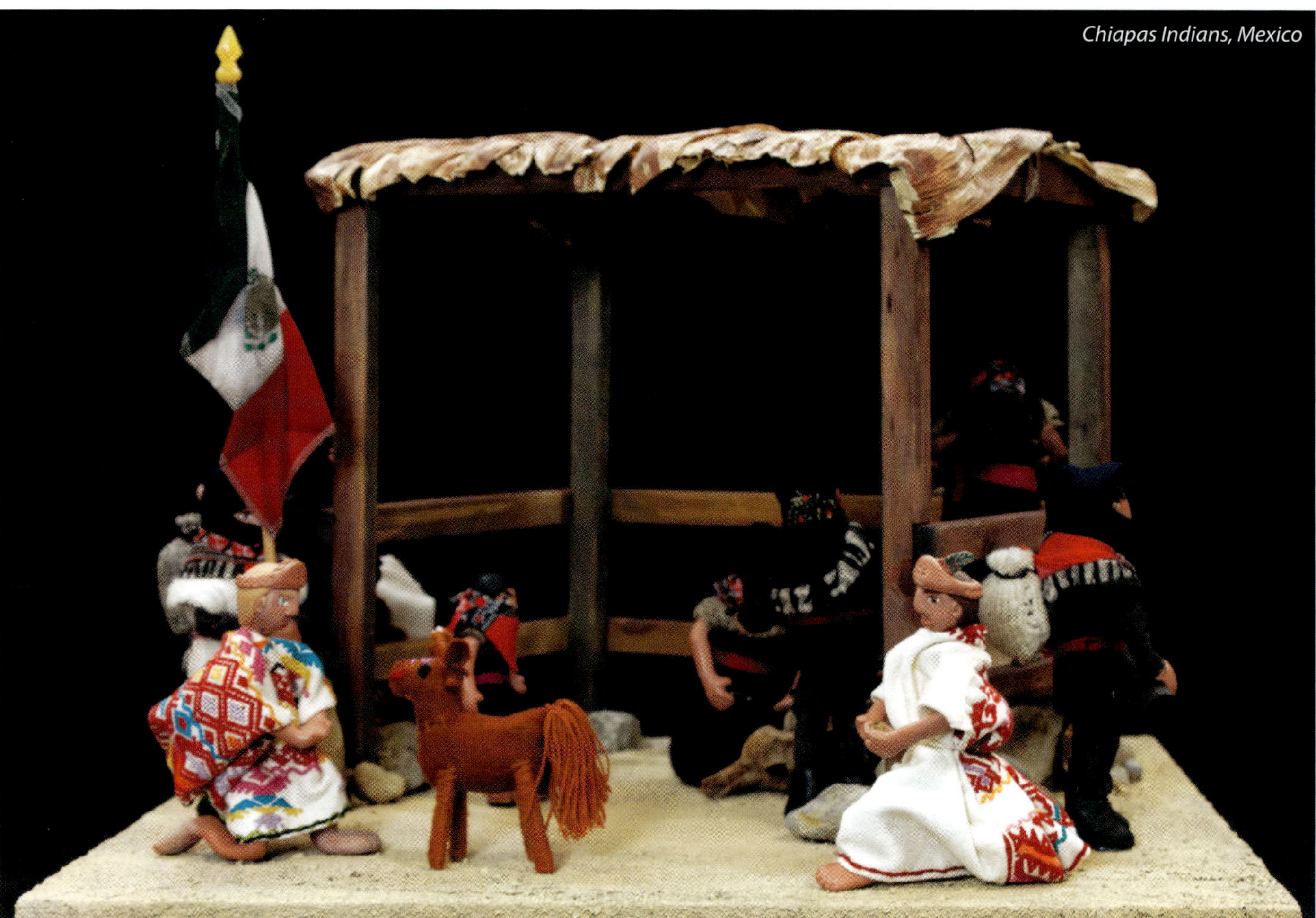

Chiapas Indians, Mexico

Protest Against Injustice

The primitive hut covered with banana leaves is the scene of a potentially violent drama. The quarreling factions can be distinguished by their dress code and hands. Those in rich white garb have empty hands, some of the others, muffled in red and black with balaclavas partially covering their faces, carry guns. Jesus and his parents are among the latter – they are the good guys. The bad guys are roaming around the hut with evil eyes. In vain they disguise themselves as the wise and generous magi. They are wolves in sheepskin, hypocrites and usurpers. They are charlatans; the clump of gold in their hands is fake. Such at least is the perception of the good guys, the downtrodden and poor. They carry backpacks and guns – symbols of revolt and despair. This nativity set has roots in contemporary history. It comes from Chiapas, a southern region of Mexico, and makes allusion to the Zapatista insurrection of past years. If Christmas means universal healing in mind and body, then the righting of wrong is necessarily part of the program of redemption. But Christmas is also a lesson about method. In the end, it is the babe in the manger and the man on the cross who bring about salvation.

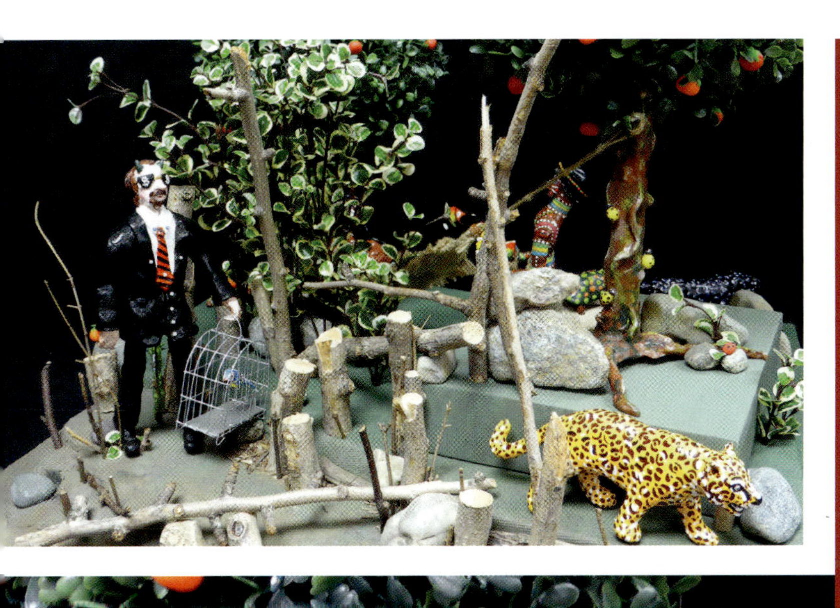

Against the Destruction of Nature

This nativity set shows the two faces of a same reality. It presents the life of the Xingu tribe hiding away in the Brazilian Amazon region. Surrounded by mango trees where a colorful population of Tucano and Tuiuiu birds compete with black and yellow panthers, turtles, snake and monkey, people live a life in harmony with nature. Mary is resting in a hammock, the child lying on her breasts. Joseph is serving a fruit platter with melon, banana, caju, abacate, and mango. Faces and bodies are painted blue, yellow, and green, the tribal colors of married couples. The scene suggests a little Eden. Alas, there is the other face of reality: the barren land, the developer in suit and tie, greed in his eyes and destruction in his wake. The battle between good and evil, in whatever suit or body paint, is at the very center of what the Incarnation stands for.

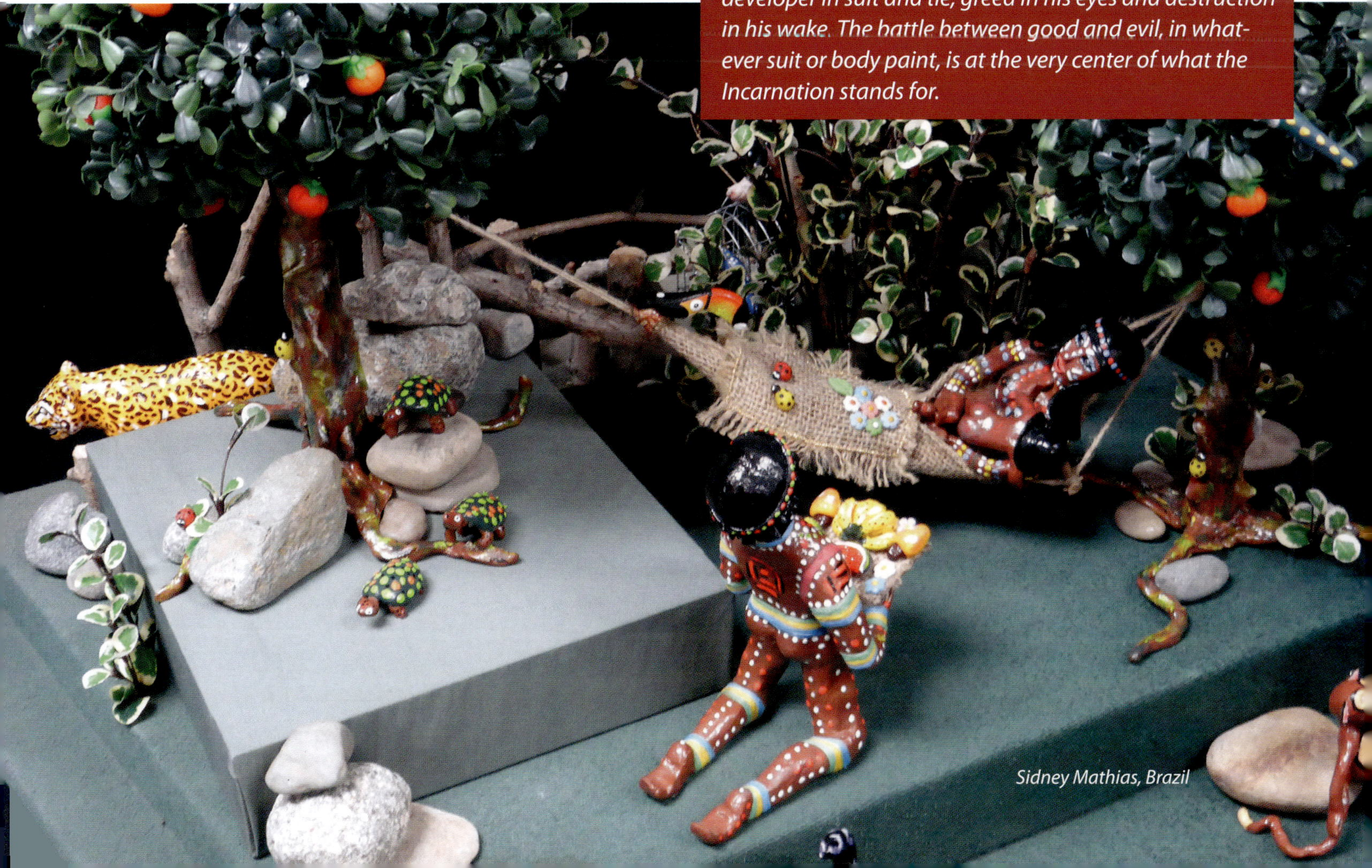

Sidney Mathias, Brazil

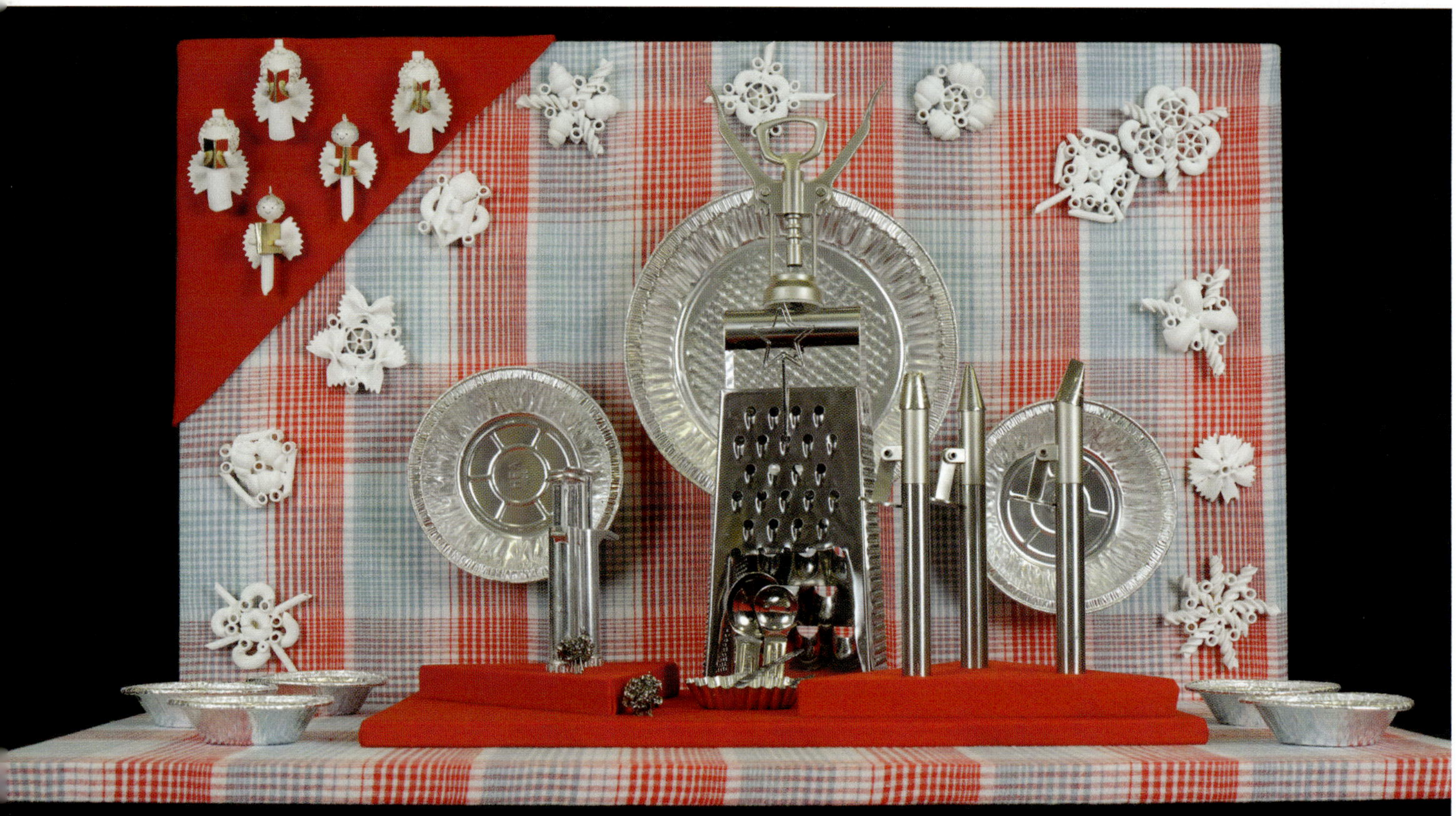

Joannah Thelin Soderborg, United States

Against Materialism and Hedonism

You will find Jesus in the manger, Mary and Joseph, the angel, and the magi, if you put yourself in the mind of the artist. This nativity set was inspired by a "corkscrew I picked up -- says the artist -- and looked like an angel with arms in celebration." The moment of discovery and wonderment led to an onslaught of creative associations: "The stable is a cheese grater, the holy parents are measuring spoons and baby Jesus is a strawberry huller nestled in a mini tart pan. The shepherds are decorating tools with the sheep made from steel wool and mini nails for the legs. The wisemen are part of a kitchen tool complete with cake decorating tips used as crowns."

If you share the imagination of the artist you may find yourself sitting at the table of an Italian trattoria, in front of you a dish of pasta. But, this set is a manifesto against materialism. There is also the silent reminder: Christmas is more than eating and drinking.

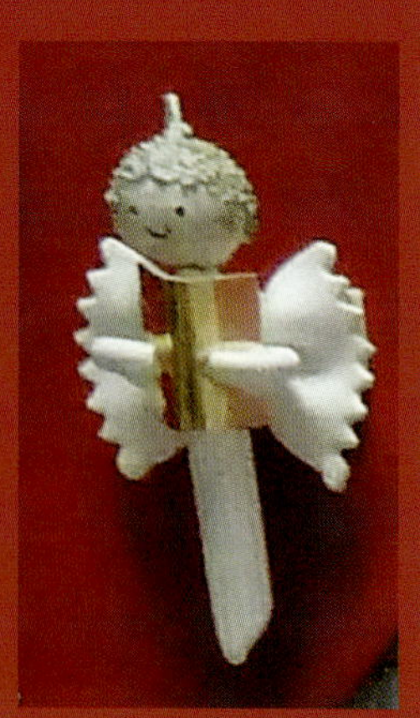

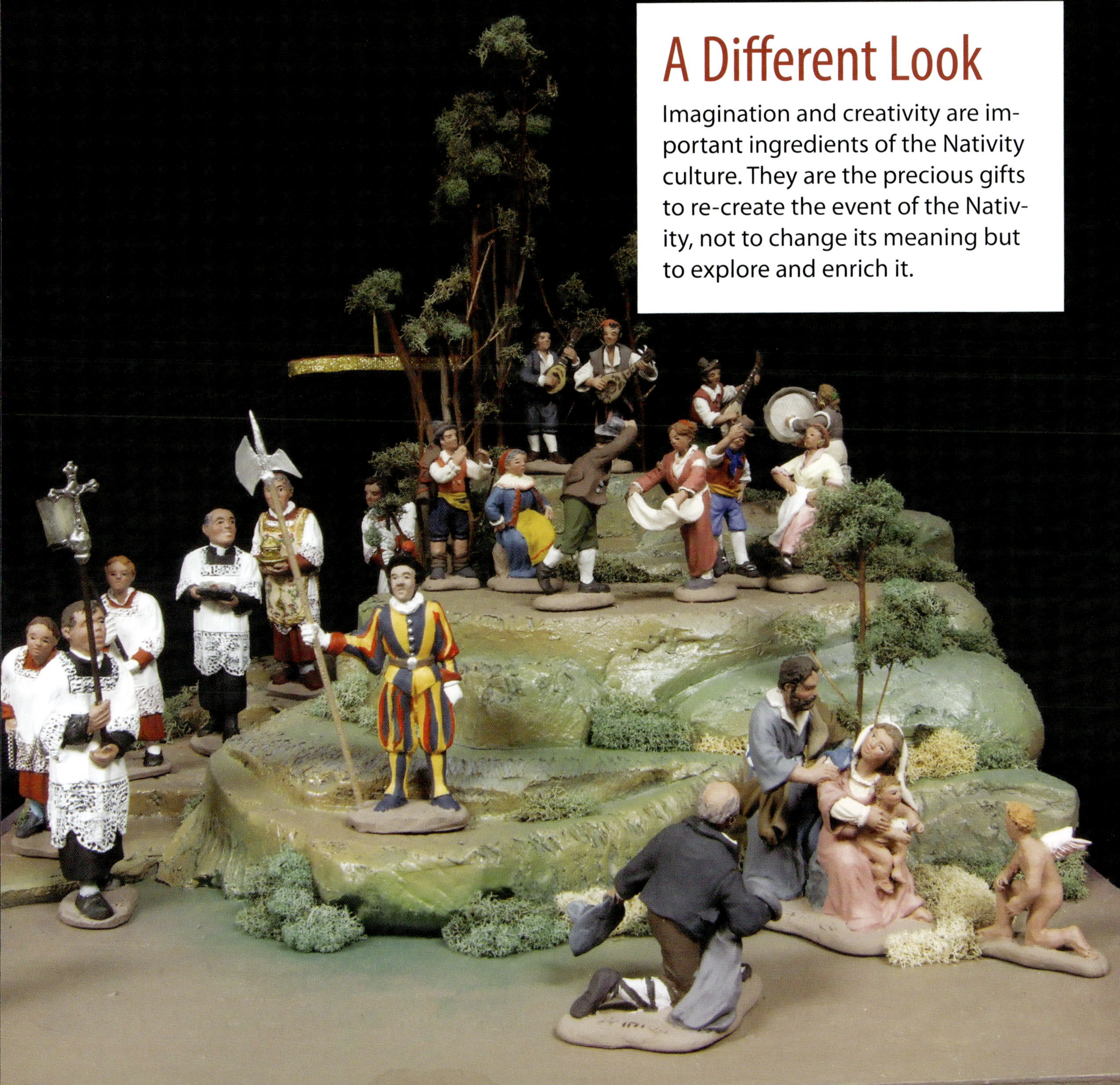

A Different Look

Imagination and creativity are important ingredients of the Nativity culture. They are the precious gifts to re-create the event of the Nativity, not to change its meaning but to explore and enrich it.

There is a way of looking at a new Christmas with the same Jesus

A Different Look

Creativity is eagerly looking out for ever new possibilities to imagine and fashion the same mystery, the Nativity age-old and never old. The query for a different or new look is inspired by a number of reasons, most of them cultural, others to convey a special interest or message. These attempts at re-imaging the Nativity are no threat to the Christmas tradition as we know it. Most of the time a different look is new for a season. Only a few of these creations outlive the time of a fad and establish a new tradition. There is frequently a touch of humor hidden in what we call a different look.

Has Jesus always been a baby? Then why not imagine him as a toddler?

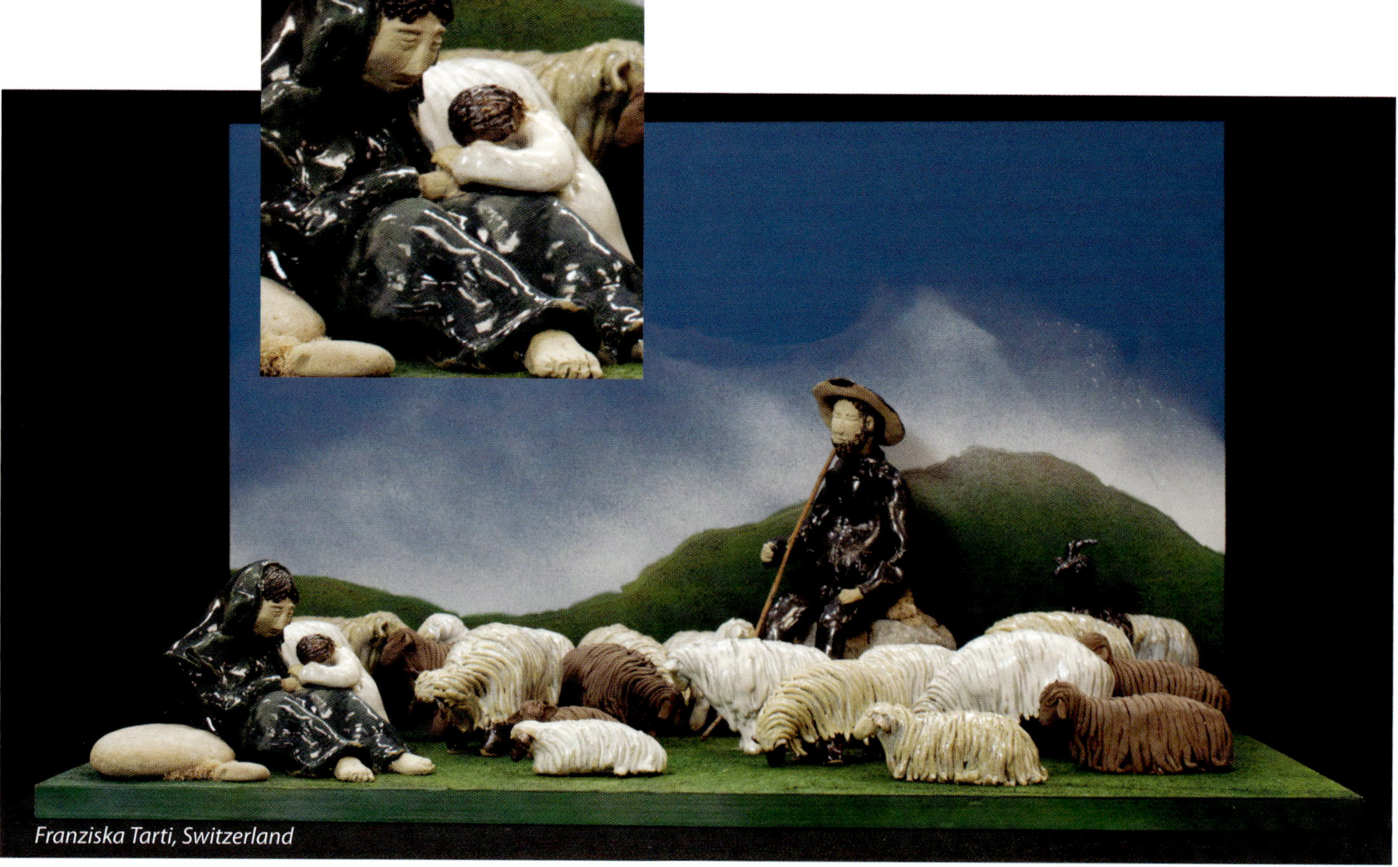

Franziska Tarti, Switzerland

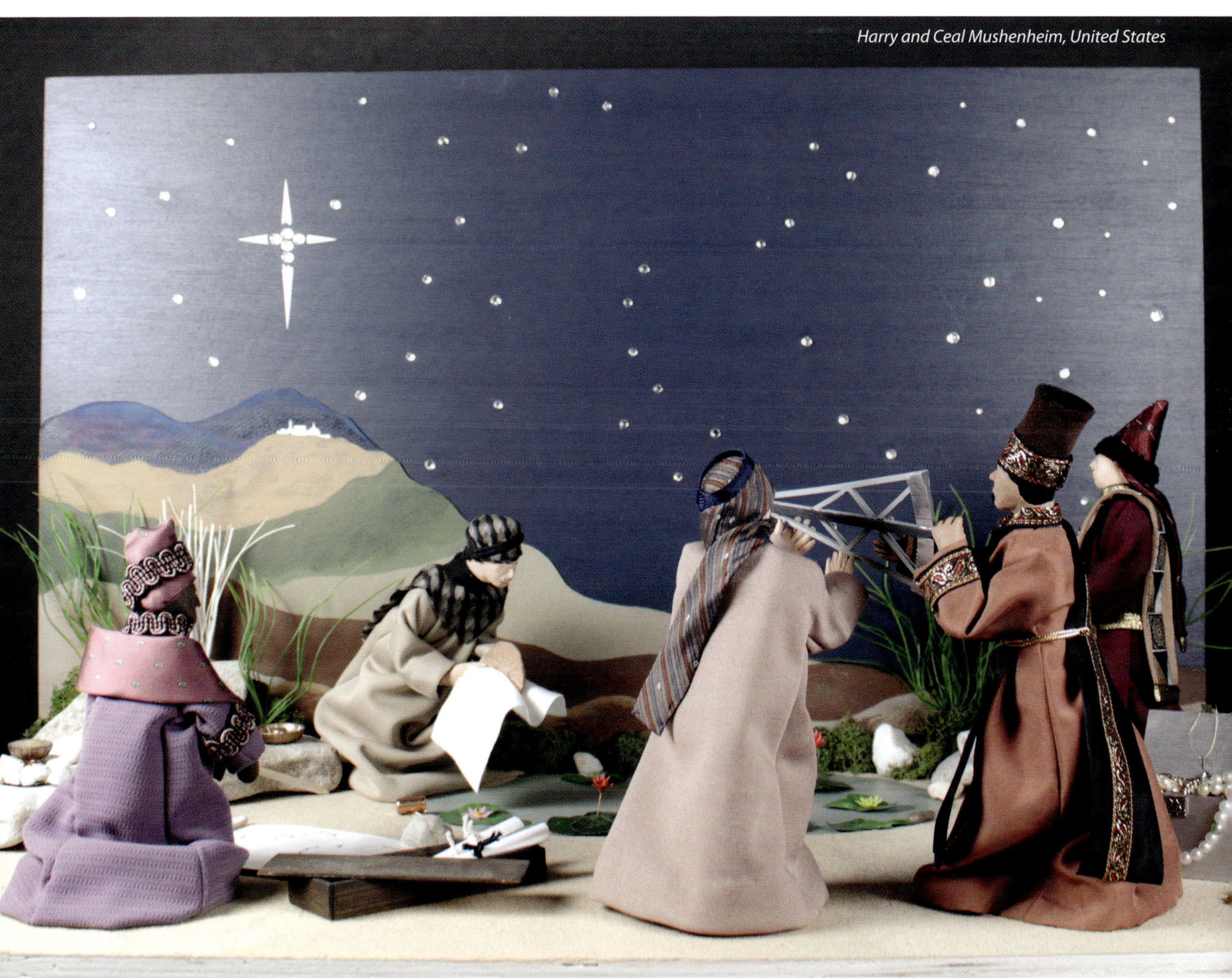

We are used to see the magi on arrival at the manger, and we forget that seeking and finding can be a cumbersome process.

Why shouldn't the baby be much bigger than all other figures? Is he not the center of attention, and the newborn King?

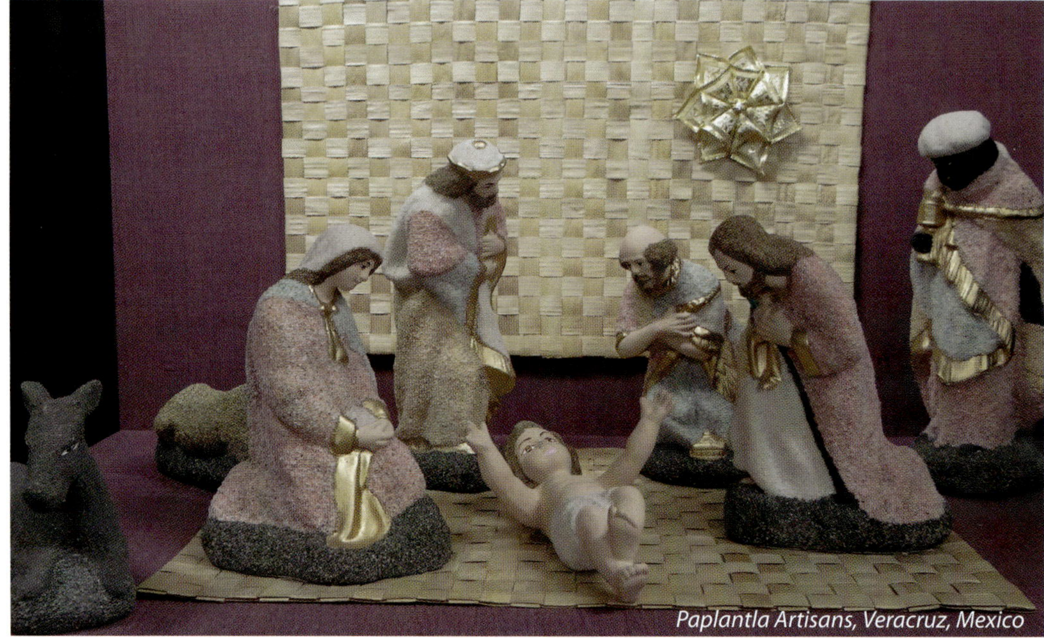

Paplantla Artisans, Veracruz, Mexico

Michael Ayala, Ecuador

Is not the mother the one who is exhausted and tired? There is a division of labor at the manger.

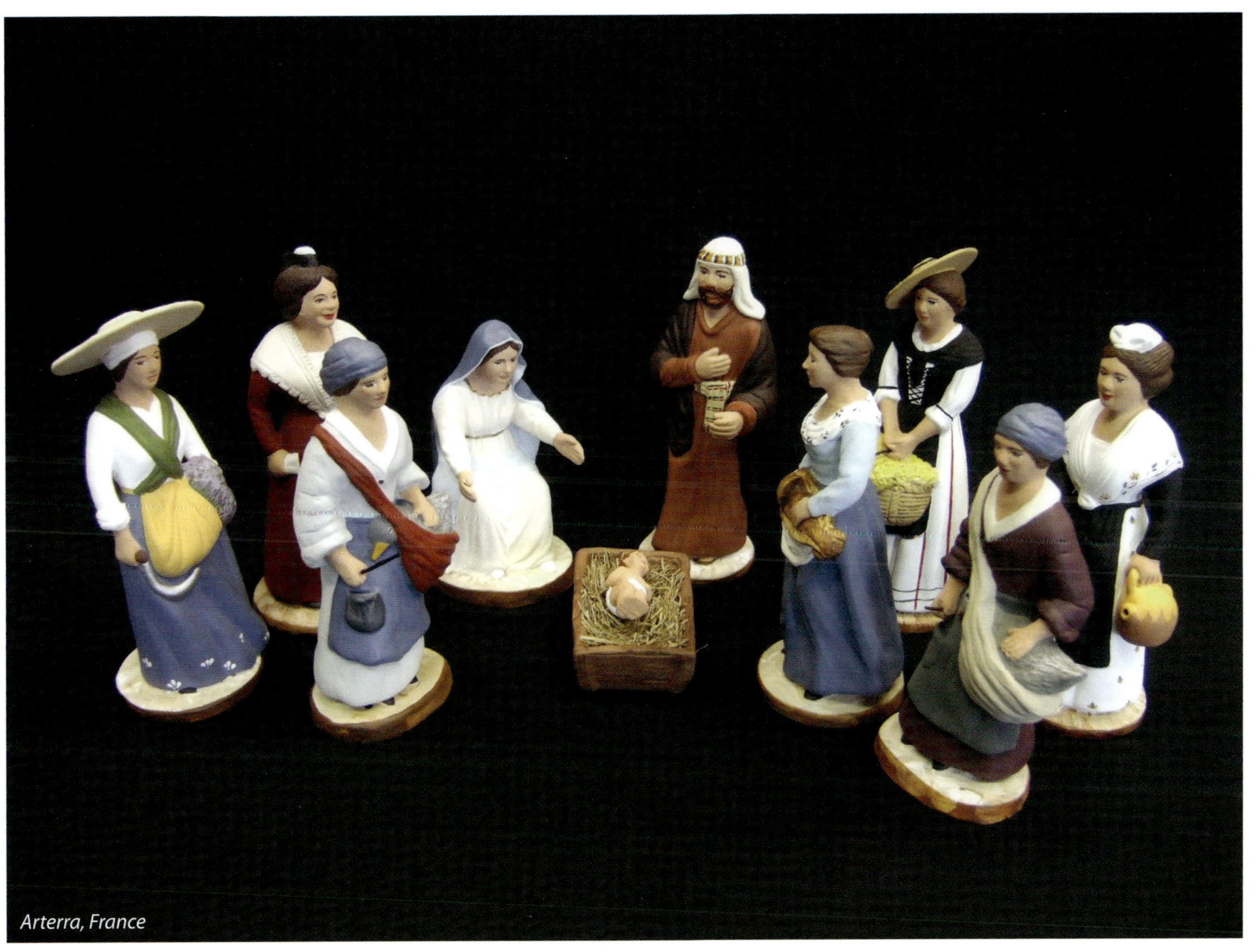
Arterra, France

Why should there always be mostly men at the manger? Could we not imagine Mary inviting women, women only, to rejoice and compare notes?

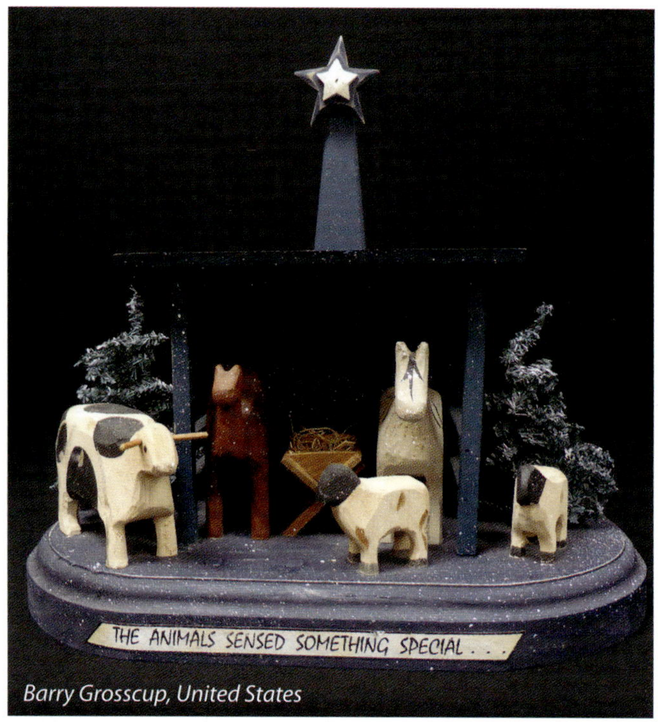

Barry Grosscup, United States

An empty manger? There was a time of waiting and expectation, as we know. Even the animals seemed to know about Advent, and they sensed something special.

They never met, but have much in common, and they like Christmas: Santa Claus and Baby Jesus.

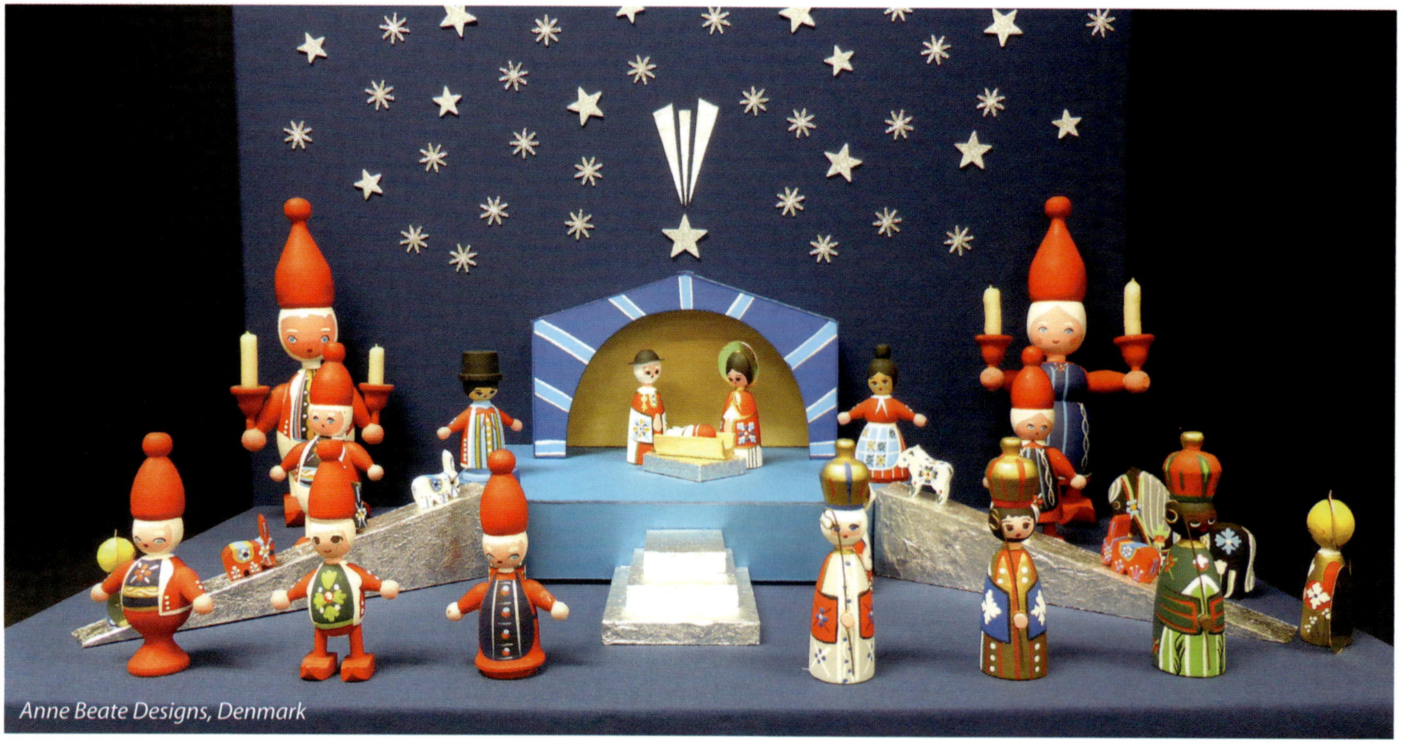

Anne Beate Designs, Denmark

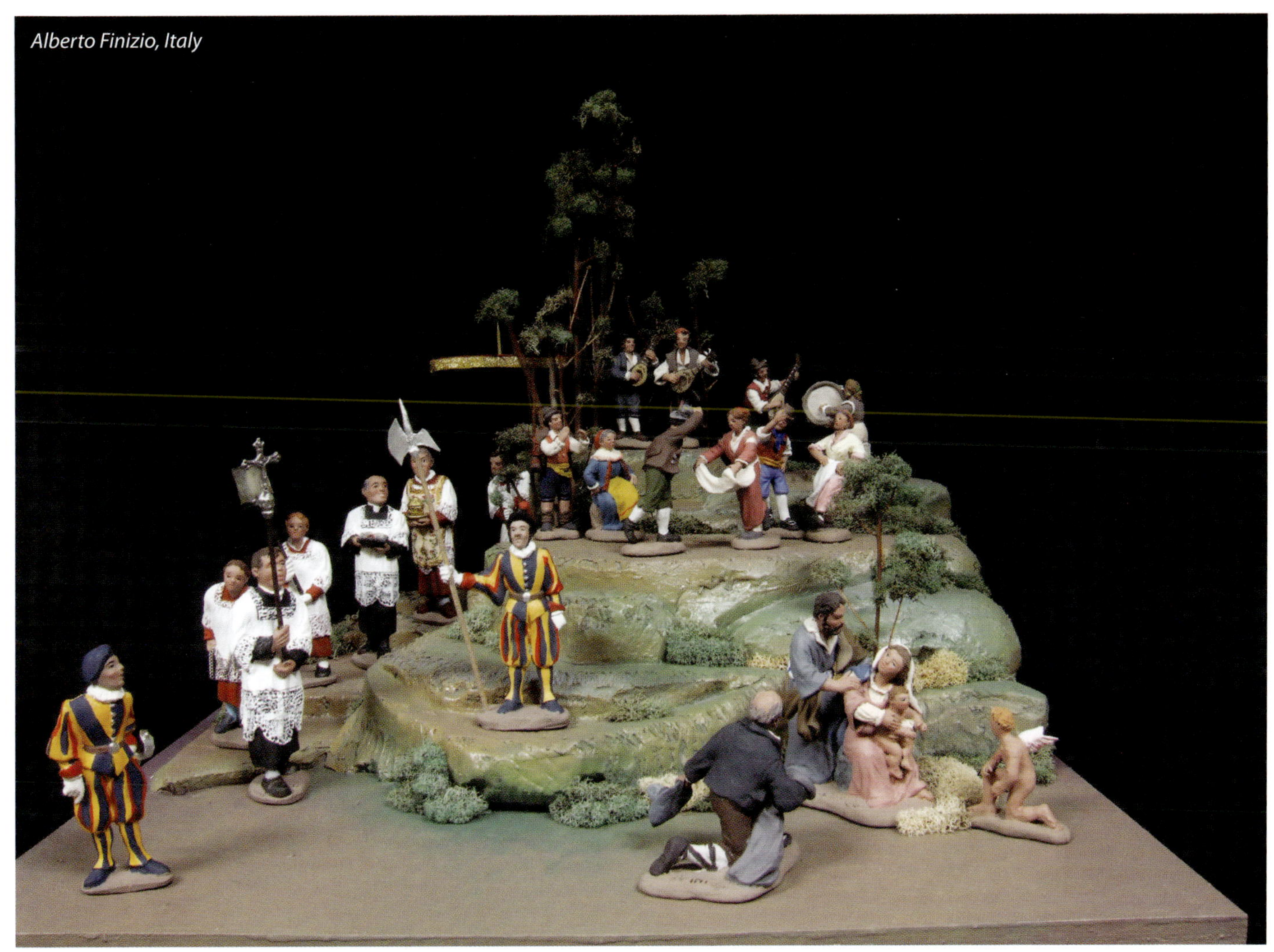
Alberto Finizio, Italy

Christmas is not the end. There is a way of looking at a new Christmas with the same Jesus, the Eucharistic Jesus.

Odd or regular, in the end nobody is missing at the great reunion around the manger

The Odd Figure

There is nothing odd about Nativity figures. All characters are welcome at the manger. They all bring their own life and message to the Christchild. Some of these odd personages are present at the manger to publicize local traditions or to add humor to piety. Others contribute historical information or spiritual insights. As to the latter, there is *Anastasia*, an early martyr, whose feast was never celebrated because it fell on the day of Christmas. Out of the Old Testament and braving the times we have Moses' explorers carrying a giant grape proof of the promised land flowing with "milk and honey". Admire a high level conversation between Saint Francis and Mister Fontanini, founder of the Fontanini Collectibles. The content of their conversation remains secret, but the meaning seems obvious: the Christmas tradition inaugurated in part by Francis remains intact, however, its mass marketing is more than a minor concern for the beloved saint. Saint Nicholas and Mozart together with the Christchild celebrating a reunion of child prodigies? What brings them together? They all had a generous heart. Well known in the Provençal tradition, the *Ravi*, the exalted one, has a similarly generous heart for the newborn king. He is the simpleton of the village but he is also the first to sense that there is more than an ordinary baby. And so he shouts his joy. On a lighter note, bringing commedia dell'arte to the manger, we have Pierrot, the bouffon. The chimney sweepers, on the contrary, play a questionable role. They are Joseph II's spies to check on families who have a forbidden manger in their home.

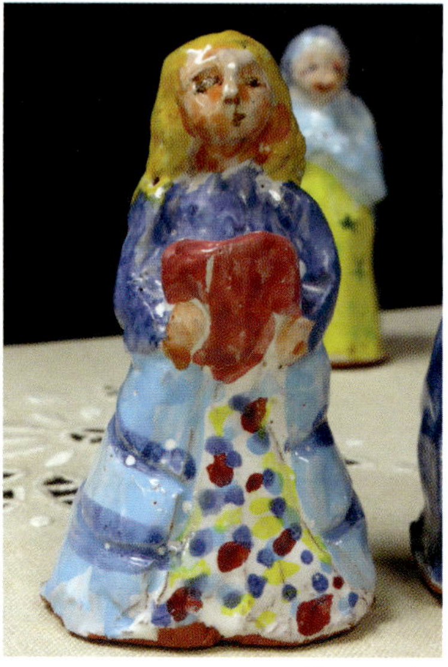

Anastasia.
Beth Watson , United States

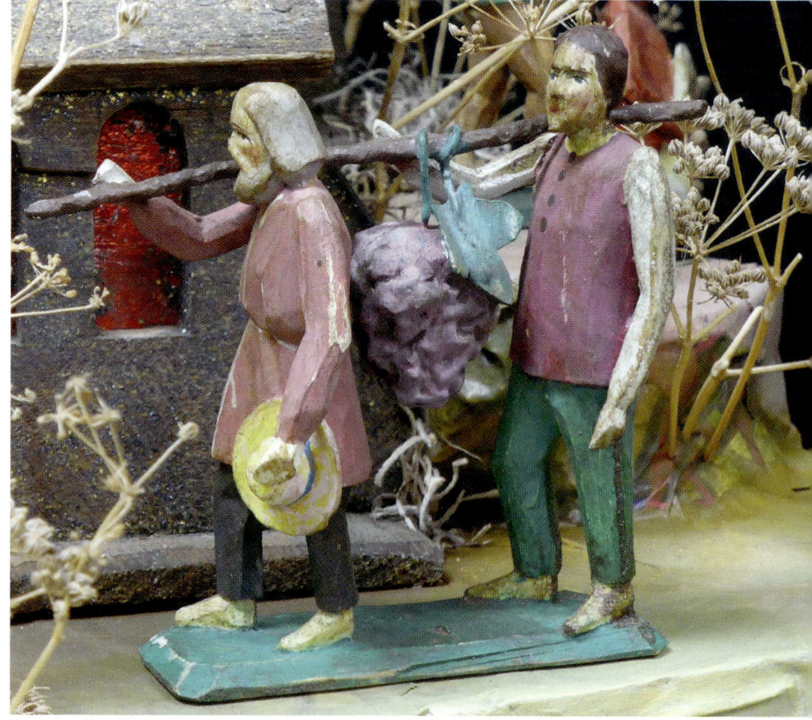

Moses' explorers of the Holy Land. Grulich Tradition

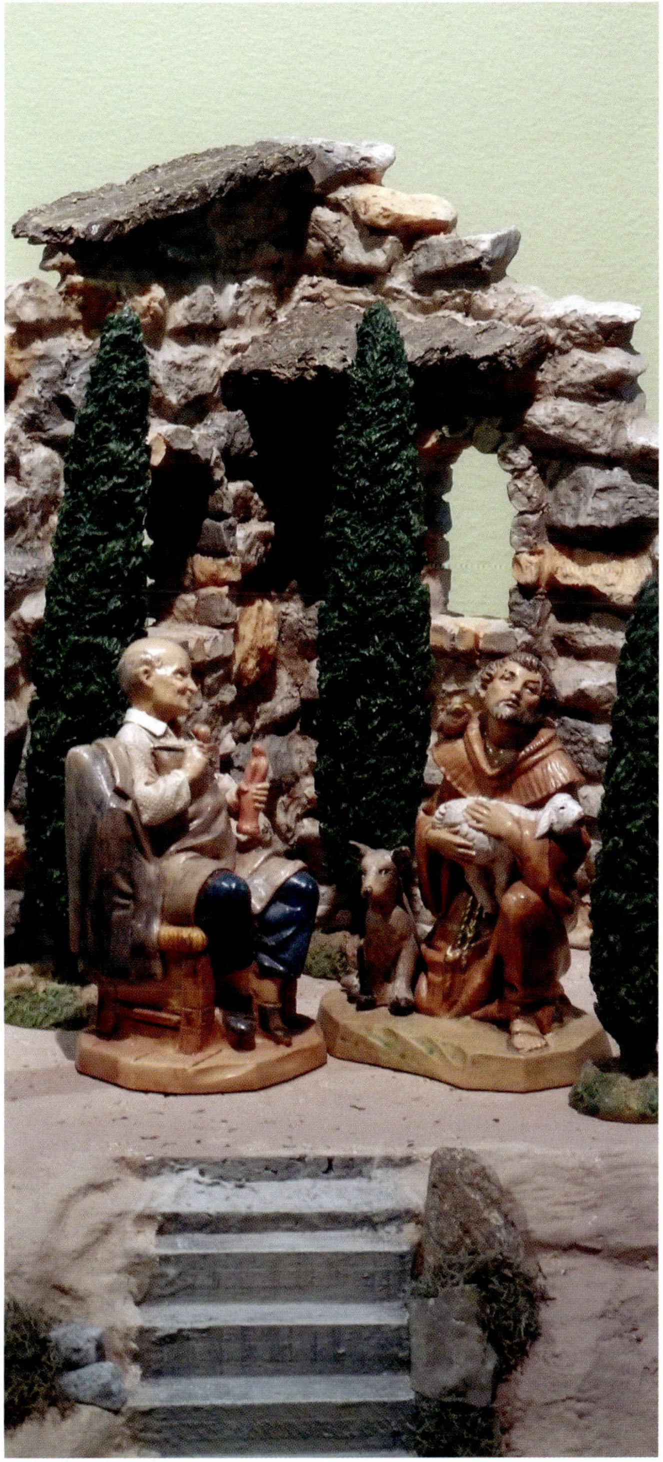

St. Francis and Mister Fontanini. Fontanini Collectibles

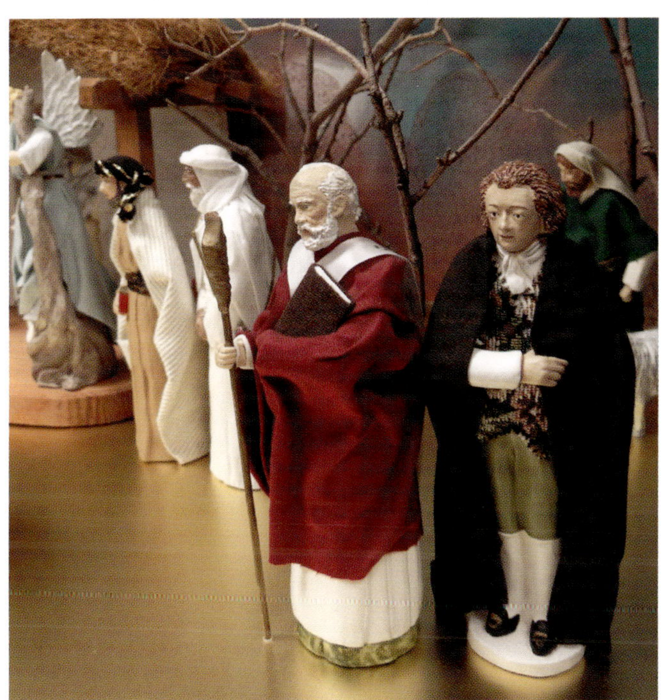

Saint Nicholas and Mozart. Hestia Creations, United States

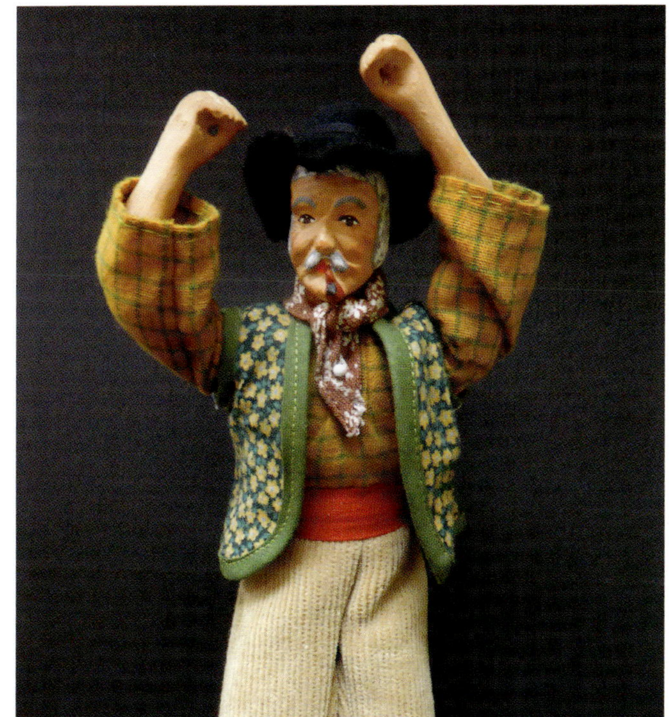

Ravi, the village simpleton. Provençal clothed figure

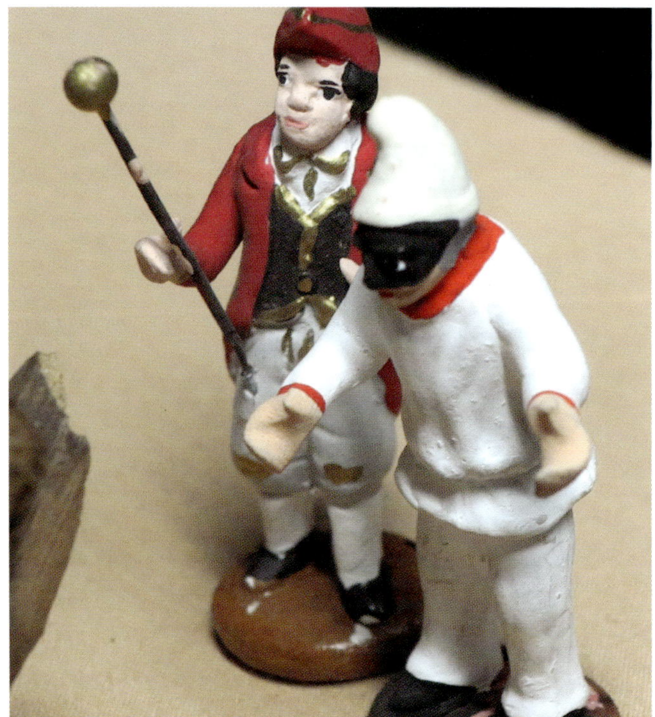

Pierrot. Unkown artist, Italy

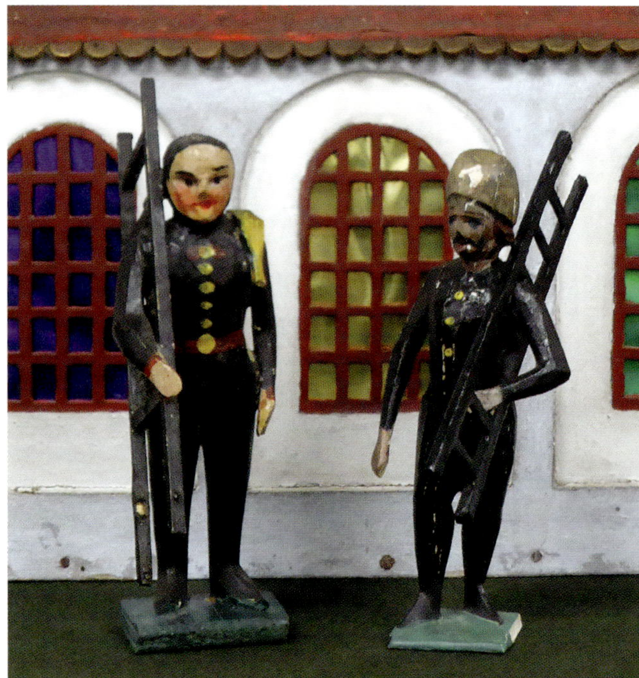

Chimney Sweeps. Grulich Tradition

There are many more of these odd figures, like Artaban, the fourth king, who never made it to the manger but caught up with Christ at the crucifixion, or the communist mayor, quarreling constantly with the parish priest but in the end present at the manger. Indeed, odd or traditional figure, in the end nobody is missing at the great reunion at the manger.

Artaban.
Grulich Tradition

From the birth of Christ to a time of associations and conferences.

Timetable of the Nativity Culture

It was not possible to evaluate the historical accuracy of each and every date of the timeline offered here. The information was gathered from a number of sources, most important among them Bogner's Krippenlexikon (2003). The main purpose of these annals is to convey a sense of the development, of growth but also decline, of stations and major players, of countries and styles making up the culture of the crèche during centuries past.

The Birth of Christ: Reminiscence and Date

6-5 B.C. Birth of Jesus in Bethlehem.

155 Justin Martyr mentions that Jesus was born in Bethlehem.

220 Origen visits the grotto of Christ's birth in Bethlehem which has been converted into a shrine in honor of Tammuz-Adonis.

250-400 Stone sarcophagi are decorated with the scene of the Holy Family surrounded by ox, donkey, shepherds and the Magi.

326 The Empress Helena visits Jerusalem and Bethlehem and returns to Constantinople with numerous relics of the Nativity and Christ's Passion.

330 The Emperor Constantin moves the capital of the Roman empire to Constantinople and through the influence of his mother Helena erects a Basilica in Bethlehem, at the place of Christ's birth.

340 The Adelphia sarcophagus in Syracuse depicts Mary with the Christchild along with ox, donkey and the shepherds.

354 Pope Liberius moves the Feast of the Birth of Jesus from January 6 to December 25, the old Roman day of Sol Invictus.

After 360 the worship by the Magi is depicted in the Roman catacombs and elsewhere on stone sarcophagi, on wall frescoes and on liturgical vessels.

Ca. 370 In a painting in the Sebastian catacombs, the Manger is presented for the first time in the form of a trough.

390 Christmas is definitively established as the Feast of the Birth of Jesus.

440 Pope Sixtus II places a wooden relic of the Manger in the Church of Santa Maria Maggiore.

565 Death of the Emperor Justinian, who erected a church to Mary in Carthage which contained a slab of marble with representations of the Annunciation to the shepherds, the Magi and the disappearance of the Star over Bethlehem.

From Relics to Early Representations

1160 The Abbot Gerhoh von Reichersberg in Austria describes representations in churches of the Manger, the crying Christchild, the Virgin Mother, and the Slaughter of the Innocents.

1170 The earliest dated examples of silver and crystal "original" wooden portions of the Manger are placed under the main altar of Santa Maria Maggiore.

The Bavarian minstrel Spervogel uses the expression "born on Christmas" for the first time in a poem.

1223 With the permission of Pope Honorius II, St. Francis of Assisi, after returning from a trip to Palestine, creates in a small wood near Rieti a Manger scene with living persons and animals.

1291 The Canon Pandolfo commissions Arnolfo di Cambio to create for the northern lateral aisle of Santa Maria Maggiore a representation of the Nativity, with Mary, Joseph, Isaiah and David, placed in a small house next to the reliquary from Bethlehem.

1291 Cardinal Colonna authorizes the renovation of the gold and silver version of the five "original" wooden pieces of the Manger in Santa Maria Maggiore.

1306 Epiphany Caroling (Sternsinger) is approved in Upper Austria (temporarily forbidden in 1622).

1310 or later The oldest Manger altar with tall painted figures appears in the enclosure of the Women's Convent of St. Chiara in Naples.

1336 In Milan, a Dominican procession on the Feast of Epiphany includes three finely dressed Magi with their entourage, music, and unusual animals.

1360 The German Emperor Karl IV receives from Pope Urban V the relic of a shaving from the Manger and adds it as royal insignia to the Imperial treasure.

1372 St. Bridget of Sweden makes a pilgrimage to Bethlehem and has a vision of Mary kneeling, and the child Jesus lying naked by the Manger, surrounded by angels in a circle of light.

1392 In Bavaria, a market dedicated to St. Nicholas is a forerunner of later Christmas market celebrations.

Before 1400 During a Mass at the Cathedral in Padua, the Flight to Egypt is represented with a live donkey.

1419 The first Christmas tree, decorated with fruit, pastries and paper, is made by a group of bakers in Freiburg.

From Manger to Nativity Set

1453 In the sacristy of St. Lawrence Church in Florence, first known example of an elaborately clothed Christchild is maintained for exhibition near the Christmas altar.

1480 In Rome, a Franciscan brother brings to the Basilica of St. Mary in Aracoeli a woodcarving of the holy Christchild made from the wood of an olive tree in Gethsemane.

In Southern Germany, altars are created with free standing figures of the three Magi.

In the Hospital Church of Palma di Mallorca, a Nativity representation is assembled using wooden figures from Naples; later additions are made in 1536 through a vow by sea captain Domingo Jacobo.

1491 Kunigunde von Bayern, the daughter of Emperor Friedrich III, receives as a Christmas gift a Manger containing the Christchild.

In Varallo, Piedmont, Franciscan Bernardino Caimi and the artist Gaudenzio Ferrari erect the first "Sacred Mountain," an ascending pathway with 500 life-sized figures and 45 house-sized chapels depicting events from the life of Christ.

Around 1500 In Italy, a glass and clay relief Nativity appears as a forerunner of the Nativity Mountain (Krippenberg).

In the lower Rheinland, clay figures appear of the angel of the Annunciation, of the flight to Egypt, and of an angel holding the instruments of the Passion.

Ca. 1510 St. Cajetan von Thiene, founder of the Theatines, is one of the first to make a small Nativity set for private veneration in the home.

1534 Martin Luther writes the Christmas song "Vom Himmel hoch, da komm ich her." The first mention of a Christmas tree in the Cathedral of Strasbourg.

1552 In Cologne, the Gymnasium Tricoronatum, the first Jesuit school in Germany, is founded, along with the introduction of spiritual theater plays, a culture spearheaded by the Jesuits.

1560 In Celano, Italian house nativity sets appear for the first time in the inventory listing of Duchi di Amalfi. One has 116 figures, including some with mechanically moving parts.

To the Ends of the World with the Jesuits

The Jesuits bring representation of the Nativity to Latin America.

First Jesuit Nativity appears in Vienna.

In Catalonia, the Canon Pere de Bonavia possesses the first known home Nativity in Spain.

1561 At the Gymnasium Tricoronatum, the Christmas Story is presented regularly with dialogue and music in front of the Manger scene.

1562 In the Church of St. Clement in Prague, the Jesuits present the Nativity scene, along with the Last Supper and the Agony in the Garden, using live figures.

1563 The Council of Trent instructs Bishops to use representations of the Nativity for recatholicization and missionary work. In Munich, the Jesuit Father Heinrich Samerius reports that even Protestants are attracted by Christmas displays in Catholic Churches.

1570 The promulgation of the Roman Missal by Pius V impacts the crèche culture thanks to the selection of various gospel texts relating the Infancy Narratives.

1571 The altar of the Schlosskapelle in Innsbruck is decorated with representations of the Annunciation, Visitation, the Birth of Christ, and the Adoration of the Magi.

In Prague, the Jesuit college records for the second time the exhibition of a Nativity, before which a midnight mass followed by many other masses were celebrated until morning.

1574 The parish priest of the Church of St. George in Genoa orders from Matteo Castellino in Naples a Nativity set with the Holy Family and angels.

Erasmus Obrist provides the earliest reliable report of a Nativity in the Tyrol.

1577 In Munich, the Archduke William V of Bavaria and Duchess Maria of Steiermark exchange letters regarding how to expand creation and devotion to the Nativity culture.

1578 At the Court of Bavaria in Munich, a Nativity with fully dressed moving figures is mentioned for the first time.

1579 In Brazil, the Jesuits organize an exhibition of Nativity sets.

At the Jesuit seminary chapel in Graz (Austria), the first nativity appears which was visited by the Ducal family.

In the year of his death, the Bavarian Duke Albrecht V authorizes a finely constructed silver Nativity set with 14 figures.

1583 Fra Luis de Granada designates in writing the location where the Cistercian visionaries of Goz, near Alcobaca Portugal, placed the Holy Manger.

1587 Pope Sixtus V provides a chapel dedicated to the Nativity for Santa Maria Maggiore Church in Rome.

1592 In response to controversy regarding the use of Nativities in mission work, the General of the Jesuit order, Claudio Aquaviva, issues detailed instructions approving the use of Nativities with moderation.

1595 In Japan, Jesuit missionaries, who have celebrated Christmas there since 1556, erect the first Nativity set.

In northern Bohemia, the Jesuits exhibit Nativities for the first time, with the result that Nativities spread throughout the Erzgebirge.

1599 In Lahore and at Kochi College, India, Jesuit missionaries show the Christmas Nativity for the first time and draw 3,000-4,000 visitors.

Magnificently constructed Jesuit Nativities for the native people are reported in Rio de Janeiro.

The Jesuits bring the Nativity to Moscow.

A Growing Tradition in Church, School, and Castle

1607 In Akra, West Indies, the Jesuit Fathers celebrate Christmas with great veneration and on the altar erect a Nativity which attracts a large crowd.

In the Jesuit Church of St. Michael in Munich, a large Nativity appears on the monumental stairway, with fully dressed and moveable figures in changing scenes from the Birth of Christ to Flight to Egypt.

1611 In the vicinity of Rio de Janeiro, Nativity sets are again set up by the Jesuits for the native people.

In Rennes, France, the Jesuits put a stop to the "Shepherd's Dance."

The Jesuit erect a "Nativity Theater" in Montreal.

Additional figures are added to a Nativity set created in 1609 in Messina, Sicily.

1613 A Nativity set is created for the Women Convent Damenstift of Innsbruck; additional figures are added in the immediately following years.

Numerous Nativity figures are found when the will of the Spanish poet Lope de Vega is executed.

The Jesuits construct a Lenten Nativity (Fastenkrippe) in Kitzbühl, Tyrol.

1615 A "Theater for the Feast of Christ's Birth," which includes a Nativity House with wooden boards, straw and the wooden heads of oxen and donkey, appears in Bamberg at the Jesuit Church of Old St. Martin.

In Brazil, Jesuits bring sick children to the Nativity for healing.

To increase the devotion of the people, the first Nativity is erected at the Benedictine Convent Nonnberg in Salzburg.

The Nativity in the residence of the Servites in Innsbruck is enlarged.

The Church of St. Martin in Bamberg makes wooden heads of oxen and donkey, which are added to a figure of the Christchild, the remaining figures are represented by living persons.

1616 Duke Ferdinand of Bavaria sends an automatic clock with the representation of the Christmas Story as a gift to the Chinese Emperor.

Duke Maximilian I of Bavaria orders the construction of a Christmas Nativity. At first the set includes only the Child, a mountain and cave; in later years other figures are added.

In Innsbruck, the churches of the Franciscans, Capuchins, and Augustinians have Nativities with changing representations.

1619 The Jesuit Philippe de Berlaymont publishes his work "Paradise of the Children" as a defense of the Nativity culture. He thereby develops the first "philosophy of the crèche."

In Upper Austria, George Scheible from Wellheim paints big Christmas paintings for the monastery of Kremsmünster.

The Golden Century of the Nativity

1620 After all Western monks are taken into captivity, Armenians, instead of Franciscans, administer the Church of the Nativity in Bethlehem.

The Augsburg goldsmith Abraham Lotter makes two silver Nativity sets (Bethlehem); one is donated to the Loreto Church in Prague, the other, on loan from the Bavarian National Museum, was stolen in 1967 from an exhibition in Montreal.

The Bavarian Duke Maximilian I purchased Nativities for his three children.

A Nativity and Holy Tomb are erected at Heilig-Geist Spital in Ingolstadt.

1621 At Neustift bei Brixen, in the Southern Tyrol, the first Nativity is erected.

In Amberg (Bavaria), soldiers help to erect the first Nativity at the castle of the Elector.

1624 In Lisbon, the Dominican sisters of San Salvador, after one of them receives a vision, construct a Nativity in their convent.

1625 Father Joseph Brandstaetter, who had supported Nativity displays throughout upper Germany, dies at age 84 in Ingolstadt. He was known as "Praesepiorum Christi nascentis auctor."

1628 Princess Polyxena von Lobowitz donates a foot-long, wooden, wax-covered figure of the three year old Christchild to the Church of "Our Lady of Victory in the Carmelite convent in Prague. It was and still is the famous "Infant of Prague."

1638 On December 25 and 27, a fire, which is attributed to the presence of Nativities, destroys a house in the Benedictine convent at Trastevere in Rome.

1642 The Jesuit Father Jean de Brebeuf exhibits a Nativity set for the Huron and Algonquin Indian tribes in Canada.

1644 The English protestant traveler John Evelyn, while visiting Rome, sees a large Nativity set in the Church of Santa Maria sopra Minerva, and also other Nativities throughout the city; this discovery gives him a powerful experience of Christmas Eve night.

1647 An extensively laid out Nativity set is placed in the Carmelite Church of San Martino dei Monti in Rome.

1650 In Provence in France, through the sculpture workshops of monasteries, especially those of the Carmelites and the Carthusians, a Nativity tradition emerges of sober and sturdy wooden and wax figures; only a few home Nativities are extant.

In Spain, Nativity sets made from ivory and alabaster are popular both among religious communities and in prosperous private households.

1661 In the Church of San Paolo Naples, the Brotherhood of Goldsmiths erects a Nativity set to exhibit the jewelry of the rich; the eight figures are adorned with precious stones such as smaragd, sapphire and pearls.

1662 The residents of Agana in the Mariana Islands in the Pacific flock to a Nativity set regularly displayed until 1672 by the Jesuit Father Diego San Vittores.

In the vicinity of Grulich in Bohemia, the Jesuits erect the first Nativities and establish what would later become the extremely fruitful wood carving tradition of the Grulich Nativities.

1665 In Rottweil, Württemberg, the first wax Nativities are known; from them will arise a hundred years later the tradition of wax figures of the infant Jesus, known as "Fatschenkinder." (Christchild in swaddling clothes).

The Franciscan Father Justinus erects the first Nativity in Parkstein, Oberpfalz.

1670 In Austria, Nativities are forbidden for the first time, in order to limit all too wordy representations in church Nativities and to contain the stream of visitors.

1680 An unknown travelling worker, while making a Nativity for the town of Isareck-Volkmannsdorf bei Freising in upper Bavaria, uses glass eyes for the first time.

1688 After the Elector Max Emanuel captures the Turkish held citadelle in Belgrade, the clothing and equipment of the Turks influences the European style of representations of the Magi and their entourage.

1690 In Bethlehem, the rights of the Franciscans to the Church of the Nativity are reestablished (reconfirmed 1756), although all three confessions (Greek, Armenian and Latin) receive a key to the building. This gives new attention to the Nativity and the Crèche culture.

1700 In Rome, the popularity of Nativities reaches a highpoint. In Rome, hallways, staircases, and rooms of palaces serve as a location for the exhibit of Christmas nativities, through which invited guests can wander to the accompaniment of music.

In Provence, a tradition is established of handmade glass Nativities in wooden boxes; this leads to the development of boxed Nativities (Kastenkrippen). Since they are made to extraordinarily demanding standards and possess richly decorated landscapes and figures, they will eventually compare favorably to those of Naples.

In the vicinity of Avignon and Comtat, individual families begin to acquire home Nativities with ornately dressed puppet-like figures which are strikingly expressive and display lifelike movement.

On January 4, at Tegernsee in upper Bavaria, the Benedictines of the monastery construct a circular walk around a Nativity.

In Balzhausen, Swabia, Nativities are erected for the first time.

Johann Karl Stilp, the first carver of wooden nativities who is known by name in Egerland, works for the seminary in Waldsassen.

Historical records indicate that nativities are widespread in the area of the Erzgebirge Mountains, Königgrätz and Grulich in Bohemia and Moravia.

Flat or two-dimensiional figure Nativities (Flachfigurenkrippe) are widespread in the Erzgebirge and Orlické mountains.

Woodcarving grows rapidly in the vicinity of Grulich because of the availability of rich forest resources, the presence of organ makers and turners, and the need to support pilgrimages to the "Mountain of the Mother of God" built by Bishop Tobias Becher.

Variety in Style and Numbers

1702 During a visit to Naples, the Spanish King Philip V receives from the wealthy citizen Niccolo Speruti the gift of a Nativity; the King publicly exhibits it every year in his palace, whereby his young son, the later King Karl III of Naples, is influenced to support nativities in Naples.

1704 In the convent church at Gutenzell, upper Swabia, the Abbess Maria Victoria supervises the construction of the first Baroque Nativity with changing Christmas scenes on a stage.

1723 Mechanical Nativities become fashionable in Bohemia at the pilgrimage churches of Maria-Schein and Maria-Sorg as well as many other places.

1736 To prevent destructive secular influences, Bishop Teodor Czartoryski forbids the performance of Christmas plays with the exception of non-moving Nativity figures and requires the plays be performed on the grounds in front of a church building.

First in the Erzgebirge Mountains (Eastern Moravia) and then in surrounding areas, Nativities appear which use background scenery consisting of painted buildings and landscapes.

1750 The highpoint of Nativities in Sicily is reached.

In Milan, private entrepreneurs charge a fee to visit Nativities; the government bans this practice in 1761 and places all nativities under the control of Church authorities.

In Provence, a Nativity appears which is made out of paper-maché.

A Nativity in Rococo style appears at the convent of the Servites in Innsbruck.

On a commission from the mining family Fugger, the sculptor Franz Spindler constructs a Nativity oriented towards mining for the village church in Rinn in Tyrol.

The first Nativity market takes place in Vienna.

At Castle Ellwangen in Württemberg, a Nativity appears from which one hundred of the foot high statues are still extant.

At Kümmeratzhofen, Swabia, the carpenter Franz Josef Sohn begins to make clay figures from models, later his son will use them to create grotesque representations which earn him the title of "Bildermann of Zizenhausen."

In Egerland, nativities are found in private residences.

In the Bohemian Forest, development takes place of the year-long Nativity (Jahreskrippe) with changing representations from Christmas to Easter.

Engraved paper representations from studios in Augsburg, Nuremberg, Regensburg, and Vienna appear in markets in Tyrol; and will spread to the Oberpfalz and Bohemia.

A new art form of nativity making begins in Westfalen with the development of open shrine nativities (Krippenschrein) and boxed nativities (Kastenkrippen). They take the form of a peasant house with steep gables and a front side made of glass, within which stand clothed wax figures.

1758 In Munich, a Lenten Nativity (Fastenkrippe) appears with 4 feet high wooden, clothed dolls whose eyes are made of Venetian glass.

On September 19, at Sterzing in the southern Tyrol, Augustin Alois Probst is born; later he will become famous as the maker of wooden nativities for the Archbishop Franz Carl von Lodron in Brixen.

To fulfill a commission by the Archbishop Franz Carl von Lodron for the chapel of the main castle in Brixen, Franz Xaver Nißl carves a Nativity for Christmas and Lent (Fastenkrippe) with 4 to 6 inch figures; figures which establish a new style in Tyrol.

1760 Two Nativities are present in the Portuguese Royal Palace. Nativities in the style of Estremoz (crèches in roadside altar style) appear in the Museum of Art in Lisbon.

1761 Lasting until 1787, the "Royal Nativity" of Ferdinand of Naples contains 135 figures, 73 animals, 350 sets of horse equipment and 34 musical instruments of extraordinary quality.

In Wuppertal, the Jesuits present a catechetical play for children in the form of a Nativity play, which is repeated for Christmas in 1763, 1766, 1770 and 1772.

1765 The woodcarver and Nativity maker Johann Georg Schwanthaler makes a six-part Nativity with 10 inch high figures for the town of Kematen in the Tyrol.

1766 For the Cathedral in Lisbon, Joaquim Machado de Castro finishes a much admired Nativity with colorfully painted figures 1-2 inches high.

Ban on Nativities

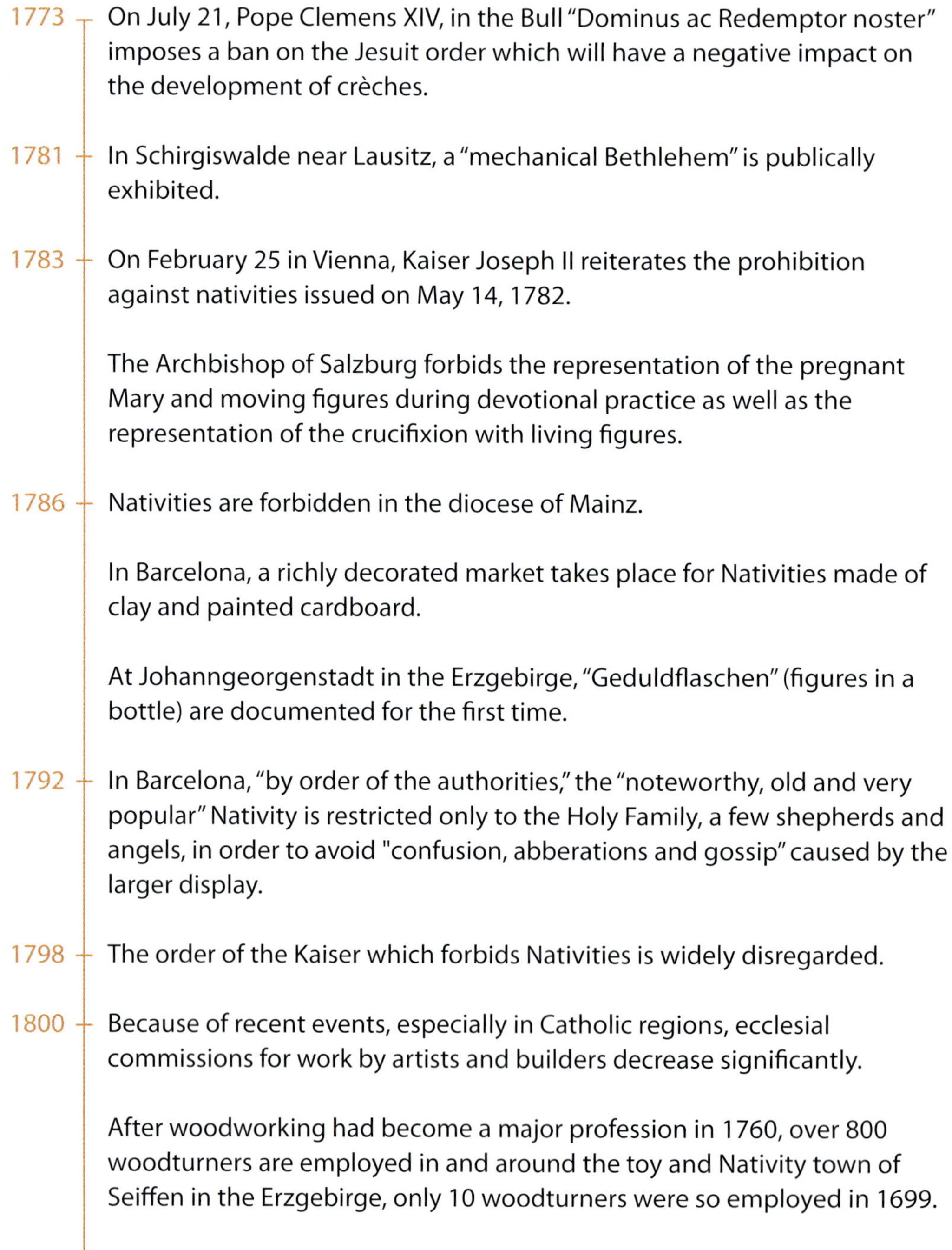

1773 On July 21, Pope Clemens XIV, in the Bull "Dominus ac Redemptor noster" imposes a ban on the Jesuit order which will have a negative impact on the development of crèches.

1781 In Schirgiswalde near Lausitz, a "mechanical Bethlehem" is publically exhibited.

1783 On February 25 in Vienna, Kaiser Joseph II reiterates the prohibition against nativities issued on May 14, 1782.

The Archbishop of Salzburg forbids the representation of the pregnant Mary and moving figures during devotional practice as well as the representation of the crucifixion with living figures.

1786 Nativities are forbidden in the diocese of Mainz.

In Barcelona, a richly decorated market takes place for Nativities made of clay and painted cardboard.

At Johanngeorgenstadt in the Erzgebirge, "Geduldflaschen" (figures in a bottle) are documented for the first time.

1792 In Barcelona, "by order of the authorities," the "noteworthy, old and very popular" Nativity is restricted only to the Holy Family, a few shepherds and angels, in order to avoid "confusion, abberations and gossip" caused by the larger display.

1798 The order of the Kaiser which forbids Nativities is widely disregarded.

1800 Because of recent events, especially in Catholic regions, ecclesial commissions for work by artists and builders decrease significantly.

After woodworking had become a major profession in 1760, over 800 woodturners are employed in and around the toy and Nativity town of Seiffen in the Erzgebirge, only 10 woodturners were so employed in 1699.

The protestant Princess Caroline von Baden brings the Christmas tree to the royal residence in Munich and thereby introduces it to Bavaria.

In many localities along the railroad in the vicinity of Steyr, Austria, manufacturing begins of "Loahmmandl" (little clay figures) for box nativities (Kastenkrippen), while nail smiths and knife makers develop their own tradition of home nativities.

In Westfalen, free-standing, clothed wax Nativity figures, about 80 cm high and accompanied by figures dressed in peasant garb, appear in churches. This leads to a change in the use of wooden or paper-maché figures covered with paint and cloth.

From Churches to Homes

1808 In Marseilles, "Santons," a clay cold painted figure developed after the closing of Churches during the French Revolution, appear as merchandise in markets.

1818 On Christmas Eve in the Church of Oberndorf Laufen an der Salzach (Austria), the carol "Silent Night" is created, with the words by the priest Joseph Mohr and the music by organist Franz Gruber.

In Schluckenau, northern Bohemia, woodcarvers, give a Southern European imprint to the Nativity construction, which supercedes the oriental style of the Nazareans throughout the Erzgebirge and the Bohemian lowlands.

1820 In Ebensee, Nativities reflecting the local culture, with a large setting, develops from the smaller "Corner Nativity" (Eckkrippe), and spreads throughout the surrounding region to Bad Ischl.

In Dörflas near Marktredwitz, the potter Johann Meyer creates fully plastic and colorfully painted Nativity figures out of white porcelain.

The production of nativity figures out of paper-maché commences in the Erzgebirge.

1826 The Bamberg Cathedral vicar Johann Baptist Cavallo publishes a pamphlet "Short Instruction concerning the Use of Nativities at Christmastime," in which he makes a passionate plea for their reintroduction.

The December 1 edition of the "Münstrischen Intelligenzblatt," presumably as a consequence of secularization, contains the advertisement "an almost complete Nativity, which would be very useful in a church, is available for viewing and for sale."

1830 In Marseille, a trader from Naples offers Nativity figures at the "Santi Belli" market, as a result of which the Nativity Tradition of Provence, interrupted since the French Revolution, is reestablished.

1843 The wealthy London businessman Sir Henry Cole has the draftsman John Calcott Horsley draw, hand color and print a thousand of the world's first Christmas card; unneeded cards are sold for one shilling piece.

The Popular Revival

1847 The Crimean War between Russia and Turkey is instigated when the silver star over the birthplace of Jesus in the Grotto of the Nativity in Bethlehem is stolen. The Sultan has the star replaced.

1850 In Rome and Naples, the production of Nativities ceases and is replaced by the collection of older Nativity figures which are arranged in scenes in a glass case or "scarabattola."

In Alpine countries, especially between Nassereith and Innsbruck, Nativity sets with clay model figures appear in markets during Advent.

In Grulich, Moravia, House Nativities change from figures 100-150 cm high to smaller ones 25-30 centimeters high.

The first and very active Nativity market appears in Spain.

1856 180,000 "Santons" are sold at a Christmas market in Marseilles.

1863 An Association of Friends of the Nativity is founded in Barcelona.

1856 In Vienna, Joseph von Führich paints a paper Nativity with 25 cm high figures in bright colors; this Nativity is the forerunner of the later widespread and stylistically influential Nazarean cardboard cutout Nativity sheets (Krippenbögen).

1891 The oldest Nativity in France, in the Church of St. John the Baptist in Chaource (Aube), is declared a national monument.

1897 In the vicinity of Steyr and Garsten in Austria, "Loahmmandl" Nativities, homemade by nail smiths and knife makers, go out of style.

A Time of Associations and Conferences

1919 The Association of Friends of the Nativity is founded in Vienna. Additional associations are formed in Bamberg, Augsburg, Aschaffenburg, Traunstein, Bohemia. Another association is founded in Spokane, Washington, which only lasts for ten years.

The sculptor Jakob Holtmann begins seven years of work on a Christmas Nativity for the cathedral in Osnabrück.

1920 The construction of Nativities in northeast Bavaria, which was languishing because of the First World War, is revived when cutout nativity sheets are published in Munich.

In the Erzgebirge region, makers of Nativities change back from an "oriental" to a local style.

1923 After a jubilee exhibition at the folk art museum in Prague, Nativities which have a Slavic motif and reflect everyday life become more common in Bohemia.

1929 In Innsbruck, Franciscan tertiaries, wishing to revive Lenten Nativities, offer a course for their construction.

1931 The Tyrol Nativity Association in Innsbruck publishes a guide to the 500 most beautiful and largest Christmas Nativities in the Tyrol.

The Northern and Southern German Nativity Associations agree to merge and decide to publish a magazine and yearbook dedicated to Nativities.

In Arnhem, the "Society of the Friends of Nativities in the Netherland" is formed.

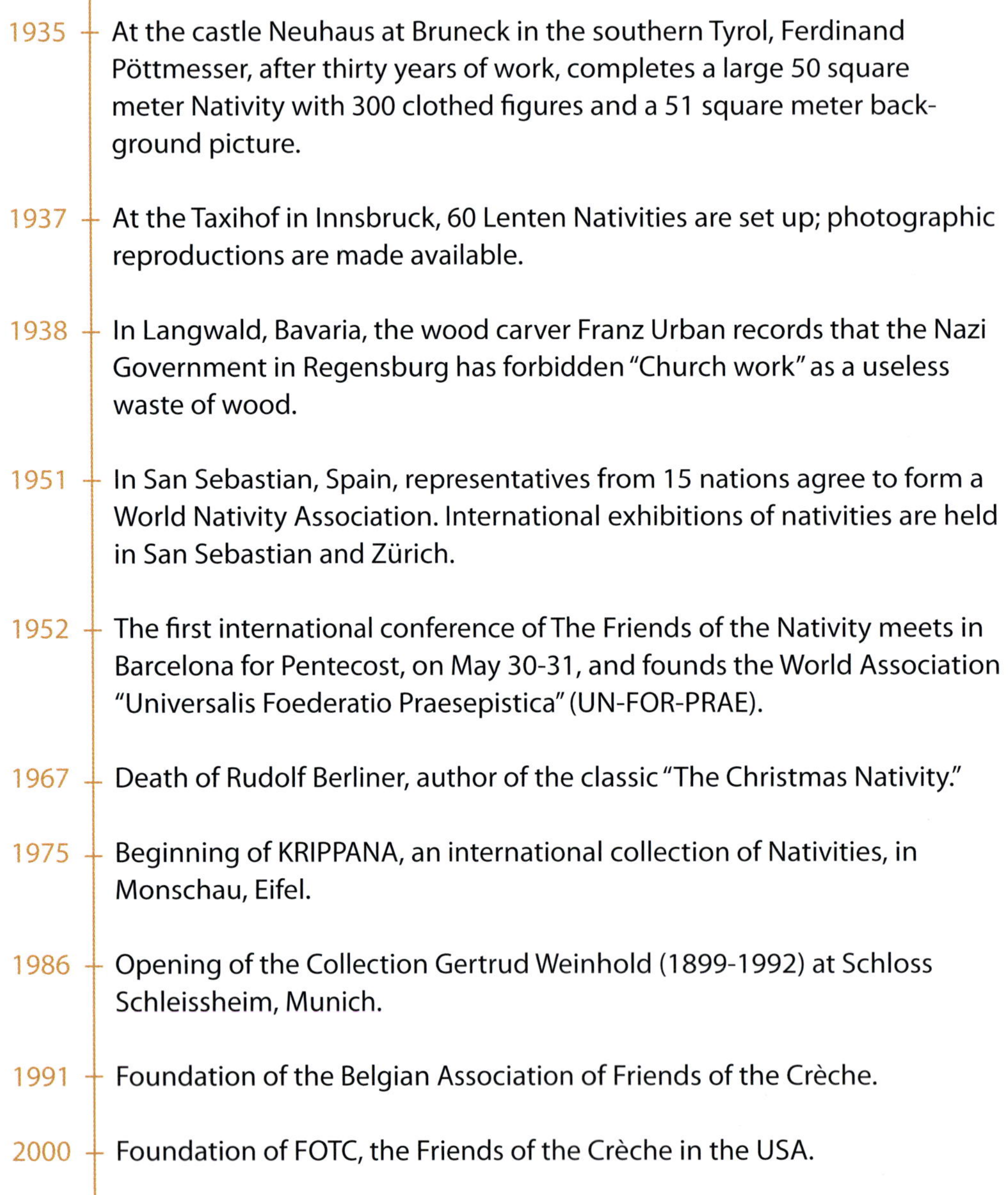

1935 At the castle Neuhaus at Bruneck in the southern Tyrol, Ferdinand Pöttmesser, after thirty years of work, completes a large 50 square meter Nativity with 300 clothed figures and a 51 square meter background picture.

1937 At the Taxihof in Innsbruck, 60 Lenten Nativities are set up; photographic reproductions are made available.

1938 In Langwald, Bavaria, the wood carver Franz Urban records that the Nazi Government in Regensburg has forbidden "Church work" as a useless waste of wood.

1951 In San Sebastian, Spain, representatives from 15 nations agree to form a World Nativity Association. International exhibitions of nativities are held in San Sebastian and Zürich.

1952 The first international conference of The Friends of the Nativity meets in Barcelona for Pentecost, on May 30-31, and founds the World Association "Universalis Foederatio Praesepistica" (UN-FOR-PRAE).

1967 Death of Rudolf Berliner, author of the classic "The Christmas Nativity."

1975 Beginning of KRIPPANA, an international collection of Nativities, in Monschau, Eifel.

1986 Opening of the Collection Gertrud Weinhold (1899-1992) at Schloss Schleissheim, Munich.

1991 Foundation of the Belgian Association of Friends of the Crèche.

2000 Foundation of FOTC, the Friends of the Crèche in the USA.